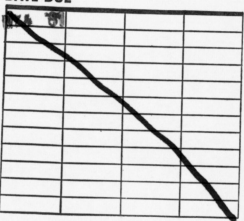

NEW PERSPECTIVES ON THE HOUSE OF REPRESENTATIVES

NEW PERSPECTIVES ON THE
HOUSE OF REPRESENTATIVES

Second Edition

Edited by:

Robert L. Peabody
The Johns Hopkins University

and

Nelson W. Polsby
*The University of California,
Berkeley*

RAND MᶜNALLY & COMPANY · CHICAGO

RAND McNALLY POLITICAL SCIENCE SERIES

PREFACE TO SECOND EDITION

Since we prepared the first edition of this book, a great deal has happened to the House and to research about the House. Successive waves of organizational change, of which the first was the 1961 fight over Rules Committee enlargement discussed in Chapter 11, and the last was the aftermath of the 1964 elections, for a time turned the House into a somewhat more enthusiastic partner of an activist President and liberal Senate than had been true for many a year. In this same 89th Congress, the House Republican minority, in a series of pitched battles, reorganized their party leadership (See Chapter 14). A Joint Committee on the Organization of Congress was constituted, held hearings, and blossomed forth with recommendations for reform. As we write, these are stalled in the Rules Committee. The President of the United States, in his 1966 State of the Union address, proposed a Constitutional Amendment providing for a four-year term for Congressmen, but nothing further came of that. *Plus ça change, plus c'est la même chose,* more or less.

Rather than advocate reform or the status quo, we have in this second edition once again tried to find selections from contemporary research which we thought would add to a reader's factual knowledge and intuitive understanding of the House. When we first began to study the House, in 1960 and 1961, information was scarce about how it was organized and how it ran. Since then, a great many researchers have "discovered" the House, much as we did ourselves, and in increasing numbers have been publishing on the subject. The American Political Science Association, under a grant from the Carnegie Corporation, has undertaken a Study of Congress which is bound to contribute further knowledge. It is a good time to be reading and writing about the U.S. House of Representatives.

Washington, D.C.   R.L.P.
Berkeley, California   N.W.P.
January, 1968

PREFACE TO FIRST EDITION

WITH TWO exceptions, the selections in this volume represent what seems to us to be an extraordinary reawakening of scholarly interest in the United States House of Representatives. The awakening is long overdue, for many reasons. The House is a superbly interesting institution, ancient in its customs, intricate in its byways, colorful in its rituals and practices, rich in controversy and in the display of all the arts and crafts of politics. Since 1937, it has been a kind of policy bottleneck in the federal system—the only institution of government which regularly has thwarted the enactment of the major domestic policies of activist Presidents. And yet, aside from exceptions such as the two classic studies which begin and end this book, the scholarly literature on the House—indeed the total amount of *all* discussion of the House—has, until quite recently, been exceedingly thin.

Although the state of knowledge about the House has improved markedly over the past few years, it has apparently not improved to the point where a summary statement pretending to comprehensiveness and accuracy can be made about its contemporary politics. And so it seems to us that a more preliminary treatment, embodying a variety of perspectives, is appropriate at this time. The rationale for such a procedure was admirably stated by Woodrow Wilson many years ago:

> Like a vast picture thronged with figures of equal prominence and crowded with elaborate and obtrusive details, Congress is hard to see satisfactorily and appreciatively at a single view and from a single stand-point. Its complicated forms and diversified structure confuse the vision, and conceal the system which underlies its composition. It is too complex to be understood without an effort, without a careful and systematic process of analysis. Consequently, very few people do understand it, and its doors are practically shut against the comprehension of the public at large.[1]

Our purpose in presenting this collection is, then, to call the attention of our students, our colleagues, and our neighbors to the

---

[1] *Congressional Government* (New York: Meridian, 1956 [First published, 1885]).

House as a political institution, and to invite their interest. A second purpose is to circulate in a handy form the results of current political research on the House in the hope that other research similarly oriented to the production of middle-range theories and general descriptive statements may be encouraged. And finally, not the least of our hopes is that our long-suffering friends and mentors on Capitol Hill, the congressmen themselves and their staff aides, may observe that their kindness and patience to each of the authors represented here—and to others equally astute and productive not included in this collection—has not been wholly in vain.

A brief word about the principles of selection we employed. We tried to include articles which would give our readers a "feel" for the politics of the House, a sense of its variety and diversity, and which would give as contemporary and accurate a portrait as we could manage in a short compass. The necessity for brevity led us to choose fewer selections than we might have, since we wanted to present them whole and with footnotes intact. To mitigate at least partially our inevitable sins of omission, we have appended a brief bibliography which will bring interested readers into touch with a wider range of materials than could be presented in full here.

Washington, D.C.   R.L.P.
July, 1962   N.W.P.

TABLE OF CONTENTS

PART ONE

Congressmen and their Constituents

THE REPRESENTATIVE AND HIS DISTRICT*

Lewis Anthony Dexter

I
INTRODUCTION

WE TALK frequently of a representative or senator "representing" or "failing to represent" his constituents. This is shorthand. The fact is the congressman represents his image of the district or of his constituents (or fails to represent his, or our, image of them). How does he get this image? Where does it come from?[1]

On numerous important policy matters, he hears nothing from his constituency.[2] But whether he hears anything on an issue, what he hears, whom he hears from, or how he interprets what he hears all *vary* depending upon the kind of person he is, the kind of associations he has had and has in the constituency and in Washington, the public image of his interests and concerns, and the background information or misinformation which he possesses. An editorial summary of an earlier draft of this paper said, "Congressmen make choices about which people communicate with them. . . ."[3]

---

* Reprinted by permission of the author. Part of this article appeared originally in *Human Organization*, 16 (1947), pp. 2–13. Copyright by Lewis Anthony Dexter. An extended discussion of some of this material appears in R. Bauer, L. Dexter, and I. Pool, *American Business and Public Policy* (New York: Atherton, 1963), especially Part V and the chapters on Delaware, Appalachian City, and the 53rd District. Indebtedness to Ithiel Pool is gratefully acknowledged.

[1] The present analysis is based upon 650 interviews, from 1953 to 1957 (420 of them by the author) with politicians, businessmen, trade union leaders, and departmental officials, about the influences impinging upon the formulation of policy. More than 100 interviews were conducted with members of Congress and 40 with executive assistants on Capitol Hill. Four-hundred of the interviews utilized dealt with formation of policy or communication of preference on the Reciprocal Trade Extension Acts of 1953, 1954, and 1955, and it is around these that the analysis is chiefly organized. Considerable use has been made of the writer's own participation in politics, in, for example, the State Government of Massachusetts, September, 1956–August, 1957, the Stevenson primary campaign of 1956, and an effort to arouse public interest in a civil defense bill.

[2] See L. A. Dexter, "Candidates Make the Issues and Give Them Meaning," *Public Opinion Quarterly*, 19 (1955–56), pp. 408–414, for supporting data; and "What Do Congressmen Hear: The Mail," *op. cit.*, 20 (1956–57), pp. 16–27.

[3] Either by consciously providing distracting stimuli or by consciously exposing themselves to countervailing viewpoints.

In large part this is also a manner of speaking. It would be more precise to say that the people in electing a congressman have chosen one sort of recording instrument or another, and that while one instrument may be adjusted to catch or hear one sort of communication, another will hear a different sort, and so on. Although congressmen do, to a small degree, consciously choose what they will hear, it is probably more significant that in large measure their personalities, careers, and public images make them choose what they hear and how they interpret it.

A good many congressmen believe that their districts feel very strongly on this, that, or the other issue, and that they are constrained, therefore, to vote a certain way. The more sophisticated realize, of course, that legislative procedures and processes are so complex that it is more often than not possible to go through the motions of conforming to such views without helping to enact them when they believe the public preference to be wrong.[4] On most issues, out of a desire to serve the district or from indifference, many congressmen do go along with any view which they believe "the district" holds strongly. When the chips are down, and they have to declare themselves, some will vote against their convictions and for their constituents' (presumed) preferences.

This situation has led to a series of classical utterances on the moral problem of the representative: *Should he sacrifice his judgment to his constituents' inclinations as he conceives them or not?* It would be more accurate to emphasize the ways in which representatives' beliefs about constituent preference are functions of the channels of communication and the special processes of transaction between constituents and representatives.

If this is so, more students of representation and representatives would concur with the late Congressman Eberharter's interpretation of the representative-constituent picture. The latter for years was at the center of the legislative issues which provoke the most comment by critics of "pressure," and he told me early in my study of reciprocal trade:

> You know I am sure you will find out a congressman can do pretty much what he decides to do and he doesn't have to

---

[4] See L. A. Dexter, *Congressmen and the People They Listen To* (Cambridge: Center for International Studies, Massachusetts Institute of Technology, Dittoed, 1956), Ch. III, *passim*. M. I. T. has no further copies of this, but it is copyrighted and was also submitted as a doctoral dissertation (Columbia, Sociology, 1960) and therefore is available at the Library of Congress and various libraries.

bother too much about criticism. I've seen plenty of cases since I've been up here where a guy will hold one economic or political position and get along all right; and then he'll die or resign and a guy comes in who holds quite a different economic or political position and he gets along all right too. That's the fact of the matter.

II

The first difference between some congressmen and others is how (consciously or unconsciously) they define their responsibilities.

Many of the congressmen interviewed about both tariff and defense matters referred to a personal conception of what they owe their job, of what in some circles would be called "professional obligation." A few made explicit and many apparently hold implicit theories of representation. These theories of representation were not, except for a few instances, so far as I could tell directly derived from philosophical or academic sources. They resulted from the experiences of men facing the actual moral complexities of a job.

Some members expressed themselves in terms of their obligation to select the right course, regardless of the views of their constituents. For instance, Congressman Stubborn[5] has for a good many years represented a district which (according to interviews with business interests in the district and from an economic analysis of its industrial situation) is inclined to favor the reciprocal trade program. Nevertheless, he says:

> Oh, knowing my stubborn characteristics, no one ever thinks he can change me, you know . . . some of my people say, "You may not agree with this man, 'Stubborn,' but you know where he stands."

Mr. Stubborn agreed that if fate were to select as his successor a Clarence Randall-type "free trader," such a man would be able to vote for a reciprocal trade program without much difficulty, but Stubborn interrupted an effort to probe this point further by declaring:

> That's because they [my constituents] do not really understand the matter. During the twenty-one years reciprocal trade

---

[5] Except for deceased interviewees and (by special permission) Congressman Warburton (R., Del.), the names of all those interviewed and quoted are disguised.

has been in effect, it has had . . . [and he named various alleged or actual consequences which he regards as evil]. . . . There isn't any use trying to change *me!*

Congressman Emphatic on the other hand voted the same way as Mr. Stubborn on the Reciprocal Trade Extension Act of 1955 because of a quite different definition of his responsibility. He said:

My first duty is to get re-elected. I'm here to represent my district. . . . This is part of my actual belief as to the function of a congressman. . . . What is good for the majority of districts is good for the country. What snarls up the system is these so-called statesmen—congressmen who vote for what they think is the country's interest . . . let the Senators do that. . . . They're paid to be statesmen; we [members of the House] aren't.

(This was said sarcastically, but without humorous intent.)

Mr. Leader, as strong a supporter of reciprocal trade as Mr. Stubborn is an opponent of it, comes fairly close to Mr. Stubborn in his attitude towards constituent opinion. Said Leader:

You're not identifying me on this, of course? It's strictly confidential? Always bear in mind there are those in Congress who lead their districts and those who are led by them. . . . It makes a lot of difference. . . . The "ruanga" growers of my district never opposed *me* on reciprocal trade. . . . The answer is government stockpiling for them. . . . I think I have convinced these men that a program of high tariffs would not assist them and I think my viewpoint has gained general acceptance from them.

Several times he spoke of himself as having "straightened out" people who had seen the matter "wrongly." But Mr. Leader and Mr. Stubborn do not essentially disagree. In another interview during the same session but dealing with an unrelated piece of legislation in which he had also played a prominent part, Mr. Leader showed his conception of his role on this matter to be very similar.

The reciprocal trade issue is so well known, the origin of Mr. Leader's views so deeply based, and his technical knowledge of the field so considerable that he is probably right in his contemptuous dismissal of the possibility that any lobbying or "pressure" could change his position. However, regarding the other legislation, it is entirely probable that a skillful public relations campaign did manipulate *the facts* which came to his attention and to the attention of some of his colleagues, much as we shall see Mr. Fourth was influenced on the reciprocal trade issue.

Mr. Fourth represents a district in which there is vociferous anti-reciprocal trade sentiment. This district also has strong economic reasons for supporting reciprocal trade and a particularly influential number of intellectuals predisposed toward reciprocal trade. Mr. Fourth showed how a portion of the district can influence a man when he said:

> My impulses when I came down here were in favor of trade not aid, until I started to hear all sorts of things from my district. . . . So, actually, when you stack all these things together, well you're in favor of trade not aid, but, goodness, there comes a time . . . if trade means wholesale layoffs in your district. . . . I've got any number of letters against it . . . carpets, imported rugs . . . there've been around 300 layoffs in a local bicycle plant . . . textiles . . . chemicals . . . electrical equipment . . . glass salesmen. It's difficult to get figures. I assume the Randall Commission report has them. . . . I haven't had time to read it. I don't know. . . . I assume that the people I hear from exaggerate the seriousness of the situation but still that it is serious.

Mr. Fourth ultimately voted against reciprocal trade on the key votes; the decisive factor appears to have been his unwillingness to separate himself from several members from his state, also of junior status, who were definite in their opposition to reciprocal trade. Mr. Fourth, according to his colleagues was wavering as late as two hours before the vote. Had the chairman of his state delegation (who strongly supported reciprocal trade) personally requested his support, he might well have voted the other way. But he was obviously uncertain, *on the reciprocal trade issue,* whether to adopt the role of servant of his district (as he conceived its desires) or to think in terms of the ideology, implied by the phrase "trade not aid." How he would vote was therefore completely unpredictable. Had he stumbled into any one of three congressmen with strong pro-reciprocal trade views in the lobby or the corridors just before the vote, he might have voted the other way.

Congressman Fourth's vote was unpredictable because on this particular issue he does not have a clear conception of what his obligations are. On some issues—flood control or taxes affecting the major agricultural product of the district—one can predict that he would see his responsibility as being almost exclusively to the district. On others—particularly those under consideration by the very important subcommittee of which he is a member—he would be strongly inclined to emphasize national interest in some form as against district concern.

III

Congressmen tend to see their obligations as being either to the nation or to their constituency—other equally possible obligations are seemingly not considered.

Obligation seemed to be conceived as national interest versus district interest (district interest was often, as in the case of Mr. Emphatic, related to re-election and therefore to self-interest). No congressman interviewed indicated any feeling of moral obligation to our allies or to any other country, although our allies are regarded instrumentally as means. This is contrary to a theory sometimes expressed that Americans tend to adopt some favorite foreign country as "theirs." Also, reference to representing a region (the South, the West, New England) was very slight.

The congressman's definition of national interest and responsibility on a particular issue depends in large measure upon his understanding of the facts of a particular issue.

Both Congressman Leader and Congressman Stubborn are quite clear on what they believe are the facts of the reciprocal trade question, and they have no doubt about the effects of the legislation (although their "facts" are to a great extent contradictory, and their conclusions are opposite). Congressman Fourth, on the other hand, was susceptible to influence from either side because he lacked any clear idea of what reciprocal trade legislation means or entails. His sympathy for the phrase "trade not aid" came from a diffuse and generalized acceptance of a *slogan* rather than from an understanding of facts or consequences. He was really uncertain what, if any, difference his vote on reciprocal trade makes to the national welfare. Thus, he much more easily than Mr. Leader or Mr. Stubborn can see the matter as one of simply performing a service for discontented people in his district. It is far less likely that he will —in the absence of external stimuli—feel any strong need to learn the facts. On *service* matters—and much of a congressman's job is service[6]—most congressmen are willing to go along with those con-

---

[6] Cf. J. F. Kennedy, *Profiles in Courage* (New York: Harpers, 1955), esp. pp. 12–21.

stituents who seem to know what service they want performed, and how it is to be performed (provided, of course, nothing irregular is requested). But if, for instance, Mr. Fourth were a New Deal "intellectual"—and his district is one which might easily elect such a person—he would have interpreted the same situation quite differently. And, if he were a politically astute New Deal "intellectual," he would have shown that the major agricultural crop of the district is exported, that several large industries in the area depend on foreign trade, and so forth.

A congressman's conception of his district confirms itself, to a considerable extent, and may constitute a sort of self-fulfilling prophecy.

Within the limits of the morally and sociologically conceivable (no congressman from Alabama in 1942 could have advocated racial integration, for instance!), a congressman has a very wide range of choices on any given issue, *so far as his constituency is concerned.* His relationships in the House or Senate and with party leadership, of course, limit these choices severely. It is a fact, however, that there is no district viewpoint *as such* to be represented on the overwhelming majority of issues. A few will care one way and a few the other, but the issue will be insignificant or unknown to the great majority. Indeed, in many districts, only a fraction of the voters know the name of their congressman, let alone how he voted on a particular issue.

A congressman of my acquaintance took about 100 letters which he received on a particular issue and checked the registration of the writers. He found that almost three-quarters of them were not registered in his district. What difference, then, would their views make with respect to his prospects for re-election?

Mr. Emphatic, who insisted that he was representing his district's desires, was led nevertheless, by my questions, to admit that more than likely none of the workers presumably represented by him actually knew how he had voted. "Not a single one of them," he complained, "wrote in to thank me, though hundreds had written asking me to vote their way." He attributed this in large measure to the allegation that the largest newspaper in the district is "anti-Emphatic." However, since newspapers published outside the district, which gave front page publicity to his stand, have far greater circulation in the district than does the anti-Emphatic "News," this seems an unsound explanation.

Actually, most of the letters Mr. Emphatic received and most of the comments he heard originated in three large plants in the district, and they represented less than 7 per cent of the voters of the district. These plants are organized by national unions which, ironically enough, in chalking up Mr. Emphatic's score in 1956, were inclined to regard his vote against reciprocal trade as an anti-labor vote. Fortunately for him, his stands on other matters and his personal contacts offset this factor. Of the groups in the district, only members of the League of Women Voters wrote to him in favor of reciprocal trade. "They aren't," he averred, "God knows, a potent political force, and all their letters are damn stilted, right out of the same handbook." However, it was likely that the League members *would* remember in 1956, and perhaps again in 1958, how he voted. And, because of the racial and academic composition of the district, League members may have some influence outside their own membership.

It would have been perfectly possible for Mr. Emphatic to take the reverse position favoring reciprocal trade and still regard himself as representing his district—particularly since the area also has a strong port interest.

A congressman has great difficulty in deciding what the viewpoint of the district is even on such an issue as reciprocal trade. Most persons with an interest or belief in the tariff will have interests or beliefs in other issues as well. Thus, the most effective representation of their overall interests may necessitate concessions on some matters, in order to get along with party leadership, colleagues, or prominent committee members in the Congress. "Joe Martin and Charlie Halleck in their heart of hearts," said a prominent Republican, "certainly go along with us, not with the White House on this; and they can swing twenty-five votes, at least, anytime they want; we lost by less than twenty-five votes, so they beat us." Until 1958 Martin was the Republican leader; Halleck became his successor in the 86th Congress. Is a congressman doing a better job of representing his district when he keeps in the good graces of such powerful men (and thereby helps to get a bridge or a new post office or a dam for his district) or when he opposes them on an issue, the details of which few will remember six months later? The Republican who told me about Martin and Halleck is one of the most persistent enemies of reciprocal trade in the party, and he is probably the most effective in a quiet way. He is opposed to reciprocal trade in part because of its "harmful" effect on his district.

However, he cheerfully admitted, "It wouldn't make any difference what my congressman does in this matter," insofar as his reelection is concerned. Afterwards he qualified this by saying that perhaps the incumbent ought not stick his neck out strongly *for* reciprocal trade, but there is no call for activity of any kind.

IV

A congressman hears most often from those who agree with him.
A congressman's relationships with his district tend to be maintained through a small group whom he knew before he was elected or through a group who have since then worked closely with him. Generally speaking, the views of those whom he knew prior to his election tend to be more like his than do the views of the "average" voter. It is a well-known fact that we tend to be like the people with whom we associate and vice-versa. Also, most of the people who have worked closely with the congressman since his election—because he is a congressman—have a particular ax to grind. They will naturally tend to stress agreement with him on issues about which they are not concerned—just as salesmen typically do not disagree with their customers on politics. For several years, I wondered about the unfavorable references congressmen frequently made to the League of Women Voters and several times to delegations from labor unions. Ultimately, it occurred to me that these two groups are probably the only ones which seriously, on a face-to-face basis, year after year, go over with a congressman the issues on which they disagree with him. Because their efforts cannot be entirely discounted as "politics," they make congressmen uncomfortable.

Congressmen may also have a few close supporters upon whom they rely who tend to become "their" men, and who shift as they shift. This is not always just a matter of holding on to a job, but may represent confidence in a man, prestige gained by association with him, or an unwillingness to sacrifice an investment in goodwill which may be utilized for better public or personal purposes in the future. Such supporters are likely to couch any criticism in tactical terms, and ultimately, to follow the leader.[7]

Some men automatically interpret what they hear to support their own viewpoints.

---

[7] Dexter, *Congressmen and the People They Listen To*, Chs. II–III.

Mr. First of New Hungary does not think he hears much about foreign imports. Mr. Second, coming from the same sort of district in the same city, says:

It's either the first or second most important issue with me. Unemployment is the other. And, of course, they're really the same thing.

The last sentence is the clue to why Mr. Second hears so much more than Mr. First about foreign imports. When Mr. First hears about unemployment, he hears just about unemployment, or just about the declining industries of the area, or just about the invidious differential effect which accelerated amortization and certain other tax provisions have had on industry in the area. In fact, when I talked to him about tariff, he advised me that I really ought to study accelerated amortization. Mr. Second, however, interprets almost any statement about unemployment as a plea for relief from foreign imports. Sometimes it is, but sometimes it isn't. So, seeing the same men and hearing the same things said, Mr. Second will "hear" about tariff matters, Mr. First will not. Mr. Third, their colleague from an adjoining district, is vitally interested in wilderness preservation, hunting, and fishing. He sees many of the same men, but they are likely to talk to him about his interests, and if they do talk to him about unemployment, he is less likely to draw any special conclusions from the talk.

In more general terms, what congressmen hear and how they interpret what they hear depends on who they are.

Conventional discussion of the relationship between congressmen and constituents assumes that the kind of man the congressman is does not influence what he hears from the district and that the question is whether he follows or contravenes district sentiment. The notion of the congressman representing "the" district at least needs restatement *in terms of a particular congressman who represents what he hears from the district as he interprets it.* And his interpretation results from his being the particular kind of person he is and is reputed to be.

Of course, congressmen will hear many of the same things. The similarity is very great since there are common factors in the careers of American politicians, and since Congress is a continuing social group where habits and attitudes are likely to persist. The old hands (staff, lobbyists, and active constituents as well as members) teach the newer ones. Furthermore, and not surprisingly, within any given district the balance of forces may continue so that several successive congressmen will belong to the same politico-social group (sometimes even when they are members of different parties). The real test of how successfully the district exerts an inescapable "pressure" upon the congressman comes when, without any sharp shift in population characteristics in the district, the congressman comes from a different social grouping.

Students of comparative politics have, however, much more manageable ways of exploring this problem than by studying the activities of congressmen from the same district at different times. For instance, even in terms of our foci upon substantive issues, if I had realized the significance of knowing how a congressman's interpretation of what he hears is affected by his perception of the job, the constituency, and the facts, I could have tried to find out how senators of the same party and from the same state (but representing different factions and obviously looking at the world differently) understood the reciprocal trade question. It is almost incredible that Wiley, Republican of Wisconsin, and McCarthy, Republican of Wisconsin, could have heard the same messages on domestic security and international relations. It would have been interesting, therefore, to find out whether Wiley was as "convinced" as McCarthy was of the vital need for protecting Wisconsin's fur-bearing mammal growers or trappers against foreign competition. Robertson and Byrd of Virginia, Johnson and Daniel of Texas, Beall and Butler of Maryland, Martin and Duff of Pennsylvania, Cotton and Bridges of New Hampshire, Morse and Neuberger of Oregon, would all have made interesting studies from this standpoint. As it happened, I did most of my interviewing with representatives simply because senators' schedules are so much more complex, and it is more difficult to see them. A first-term senator may serve on as many as fourteen subcommittees, something unimaginable in the House.

For those whose focus is on the communication between a representative and his district, and who are not necessarily confined to a particular issue, there are still better cases for study. For instance, several districts in Maryland elect seven members to its Lower House, and Massachusetts has a number of three- and two-member districts (as have other states and cities). Considering the wide factional and personality differences of incumbents at the same time, an analysis of the messages they "hear" from their districts would be of considerable value.

V

How a congressman was "influenced" by his district: A transactional relationship.

Mr. Serious-Consideration provides a very good case study of how a particular constellation of factors in the district may lead to a particular vote. The vote cannot be understood unless we recognize that both a congressman—as a personality and at a particular time— and the "district," as understood by him, are variables.

During the spring of 1954, my old friend Mr. Straightforward did considerable canvassing in the district with a view to running for Congress in the primary against Mr. Serious-Consideration. Mr. Straightforward, incidentally, has held public office in the area several times before. He told me, in effect:

> There's practically no interest in trade or tariff matters in the district; if you are thinking as we were of interviewing businessmen and labor leaders about it, don't bother. None of them know anything about it; it just doesn't bulk large in their sight.

Mr. Serious-Consideration, however, in the same year reported that in his view it was one of the most significant issues to his constituents.

Why the difference? It can be explained, I think, partly by the fact that Mr. Serious-Consideration is, consciously, or unconsciously, looking for ways in which he can appeal to local labor without offending local business. Protection against "low-wage foreign imports" is, as trade association executives have pointed out to us, an excellent issue for *uniting* labor and management in depressed or dying industries (of which there are several in the district). Mr. Straightforward, on the other hand, has a program for economic redevelopment and reform of labor legislation which deflects the attention of those whom he meets, whether they agree with him or not, from such issues as the tariff. He, therefore, rarely hears about the tariff as an issue. Then, too, in manner and bearing, Mr. Straightforward is clearly an intellectual, and one of the popular conceptions of the intellectual is his belief in free trade.[8] Mr. Serious-Consideration is not at all of this type. Finally, Mr. Straightforward's worst fault as a politician is a rather curt dismissal of anything he regards as nonsense. Mr. Serious-Consideration, on the other hand, might justly be criticized for not being able to distinguish between more or less unmotivated grumbling and serious pleas for effective action.

Mr. Serious-Consideration is a worrier. He seems genuinely to believe that we must shore-up NATO by strengthening trade relations. Therefore, he called a meeting of everyone in his district who might be interested and wanted to come to discuss the problem. After this meeting, his office, which had already received a good deal of mail on the subject, was simply overwhelmed by protectionist mail. This came about because people who had attended the meeting told their friends and business acquaintances about his indecision. Mr. Serious-Consideration had called upon persons whom he thought might be interested. Naturally most of those who turned up were from protection-minded industries. It is much easier for the businessman who is, or thinks he is, in considerable economic danger from foreign imports to take a day off to attend a meeting on trade and tariffs called by the congressman (he can charge this as a business expense) than it is for the businessman who *might* benefit economically if international trade were increased in total. It is more difficult, of course, for nonbusinessmen to take such time off and it is usually quite impossible for them to charge the cost off as business expense.

So this meeting was "stacked" in this particular district. If, on the other hand, Congressman Lankford of the Fifth Maryland had called such a meeting it might well have been stacked the other way. His district is a big tobacco-growing area which is well aware of its dependence on sales to Switzerland, and there have been Swiss threats to cut off purchases unless the U.S. withdrew its trade barriers to Swiss watches. Congressman Serious-Consideration or Congressman Lankford, however, by some planning could have gotten a more balanced attendance. A different picture would have developed if leaders of those unions in the district whose headquarters favor reciprocal trade had been consulted; and if the several college

---

[8] See Dexter, *Congressmen and the People They Listen To*, Ch. XIX; and "Where the Elephant Fears to Dance Among the Chickens: Business in Politics? The Case of DuPont," *Human Organization*, 19 (1960–61), pp. 188–194.

professors of economics in the district and representatives of the Grange and the Farm Bureau had been invited. Or several organizations could have been asked to do what the League of Women Voters has done in some areas—study the dependence of the local industries on foreign trade.

Mr. Serious-Consideration would have had to be a different kind of man to provide wider representation at his meeting. However, three or four imaginative supporters of reciprocal trade could have produced the same result. And if the agricultural commodity in which Mr. Serious-Consideration himself has had an interest were on an export basis (as it was prior to World War II), his picture of the situation might well have been altered. He would then have been hearing from his own associates in his own trade association.

Mr. Serious-Consideration finally decided to vote against the party leadership on the key votes on reciprocal trade. He justified himself by objecting to various procedural aspects of the legislation—for instance the so-called "gag rule" under which the bill was brought to the floor. But he had not objected to this gag rule, which is standard parliamentary practice, in other cases where it was invoked. He continues to regard himself as a strong advocate of reciprocal trade.

When a congressman was not much influenced by his district.

Representative Warburton (R., Del., 1953–5) provided a particularly clear example of the way in which a congressman may select the kind of communications he hears. In answer to a question from me, he said to his secretary, "Am I right? We haven't received mail from more than five people on this tariff business." I looked somewhat astounded and she replied, "Yes, except of course for the pressure groups." The congressman had instructed her to segregate all recognized pressure-group mail. And he added, quite offhandedly, that he would discount, "because of his self-interest," one out of the five people who had written him about the tariff. His attitude may, in part at least, explain why the chemical companies and other industries in the state had never given him "any particular specifications" on the tariff. It certainly clarifies his assertion that his approach to the problem of communications had "choked off" pressure-group mail.

Such an approach is relatively easy in Delaware,[9] where DuPont,

---

[9] *Ibid.*

because of its tremendous size and consciousness of its own vulnerability, has developed a practice and to some extent a doctrine of self-restraint. In a sense, Congressman Warburton's procedure[10] was made much easier because of the effect upon DuPont of the munitions investigations of twenty years ago and its subsequent earnest effort never, never, never to get into that sort of trouble again. Thus it could happen when a prominent Delaware Democrat was asked why DuPont had not put on a campaign in regard to tariff matters (if, as it was reported, DuPont was hostile to the Reciprocal Trade Extension Act) that he said in a genuinely shocked voice, "Oh, the company would never allow that, two or three letters at the most."

A congressman's reputation among those who might want to influence him, determines in large measure what actually is said to him.

Most lobbyists appear to follow the principle of going to see only those who already agree with them. "Work with your friends, but don't stir up your enemies" is a principle fairly widely believed by Capitol Hill lobbyists. There is a reason for this prudence. Most investigations of lobbying and of particular lobbyists seem to have been started by congressmen who were annoyed at being continually approached by lobbyists with whom they disagreed. There is also another possible reason—it makes the job easy for the lobbyist. Representatives of the League of Women Voters and of labor union councils, who do not follow this principle, make themselves unpopular in some quarters. In other words, survival and comfort for the lobbyist may depend upon not lobbying very much—and it is safer to stay away from somebody who may be an enemy and react negatively than to take a risk.

The tendency to abstain from trying to influence those whom you believe to be against you affects the districts back home as well as professional Capitol Hill lobbyists. The Farm Bureaus in Congressman Stubborn's district, like most Farm Bureaus, were definitely committed to the reciprocal trade program. Nevertheless, when a delegation went to see him, they made no effort to talk in favor of

---

[10] Congressman Warburton followed the same procedure on other matters. He was, it is true, rather badly beaten in his try for the Senate in 1954 by the incumbent Democrat, Frear, but there is no reason to suppose that this handling of communications had anything to do with the outcome. Far more significant political factors, such as the opposition to integration, probably explain that.

reciprocal trade. Our correspondent in Mr. Stubborn's district inquired of Farm Bureau representatives why they made no such effort and he summarized their attitude as follows:

> The farmers deliberately avoided mention of tariffs; when I asked one of them why he didn't beard old "Stubborn" in his high-tariff den, he replied, "Nothing in the world will change his thinking on tariffs, so why bother? He knows how we feel and can't help but feel a little nervous about the situation. So we can take that nervousness and get him to go along with us on things he isn't so dead-set against."

The probability is that they didn't *change* him on anything, but that they may have influenced him to take a more aggressive and effective part on an issue of importance to them—an issue on which he did not disagree, but which he considered less important than they did.

In another instance, the congressmen from a certain area are inclined to be rather blunt and not to rely on any indirection. Before the 1955 vote on reciprocal trade, the Farm Bureau sent representatives in to talk with these congressmen. One of them, Congressman Ridge, told me that the farmers said, "National asked us to pass the word along that we're in favor of reciprocal trade—but we shan't be mad if you vote against it." Then, according to Mr. Ridge, one of the congressmen asked the Farm Bureau men if any one of them really favored reciprocal trade. Anyone who knows the congressmen present can be sure that at least two of them would look ready to slay on the spot any farmer bold enough to say "Yes." Apparently no one did say "Yes," and the reason may have been similar to that advanced by the Farm Bureau member from Mr. Stubborn's district. So Mr. Ridge, who is not as strongly opposed to reciprocal trade as some of his colleagues, was pushed to this conclusion: "Everybody in my state is against reciprocal trade. . . . The only ones for it would be the ultra-internationalists." Of course, if Mr. Ridge were a devoted supporter of reciprocal trade, or if he were a really sophisticated analyst of interpersonal relations, he might well have felt that the conclusion is not that easy. But he is neither of these and so he allied himself entirely with his colleagues' opposition to the reciprocal trade program.

Several congressmen told me, in effect, that they tell their constituents: "I want a letter of such and such a kind, or I won't pay any attention to it."

One of the most dedicated opponents of reciprocal trade in the country is a man who has often pointed out that reciprocal trade is really an invention of Karl Marx himself, designed to "make us captives of the Kremlin," developed and implemented by Harry Dexter White. This congressman states that he tells his constituents that he is only interested in "factual, thoughtful" letters, nothing mass-produced or propagandistic. He also told me that in three months he had not received one single letter opposing his views on reciprocal trade; he had received over 2,000 supporting his position, 1,750 of which were definitely individual letters. The very extremity of his position apparently leads those who might disagree with him to feel, "Oh, what's the use?" Senators who make statements of this kind, however, may simply not know what mail they receive, since the mail clerks handle it. Most members of the House do have a fairly good idea of what is coming in to them. Of course, protectionist mail was mass-produced in a way that reciprocal trade mail was not, and it is far more likely that a protectionist congressman would receive nothing in opposition to his stand rather than the reverse. Oil interests on the Atlantic seaboard did mass-produce mail protesting the fuel-oil quota, but few of the congressmen to whom they wrote favored a fuel-oil quota, whatever their general tariff views.

We need more studies of what the image of a person to whom a communication is sent is in the minds of the sender.[11] By and large, I strongly suspect that the bulk of political communications in the United States today tends to be addressed to those believed most likely to be sympathetic. Exceptions may occur when an issue becomes one of great involvement (as reciprocal trade did *not*, in 1953–1955), or of interest to persons politically very unsophisticated who have no image of specific political figures. (Occasionally, too, a writer may regard his request as one for a personal service but in the recipient's view, it may involve an issue. A sympathetic response is expected, of course, to a request for a personal service.)

Some communications tend to be unclear in their meaning.

A good deal of so-called "lobbying" by constituents tends to be nothing more than a social visit and a general discussion. One senator's assistant said:

---

[11] The work of Erving Goffman, *The Presentation of Self in Everyday Life* (Garden City: Doubleday-Anchor, 1960), seems to me to be methodologically of extreme value for this purpose, as is also that of Everett C. Hughes, *Men and Their Work* (Glencoe: The Free Press, 1958).

> You know, many of these guys who come in here from back home never talk about issues at all. I've seen lots of them supposedly lobbying. Now, "Roughie," [the senator] takes me to lunch with them and we go out to lunch, but they don't necessarily talk about anything. "Roughie," just knows a good guy may be going out of business because he doesn't get more trade or so. It's the spirit that influences him.

Interestingly enough, some weeks later I found that this particular assistant was completely ignorant of the quite strong feelings (verbalized in other quarters) on tariff matters of an important industry in the state. This is an industry whose representatives had visited him and the senator, and in whose behalf he personally had spent many hours performing other chores in administrative agencies.

Mr. Busy represents a district very much like those of Messrs. First, Second, and Third discussed above, and he is home every weekend. He was professedly strongly opposed to reciprocal trade, but when I questioned him, he said he really did not know whether people talk about the tariff with him or not. At first, it seemed as though this might be because of his schedule which is so heavy that most men could not stand it, and he must be, as a result, always fatigued. But the real point appears to be that Mr. Busy's focus and attention in oral conversations back home are given to requests for personal services. He is the archtype of the errandboy congressman and the only things he seems attuned to hear are requests for personal services. He shunts comments on issues to one side or regards them as preliminaries to requests for favors. When Mr. Second hears someone talk about unemployment caused by foreign imports, he regards this as a request to fight reciprocal trade. Mr. First regards it as nonsense, although possibly nonsense of which he should be cognizant. But Mr. Busy pays only vague attention to it except insofar as it leads or may lead to a request for him to perform a service. In this he may well be correct, for very few constituents talk about an issue with a congressman just to talk about the issue. I spent about twenty man-days in the winter of 1956 acting as co-manager of a candidate in a congressional primary campaign and about half of this time I was actually with the candidate. During the entire twenty days only four people raised any national or international issues whatsoever with him or me. (Others who worked for him at the same time and in the same area had similar reports to make.)

It's partly accident if anybody's listening.

There is a highly unpredictable element in the kind of response a particular communication will get. As a senatorial assistant said:

> I've seen it a dozen times. One time some letter or call will come in from "Minerville" and nobody will pay any attention to it. They might say, for instance, the miners are all worried about this foreign fuel oil. Another time a call will come in in the same words almost and everybody will get worried as hell about it; it might be that the State Chairman was in the day before and says, "We're not doing so well in 'Coal County'" so we all jump to the conclusion that it's fuel oil that is hurting us there. Or it may be just accident; one time the Senator is preoccupied, another in a relaxed mood, but the third time he listens eagerly. You know how it is.

VI

Important instances when congressmen were changed by their districts.

The two statistically notable shifts on reciprocal trade in 1955 as compared with previous years were: (1) Southern congressmen, mostly representing textile manufacturing districts, who for the first time voted against the Hull reciprocal trade program, in spite of a traditional veneration for free trade in the South; and (2) Farm Belt congressmen, from districts where "isolationist" sentiment had been fairly strong, who for the first time supported reciprocal trade on the key votes. The latter were presumably influenced by the organized efforts of national Farm Bureau leaders to get their local leaders to understand the (actual or alleged) dependence of farm prosperity upon international trade and the (actual or alleged) values of a trade not aid program. But those who were influenced were not, so far as is known, men to whom the issue mattered much one way or another.

In the case of the Southern congressmen the matter is clearer. Here "pressure education"—agitation in the district—worked. They broke with the leadership of Speaker Rayburn, generally said to be the most powerful Speaker since Speaker Cannon. They broke with the Southern tradition and the tradition of Cordell Hull, the father of reciprocal trade. They challenged and to some degree pressured that highly respected Southern Senator, Walter George, on his long-standing pro-reciprocal trade position. And they gave, in this case, a weapon to Herman Talmadge, George's potential opponent in the senatorial primary in 1956, in spite of the fact that practically none of them would have preferred Talmadge to George. This breaking with precedent was chiefly the result of the communications they received from their districts, largely from textile interests. Some Southern congressmen received more mail on the reciprocal trade question in a few weeks than they normally do in months on all issues combined. That the mail was more or less synthetic and stimulated is shown by the fact that some congressmen, whose positions are known to be unchangeable, received not a single letter! For these Southern congressmen, such a flood of mail was apparently like the first engagement in a war for inexperienced troops. They had never seen anything of the sort before. The results: most of the Georgia delegation opposed reciprocal trade on the key votes. Hugh Alexander, successor to "Muley" Doughton who as leader of Ways and Means had year after year pushed reciprocal trade through committee and the House much as Cordell Hull wanted it, voted against the program of Hull and Doughton similarly.

This does not controvert what has been said before. Most of these men, although traditionally "free-traders," care very little about the issue one way or the other. If industry and the workers in their district are convinced that reciprocal trade will hurt them, they are willing enough to go along—just as most of them would go along with their farmers if the latter wanted new soil conservation legislation. In either case, they would regard themselves simply as serving their constituents.

Mr. Lanham's shift.

The leader of the Southeastern congressmen was the late Henderson Lanham of Georgia. He played a part, perhaps a large part, in making it respectable for ten to fifteen men from his section to reject the leadership of Sam Rayburn, Jere Cooper, and Wilbur Mills, and support the textile industry's protectionist claims. How did he happen to bolt?

In January, 1955, he received a large quantity of mail from workers in the textile industry saying that they wanted protection against foreign goods. Shrewd enough to realize that they must have been "put up to it" by manufacturers, Mr. Lanham said:

> I did not appreciate it. I wrote to a friend of mine who is in business, saying, in effect, "call your fellows off." I asked

my friend, "Don't peril point and escape clause protect you?"
He replied, "No, they don't." That shocked me. I started making inquiries. I found out I'd been pretty naive. Peril point
and escape clause did not protect our people.

(Peril point and escape clause refer to provisions of earlier Reciprocal Trade Acts, professedly designed to protect U.S. industry against
"ruination" through goods introduced under the Reciprocal Trade
Act.)

It is significant that the congressman made his inquiries in his
home state almost (if not quite) entirely among people in the
textile industry. Despite the fact that at least half of the economy
of his district is agricultural, producing cotton among other commodities, he made no inquiry among his farmers. A superficial
analysis, however, would suggest that most of his farmers profit
from foreign trade, directly or indirectly, and that many of them
are affiliated with farm organizations which have endorsed reciprocal
trade. Mr. Lanham actually represented the town more than the
countryside. The town is where his roots were, where his friends
were, and he thought in its terms. Populationwise, it would be perfectly conceivable that his district and several other districts over
whose congressmen he had influence, might be represented by men
to whom the farmer is more important than the manufacturer. Although I cannot prove it to be so, and I did not realize its significance until 1959, I suspect that the Talmadge-George senatorial
rivalry was a very significant matter to Mr. Lanham and his Georgia colleagues. Walter George had won national renown as a
"world-minded" statesman; Herman Talmadge intended to challenge him for the Senate. The most vulnerable—in terms of local
interests and concerns—aspect of George's internationalist position
was his support of reciprocal trade. In whatever manner he responded to the organized pressure from back home on protection
for textiles he would be weaker. (George himself, as late as 1954,
was, as my interview with him suggested, probably quite ignorant
of the potential strength of the drive for textile protection.) Consequently, Talmadge in the nature of the case espoused the interests
of the textile industry as that industry interpreted them; and,
naturally, Congressmen from the state would have been inclined
to feel that if they continued to support reciprocal trade they might
be out on a limb which Talmadge (a younger, politically stronger,
and probably more organization-minded man than George) could
saw off.

VII

Reverse English.

When Mr. Lanham became convinced that there was merit to the contention of the textile and allied industries, he then went to the state organization representing textiles. According to his account, he politely pointed out to them that they really hadn't been on the ball—he should have heard more about the matter and so should his colleagues. Presumably, this did increase the communications on the subject, by mail and personal visits, to his colleagues.

Reverse lobbying—from congressmen to interest groups—is by no means unusual. I asked another prominent congressman how much he heard from the organizations on his side of the issue.

> Hell no, it's just the other way. It's me calling them up and trying to shaft them to get off their fat asses and get out and do something.

More common, probably, is the senator or representative who asks the lobbyists on his side to do something which they then generalize. A senatorial assistant needed some figures in preparing a speech and tried to get them from the lobbying group: "I absolutely had to beat them over the head to get those things." But not long after, the same figures were cited by the organization as "proving" their point.

VIII

Pressure is how you see it.

"Pressure" and "pressure politics" are regarded by most "sophisticated" people today as "explaining" a great deal that happens. But it was frequently impossible to find any admission of or apparently any awareness of "pressure." That was not because shrewd and worldly politicians were concealing what really goes on from this naive and innocent interviewer and his naive and innocent colleagues.[12]

---

[12] On Beacon Hill in Massachusetts, when with Governor Furcolo (D.), and to a lesser extent with Governor Volpe (R.), the writer noted pressure, possibly which conforms more to the traditional view of "pressure." The journalistic, traditional notion of pressure certainly seemed to apply to highway contracts and some patronage matters in the Furcolo administration. In all probability, the pressure (not so much on congressmen but on the relevant officials in the Defense Department) on defense contracts might be much "rougher" than any-

The reason is explained by Senator Service's assistant:

> There are very few people actually pressuring us, even if you count all we hear about all issues. Seriously, the sense of being pressured is a matter of reaction. Other people who get no more mail than we do in this office would say, "See how much pressure is on me." We don't feel it. . . . Sure, you get mail. It's just that so-and-so makes more 'phone calls than somebody else. The result is purely physical. It isn't a representation of what or how or when people are going to vote in elections. . . . My personal opinion is that members of most organizations make up their minds on what they read in the papers without reference to organizations.

With this theory of voting behavior, Senator Service's assistant naturally will not be too much worried by a good deal of effort to get him or his boss to change policies—he simply will not regard it as pressure.

Congressman Widesight amusingly illustrated the point made by Service's assistant. Mr. Widesight has moods when he reaches way out into left field looking for things to worry about, things which might possibly defeat him. One day, discussing reciprocal trade, he said that things were very bad indeed. His reason was that he was getting "so much" mail against it. "I, whom they never used to bother at all." When I checked with his secretary later, I found he couldn't possibly have received more than fifty letters opposing reciprocal trade. This was only a fraction of the mail Senator Service received on the same matter. It was also a fraction of what Congressman Widesight himself has several times heard on other matters such as postal pay increases. However, Widesight is accustomed to communications on that issue and he wasn't accustomed to them on the reciprocal trade issue.

As a matter of fact, on the reciprocal trade issue, most of the congressmen interviewed reported that no one had come to see them. Several of them expressed the wish that someone would make the issue clear. This does not mean, of course, that they were not approached; but simply that they had forgotten the approach or had not realized its purpose. Some of them tried to question me about the matter in what I think was a serious effort to get some guidance.

---

thing congressmen generally experience on reciprocal trade. But it will be noted that contracts and patronage are matters of direct, demonstrable interest to determinate people. Reciprocal trade is *general* legislation.

Our interviews confirmed the observation of the late Sam Jacobs, then newly appointed to the staff of Senator McNamara (D., Mich.), who said, speaking generally and not talking just about reciprocal trade:

> I was very much surprised how few representatives of organizations come around to make themselves known. The Senator is, as you know, on the subcommittee dealing with "ruanga" and "minorca" manufacturing; yet nobody came around to see us either from the Ruanga Makers, AFL, or the Minorca Setters, CIO. I raised hell with them about that because I know some of their top guys through AVC; but some, who should have been here, haven't been. . . . Of course, there might have been some reason they hesitated, although, hell, they ought to know the Senator is pro-labor if anybody is; and if they were in any doubt as to how they might be received, there are a dozen ways of throwing your hat in to see if it gets tossed back.

Later he continued:

> You know we are very much interested in educational legislation. I had some representatives of . . . organizations here to talk with us. I sent for them, they didn't try to see us. We thought about some changes in the educational bill which looked desirable in terms of their program and worked them out. We did get their O.K. They went along with us.

The question here is: How much lobbying or pressure was there?

Even where there is a considerable amount of what the outsider would consider pressure, the point made by Senator Service's assistant is entirely valid. What you call pressure, or what you feel to be pressure, depends on how thick your skin is. Mr. Second, for instance, told me that he had been subject to no "pressure—that is, no threats." To many men in politics, threats alone represent real pressure because they know very well that few votes are actually lost on any one given issue such as reciprocal trade. But, of course, what is a threat to one man is not a threat to another.

The most strongly felt kind of "pressure" on the reciprocal trade issue came, apparently, from Speaker Rayburn and the Democratic leadership against the potentially recalcitrant Democrats. Speaker Rayburn attended a breakfast for freshmen congressmen shortly before the vote and said, in effect, that he's discovered that those who go along, get along. One new member regarded this as pressure—a threat. Another new member (actually probably more vulnerable in terms of his factional position and his position within the delegation) did not. Both of them failed to "go along." Aside from this speech, most of the "pressure" on the doubtful members seems to have come through the grapevine or from their own apprehensions as to what might happen if they bolted the party leadership. One reason why fairly few members seem to have felt pressure on this matter is to be explained in terms of their background and associations in local politics. In many states, "pressure" on matters like highway contracts or patronage, or even for or against gubernatorial programs, must be relatively heavy—that is, threats are far more common at the state level than they are in Washington. Many congressmen come from such a background and a good many are still involved in local conflicts about patronage, contracts, etc. As a result, Washington to them seems mild.

It should never be forgotten that most congressmen respect—although in an inarticulate or almost subconscious way—the right of petition. They have a general feeling that everyone should have a right to talk or write to them about any public issue—that's what they're there for. But they aren't as worried about each communication as college professors might expect. They generally feel they have an equal right to disregard the petitioner's point, once it has been courteously received and acknowledged. Until a congressman definitely makes up his mind, it isn't pressure—it's communication or instruction. Much of what Mr. Fourth, for instance, believes about reciprocal trade he learned from his mail.

IX

Opportunism is also where you see it.

Outsiders, nonpoliticians, tend to attribute many political decisions to opportunism. Also, opponents in politics sometimes attribute the decisions of the other party or faction to "opportunism." However, in the interviews which I conducted, few congressmen attributed their friends' decisions or their own to opportunism. When friends differ on a particular issue it may be explained in terms of "the heat being on." Whether any significant number of politicians anywhere would have an image of themselves as opportunists, I do not know. It is certainly true that in these interviews many men were amazingly—and often embarrassingly—frank about events, relationships, and personal opinions. But insofar as the overt picture which they have of themselves is concerned, opportunism does not play a prominent role. Even Congressman District, who related his obligation to his district directly to his chances for reelection, spoke of his "duty" to get reelected. No one used a systematically opportunistic vocabulary of motives to explain himself or his action. Perhaps a different type of interview, some sort of "depth-interviewing," would bring out a hidden set of self-images at variance with this surface picture. However, I have no evidence to that effect and am inclined to doubt it.

* * *

X
CONCLUSION

Attention has been focused in the present study on the ways congressmen view representation and on the ways in which their pictures of the world determine what they hear, how they interpret it, whom they represent, how they influence representation by others, and how they view other representatives. It omits many equally significant facets of the representative process—for example, the formal and informal structure of the congressional system. Elsewhere[23] I have discussed the formal structure. It is obvious that there is an informal structure and that it is highly significant. That it is an exceptionally complex structure to study, because congressmen are members of several different groups simultaneously, is also apparent. I have made only random observations concerning it.

Obviously, it would be enlightening and helpful to have comparative studies of state legislatures to follow up the brilliant work of Garceau and Silverman.[24] It would also be useful to have additional studies of other issues coming before Congress.

The study here reported was defective in that it lacked the precision of, for example, many sociological reports on industrial plants. One reason for this is the problem of anonymity. To describe the factional conflicts in a particular congressional district, or even more personal interrelationships within a congressional committee, could hardly be done with fairness to the subjects of

---

[23] Dexter, *Congressmen and the People They Listen To.*
[24] Oliver Garceau and Corinne Silverman, "A Pressure Group and the Pressured," *American Political Science Review,* 48 (1954), pp. 672–691.

the study. Such details are safe enough when the study concerns a factory. But aside from this problem, the "group memberships," reference groups, and so on, of politicians, are substantially more complex than those reported in many professional journals. Our reciprocal trade study devoted an unusual degree of attention to the districts from which some of the congressmen we interviewed came. However, we devised no technique for observing the relationship between a congressman and his constituency in detail over a period of time. Probably, considering the workload of congressmen, this can only be done by those who become helpers and thereby preclude themselves from reporting. Studies of state and city legislatures and of the representative process therein offer more hope for the development of a sociology of representation. It should be remembered that representation exists in many cultural frameworks. How for instance, does all that is said here apply to other systems? In connection, it is noted that the representative process exists in the church, in trade unions, in trade associations, and in fraternal organizations. So far, the process has been studied only occasionally in such contexts.

CONSTITUENCY INFLUENCE IN CONGRESS*

Warren E. Miller and Donald E. Stokes

SUBSTANTIAL CONSTITUENCY influence over the lower house of Congress is commonly thought to be both a normative principle and a factual truth of American government. From their draft constitution we may assume the Founding Fathers expected it, and many political scientists feel, regretfully, that the Framers' wish has come all too true.[1] Nevertheless, much of the evidence of constituency control rests on inference. The fact that our House of Representatives, especially by comparison with the House of Commons, has irregular party voting does not of itself indicate that Congressmen deviate from party in response to local pressure. And even more, the fact that many Congressmen *feel* pressure from home does not of itself establish that the local constituency is performing any of the acts that a reasonable definition of control would imply.

I. CONSTITUENCY CONTROL IN THE NORMATIVE THEORY OF REPRESENTATION

Control by the local constituency is at one pole of *both* the great normative controversies about representation that have arisen in modern times. It is generally recognized that constituency control is opposite to the conception of representation associated with Ed-

* Reprinted from *The American Political Science Review*, Vol. LVII, No. 1, March, 1963.

The research reported here was made possible through grants of the Rockefeller Foundation and the Social Science Research Council, whose support is gratefully acknowledged. The authors are indebted also to Ralph Bisco and Gudmund R. Iversen for invaluable assistance.
[1] To be sure, the work of the Federal Convention has been supplemented in two critical respects. The first of these is the practice, virtually universal since the mid-19th Century, of choosing Representatives from single-member districts of limited geographic area. The second is the practice, which has also become virtually universal in our own century, of selecting party nominees for the House by direct primary election.

mund Burke. Burke wanted the representative to serve the constituency's *interest* but not its *will,* and the extent to which the representative should be compelled by electoral sanctions to follow the "mandate" of his constituents has been at the heart of the ensuing controversy as it has continued for a century and a half.[2]

Constituency control also is opposite to the conception of government by responsible national parties. This is widely seen, yet the point is rarely connected with normative discussions of representation. Indeed, it is remarkable how little attention has been given to the model of representation implicit in the doctrine of a "responsible two-party system." When the subject of representation is broached among political scientists the classical argument between Burke and his opponents is likely to come at once to mind. So great is Burke's influence that the antithesis he proposed still provides the categories of thought used in contemporary treatments of representation despite the fact that many students of politics today would advocate a relationship between representative and constituency that fits *neither* position of the mandate-independence controversy.

The conception of representation implicit in the doctrine of responsible parties shares the idea of popular control with the instructed-delegate model. Both are versions of popular sovereignty. But "the people" of the responsible two-party system are conceived in terms of a national rather than a local constituency. Candidates for legislative office appeal to the electorate in terms of a *national* party program and leadership, to which, if elected, they will be committed. Expressions of policy preference by the local district are reduced to endorsements of one or another of these programs, and the local district retains only the arithmetical significance that whichever party can rally to its program the greater number of supporters in the district will control its legislative seat.

No one tradition of representation has entirely dominated Amer-

---

[2] In the language of Eulau, Wahlke, *et al.,* we speak here of the "style," not the "focus," of representation. See their "The Role of the Representative: Some Empirical Observations on the Theory of Edmund Burke," *APSA Review,* Vol. 53 (September, 1959), pp. 742–756. An excellent review of the mandate-independence controversy is given by Hanna Fenichel Pitkin, "The Theory of Representation" (unpublished doctoral dissertation, University of California, Berkeley, 1961). For other contemporary discussions of representation, see Alfred de Grazia, *Public and Republic* (New York, 1951), and John A. Fairlie, "The Nature of Political Representation," *APSA Review,* Vol. 34 (April–June, 1940), pp. 236–48, 456–66.

ican practice. Elements of the Burkean, instructed-delegate, and responsible party models can all be found in our political life. Yet if the American system has elements of all three, a good deal depends on how they are combined. Especially critical is the question whether different models of representation apply to different public issues. Is the saliency of legislative action to the public so different in quality and degree on different issues that the legislator is subject to very different constraints from his constituency? Does the legislator have a single generalized mode of response to his constituency that is rooted in a normative belief about the representative's role or does the same legislator respond to his constituency differently on different issues? More evidence is needed on matters so fundamental to our system.

II. AN EMPIRICAL STUDY OF REPRESENTATION

To extend what we know of representation in the American Congress the Survey Research Center of The University of Michigan interviewed the incumbent Congressman, his nonincumbent opponent (if any), and a sample of constituents in each of 116 congressional districts, which were themselves a probability sample of all districts.[3] These interviews, conducted immediately after the

[3] The sampling aspects of this research were complicated by the fact that the study of representation was a rider midway on a four-year panel study of the electorate whose primary sampling units were not congressional districts (although there is no technical reason why they could not have been if the needs of the representation analysis had been foreseen when the design of the sample was fixed two years before). As a result, the districts in our sample had unequal probabilities of selection and unequal weights in the analysis, making the sample somewhat less efficient than an equal-probability sample of equivalent size.

It will be apparent in the discussion that follows that we have estimated characteristics of whole constituencies from our samples of constituents living in particular districts. In view of the fact that a sample of less than two thousand constituents has been divided among 116 districts, the reader may wonder about the reliability of these estimates. After considerable investigation we have concluded that their sampling error is not so severe a problem for the analysis as we had thought it would be. Several comments may indicate why it is not.

To begin with, the weighting of our sample of districts has increased the reliability of the constituency estimates. The correct theoretical weight to be assigned each district in the analysis is the inverse of the probability of the district's selection, and it can be shown that this weight is approximately proportional to the number of interviews taken in the district. The result of this is that the greatest weight is assigned the districts with the largest number of interviews and, hence, the most reliable constituency estimates. Indeed, these weights

congressional election of 1958, explored a wide range of attitudes and perceptions held by the individuals who play the reciprocal roles of the representative relation in national government. The distinguishing feature of this research is, of course, that it sought direct information from both constituent and legislator (actual and aspiring). To this fund of comparative interview data has been added information about the roll call votes of our sample of Congressmen and the political and social characteristics of the districts they represent.

Many students of politics, with excellent reason, have been sensitive to possible ties between representative and constituent that have little to do with issues of public policy. For example, ethnic identifications may cement a legislator in the affections of

---

increase by half again the (weighted) mean number of interviews taken per district. To put the matter another way: the introduction of differential weights trades some of our sample of congressional districts for more reliable constituency estimates.

How much of a problem the unreliability of these estimates is depends very much on the analytic uses to which the estimates are put. If our goal were case analyses of particular districts, the constituency samples would have to be much larger. Indeed, for most case analyses we would want several hundred interviews per district (at a cost, over 116 districts, of several small nuclear reactors). However, most of the findings reported here are based not on single districts but on many or all of the districts in our sample. For analyses of this sort the number of interviews per district can be much smaller.

Our investigation of the effect of the sampling variance of the constituency estimates is quite reassuring. When statistics computed from our constituency samples are compared with corresponding parameter values for the constituencies, the agreement of the two sets of figures is quite close. For example, when the proportions voting Democratic in the 116 constituencies in 1958, as computed from our sample data, are compared with the actual proportions voting Democratic, as recorded in official election statistics, a product moment correlation of 0.93 is obtained, and this figure is the more impressive since this test throws away non-voters, almost one-half of our total sample. We interpret the Pearsonian correlation as an appropriate measure of agreement in this case, since the associated regression equations are almost exactly the identity function. The alternative intraclass correlation coefficient has almost as high a value.

Although we believe that this analysis provides a textbook illustration of how misleading intuitive ideas (including our own) about the effects of sampling error can be, these figures ought not to be too beguiling. It is clear that how close such a correlation is to 1.0 for any given variable will depend on the ratio of the between-district variance to the total variance. When this ratio is as high as it is for Republican and Democratic voting, the effect of the unreliability of our constituency estimates is fairly trivial. Although the content of the study is quite different, this sampling problem has much in common with the problem of attenuation of correlation as it has been treated in psychological testing. See, for example, J. P. Guilford, *Fundamental Statistics in Psychology and Education* (New York, 1956), pp. 475–78.

his district, whatever (within limits) his stands on issues. And many Congressmen keep their tenure of office secure by skillful provision of district benefits ranging from free literature to major federal projects. In the full study of which this analysis is part we have explored several bases of constituency support that have little to do with policy issues. Nevertheless, the question how the representative should make up his mind on legislative issues is what the classical arguments over representation are all about, and we have given a central place to a comparison of the policy preferences of constituents and Representatives and to a causal analysis of the relation between the two.

In view of the electorate's scanty information about government it was not at all clear in advance that such a comparison could be made. Some of the more buoyant advocates of popular sovereignty have regarded the citizen as a kind of kibitzer who looks over the shoulder of his representative at the legislative game. Kibitzer and player may disagree as to which card should be played, but they were at least thought to share a common understanding of what the alternatives are.

No one familiar with the findings of research on mass electorates could accept this view of the citizen. Far from looking over the shoulder of their Congressmen at the legislative game, most Americans are almost totally uninformed about legislative issues in Washington. At best the average citizen may be said to have some general ideas about how the country should be run, which he is able to use in responding to particular questions about what the government ought to do. For example, survey studies have shown that most people have a general (though differing) conception of how far government should go to achieve social and economic welfare objectives and that these convictions fix their response to various particular questions about actions government might take.[4]

What makes it possible to compare the policy preferences of constituents and Representatives despite the public's low awareness of legislative affairs is the fact that Congressmen themselves respond to many issues in terms of fairly broad evaluative dimensions. Undoubtedly policy alternatives are judged in the executive agencies and the specialized committees of the Congress by criteria that are

---

[4] See Angus Campbell, Philip E. Converse, Warren E. Miller, and Donald E. Stokes, *The American Voter* (New York, 1960), pp. 194–209.

relatively complex and specific to the policies at issue. But a good deal of evidence goes to show that when proposals come before the House as a whole they are judged on the basis of more general evaluative dimensions.[5] For example, most Congressmen, too, seem to have a general conception of how far government should go in the area of domestic social and economic welfare, and these general positions apparently orient their roll call votes on a number of particular social welfare issues.

It follows that such a broad evaluative dimension can be used to compare the policy preferences of constituents and Representatives despite the low state of the public's information about politics. In this study three such dimensions have been drawn from our voter interviews and from congressional interviews and roll call records. As suggested above, one of these has to do with approval of government action in the social welfare field, the primary domestic issue of the New Deal-Fair Deal (and New Frontier) eras. A second dimension has to do with support for American involvement in foreign affairs, a latter-day version of the isolationist-internationalist continuum. A third dimension has to do with approval of federal action to protect the civil rights of Negroes.[6]

---

[5] This conclusion, fully supported by our own work for later Congresses, is one of the main findings to be drawn from the work of Duncan MacRae on roll call voting in the House of Representatives. See his *Dimensions of Congressional Voting: A Statistical Study of the House of Representatives in the Eighty-First Congress* (Berkeley and Los Angeles: University of California Press, 1958). For additional evidence of the existence of scale dimensions in legislative behavior, see N. L. Gage and Ben Shimberg, "Measuring Senatorial Progressivism," *Journal of Abnormal and Social Psychology*, Vol. 44 (January 1949), pp. 112–117; George M. Belknap, "A Study of Senatorial Voting by Scale Analysis" (unpublished doctoral dissertation, University of Chicago, 1951), and "A Method for Analyzing Legislative Behavior," *Midwest Journal of Political Science*, Vol. 2 (1958), pp. 377–402; two other articles by MacRae, "The Role of the State Legislator in Massachusetts," *American Sociological Review*, Vol. 19 (April 1954), pp. 185–194, and "Roll Call Votes and Leadership," *Public Opinion Quarterly*, Vol. 20 (1956), pp. 543–558; Charles D. Farris, "A Method of Determining Ideological Groups in Congress," *Journal of Politics*, Vol. 20 (1958), pp. 308–338; and Leroy N. Rieselbach, "Quantitative Techniques for Studying Voting Behavior in the U. N. General Assembly," *International Organization*, Vol. 14 (1960), pp. 291–306.

[6] The content of the three issue domains may be suggested by some of the roll call and interview items used. In the area of social welfare these included the issues of public housing, public power, aid to education, and government's role in maintaining full employment. In the area of foreign involvement the items included the issues of foreign economic aid, military aid, sending troops abroad, and aid to neutrals. In the area of civil rights the items included the issues of school desegregation, fair employment, and the protection of Negro voting rights.

Because our research focused on these three dimensions, our analysis of constituency influence is limited to these areas of policy. No point has been more energetically or usefully made by those who have sought to clarify the concepts of power and influence than the necessity of specifying the acts *with respect to which* one actor has power or influence or control over another.[7] Therefore, the scope or range of influence for our analysis is the collection of legislative issues falling within our three policy domains. We are not able to say how much control the local constituency may or may not have over *all* actions of its Representative, and there may well be pork-barrel issues or other matters of peculiar relevance to the district on which the relation of Congressman to constituency is quite distinctive. However, few observers of contemporary politics would regard the issues of government provision of social and economic welfare, of American involvement in world affairs, and of federal action in behalf of the Negro as constituting a trivial range of action. Indeed, these domains together include most of the great issues that have come before Congress in recent years.

In each policy domain we have used the procedures of cumulative scaling, as developed by Louis Guttman and others, to order our samples of Congressmen, of opposing candidates, and of voters. In each domain Congressmen were ranked once according to their roll call votes in the House and again according to the attitudes they revealed in our confidential interviews. These two orderings are by no means identical, nor are the discrepancies due simply to uncertainties of measurement.[8] Opposing candidates also were

---

[7] Because this point has been so widely discussed it has inevitably attracted a variety of terms. Dahl denotes the acts of *a* whose performance *A* is able to influence as the *scope* of *A*'s power. See Robert A. Dahl, "The Concept of Power," *Behavioral Science*, Vol. 2 (July 1957), pp. 201–215. This usage is similar to that of Harold D. Lasswell and Abraham Kaplan, *Power and Society* (New Haven: Yale University Press, 1950), pp. 71–73. Dorwin Cartwright, however, denotes the behavioral or psychological changes in *P* which *O* is able to induce as the *range* of *O*'s power: "A Field Theoretical Conception of Power," *Studies in Social Power* (Ann Arbor: Research Center for Group Dynamics, Institute for Social Research, The University of Michigan, 1959), pp. 183–220.

[8] That the Representative's roll call votes can diverge from his true opinion is borne out by a number of findings of the study (some of which are reported here) as to the conditions under which agreement between the Congressman's roll call position and his private attitude will be high or low. However, a direct confirmation that these two sets of measurements are not simply getting at the same thing is given by differences in attitude-roll call agreement according to the Congressman's sense of how well his roll call votes have expressed his real views. In the domain of foreign involvement, for example, the correlation of our attitudinal and roll call measurements was .75 among Representatives who said

ranked in each policy domain according to the attitudes they revealed in our interviews. The nationwide sample of constituents was ordered in each domain, and by averaging the attitude scores of all constituents living in the same districts, whole constituencies were ranked on each dimension so that the views of Congressmen could be compared with those of their constituencies.[9] Finally, by considering only the constituents in each district who share some characteristic (voting for the incumbent, say) we were able to order these fractions of districts so that the opinions of Congressmen could be compared with those, for example, of the dominant electoral elements of their districts.

In each policy domain, crossing the rankings of Congressmen and their constituencies gives an empirical measure of the extent of policy agreement between legislator and district.[10] In the period

---

that their roll call votes had expressed their real views fairly well. But this correlation was only .04 among those who said that their roll call votes had expressed their views poorly. In the other policy domains, too, attitude-roll call agreement is higher among Congressmen who are well satisfied with their roll call votes than it is among Congressmen who are not.

[9] During the analysis we have formed constituency scores out of the scores of constituents living in the same district by several devices other than calculating average constituent scores. In particular, in view of the ordinal character of our scales we have frequently used the *median* constituent score as a central value for the constituency as a whole. However, the ordering of constituencies differs very little according to which of several reasonable alternatives for obtaining constituency scores is chosen. As a result, we have preferred mean scores for the greater number of ranks they give.

[10] The meaning of this procedure can be suggested by two percentage tables standing for hypothetical extreme cases, the first that of full agreement, the second that of no agreement whatever. For convenience, these illustrative tables categorize both Congressmen and their districts in terms of only three degrees of favor and assume for both a nearly uniform distribution across the three categories. The terms "pro," "neutral," and "con" indicate a relative rather than an absolute opinion. In Case I, full agreement, all districts relatively favorable to social welfare action have Congressmen who are so too, etc.; whereas in Case II, or that of no agreement, the ordering of constituencies is independent in a statistical sense of the ranking of Congressmen: knowing the policy orientation of a district gives no clue at all to the orientation of its Congressman. Of course, it is possible for the orders of legislators and districts to be *inversely* related, and this possibility is of some importance, as indicated below, when the policy position of non-incumbent candidates as well as incumbents is taken into account. To summarize the degree of congruence between legislators and voters, a measure of correlation is introduced. Although we have used a variety of measures of association in our analysis, the values reported in this article all refer to product moment correlation coefficients. For our hypothetical Case I a measure of correlation would have the value 1.0; for Case II, the value 0.0. When it is applied to actual data this convenient indicator is likely to have a value somewhere in between. The question is where.

Case I: Full Policy Agreement

Congressmen	Constituencies			
	Pro	Neutral	Con	
Pro	33	0	0	33
Neutral	0	34	0	34
Con	0	0	33	33
	33	34	33	100%

Correlation = 1.0

Case II: No Policy Agreement

Congressmen	Constituencies			
	Pro	Neutral	Con	
Pro	11	11	11	33
Neutral	11	12	11	34
Con	11	11	11	33
	33	34	33	100%

Correlation = 0.0

of our research this procedure reveals very different degrees of policy congruence across the three issue domains. On questions of social and economic welfare there is considerable agreement between Representative and district, expressed by a correlation of approximately 0.3. This coefficient is, of course, very much less than the limiting value of 1.0, indicating that a number of Congressmen are, relatively speaking, more or less "liberal" than their districts. However, on the question of foreign involvement there is no discernible agreement between legislator and district whatever. Indeed, as if to emphasize the point, the coefficient expressing this relation is slightly negative (-0.09), although not significantly so in a statistical sense. It is in the domain of civil rights that the rankings of Congressmen and constituencies most nearly agree. When we took our measurements in the late 1950s the correlation of congressional roll call behavior with constituency opinion on questions affecting the Negro was nearly 0.6.

The description of policy agreement that these three simple correlations give can be a starting-point for a wide range of analyses. For example, the significance of party competition in the district for policy representation can be explored by comparing the agreement between district and Congressman with the agreement between the district and the Congressman's non-incumbent opponent.

Alternatively, the significance of choosing Representatives from single-member districts by popular majority can be explored by comparing the agreement between the Congressman and his own supporters with the agreement between the Congressman and the supporters of his opponent. Taking *both* party competition and majority rule into account magnifies rather spectacularly some of the coefficients reported here. This is most true in the domain of social welfare, where attitudes both of candidates and of voters are most polarized along party lines. Whereas the correlation between the constituency majority and congressional roll call votes is nearly $+0.4$ on social welfare policy, the correlation of the district majority with the non-incumbent candidate is -0.4. This difference, amounting to almost 0.8, between these two coefficients is an indicator of what the dominant electoral element of the constituency gets on the average by choosing the Congressman it has and excluding his opponent from office.[11]

These three coefficients are also the starting-point for a causal analysis of the relation of constituency to representative, the main problem of this paper. At least on social welfare and Negro rights a measurable degree of congruence is found between district and legislator. Is this agreement due to constituency influence in Congress, or is it to be attributed to other causes? If this question is to have a satisfactory answer the conditions that are necessary and sufficient to assure constituency control must be stated and compared with the available empirical evidence.

III. THE CONDITIONS OF CONSTITUENCY INFLUENCE

Broadly speaking, the constituency can control the policy actions of the Representative in two alternative ways. The first of these is for the district to choose a Representative who so shares its views that in following his own convictions he does his constituents' will. In this case district opinion and the Congressman's actions are connected through the Representative's own policy attitudes. The second means of constituency control is for the Congressman to

---

[11]A word of caution is in order, lest we compare things that are not strictly comparable. For obvious reasons, most non-incumbent candidates have no roll call record, and we have had to measure their policy agreement with the district entirely in terms of the attitudes they have revealed in interviews. However, the difference of coefficients given here is almost as great when the policy agreement between the incumbent Congressman and his district is also measured in terms of the attitudes conveyed in confidential interviews.

follow his (at least tolerably accurate) perceptions of district attitude in order to win re-election. In this case constituency opinion and the Congressman's actions are connected through his perception of what the district wants.[12]

These two paths of constituency control are presented schematically in Figure 1. As the figure suggests, each path has two steps, one

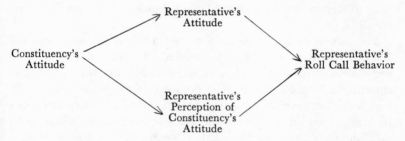

FIGURE 1. Connections between a constituency's attitude and its Representative's roll call behavior.

connecting the constituency's attitude with an "intervening" attitude or perception, the other connecting this attitude or perception with the Representative's roll call behavior. Out of respect for the processes by which the human actor achieves cognitive congruence we have also drawn arrows between the two intervening factors, since the Congressman probably tends to see his district as having the same opinion as his own and also tends, over time, to bring his own opinion into line with the district's. The inclusion of these arrows calls attention to two other possible influence paths, each consisting of *three* steps, although these additional paths will turn out to be of relatively slight importance empirically.

Neither of the main influence paths of Figure 1 will connect the final roll call vote to the constituency's views if either of its steps is blocked. From this, two necessary conditions of constituency

---

[12] A third type of connection, excluded here, might obtain between district and Congressman if the Representative accedes to what he thinks the district wants because he believes that to be what a representative *ought* to do, whether or not it is necessary for re-election. We leave this type of connection out of our account here because we conceive an influence relation as one in which control is not voluntarily accepted or rejected by someone subject to it. Of course, this possible connection between district and Representative is not any the less interesting because it falls outside our definition of influence or control, and we have given a good deal of attention to it in the broader study of which this analysis is part.

influence can be stated: *first,* the Representative's votes in the House must agree substantially with his own policy views or his perceptions of the district's views, and not be determined entirely by other influences to which the Congressman is exposed; and, *second,* the attitudes or perceptions governing the Representative's acts must correspond, at least imperfectly, to the district's actual opinions. It would be difficult to describe the relation of constituency to Representative as one of control unless these conditions are met.[13]

Yet these two requirements are not sufficient to assure control. A *third* condition must also be satisfied: the constituency must in some measure take the policy views of candidates into account in choosing a Representative. If it does not, agreement between district and Congressman may arise for reasons that cannot rationally be brought within the idea of control. For example, such agreement may simply reflect the fact that a Representative drawn from a given area is likely, by pure statistical probability, to share its dominant values, without his acceptance or rejection of these ever having been a matter of consequence to his electors.

IV. EVIDENCE OF CONTROL: CONGRESSIONAL ATTITUDES AND PERCEPTIONS

How well are these conditions met in the relation of American Congressmen to their constituents? There is little question that the first is substantially satisfied; the evidence of our research indicates that members of the House do in fact vote both their own policy views and their perceptions of their constituents' views, at least on issues of social welfare, foreign involvement, and civil rights. If these two intervening factors are used to predict roll call votes, the prediction is quite successful. Their multiple correlation with roll call position is 0.7 for social welfare, 0.6 for foreign involvement, and 0.9 for civil rights; the last figure is especially persuasive. What is more, both the Congressman's own convictions and his perceptions of district opinion make a distinct contribution to his roll

---

[13] It scarcely needs to be said that demonstrating *some* constituency influence would not imply that the Representative's behavior is *wholly* determined by constituency pressures. The legislator acts in a complex institutional setting in which he is subject to a wide variety of influence. The constituency can exercise a genuine measure of control without driving all other influences from the Representative's life space.

call behavior. In each of the three domains the prediction of roll call votes is surer if it is made from both factors rather than from either alone.

Lest the strong influence that the Congressman's views and his perception of district views have on roll call behavior appear somehow foreordained—and, consequently, this finding seem a trivial one—it is worth taking a sidewise glance at the potency of possible other forces on the Representative's vote. In the area of foreign policy, for example, a number of Congressmen are disposed to follow the administration's advice, whatever they or their districts think. For those who are, the multiple correlation of roll call behavior with the Representative's own foreign policy views and his perception of district views is a mere 0.2. Other findings could be cited to support the point that the influence of the Congressman's own preferences and those he attributes to the district is extremely variable. Yet in the House as a whole over the three policy domains the influence of these forces is quite strong.

The connections of congressional attitudes and perceptions with actual constituency opinion are weaker. If policy agreement between district and Representative is moderate and variable across the policy domains, as it is, this is to be explained much more in terms of the second condition of constituency control than the first. The Representative's attitudes and perceptions most nearly match true opinion in his district on the issue of Negro rights. Reflecting the charged and polarized nature of this area, the correlation of actual district opinion with perceived opinion is greater than 0.6, and the correlation of district attitude with the Representative's own attitude is nearly 0.4, as shown by Table I. But the comparable correlations for foreign involvement are much smaller—indeed

TABLE I

Correlations of Constituency Attitudes

Policy Domain	Correlation of Constituency Attitude with	
	Representative's Perception of Constituency Attitude	*Representative's Own Attitude*
Social welfare	.17	.21
Foreign involvement	.19	.06
Civil rights	.63	.39

almost negligible. And the coefficients for social welfare are also smaller, although a detailed presentation of findings in this area would show that the Representative's perceptions and attitudes are more strongly associated with the attitude of his electoral *majority* than they are with the attitudes of the constituency as a whole.

Knowing this much about the various paths that may lead, directly or indirectly, from constituency attitude to roll call vote, we can assess their relative importance. Since the alternative influence chains have links of unequal strength, the full chains will not in general be equally strong, and these differences are of great importance in the relation of Representative to constituency. For the domain of civil rights Figure 2 assembles all the intercorrelations of

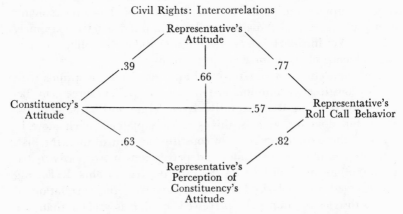

FIGURE 2. Intercorrelations of variables pertaining to Civil Rights.

the variables of our system. As the figure shows, the root correlation of constituency attitude with roll call behavior in this domain is 0.57. How much of this policy congruence can be accounted for by the influence path involving the Representative's attitude? And how much by the path involving his perception of constituency opinion? When the intercorrelations of the system are interpreted in the light of what we assume its causal structure to be, it is influence passing through the Congressman's perception of the district's views that is found to be preeminently important.[14] Under the

[14] We have done this by a variance-component technique similar to several others proposed for dealing with problems of this type. See especially Herbert A. Simon, "Spurious Correlation: A Causal Interpretation," *Journal of the American Statistical Association,* Vol. 49 (1954), pp. 467–479; Hubert M. Bla-

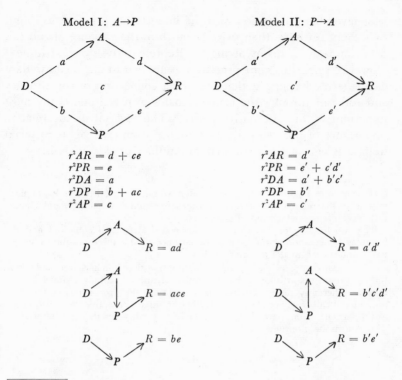

Model I: $A \rightarrow P$

Model II: $P \rightarrow A$

$r^2AR = d + ce$
$r^2PR = e$
$r^2DA = a$
$r^2DP = b + ac$
$r^2AP = c$

$r^2AR = d'$
$r^2PR = e' + c'd'$
$r^2DA = a' + b'c'$
$r^2DP = b'$
$r^2AP = c'$

$D \nearrow A \searrow R = ad$

$D \searrow A \nearrow R = a'd'$

$D \nearrow A \downarrow P \nearrow R = ace$

$D \searrow A \uparrow P \nearrow R = b'c'd'$

$D \searrow P \nearrow R = be$

$D \searrow P \nearrow R = b'e'$

lock, Jr., "The Relative Importance of Variables," *American Sociological Review,* Vol. 26 (1961), pp. 866–874; and the almost forgotten work of Sewall Wright, "Correlation and Causation," *Journal of Agricultural Research,* Vol. 20 (1920), pp. 557–585. Under this technique a "path coefficient" (to use Wright's terminology, although not his theory) is assigned to each of the causal arrows by solving a set of equations involving the correlations of the variables of the model. The weight assigned to a full path is then the product of its several path coefficients, and this product may be interpreted as the proportion of the variance of the dependent variable (roll call behavior, here) that is explained by a given path.

A special problem arises because influence may flow in either direction between the Congressman's attitude and his perception of district attitude (as noted above, the Representative may tend both to perceive his constituency's view selectively, as consistent with his own, and to change his own view to be consistent with the perceived constituency view). Hence, we have not a single causal model but a whole family of models, varying according to the relative importance of influence from attitude to perception and from perception to attitude. Our solution to this problem has been to calculate influence coefficients for the two extreme models in order to see how much our results could vary according to which model is chosen from our family of models. Since the systems of equations in this analysis are linear it can be shown that the coefficients we seek have their maximum and minimum values under one or the other of the limiting models. Therefore, computing any given coefficient for each of these limiting cases defines an interval in which the true value of the

least favorable assumption as to its importance, this path is found to account for more than twice as much of the variance of roll call behavior as the paths involving the Representative's own attitude.[15] However, when this same procedure is applied to our social welfare data, the results suggest that the direct connection of constituency and roll call through the Congressman's own attitude is the most important of the alternative paths.[16] The reversal of the relative importance of the two paths as we move from civil rights to social welfare is one of the most striking findings of this analysis.

-----

coefficient must lie. In fact these intervals turn out to be fairly small; our findings as to the relative importance of alternative influence paths would change little according to which model is selected.

The two limiting models with their associated systems of equations and the formulas for computing the relative importance of the three possible influence paths under each model are given below.

[15] By "least favorable" we mean the assumption that influence goes only from the Congressman's attitude to his perception of district attitude (Model I) and not the other way round. Under this assumption, the proportions of the variance of roll call behavior accounted for by the three alternative paths, expressed as proportions of the part of the variance of roll call votes that is explained by district attitude, are these:

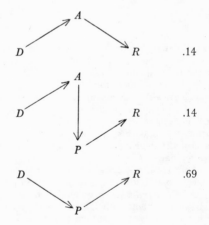

Inverting the assumed direction of influence between the Congressman's own attitude and district attitude (Model II) eliminates altogether the effect that the Representative's attitude can have had on his votes, independently of his perception of district attitude.

[16] Under both Models I and II the proportion of the variance of roll call voting explained by the influence path involving the Representative's own attitude is twice as great as the proportion explained by influence passing through his perception of district attitude.

V. EVIDENCE OF CONTROL: ELECTORAL BEHAVIOR

Of the three conditions of constituency influence, the requirement that the electorate take account of the policy positions of the candidates is the hardest to match with empirical evidence. Indeed, given the limited information the average voter carries to the polls, the public might be thought incompetent to perform any task of appraisal. Of constituents living in congressional districts where there was a contest between a Republican and a Democrat in 1958, less than one in five said they had read or heard something about both candidates, and well over half conceded they had read or heard nothing about either. And these proportions are not much better when they are based only on the part of the sample, not much more than half, that reported voting for Congress in 1958. The extent of awareness of the candidates among voters is indicated in Table II. As the table shows, even of the portion of the public

TABLE II

Awareness of Congressional Candidates Among Voters, 1958

		Read or Heard Something About Incumbent[a]		
		Yes	*No*	
Read or Heard Something About Non-Incumbent	Yes	24	5	29
	No	25	46	71
		49	51	100%

[a] In order to include all districts where the House seat was contested in 1958 this table retains ten constituencies in which the incumbent Congressman did not seek re-election. Candidates of the retiring incumbent's party in these districts are treated here as if they were incumbents. Were these figures to be calculated only for constituencies in which an incumbent sought re-election, no entry in this four-fold table would differ from that given by more than two percent.

that was sufficiently interested to vote, almost half had read or heard nothing about either candidate.

Just how low a hurdle our respondents had to clear in saying they had read or heard something about a candidate is indicated by detailed qualitative analysis of the information constituents *were* able to associate with congressional candidates. Except in rare cases, what the voters "knew" was confined to diffuse evaluative judgments about the candidate: "he's a good man," "he understands the problems," and so forth. Of detailed information about policy stands not more than a chemical trace was found. Among the comments about the candidates given in response to an extended series of free-answer questions, less than two percent had to do with stands in our three policy domains; indeed, only about three comments in every hundred had to do with legislative issues of *any* description.[17]

This evidence that the behavior of the electorate is largely unaffected by knowledge of the policy positions of the candidates is complemented by evidence about the forces that *do* shape the voters' choices among congressional candidates. The primary basis of voting in American congressional elections is identification with party. In 1958 only one vote in twenty was cast by persons without any sort of party loyalty. And among those who did have a party identification, only one in ten voted against their party. As a result, something like 84 percent of the vote that year was cast by party identifiers voting their usual party line. What is more, traditional party voting is seldom connected with current legislative issues. As the party loyalists in a nationwide sample of voters told us what they liked and disliked about the parties in 1958, only a small fraction of the comments (about 15 per cent) dealt with current issues of public policy.[18]

Yet the idea of reward or punishment at the polls for legislative stands is familiar to members of Congress, who feel that they and their records are quite visible to their constituents. Of our sample of Congressmen who were opposed for re-election in 1958, more than four-fifths said the outcome in their districts had been strongly influenced by the electorate's response to their records and personal standing. Indeed, this belief is clear enough to present a notable contradiction: Congressmen feel that their individual legislative actions may have considerable impact on the electorate, yet some simple facts about the Representative's salience to his constituents imply that this could hardly be true.

In some measure this contradiction is to be explained by the tendency of Congressmen to overestimate their visibility to the local

---

[17] What is more, the electorate's awareness of Congress as a whole appears quite limited. A majority of the public was unable to say in 1958 which of the two parties had controlled the Congress during the preceding two years. Some people were confused by the coexistence of a Republican President and a Democratic Congress. But for most people this was simply an elementary fact about congressional affairs to which they were not privy.

[18] For a more extended analysis of forces on the congressional vote, see Donald E. Stokes and Warren E. Miller, "Party Government and the Saliency of Congress," *Public Opinion Quarterly*, Vol. 26 (Winter 1962), pp. 531–546.

public, a tendency that reflects the difficulties of the Representative in forming a correct judgment of constituent opinion. The communication most Congressmen have with their districts inevitably puts them in touch with organized groups and with individuals who are relatively well informed about politics. The Representative knows his constituents mostly from dealing with people who *do* write letters, who *will* attend meetings, who *have* an interest in his legislative stands. As a result, his sample of contacts with a constituency of several hundred thousand people is heavily biased: even the contacts he apparently makes at random are likely to be with people who grossly over-represent the degree of political information and interest in the constituency as a whole.

But the contradiction is also to be explained by several aspects of the Representative's electoral situation that are of great importance to the question of constituency influence. The first of these is implicit in what has already been said. Because of the pervasive effects of party loyalties, no candidate for Congress starts from scratch in putting together an electoral majority. The Congressman is a dealer in increments and margins. He starts with a stratum of hardened party voters, and if the stratum is broad enough he can have a measurable influence on his chance of survival simply by attracting a small additional element of the electorate—or by not losing a larger one. Therefore, his record may have a very real bearing on his electoral success or failure without most of his constituents ever knowing what that record is.

Second, the relation of Congressman to voter is not a simple bilateral one but is complicated by the presence of all manner of intermediaries: the local party, economic interests, the news media, racial and nationality organizations, and so forth. Such is the lore of American politics, as it is known to any political scientist. Very often the Representative reaches the mass public through these mediating agencies, and the information about himself and his record may be considerably transformed as it diffuses out to the electorate in two or more stages. As a result, the public—or parts of it—may get simple positive or negative cues about the Congressman which were provoked by his legislative actions but which no longer have a recognizable issue content.

Third, for most Congressmen most of the time the electorate's sanctions are potential rather than actual. Particularly the Representative from a safe district may feel his proper legislative strategy is to avoid giving opponents in his own party or outside of it material they can use against him. As the Congressman pursues this strategy he may write a legislative record that never becomes very well known to his constituents; if it doesn't win votes, neither will it lose any. This is clearly the situation of most southern Congressmen in dealing with the issue of Negro rights. By voting correctly on this issue they are unlikely to increase their visibility to constituents. Nevertheless, the fact of constituency influence, backed by potential sanctions at the polls, is real enough.

That these potential sanctions are all too real is best illustrated in the election of 1958 by the reprisal against Representative Brooks Hays in Arkansas' Fifth District.[19] Although the perception of Congressman Hays as too moderate on civil rights resulted more from his service as intermediary between the White House and Governor Faubus in the Little Rock school crisis than from his record in the House, the victory of Dale Alford as a write-in candidate was a striking reminder of what can happen to a Congressman who gives his foes a powerful issue to use against him. The extraordinary involvement of the public in this race can be seen by comparing how well the candidates were known in this constituency with the awareness of the candidates shown by Table II above

TABLE III

Awareness of Congressional Candidates Among Voters in Arkansas Fifth District, 1958

		Read or Heard Something About Hays		
		Yes	No	
Read or Heard Something About Alford	Yes	100	0	100
	No	0	0	0
		100	0	100%

for the country as a whole. As Table III indicates, not a single voter in our sample of Arkansas' Fifth District was unaware of either candidate.[20] What is more, these interviews show that Hays

---

[19] For an account of this episode see Corinne Silverman, "The Little Rock Story," Inter-University Case Program series, reprinted in Edwin A. Bock and Alan K. Campbell, eds., *Case Studies in American Government* (Englewood Cliffs, 1962), pp. 1–46.

[20] The sample of this constituency was limited to twenty-three persons of whom thirteen voted. However, despite the small number of cases the prob-

was regarded both by his supporters and his opponents as more moderate than Alford on civil rights and that this perception brought his defeat. In some measure, what happened in Little Rock in 1958 can happen anywhere, and our Congressmen ought not to be entirely disbelieved in what they say about their impact at the polls. Indeed, they may be under genuine pressure from the voters even while they are the forgotten men of national elections.[21]

VI. CONCLUSION

Therefore, although the conditions of constituency influence are not equally satisfied, they are met well enough to give the local constituency a measure of control over the actions of its Representatives. Best satisfied is the requirement about motivational influences on the Congressman: our evidence shows that the Representative's roll call behavior is strongly influenced by his own policy preferences and by his perception of preferences held by the constituency. However, the conditions of influence that presuppose effective communication between Congressman and district are much less well met. The Representative has very imperfect information about the issue preferences of his constituency, and the constituency's awareness of the policy stands of the Representative ordinarily is slight.

The findings of this analysis heavily underscore the fact that no single tradition of representation fully accords with the realities of American legislature politics. The American system *is* a mixture,

---

ability that the difference in awareness between this constituency and the country generally as the result only of sampling variations is much less than one in a thousand.

[21] In view of the potential nature of the constituency's sanctions, it is relevant to characterize its influence over the Representative in terms of several distinctions drawn by recent theorists of power, especially the difference between actual and potential power, between influence and coercive power, and between influence and purposive control. Observing these distinctions, we might say that the constituency's influence is *actual* and not merely *potential* since it is the sanction behavior rather than the conforming behavior that is infrequent (Dahl). That is, the Congressman is influenced by his calculus of potential sanctions, following the "rule of anticipated reactions" (Friedrich), however oblivious of his behavior the constituency ordinarily may be. We might also say that the constituency has *power* since its influence depends partly on sanctions (Lasswell and Kaplan), although it rarely exercises *control* since its influence is rarely conscious or intended (Cartwright). In the discussion above we have of course used the terms "influence" and "control" interchangeably.

to which the Burkean, instructed-delegate, and responsible-party models all can be said to have contributed elements. Moreover, variations in the representative relation are most likely to occur as we move from one policy domain to another. No single, generalized configuration of attitudes and perceptions links Representative with constituency but rather several distinct patterns, and which of them is invoked depends very much on the issue involved.

The issue domain in which the relation of Congressman to constituency most nearly conforms to the instructed-delegate model is that of civil rights. This conclusion is supported by the importance of the influence-path passing through the Representative's perception of district opinion, although even in this domain the sense in which the constituency may be said to take the position of the candidate into account in reaching its electoral judgment should be carefully qualified.

The representative relation conforms most closely to the responsible-party model in the domain of social welfare. In this issue area, the arena of partisan conflict for a generation, the party symbol helps both constituency and Representative in the difficult process of communication between them. On the one hand, because Republican and Democratic voters tend to differ in what they would have government do, the Representative has some guide to district opinion simply by looking at the partisan division of the vote. On the other hand, because the two parties tend to recruit candidates who differ on the social welfare role of government, the constituency can infer the candidates' position with more than random accuracy from their party affiliation, even though what the constituency has learned directly about these stands is almost nothing. How faithful the representation of social welfare views is to the responsible-party model should not be exaggerated. Even in this policy domain, American practice departs widely from an ideal conception of party government.[22] But in this domain, more than any other, political conflict has become a conflict of national parties in which constituency and Representative are known to each other primarily by their party association.

It would be too pat to say that the domain of foreign involvement conforms to the third model of representation, the conception promoted by Edmund Burke. Clearly it does in the sense that the

[22] The factors in American electoral behavior that encourage such a departure are discussed in Stokes and Miller, *loc. cit.*

Congressman looks elsewhere than to his district in making up his mind on foreign issues. However, the reliance he puts on the President and the Administration suggests that the calculation of where the public interest lies is often passed to the Executive on matters of foreign policy. Ironically, legislative initiative in foreign affairs has fallen victim to the very difficulties of gathering and appraising information that led Burke to argue that Parliament rather than the public ought to hold the power of decision. The background information and predictive skills that Burke thought the people lacked are held primarily by the modern Executive. As a result, the present role of the legislature in foreign affairs bears some resemblance to the role that Burke had in mind for the elitist, highly restricted *electorate* of his own day.

III

SAFE SEATS, SENIORITY, AND POWER IN CONGRESS*

Raymond E. Wolfinger and Joan H. Hollinger

THE PRESIDENT's difficulties in inducing Congress to pass his legislative program are usually ascribed to the different constituencies
of the two institutions. This difference would make for disharmony
under any circumstances, but it is said to be particularly important
because the seniority system bestows the most power on congressmen whose constituencies are most unlike the president's. His policy
commitments are responses to the needs of a heterogeneous, indus-
trialized, urban society. The occupants of the most influential congressional positions come from districts that re-elect them regardless
of national political trends. The representative from such a district
"views with alarm the great issues that sweep the nation and
threaten to disrupt the familiar and comfortable politics of his district,"[1] which is usually characterized as a rural backwater.

Both political parties are described this way. Because the Democrats have controlled Congress for all but four of the past 36 years,
most illustrations of this thesis are drawn from conflicts between
Democratic presidents and Democratic congresses. More specifically,
the focus of attention is usually on the refusal of southern Democratic congressional leaders to support presidential legislative requests. In this article we will be concerned with this phenomenon

* Reprinted from *The American Political Science Review*, Vol. LIX, No. 2,
June, 1965.

We were aided in gathering data by Milton Cummings and Richard Scam-
mon. Many helpful comments on an earlier draft of this article were made by
Richard F. Fenno, Jr., Fred I. Greenstein, Duncan MacRae, Jr., Donald
Matthews, Nelson W. Polsby, Randall Ripley, Alan Rosenthal, Stephen Smith,
Leo M. Snowiss, Aaron B. Wildavsky, and Barbara Kaye Wolfinger. We are
grateful for financial support from the Edgar Stern Family Fund, the John
Simon Guggenheim Memorial Foundation and the Committee on Political Behavior of the Social Science Research Council, and to the Brookings Institution
for use of its facilities.
[1] James MacGregor Burns, *The Deadlock of Democracy,* rev. Spectrum ed.
(Englewood Cliffs, N.J., 1963), p. 244.

in the House of Representatives. The thesis we examine may be restated as follows: lack of responsibility in the Democratic party is due to control of Congress by Southerners. Their influence is due to their seniority, which is a result of the lack of party competition in the South. Most academic descriptions of American politics include this thesis.[2] It is particularly common in textbooks. We will call it the "textbook theory."

Another interpretation of congressional behavior, that might be called the "insiders' theory," has a good deal of currency in Washington circles close to Congress.[3] The insiders concede both the one-party South and southern congressional power, but they say that the former is not a sufficient cause of the latter, and introduce other considerations to explain it. Southern influence in Congress, according to the insiders, is not due just to the lack of party competition in the South, since there are many safe Democratic seats in the North. The men in these northern seats allegedly do not, however, make use of their "potential seniority." They are less interested in congressional careers and tend to "committee hop," thus losing the benefit of whatever seniority they have accrued. Many of these congressmen come from machine-dominated big cities where command of local patronage and contracts is the real sign of status and power. When an opportunity for such a position opens up back home, they desert the House for state or local government.

In the insiders' view, Southerners value a career in the House of Representatives more highly than do Northerners. One presumed reason is that the South, less developed industrially than the rest of the country, offers fewer alternate careers to ambitious young men. A second explanation is that the plantation owners' traditional *noblesse oblige* has made politics a more highly valued activity in the South, attracting some of the most able men from all walks of life. In the North politics has been not so much a gentleman's calling as a channel of social mobility for underprivileged ethnic groups.

The central proposition of the insiders' theory is that the level of southern influence in Congress is due to more than the "natural"

---

[2] Burns is probably the best-known contemporary advocate of this point of view.

[3] While the insiders' theory is probably the prevailing one among Washington *cognoscenti*, it has not been given the literary circulation of the textbook theory. Hints and scraps of it may be found in the writings of William S. White; see particularly *Citadel* (New York, 1956).

consequences of the lack of party competition in the South. More generally, the insiders' theory raises a number of questions about the relationship between types of party systems and effective legislative representation, and between career alternatives and types of legislative behavior. It suggests that the constituent environment may influence not only the direction of congressional behavior (for example, votes pro or con), but also the roles played by legislators from different types of party systems.[4]

Most of the empirical propositions and assumptions in the two theories are readily verifiable. Yet published evidence on them is surprisingly scarce. Their evaluation involves answering the following questions:

1. Do congressmen in southern safe seats have more congressional seniority than those in northern safe seats?
2. Do the career patterns of the Northerners indicate any greater willingness to leave the House?
3. Do congressmen from southern safe districts have more committee seniority than safe Northerners?
4. Do the Southerners have more chairmanships than they are "entitled to" by their seniority?
5. Do members of the House have more prestige in the South than in the North?

If these questions can be answered affirmatively, the insiders' explanation is a crucial modification of the textbook theory. If not, the insiders' theory is superfluous. If the insiders are right, then the growing northern Democratic representation in Congress will be partly vitiated by members who do not take full advantage of their opportunities to accrue seniority. Our purpose in this article is twofold: to examine the available data in an attempt to answer these five questions; and to explore the implications of recent shifts in the distribution of safe House seats.

I. THE REGIONAL DISTRIBUTION OF INFLUENTIAL POSITIONS IN THE HOUSE

As a prelude to examination of the relevant evidence, it is useful to review the familiar topic of alleged southern and rural domi-

[4] For an extensive treatment of this subject at the state level see John Wahlke *et al., The Legislative System* (New York, 1962). See also James Q. Wilson, "Two Negro Politicians: An Interpretation," *Midwest Journal of Political Science*, Vol. 4 (November, 1960), pp. 346–69.

nance in the House of Representatives. There were 255 Democratic Representatives on January 7, 1964.[5] Of these, 38 per cent were from southern districts.[6] Table I shows the representation of con-

TABLE I

Distribution of Democratic Congressmen in Influential Committee Positions, by Region—January, 1964

	North		South		Total	
	Urban	Rural	Urban	Rural	No.	Per cent
	(%)	(%)	(%)	(%)		
All Democratic congressmen	42	21	9	29	255	101[a]
Membership on top three committees	40	24	5	31	55	100
Major committee chairmanships	29	18	0	53	17	100
Subcommittee chairmanships	29	17	6	47	109	99[a]
Holding first three positions	37	14	4	45	51	100

[a] Does not sum to 100 because of rounding.

[5] Since minor changes in the composition of the House occur frequently, it is necessary to choose a date for any analysis of House membership. We chose January 7, 1964 because a House roster for that date was published in the *Congressional Quarterly Weekly Report,* January 10, 1964.

[6] Throughout this article the South is defined as the eleven states of the Confederacy: Alabama, Arkansas, Florida, Georgia, Louisiana, Mississippi, North Carolina, South Carolina, Tennessee, Texas, and Virginia.

We have included the five border states (Kentucky, Maryland, Missouri, Oklahoma, and West Virginia) in the North. Some observers of Congress classify some or all of these states as southern, or put them in a separate category. We saw no reason to do this, since the voting record of the 28 Democratic representatives from these states is similar to that of northern congressmen, and very different from the Southerners'. In 1963, for instance, the border congressmen had a Presidential Support score of 80, compared to 59 for the Southerners and 82 for congressmen from the northeastern states. The Presidential Opposition scores of the three groups were 9, 27, and 5, respectively. (These scores are based on individual voting records for 71 House roll calls during 1963 on proposals on which President Kennedy took a position. The support score is the percentage of the 71 roll calls on which the member supported the president. Since failure to vote lowers a member's support score, we also present the opposition scores. The individual scores are in *Congressional Quarterly Weekly Report,* March 13, 1964).

Congressional Quarterly defines as "urban" any central city with at least 50,000 population and any suburban city with 100,000 or more people. "Suburban" areas are those "closely settled areas contiguous to central cities," with the exception of cities over 100,000 in population. All other areas are classified as rural. See *CQ Census Analysis: Congressional Districts of the United States*

gressmen from different types of district (urban-rural, North-South) in influential positions. Contrary to some impressions, the Southerners did not have a disproportionate share of appointments to the Appropriations, Rules, and Ways and Means Committees, generally considered the top three committees in the House.[7] But they are significantly over-represented in other powerful posts. They account for 53 per cent of the chairmanships of the 17 major standing committees,[8] 53 per cent of the chairmen of all these 17 committees' subcommittees; and 49 per cent of all the representatives who hold the first three positions (chairman and first and second ranking majority members) on each of the 17 committees. For a variety of reasons this last measure may be the best index of committee seniority. The number of chairmanships is so small that the death or retirement of a single chairman produces a sizeable percentage change, and subcommittee chairmen are not appointed solely on the basis of seniority. The top-ranking majority members are next in line for the chairmanship. Together with the chairman and the two ranking minority members, they are usually appointed to conference committees on bills the committee has

---

(Washington, Congressional Quarterly, Inc., 1964), pp. 1786, 1792. We have combined *CQ*'s "urban" and "suburban" classifications for the purpose of testing the propositions stated in the text. We have classified districts as "rural" if they are 50% or more rural according to *CQ*, and "urban" if they are less than 50% rural.

[7] The absence of southern overrepresentation on the top three committees is due partly to the recent appointment of four Northerners to the Appropriations Committee. During most of the period from 1947 to 1963 every southern state had a representative on that committee. (We are indebted to Richard F. Fenno, Jr. for this information.) If one splits the Appropriations Committee's 30 Democratic members on the basis of seniority, the former southern advantage becomes apparent. Eight of the top-ranking 15 members are Southerners, compared to only one of the 15 most recent appointees.

Appointments to the Ways and Means Committee are made on the basis of regional zones, but it should not be thought that this guarantees equitable representation on the committee to all parts of the country. The zones are not redrawn after every election to take account of changes in state delegations, and, perhaps for this reason, there is considerable variation in the number of representatives assigned to each zone. The range was from 14 to 24 in the 86th Congress. See Nicholas A. Masters, "Committee Assignments in the House of Representatives," *APSA Review* Vol. 55 (June, 1961), p. 347.

[8] There are 20 standing committees. Members generally consider three of them unimportant: the District of Columbia, House Administration, and Un-American Activities Committees. The first of these—important to permanent residents of the District—is in effect Washington's city council, the second is occupied with housekeeping, and the third reports virtually no legislation. Membership on one of these three committees does not preclude assignment to another standing committee.

handled.[9] Among their various other advantages is first preference in questioning witnesses at hearings.

II. THE DISTRIBUTION AND CHARACTERISTICS
OF DEMOCRATIC SAFE SEATS

For the purposes of our study we defined safe Democratic seats as those which met all three of the following criteria:

(1) Won by a Democrat in every special[10] and general election since 1940.

(2) Won by an average of 60 per cent or more of the two-party vote since 1944.

(3) Won by not less than 55 per cent of the two-party vote in every election since 1946.

Changes in district boundaries proved not much of a problem in our efforts to identify safe districts. We were usually able to "follow" the incumbent. Where a change in incumbent coincided with redistricting, we used maps to trace the district's lineage. Our definition of safety turned out to be rather stringent. It excluded the seats held by three major committee chairmen: Wayne Aspinall of Colorado, Interior and Insular Affairs; George P. Miller of California, Science and Astronautics; and Clarence Cannon of Missouri, Appropriations. Cannon's winning percentage dipped below 55 per cent on two occasions, while the first two seats were held by Republicans in the 1940s. Also excluded were a number of seats which, because of redistricting or population movement, now seem to be completely safe. But the inclusion of such newly safe seats would not contribute much to our analysis of members' responses to the opportunity to accrue seniority. Implicit in our definition is the assumption that the key aspect of safety is the incumbent's belief that he can stay in his seat as long as he wants.

By our definition we counted a total of 122 safe Democratic seats in the 88th Congress, 45 in the North and 77 in the South. Table II shows how these were distributed between urban and rural constituencies: 72 are rural and a bare majority of them are both southern and rural. More than a third of the safe seats are northern. There are four urban safe seats for every rural one in the North;

---

[9] This practice is not required by the rules, but is usually followed.

[10] Two seats, one each in the North and South, were omitted because they were won by Republicans at the special election following the death of the incumbents.

TABLE II

Distribution of Democratic Safe Seats by Region and Type of Constituency

	North		South		Totals	
	Urban	Rural	Urban	Rural	No.	Per cent
	(%)	(%)	(%)	(%)		
Safe Seats	30	7	11	52	122	100
All Democratic Seats	42	21	9	29	255	101[a]

a Does not sum to 100 because of rounding.

in the South this ratio is reversed. Seven of the nine northern rural safe seats are from the border states of Kentucky, Missouri, Oklahoma, and West Virginia. The urban seats include five from Chicago, three from Detroit, eleven from New York, and three from the Los Angeles area. The boundaries of most of these Democratic city districts were drawn by Republican legislatures.

Compared to northern non-safe seats held by Democrats in 1964, the safe districts included a somewhat higher proportion of low-income families, of Negroes, and of first- and second-generation Americans, as Table III shows. These differences are not large, however, and the safe seats are no less diverse in their socio-economic characteristics than the others. The higher level of ethnicity in the safe seats is the greatest difference. Half of the safe districts in the first income quartile and 43 per cent of those in the second quartile had 40 per cent or more first- and second-generation residents. Twenty-seven of the 45 safe constituencies had 40 per cent or more foreign-stock residents or 20 per cent Negroes, or both.

We explored the textbook theory proposition that congressmen in safe seats are less likely to support their president, presumably because they are subject to different constituency pressures.[11] Tables IV and V show the Presidential Support and Opposition scores for congressmen in safe and non-safe seats with region and type of constituency controlled. Table IV suggests that Northerners in safe seats gave slightly less support than those from non-safe districts.

---

[11] See, *e.g.*, Burns, pp. 242–4. Lewis A. Froman, Jr., discusses several other propositions about relationships between competition and party loyalty at both state and national levels. See his *Congressmen and their Constituencies* (Chicago, Rand McNally, 1963), ch. 9; and the works cited there.

TABLE III

*A Socio-Economic Profile of Northern Safe and
Non-Safe Democratic Districts—1964*

	Northern Safe Democratic	Northern Non-Safe Democratic
	(%)	(%)
1959 median family income:[a]		
Per cent of districts in:		
first quartile[b]	18	31
second quartile	36	35
third quartile	31	24
fourth quartile[c]	16	10
	101[e]	100
N	(45)	(115)
Per cent Negro:		
0–4.9%	31	64
5–9.9%	27	13
10–19.9%	13	12
20–29.9%	9	4
30% and over	20	6
	100	99[e]
N	(45)	(115)
Per cent first- and second-generation:[d]		
0–9.9%	20	17
10–19.9%	9	25
20–39.9%	36	44
40% and over	36	13
	101[e]	99[e]
N	(45)	(115)
Type of constituency:		
urban	80	61
rural	20	39
	100	100
N	(45)	(115)

[a] The average median family income for the safe seats was $5506, compared to $5921 for the non-safe districts. If rural districts from the border states are eliminated from both groups, the figures are $5811 and $6099, respectively.
[b] Quartiles are based on nationwide ranking.
[c] All but one of the northern safe seats in the 4th quartile are from rural border districts.
[d] Includes all persons born abroad (except of American parents) or with at least one foreign-born parent.
[e] Does not sum to 100 because of rounding.
Sources: 1960 Census data reported in U.S. Bureau of the Census, *Congressional District Data Book (Districts of the 88th Congress)* (Washington, 1963); and *CQ Census Analysis.*

Since failure to vote lowers a member's support score and many
New York City congressmen are notorious absentees, Table V may

TABLE IV

*Presidential Support Scores of Democratic Congressmen
in Safe and Non-Safe Seats, by Region—1963*

	North		South	
	Urban	*Rural*	*Urban*	*Rural*
Safe Seats	76	77	75	55
Non-Safe Seats	83	82	61	55

be a better indicator of presidential support.[12] It shows no differences between safe and non-safe northern congressmen. The extremely spotty attendance records of two members from rural safe

TABLE V

*Presidential Opposition Scores of Democratic Congressmen
in Safe and Non-Safe Seats, by Region—1963*

	North		South	
	Urban	*Rural*	*Urban*	*Rural*
Safe Seats	5	8	14	28
Non-Safe Seats	4	8	31	36

districts account for most of the difference in the support scores of rural Northerners. The lower support by non-safe Southerners may result from Republican competition forcing these incumbents to adopt a more conservative position. In short, the level of party competition does not appear to be a useful general explanation of voting patterns among Democratic congressmen.[13]

III. CAREER PATTERNS OF SAFE SEAT HOLDERS

We come now to our major concern: the different levels of interest in a congressional career by members from different sides of

---

[12] Of course, failure to vote also lowers the Presidential Opposition score, but the rate of opposition in all northern cells is so low that 100% voting participation would not change the opposition scores significantly.

[13] After examining voting records for the 87th Congress, Froman came to the same conclusion (*ibid.*, p. 114). Other recent findings indicate that when region is controlled, length of service is not strongly related to the support that congressmen of either party give to their president. See Judson Mitchell and George Spink, "Presidential Support and Length of Service in the House of Representatives" (unpublished paper, Stanford University).

the Mason-Dixon line. Years of consecutive service is one index of this interest. If northern congressmen in safe seats were less interested in House service, then, taken as a group, they should have less congressional seniority. But as Table VI indicates, this does

TABLE VI

Years of Consecutive Service by Democratic Congressmen in Safe Seats, by Region—1964

Years of Consecutive Service	Northerners	Southerners
	(%)	(%)
0–9	38	32
10–19	33	38
20–29	25	23
30 and over	4	6
	100	99[a]
N	(45)	(77)

[a] Does not sum to 100 because of rounding.

not appear to be the case. There were no important differences in length of consecutive service between northern and southern Representatives.

According to the insiders' theory, many congressmen from urban machines are only serving time in the House until they can get a more highly prized post. The principal example offered is a tendency for New York City congressmen to quit the House abruptly when a judgeship becomes available. (These are usually elective offices, but access to them has been effectively controlled by the regular Democratic organization in New York.) By extension other northern big-city congressmen are alleged to have the same preference for careers in state and local government. In contrast, a seat in Congress is said to be the high ambition of almost any southern politician. Those fortunate few who attain this goal are content to stay in the House (unless an opportunity for the Senate presents itself), patiently going along and working their way up the ladder of seniority to a position of real influence in national affairs.

We tested this proposition by examining the circumstances under which safe-seat incumbents left their seats from January, 1947 to the beginning of 1964. In all but a few cases the reasons for leaving were either stated by the incumbent or were obvious enough, *e.g.*, death in office, defeat in a primary, retirement. In a few instances

we inferred the reason from the man's subsequent occupation.
These data, classified by region, are presented in Table VII.

TABLE VII

*Safe Seat Holders' Reasons for Leaving Congress,
by Region—1947–1964*

Reasons for Leaving	Northerners	Southerners
	(%)	(%)
Death in office[a]	37	22
Retirement due to health or age	5	12
Defeat in primary	11	26
Run for Senate	16	12
Run for state or local office	21	2
Go into business or law	3	22
Appointed to government position	8	5
	101[b]	101[b]
N	(38)	(59)

[a] See below, p. 346, for a discussion of this regional difference.
[b] Does not sum to 100 because of rounding.

Sources: *Congressional Quarterly Weekly Reports; Biographical Directory of the American Congress, 1774–1961* (Washington, G.P.O., 1961); and various issues of *Congressional Directory* (Washington, G.P.O.).

The insiders' theory is confirmed on one point: 21 per cent of
the Northerners who left the House did so to run for a state or local
office, in contrast to only one Southerner. Almost all of these Northerners were from New York City and most of the offices sought
were state or county judgeships. Quitting one's seat to go into
business also is an indication of lack of interest in a House career,
and here the regional ratio is reversed. Twenty-two per cent of
the Southerners who left Congress went into private business or
law practice, compared to just one Northerner. Since preferences
for local public office or for private business to continuing congressional service are both examples of voluntary departure, the two
categories can be combined to provide an overall measure of low
interest in a House career. When so combined, these categories account for an identical proportion of northern and southern quit-
ters: twenty-four per cent.

Fear of losing a primary may cause a member to quit in favor of
another job. Rumors have it that several congressmen, from both
North and South, have done this in the past decade. There is no
reason to believe, however, that this fear is any more prevalent
among Northerners than Southerners, or *vice versa*. One could
argue that, everything considered, primary defeat may be less of

a hazard for Northerners because of the strong political organizations in many cities. The data in Table VII support this proposition; more than twice as many Southerners were defeated in primaries.

The data presented thus far do not support the insiders' claim that Northerners evince less interest in Congress. Table VII indicates that, in fact, Northerners who leave Congress are more likely to remain in public service than Southerners. This may reflect fewer opportunities for rewarding government posts in the largely rural South. It may also be a result of the unstructured southern political parties. There appears to be much less articulation between congressional politics and state and local politics in the South.[14]

We have seen that incumbents in northern safe seats have as much seniority as their opposite numbers from the South. Seniority in Congress is useful chiefly to secure desirable committee assignments. Since committee rank is a result of consecutive service on the committee, the northern safe seat holders conceivably could dissipate their congressional seniority by "committee hopping."

The data do not support this speculation. Twenty-nine per cent of the southern safe seat holders and 31 per cent of the Northerners were in one of the top three positions on the 17 major standing committees. Of the 14 major chairmanships held by members from safe districts, Southerners held nine and Northerners five; 12 per cent of the Southerners were major committee chairmen, and 11 per cent of the Northerners.[15] The southern advantage in total chairmanships appears to be a result of their great number of safe seats, and nothing else.

Finally, we examined the proportions of the two groups of safe seat holders who were chairmen of subcommittees. Here there is a southern advantage; 36 per cent of the Northerners were subcommittee chairmen, compared to 45 per cent of the Southerners. Subcommittee chairmen are chosen by the committee chairmen, who need not make their selections solely on the basis of seniority. Favoritism by the predominantly southern committee chairmen might account for the disparity in subcommittee chairmanships.

---

[14] See V. O. Key, *Southern Politics* (New York, 1949), ch. 18 and *passim*.

[15] The figure for the Southerners would be 13% if we took account of George Mahon's accession to the chairmanship of the Appropriations Committee on the death of Clarence Cannon in May, 1964.

We tested this proposition by counting, on each of the 17 major committees, those committee members who were not subcommittee chairmen themselves but who had more seniority than the lowest ranking subcommittee chairman. A total of 28 congressmen were in this position, 18 Northerners and 10 Southerners.[16] On committees chaired by Southerners, nine Northerners and three Southerners were by-passed. With northern chairmen, the proportion was more even: nine Northerners and seven Southerners.

Favoritism may not be the only reason for setting aside seniority in appointing subcommittee chairmen. Someone with special expertise may receive such an appointment out of turn. An uninterested or hopelessly incompetent member may be passed over. Some members may be reluctant to accept the chairmanship of an undesirable subcommittee in hopes of being chosen eventually to head a more powerful one. There is no reason to believe, however, that any of these considerations would apply disproportionately more to southern than northern members. Thus while the data in the preceding paragraph cannot be considered conclusive evidence of southern favoritism, they provide at least some basis for an explanation of the disproportionate number of subcommittee chairmanships held by Southerners.

The data presented up to this point indicate that the insiders' theory is wrong on every count:

(1) Congressmen in southern safe seats do not have more congressional seniority than those in northern safe seats.

(2) The post-congressional career patterns of the two groups do not indicate any greater northern inclination to leave the House for another career.

(3) The safe Southerners do not have more committee seniority than safe Northerners.

(4) Safe Southerners have more chairmanships than they are "entitled to" only at the subcommittee level, where considerations other than seniority affect the selection process.

The final element in the insiders' theory, concerning differences in the prestige of congressmen, will be discussed in the following section.

---

[16] It might be thought that the larger number of by-passed Northerners results from the fact that there are more of them in the House. But Southerners comprise 44% of the membership of the highest-ranking half of the 17 major committees, and it is from this group that subcommittee chairmen are chosen.

IV. OTHER REGIONAL DIFFERENCES

The finding that northern safe seat holders do not quit Congress any more readily than their southern counterparts does not by itself dispose of the proposition that Southerners are more effective legislators. Is it possible to examine the proposition that while the Northerners are no less likely to leave Congress, they do not use their House positions as effectively as the Southerners? Are the Northerners, as a group, less able men? Some fragments of data can be considered.

In the first place, the role of United States Representative does not appear to be any more prestigious among the mass of southern citizens than among those in the North. In a survey conducted in 1947 the National Opinion Research Center studied a national sample's assessment of the "general standing" of 90 occupations, one of which was "United States Representative in Congress."[17] Each of the 2920 respondents was asked to rate each occupation's "general standing" on the following scale: "excellent," "good," "average," "somewhat below average," and "poor." When tabulated by region, with southern Negro respondents removed, the results do not indicate any significant regional differences in congressional prestige. Eighty-eight per cent of the white southern respondents gave "excellent" or "good" ratings to the job of congressman, compared to 92 per cent in the Midwest and 94 per cent in Northeast and West. When all occupations were ranked, congressmen were sixth in the West and Midwest and seventh in the South and Northeast.[18]

The office of representative may be accorded as much respect by the mass electorate in the North, as in every section, and yet not be as highly regarded in the specialized political milieu in which politicians are socialized. Urban political organizations control Democratic congressional nominations in many northern one-party areas. Since these machines typically are based on the tangible rewards that can be drawn from control of local government, status in them generally goes to those who distribute jobs and contracts. Positions that have a share in this distribution process are the most

---

[17] For a full description of this study see Albert J. Reiss, Jr., *Occupations and Social Status* (New York, 1961).

[18] *Ibid.*, pp. 6, 19, 200, 220. Data on white Southerners were obtained from the National Opinion Research Center through the Inter-University, Consortium for Political Research. We are grateful to Ralph L. Bisco of the Consortium and Patrick Bova of NORC for their kind help.

desirable that the machine can bestow. In such cities many people see politics as a way to make money through the exercise of discretion.

Congressmen have hardly any patronage of their own[19] and, when there is a party organization of any consequence back home, federal appointments are cleared with its leader. In any event, federal patronage is negligible compared to the jobs and contracts that any machine-influenced local government can dispense. For most politicians who have worked their way up in an urban machine, being a congressman has little appeal. Some local bosses have also been congressmen, *e.g.*, the late William Green of Philadelphia or Charles Buckley of the Bronx, but their political power was not a result of their congressional seats. In his study of the Chicago congressional delegation, Leo M. Snowiss found that in that city's powerful Democratic organization the job of congressman was not as highly prized as any of a number of party and local governmental positions.[20] Consequently, at least some congressional nominations go to less highly regarded organization figures, tired mediocrities in late middle age. Most regular machine politicians in New York City seem to have a similarly low evaluation of congressmen. Richard H. Rovere's description of Peter J. McGuinness, an old-time boss in Brooklyn, includes an interesting example of this point of view:

> Like most politicians of his school, McGuinness considers congressmen members of an inferior class. To him, the local party bosses, who pick the legislators and tell them what to do, are the elite of politics and congressmen are men who, unable to make the grade themselves, must serve as legislative secretaries to men who have made the grade. He cannot understand the tendency, comparatively recent in this city, of political bosses to take congressional nominations for themselves. "I've sent plenty of them to Albany and Washington," he says, "but I'd never be such a damn fool as to send meself. Believe me, I'm glad I was never in a fix where anyone

---

[19] In addition to nominations to the service academies (which usually are heavily dependent on objective examination scores), the average congressman is lucky if he can name a Capitol policeman, elevator operator, or page. It takes a number of terms to acquire enough seniority to have much more appointment power.

[20] Leo M. Snowiss, "Chicago and Congress: A Study of Metropolitan Representation" (unpublished doctoral dissertation, University of Chicago, 1965), ch. 2.

else could send me. If a man's a leader in New York, what the hell business has he got in Washington?"[21]

One of the authors of this article, engaged in research that provided many opportunities to observe status relations in a very cohesive traditional northeastern urban organization, noted that the local congressional candidate seemed to get very little deference from most members of the organization.

This is not to say that all big-city congressmen are incompetent. The candidate just mentioned, for instance, has become a congressman with a considerable reputation for ability and effectiveness. Many other able representatives have come to Washington from the machines. In fact, given the low value generally placed on House seats in such political *milieux,* some ambitious men probably realize that the competition for such positions is less than for more lucrative posts at home. Nevertheless, politicians, like everyone else, are partly products of their environment, and there are indications that machine-controlled districts in the North produce more than their share of ineffective congressmen.

The New York City delegation is a case in point. Its members make up the core of the "Tuesday-to-Thursday club": congressmen who are in Washington only from Tuesday morning through Thursday afternoon and spend the rest of their time back home in more congenial and profitable pursuits. This habit is so prevalent that the decision of a second-term Democratic congressman from Queens to live in Washington evoked quasi-anthropological awe from *The New York Times:* "Mr. Rosenthal is the first New York City Democrat to take this step, as far as anyone in the state delegation can recall."[22]

The best available measure of attendance is *CQ*'s voting participation score, which gives the percentage of roll calls (119 in 1963) at which each member was present.[23] A serious disadvantage of this score as a measure of interest in legislation is that the leadership, aware of the members' habits, tries to schedule roll calls when most congressmen are in Washington. Since the House has been in Democratic hands for the past ten years, votes are seldom held when many Democrats are absent. As a practical matter, this means

---

[21] Richard H. Rovere, "The Big Hello," in *The American Establishment,* Harvest edition (New York, 1962), pp. 45–6.

[22] *The New York Times,* March 16, 1964, p. 37.

[23] *Congressional Quarterly Weekly Report,* January 31, 1964.

that there is little voting except on Tuesday, Wednesday, and Thursday. If a member's score is low, his attendance must be very spotty indeed. Table VIII contains voting participation scores for

TABLE VIII

Voting Participation by Democratic Congressmen in Safe and Non-Safe Seats, by Region—1963

Type of District	Voting Participation Score
Northern Safe	79
Northern Non-Safe	86
Southern Safe	83
Southern Non-Safe	87

safe and non-safe congressmen, with region controlled. Although a safe congressman should not have to spend as much time mending fences at home, the northern safe group scored somewhat lower than the non-safe Northerners. The New York City delegation accounts for most of this difference. When they are excluded, the northern safe group's score rises from 79 to 82, virtually the same as the southern safe score.

Since a number of Southerners also have unimpressive attendance records (although no southern delegation can match the New Yorkers), it is difficult to derive marked regional differences from these data. The complaints about the New York and Chicago delegations come chiefly from people who would usually like to be able to count on their votes. Possibly conservative spokesmen are equally bitter about southern absenteeism, but do not exhibit their disappointments in print.

Another bit of evidence may be useful in determining whether there are regional differences in legislative effectiveness. Despite the intentions of the spirit, the flesh may be weak. Some congressmen might not be physically capable of working as hard as they want. Representatives in northern safe seats are more likely than their southern counterparts to begin their congressional careers at fairly advanced ages. As Table IX shows, a quarter of the present northern safe seat holders entered the House when they were fifty or older, compared to 11 per cent of the Southerners. This explains the finding in Table VII that more Northerners than Southerners die in office. The machine-dominated recruitment patterns discussed earlier may account for the regional age difference. Like

TABLE IX

Age Distribution at Beginning of Current Term of Service of Incumbents in Safe Seats, by Region—1964

Age at Entry	Northerners	Southerners
	(%)	(%)
25–34	13	17
35–39	33	32
40–44	18	29
45–49	11	10
50–54	16	10
55 and over	8	1
	99[a]	99[a]
N	(45)	(77)

[a] Does not sum to 100 because of rounding.

other rewards for faithful service, congressional nominations are not given to neophytes. The leaders of urban machines typically are older men who have put in decades of work for the party. Upstarts are not highly regarded. On the other hand, nominations for available seats in most southern districts are more often fought over by a number of ambitious young men.[24] Since this prize is seldom one that can be bestowed by a cohesive organization, precedence has less to do with who gets it.

On the basis of these scattered data, it appears that Northerners in safe seats may be somewhat less vigorous than Southerners. This difference cannot be established as either large or conclusive.

V. TRENDS IN THE COMPETITIVENESS OF CONGRESSIONAL DISTRICTS

Our definition of safe seats is static and does not take account of districts that have become non-competitive since 1946. What trends have there been since then? As Charles O. Jones has shown, the number of competitive seats has decreased since 1952.[25] What effect is this trend likely to have on the distribution of political power in the House Democratic party? Do these trends modify the

---

[24] The classic description of the unstructured politics of most southern states is Key's book. See also Julius Turner, "Primary Elections as the Alternative to Party Competition in 'Safe' Districts," *Journal of Politics,* Vol. 15 (May, 1953), pp. 197–210.

[25] Charles O. Jones, "Inter-party Competition for Congressional Seats," *Western Political Quarterly,* Vol. 17 (September, 1964), pp. 461–76.

picture of safe districts painted by Burns and other spokesmen of the textbook theory?

To explore these questions we traced the number of non-competitive Democratic districts in every congressional election from 1946 through 1964. 1946 is a good starting point for two reasons: it was the first postwar election and it marks the low point of Democratic congressional votes in the past 36 years. For purposes of this discussion we will define a non-competitive election as one in which the Democratic candidate received 65 per cent or more of the major party vote. This is an arbitrary criterion, designed only to put often uncontested southern seats in some sort of comparative framework with northern non-competitive districts.

Table X shows the distribution of non-competitive districts in every election since the war. The number of southern districts in

TABLE X

Congressional Seats Won by Democrats by at Least 65 Per Cent of the Two-Party Vote, by Year and Region—1946 Through 1964

	North				South				Total Seats Won By 65%		Total Democratic Seats Won
	Urban		Rural		Urban		Rural				
Year	No.	Per cent	No.	Per cent	No.	Per cent	No.	Per cent	No.	Per cent	
		%		%		%		%		%	
1946	16	15	7	6	11	10	76	69	110	100	188
1948	31	23	14	10	12	9	78	58	135	100	263
1950	25	19	13	10	12	9	79	61	129	99[a]	235
1952	24	20	4	3	12	10	78	66	118	99[a]	213
1954	40	28	14	10	9	6	79	56	142	100	232
1956	32	26	8	7	13	11	68	56	121	100	234
1958	61	35	20	11	20	11	75	43	176	100	283
1960	57	36	12	8	19	12	70	44	158	100	260
1962	53	39	10	7	10	7	64	47	137	100	259
1964	81	49	25	15	12	7	48	29	166	100	294

[a] Does not sum to 100 because of rounding.

Sources: for election returns, various editions of Richard Scammon, ed., *America Votes* (Pittsburgh, University of Pittsburgh Press); several editions of the *Congressional Directory;* various editions of Clerk, U.S. House of Representatives, *Statistics of the Congressional and Presidential Elections* (Washington, G.P.O.); and *Complete Returns of the 1964 Elections by Congressional District* (Washington, Congressional Quarterly, Inc., 1965). The task of classifying Congressional districts as urban or rural proved to be rather complicated. For the 1962 and 1964 elections we used *CQ Census Analysis*, and for 1956 through 1960 similar data in *Congressional Quarterly Weekly Report*, February 2, 1962. In an earlier classification published in 1956, CQ used a completely different four-point classification scheme, *Congressional Quarterly Almanac, 1956* (Washington, Congressional Quarterly, Inc., 1956), pp. 788–792. We adapted this scheme to the urban-rural one on the basis of apparent similarities in the two taxonomies. For the elections from 1946 through 1950 we used the 1956 data, modified by examination of Congressional district maps.

this category remained almost constant through 1958, with the exception of 1956, and has declined since then. The number of northern non-competitive districts has increased consistently and now exceeds the South's. The 1964 election has exaggerated these trends,[26] but the probably aberrant character of this election should not minimize the significance of the steady increase in the North's share of non-competitive districts. Since 1956 Northern districts have never comprised less than 44 per cent of all seats won by 65 per cent or more. A similar proportion of non-competitive districts has been urban since 1956. It is no longer so true that non-competitive districts "have a heavily rural bias," as Burns said in 1963.[27]

The increase in Democratic strength in the North is due in part to population growth and movement. Better-off urban residents have been moving to the suburbs. The remaining city dwellers include higher proportions of Negroes, ethnic groups, and the poor. Reapportionment after the 1950 and 1960 Censuses may also have contributed to the growth of non-competitive districts.[28] Republican state legislatures often follow a strategy of concentrating Democratic voting strength in a few districts.[29]

The increase in northern numbers has been accompanied by a decline in the southern position. In 1947 there were 103 Democratic representatives from the South and only two Republicans. By 1963 there were eleven southern Republican seats; and in 1965 there are 17 such,[30] and 89 Democratic. Some of the Republican seats gained in 1964, notably five in Alabama and one in Mississippi, *may* presently revert to the Democrats. On the other hand, Goldwater did not do as well as Eisenhower and Nixon in the peripheral southern

---

[26] There probably would be fewer southern noncompetitive seats (not to mention fewer Democratic congressmen) if there had been Republican candidates in every southern district in the 1964 election. In several southern states Republican candidates either won or held their opponents to less than 65% of the vote in every district that they contested.

[27] Burns, p. 242.

[28] The wholesale reapportionment resulting from recent Supreme Court decisions is also likely to increase urban and suburban representation in both North and South.

[29] This is an example of how a rational strategy for Republican parties at the state level—conceding a minimum number of seats to the Democrats—is harmful to the party's interests on the national level because it enables these Democrats to build up seniority in Congress.

[30] This includes Representative Albert W. Watson of South Carolina, a Democrat who backed Senator Goldwater in 1964, was stripped of his seniority for this defection by the Democratic Caucus, and then switched parties.

states. Possibly, therefore, the Democrats will recover their seats in the Deep South only to lose seats in Florida, Texas, or Virginia.* The 1964 election cost the South two of its subcommittee chairmanships.[31] These are not the only seniority losses the region has suffered. Primary losses and redistricting have also eroded its power in the House. Since 1947 eight southern congressmen have lost their seats through redistricting and 15 more have been deposed in primaries. The redistricted seats have been gained by other southern states, but the new incumbents in these 23 seats could not inherit the seniority of the supplanted congressmen.

These trends mark an important shift in the distribution of power in the Democratic party. The northern wing of the congressional party is just now recovering the ground lost in the Republican sweep of 1946. The enormous Democratic losses in that election were confined almost entirely to the North. One of the long-term consequences of the Republican landslide then was the creation of a "seniority generation" dominated by Southerners. Unless the trend depicted in Table X is reversed, northern Democrats with useful amounts of seniority will soon be as numerous as the weakened southern contingent. Within a few years the North should begin to realize in its turn the fruits of the seniority system.

The familiar debate over "party responsibility" often leads to rejoinders that fragmentation is inevitable in American political parties. Some fragmentation is unavoidable, but it is one thing to say that we cannot (or should not) have cohesive parties on the English model, and quite another to claim that any particular existing level of fragmentation is immutable. As the changes in House rules at the beginning of the 1965 session demonstrate,[32] arrangements to make the process more or less responsive to majorities can occur within the basic framework of fragmentation. A "bargaining sys-

---

* [In 1966 the Democrats recaptured four of the seven previously safe seats in Alabama, Mississippi and Georgia lost in 1964. In the same election they lost a total of five seats in Florida, Virginia and Texas.]

[31] Representatives Grant and Roberts of Alabama and Winstead of Mississippi, all defeated by Republican candidates, headed a total of four subcommittees. A fifth subcommittee was chaired by John Bell Williams of Mississippi, who shared Watson's fate (but did not switch parties). Northerners took over Williams' subcommittee and one of the two chaired by Grant.

[32] Procedures were changed to reduce the Rules Committee's power to prevent floor consideration of legislation and avoid appointing conference committees. Most Southerners resisted these actions.

tem" can be any of a variety of political orders, from just short of anarchy to something like what happens in Great Britain when one party does not have a decisive majority. All systems characterized by bargaining do not assign similar resources to the principal actors. If the effective power of the president and the majority leadership were enhanced by any of half a dozen procedural changes, *e.g.,* an item veto, it would still be necessary for the actors to bargain with each other. The change would be in the cards, not the game. This is a simple point, but it seems to be overlooked by some of the most enthusiastic academic apologists for anti-majoritarian aspects of our political system.

Dissension in the Democratic party is due largely to Southerners.[33] As the relative strength of the South decreases, the cohesive potential of the party as a whole will increase, for there is little reason to expect that the northern wing of the party will become proportionately more divided as it grows in strength.[34] To put it another way, the decline of the Southerners will be accompanied by a Democratic president's greater ability to get his way with Con-

---

[33] There are, of course, many Southerners, including powerful committee chairmen like Carl Vinson, who are (or were) loyal to Democratic presidents all or most of the time. One cannot validly label all southern congressmen as invariably dissident. Nevertheless, there is also no doubt that the southern wing of the party is the major source of deviance.

[34] Some political scientists have argued that large legislative majorities are less responsive to the president, because they lead to factionalism. It is unclear whether this proposition refers simply to a majority for the president's party, or an effective majority for his policies. Even if it refers to the latter, there are some difficulties. Most important, it would seem that the smaller the majority, the easier it is for a potential defector to impede the president's program, since he needs to win fewer other dissidents to destroy the majority. As the majority grows, so does the size of the splinter group necessary to make an impact, and hence so does the magnitude of the defector's task. For discussions of this "law of economy" see E. E. Schattschneider, *Party Government* (New York, 1942), pp. 85–96. William H. Riker, who is cited on this point, actually discusses the weakness of big majorities when they are so big that they become "a coalition of the whole." See his *A Theory of Political Coalitions* (New Haven, Yale University Press, 1962), p. 56.

Statements of this proposition are usually accompanied by reminders that President Roosevelt, having won enormous congressional majorities in 1936, found his legislative program bogged down soon thereafter. This appears to be the major item of evidence to support the proposition. It does *not* appear that presidents have restrained their efforts to elect friendly congresses for fear of suffering Roosevelt's fate. A systematic examination of the historical record found that, if anything, big majorities are better than little ones. See Jay Goodman, "Legislative Majorities and Presidential Success" (unpublished paper, Brown University).

gress. It appears, then, that present trends are in the direction of greater cohesion and "responsibility" in the Democratic party.

VI. SUMMARY

We have presented data to test two theories about southern influence in the Democratic party in the House of Representatives. The central question is whether southern power can be explained solely by the lack of party competition in the South, or whether it is due also to regional differences which result in more dedication to legislative careers on the part of Southerners. We approached this problem by comparing northern and southern occupants of safe Democratic seats. There were no regional differences in congressional or committee seniority, or in forsaking Congress for other careers. Lack of party competition, aided perhaps by southern favoritism in appointment of subcommittee chairmen—and in the wake of the northern Republican sweep in 1946—seems to be an adequate explanation for the disproportionate number of Southerners in influential positions in the House. The textbook theory, accordingly, appears to be correct on this point.

The southerners may be more vigorous in the use they make of the positions they have. If age is any indication, Northerners, while they remain in the House, may be less able and energetic than Southerners. We could find no evidence of regional differences in the prestige of congressmen among electorates. The Northerners did tend to include more absentees and more members who first entered Congress at age 50 or older. These differences are not great, however, and must be interpreted with caution.

The number and share of non-competitive seats held by the North have increased markedly in the past fifteen years. The textbook theory is becoming increasingly less valid in its description of the characteristics of non-competitive districts. Unless this trend is reversed, northern Democrats will become much more influential in the House within a few years, since the other findings of this article do not indicate that they are any less likely to accrue seniority. The effect of these trends will be a decrease in the power of the deviant wing of the Democratic party and therefore an increase in party cohesion.

PART TWO

Work Groups in the House

THE HOUSE COMMITTEE ON WAYS AND MEANS: CONFLICT MANAGEMENT IN A CONGRESSIONAL COMMITTEE*

John F. Manley

THE HOUSE committee on Ways and Means, according to its members, is assigned the responsibility of resolving some of the most partisan issues coming before Congress: questions of taxation, social welfare legislation, foreign trade policy, and management of a national debt which exceeds $300 billion.[1] Yet members of the Committee also contend, at the same time, that they handle most of these problems in a "responsible" way. A Republican member of Ways and Means echoed the views of his fellow Committee members when he said, "it's the issues that are partisan, not the members." A Democratic member went so far as to claim that Ways and Means is "as bipartisan a committee as you have in the House." And a Treasury Department official who has worked closely with Ways and Means for several years believes that it is a

* Reprinted from *The American Political Science Review,* Vol. LIX, No. 4, December 1965.

I want to thank several scholars who commented on an early version of this paper: H. Douglas Price, Richard F. Fenno, Jr., Randall B. Ripley, Robert L. Peabody, Nelson W. Polsby, Frederic N. Cleaveland, James D. Barber, Leo Snowiss, Charles O. Jones, and Lewis A. Froman, Jr. I owe a special debt to David W. West, a perceptive friend and adviser who recently left the Committee's staff.

[1] This article is based on interviews conducted during 1964 with twenty of the twenty-five members of the Committee. The average interview ran 80 minutes. Questions were open-ended, no notes were taken during the interview, and all quotations are derived from notes made immediately after each interview. In addition, staff members, lobbyists, and executive department personnel were interviewed, some at great length. As a 1963–1964 Congressional Fellow I worked with Congressmen Thomas B. Curtis (R., Mo.) and Dante B. Fascell (D., Fla.), and was able to observe the Committee directly.

partisan committee in the sense that you get a lot of partisan voting. But while you get a lot of party votes the members discuss the bills in a nonpartisan way. It's a very *harmonious* committee, the members work very well and harmoniously together. Sure there is partisanship but they discuss the issues in a nonpartisan way.

The purpose of this paper is, first, to describe and analyze some of the factors which affect the Ways and Means Committee's ability to process, in a bipartisan manner, political demands which its members regard as highly partisan issues. Ways and Means is neither racked by partisanship nor dominated by non-partisanship; conflict and consensus coexist within the Committee and the balance between them varies chiefly with the nature and intensity of the external demands which are made on the Committee. Second, an attempt is made to contribute to the development of an analytical framework, based on Fenno's study of the House Appropriations Committee, which may prove useful for the comparative analysis of congressional committees generally.[2]

For analytical purposes, the Ways and Means Committee is here conceived as a political subsystem of the House of Representatives, charged by the House with a number of tasks, but in the normal course of events enjoying a high degree of operational autonomy.[3]

---

[2] Richard F. Fenno, Jr., "The House Appropriations Committee as a Political System: The Problem of Integration," this REVIEW, Vol. 56 (June, 1962), pp. 310–24. Fenno's approach has been applied to two other committees. See Charles O. Jones, "The Role of the Congressional Subcommittee," *Midwest Journal of Political Science,* Vol. 6 (November, 1962), pp. 327–44; Harold P. Green and Alan Rosenthal, *Government of the Atom* (New York, 1963), ch. 2. Other committee studies which may serve as a basis for comparisons include Charles O. Jones, "Representation in Congress: The Case of The House Agriculture Committee," *APSA Review,* Vol. 55 (June, 1961), pp. 358–67; Robert L. Peabody, "The Enlarged Rules Committee," in *New Perspectives on the House of Representatives,* Robert L. Peabody and Nelson W. Polsby, eds. (Chicago, 1963), pp. 129–64; James A. Robinson, *The House Rules Committee* (Indianapolis, 1963); George Goodwin, "Subcommittees: The Miniature Legislatures of Congress," *APSA Review,* Vol. 56 (September, 1962), pp. 596–604; Ralph K. Huitt, "The Congressional Committee: A Case Study," *APSA Review* Vol. 48 (June, 1954), pp. 340–65. See also Fenno's forthcoming book on the House Appropriations Committee, and his study of the House Education and Labor Committee, in Frank J. Munger and Richard F. Fenno, Jr., *National Politics and Federal Aid to Education* (Syracuse, 1962), ch. 5.

[3] For the general theory behind this paper see Talcott Parsons and Edward A. Shils, eds., *Toward a General Theory of Action* (New York, 1962), pp. 3–44, 190–233; Talcott Parsons, "Some Highlights of the General Theory of Action," in Roland Young, ed., *Approaches to the Study of Politics* (Evanston, 1958), pp. 282–301; and Marion J. Levy, Jr., *The Structure of Society* (rev.

Its primary task *vis-à-vis* the House is the resolution of political demands, many of which involve high stakes in money, power or dogma. To perform this function the Committee must solve certain problems of internal organization and interaction, and these internal problems are inextricably linked to the nature of the environmental demands which the Committee is set up to process. The Ways and Means Committee, in other words, receives from its environment, and it generates internally, demands with which it must cope if it is to maintain itself as a viable subsystem of the House.

These internal and external demands give rise to a set of decision-making norms and roles which govern intra-Committee behavior and regularize its relations with outside actors. Committee norms and roles enable it to manage three distinct but related problems: (1) problems associated with tasks (instrumental interaction); (2) problems of personal gratifications and interpersonal relations (affective interaction); and (3) problems of integration.[4] All three are affected by the type of subject matter and the external demands placed on the Committee; the internal operations of the Committee cannot be fully understood apart from the tasks which the Committee is expected to perform for the House.

The need for internal organization of a heterogeneous group poses integrative problems for the Ways and Means Committee. Integration, as defined by Fenno, is

> the degree to which there is a working together or a meshing together or mutual support among roles and subgroups. Conversely, it is also defined as the degree to which a committee

---

ed., Glencoe, 1957), pp. 19–84. For discussions of functionalism see Kingsley Davis, "The Myth of Functional Analysis as a Special Method in Sociology and Anthropology," *American Sociological Review,* Vol. 24 (December, 1959), pp. 757–72; Irving Louis Horowitz, "Sociology and Politics: The Myth of Functionalism Revisited," *Journal of Politics,* Vol. 25 (May, 1963), pp. 248–64; Don Martindale, ed., *Functionalism in the Social Sciences* (Philadelphia, 1965).

[4] Parsons and Shils, *op. cit.,* pp. 208–09. These problems are also dealt with in the literature on small groups. See Sidney Verba, *Small Groups and Political Behavior* (Princeton, 1961), pp. 117–43; Josephine Klein, *The Study of Groups* (London, 1956), pp. 115–33; George C. Homans, *The Human Group* (New York, 1950), pp. 319–20; Michael S. Olmstead, *The Small Group* (New York, 1959), chs. 4, 5, 6; Barry E. Collins and Harold Guetzkow, *A Social Psychology of Group Processes for Decision-Making* (New York, 1964), chs. 3, 10; Dorwin Cartwright and Alvin Zander, eds., *Group Dynamics: Research and Theory* (Evanston, 1953); A. Paul Hare, Edgar F. Borgatta, and Robert F. Bales, eds., *Small Groups: Studies in Social Interaction* (New York, 1955).

is able to minimize conflict among its roles and its subgroups,
by heading off or resolving the conflicts that arise.[5]

Put in a somewhat different way, as Parsons notes,[6] the integration
of roles depends on motivating *individual personalities* in the requisite ways. In order to stimulate the members of a group to contribute to the group's well-being and to the realization of its goals,
they must be induced to share certain values and to behave in prescribed ways, either through the distribution of incentives or the
application of sanctions, or both.[7] Members must, in a word, be socialized if the group is to be well integrated, and in congressional
committees socialization depends on inducements.

Part I, below, deals with three interrelated variables and their
relationship to Committee integration: the norm of restrained
partisanship, the nature of the subject matter, and the external demands of the House. Part II considers the role of the chairman as
an independent variable, describes how Chairman Mills directs
the Ways and Means Committee, and offers some reasons why he
operates as he does. Part III discusses the socialization process—the
Committee's attractiveness, which predisposes the members to respond to socialization, and its ability to satisfy members' personal
and political needs. The integration of four key roles, chairman-
ranking minority member and newcomer-experienced member, is
considered in Part IV. A final section offers some suggestions for
comparative committee studies.

I

Minority reports by Republican members of the Ways and Means
Committee and motions to recommit on the House floor frequently
accompany the major bills reported by the Committee.[8] In addi-

---

[5] Fenno, *op. cit.*, p. 310.

[6] Parsons and Shils, eds., *op. cit.*, pp. 24–25.

[7] Chester I. Barnard, *The Functions of the Executive* (Cambridge, 1956),
pp. 139–60. Frank J. Sorauf has recently analyzed political parties from an
inducement-contribution perspective; see his *Political Parties in the American
System* (Boston, 1964), pp. 81–97.

[8] *E.g.*, U. S. Congress, House, Committee on Ways and Means, 85th Cong.,
2d sess., H. Rept. No. 1761, *Trade Agreements Extension Act of 1958*, pp.
55–87. *Congressional Record*, June 11, 1958, Vol. 104, pp. 10881–82. Committee on Ways and Means, 87th Cong., 2d sess., H. Rept. No. 1818, *Trade
Expansion Act of 1962*, pp. 83–104. *Congressional Record*, June 28, 1962,
Vol. 108, pp. 12089–90. Committee on Ways and Means, 87th Cong., 2d

tion, the Committee members are clearly split along general ideological lines: the Democrats now overrepresent and the Republicans underrepresent their party's support for a larger federal role.[9] These indices of partisanship do not, however, reflect a critical integrative norm which governs the behavior of members in executive session: *the norm of restrained partisanship*. In the words of one experienced staff member,

> I think you will find that Ways and Means is a partisan committee, there are usually minority views. But partisanship is not that high when they discuss the bill and legislate. About 95 percent of the time the members deliberate the bill in a nonpartisan way, discussing the facts calmly. Then toward the end Byrnes [the ranking Republican] and the Republicans may go partisan. The things the Committee deals with are big Administration issues, so you are bound to get minority views and partisanship. But Byrnes likes to take a nonpartisan attitude toward things and it gets partisan only toward the end. On some votes they go party line but on others they don't. It all depends on the issue.

A couple of Committee members feel that Ways and Means decides most issues on a partisan basis, but the preponderant view is that of a Democrat who declared that "most of the time we go along up to a certain point and then a sharp party vote will come. On the tax bill [Revenue Act of 1964] we went along for a long time without party votes, working very well, then the Republicans lined up at the end against it. There's very little partisanship up to a point, when the political factors come in, and then a partisan vote comes."[10] Or a Republican who said, "we try to write the best legis-

---

sess., H. Rept. No. 1447, *Revenue Act of 1962*, pp. B1–B28. *Congressional Record*, March 29, 1962, Vol. 108, pp. 5431–32. Committee on Ways and Means, 88th Cong., 1st sess., H. Rept. No. 749, *Revenue Act of 1963*, pp. C1–C28. *Congressional Record*, September 25, 1963, Vol. 109, pp. 18118–19.

[9] During the 87th Congress the Democratic members of the Committee averaged 81 percent on Congressional Quarterly's index of·support for a larger federal role; the Republicans averaged 17 percent. A comparable disparity, 85 percent to 27 percent, shows up during the 88th Congress. Moreover, in both congresses the Democrats and Republicans on Ways and Means now appear to be more "liberal" and less "liberal," respectively, than the rest of their party colleagues. Data compiled from *Congressional Quarterly Weekly Report*, December 28, 1962, pp. 2290–95; October 23, 1964, pp. 2549–53. This may not have been true in earlier years.

[10] This was confirmed by the Committee's ranking Republican member, John Byrnes, in the debate over the 1964 Revenue Act: "We tried to come up with as good a bill as we could. And I say to the Speaker it was not done

lation we can in a nonpartisan way—more so than any other committee. We work in a nonpartisan way. Sure there are philosophical differences but they never become the partisan legislative fighting that they do on other committees."

The norm of restrained partisanship means that members should not allow partisanship to interfere with a thorough study and complete understanding of the technical complexities of the bills they consider. Members have a bipartisan responsibility to the House and to the nation to write sound legislation. They may disagree over what decisions the Committee ought finally to make but there is a firmly rooted consensus on *how* they ought to go about making them. Several variables affect the norm of restrained partisanship but two of them are of prime importance: (1) the nature of the Committee's subject matter; (2) the relationship between the House and the Committee.

(1) Working in a "responsible" way is valued highly by members of the Ways and Means Committee, and by "responsible" they mean being "conscientious," "thorough," "careful," and "studious." They emphasize the extreme complexity and national significance of the Committee's subject matter and this realization inclines them to constrain partisanship. "We deal with the most complicated, technical subject in the Congress, in the country for that matter, we have to be thorough on Ways and Means," according to a Democrat; a Republican said simply "you just don't mess around with taxes, it can create millionaires or paupers." All the members realize that they have to be responsible, another Democrat contended, and "this means that we don't do things on the basis of partisan or political advantage. We can reach a general consensus. Sometimes what a Republican will offer will be accepted by unanimous consent." A Republican who described the ideal GOP member in terms which made him certain to be in conflict with the Democratic members of the Committee paradoxically added that "partisanship is not too high on Ways and Means—taxes, trade, and social security should not be settled on a partisan basis."

---

on a partisan basis—and that has been confirmed by the chairman. It was done on a bipartisan basis, up until the last few days. When they had almost all the drafting completed and perfected, then they said, 'Now we don't need your help any more, boys; we will put the steamroller to work.' But up until then it was on a bipartisan basis." *Congressional Record,* September 25, 1963, Vol. 109, p. 18113. Contrast this with E. E. Schattschneider's account, *Politics, Pressures and the Tariff* (New York, 1935), of the making of the Smoot-Hawley tariff in 1929–30.

Both partisan and nonpartisan tendencies permeate the Ways and Means Committee and are reflected in the Committee's operating style.

Those members who attend the protracted meetings go through a laborious process of illuminating the implications of arcane tax, tariff, debt and social security proposals. They are assisted by experts from the executive agencies, the House Legislative Counsel's Office, the staff of the Joint Committee on Internal Revenue Taxation, and at times by employees of the Library of Congress. Legislation is pondered line by line. When the Committee makes a decision it is translated into technical language by the experts ("technicians") and brought back to the Committee for final approval. The decision-making style varies somewhat from issue to issue but in general it is marked by caution, methodical repetition, and, most important, restrained partisanship.[11] "We get together and go through things as twenty five Americans all trying to do what's for the public good. It's even rare for a bill to be reported out by a 15–10 vote."

But the internal relations of the Ways and Means Committee are not devoid of partisan political or personal disputes. Restrained partisanship is the widely accepted norm governing the Committee's day-to-day operations and it does dampen partisanship and promote integration. It also, on occasion, breaks down. Not all Committee decisions are made in the full Committee meetings. Republican members frequently caucus in order to develop a united front on key pieces of legislation and party line splits are not as rare as some members imply.[12] The norm of restrained partisanship does not stifle all dissension. A Democrat, for example, complained that the "Republicans sit there in Committee, vote for things, let things go by without saying anything, and then come out on the floor with motions to recommit, simply to surprise the Democrats." Personal feuds also erupt from time to time. On the whole, however, the Committee feels that the complex political de-

---

[11] Protests about the Committee's procedure are quite rare, but see the minority views on a 1955 bill extending corporate and excise tax rates in which the Republicans complained about the way a tax credit was "rammed" through the Committee. Committee on Ways and Means, 84th Cong., 1st sess., H. Rept. No. 69, *Revenue Act of 1955,* pp. 36–38.

[12] For a discussion of recent party battles fought on the floor over Ways and Means bills see Randall B. Ripley, "The Party Whip Organizations in the United States House of Representatives," *APSA Review,* Vol. 58 (September, 1964), pp. 570–74.

mands which it must settle are of national importance and should be handled so far as possible on their merits.[13]

(2) Virtually all the major bills reported to the House by the Ways and Means Committee are considered under a closed rule which precludes all floor amendments unless they are first accepted by the Committee. There is no lack of protest against this so-called "gag" rule but many members of the Committee and of the House argue that it saves the members from themselves.[14] Tax and tariff bills are so "sensitive" and "complex" that the House insulates itself from the demands of pressure groups by channeling the pressure into the committee stage of the process. On the few occasions when Ways and Means bills have been considered under open rules, one veteran Democrat claimed, "you had chaos."[15]

---

[13] The subject matter of Ways and Means appears to be essentially different from that of the House Education and Labor Committee, at least during recent years. Education and Labor must resolve basic ideological issues whose emotional content has been higher than the issues coming before Ways and Means. For a discussion of the influence of jurisdiction on Education and Labor, see Munger and Fenno, *op. cit.*, pp. 109–12.

[14] From 1955–1965, forty-seven bills were debated under closed rules, nine under open or modified open rules, and the rest (over 350 bills) under unanimous consent or suspension of the rules. A typical statement was made by Representative Howard W. Smith in the 1955 fight over a closed rule for the Trade Act: "Mr. Speaker, I recognize the difficulty of many Members of the House on this bill; we all have our own problems in our own districts, but this is a question that affects the whole country. . . . It has been recognized ever since I have been on the Rules Committee that bills of this type should be considered, as a practical matter, under a closed rule. The original bill setting up this program, as I recall, and the extensions in 1953 and 1954 were considered under closed rules. Nobody seemed to object at that time; as a matter of fact, both the majority and minority members of the Ways and Means Committee came before the Rules Committee and joined in the usual request that that committee makes of the Rules Committee for a closed rule." *Congressional Record*, February 17, 1955, Vol. 101, p. 1676. On this occasion the closed rule was almost defeated; it was adopted by one vote only after Rayburn took the floor and told his colleagues that "the House on this last vote has done a most unusual and under the circumstances a very dangerous thing. . . . Only once in the history of the House in 42 years in my memory has a bill of this kind and character been considered except under a closed rule. How long it is going to take, how far afield you will go, I do not know. . . . So as an old friend to all of you, as a lover of the House of Representatives and its procedures, I ask you to vote down this amendment offered by the gentleman from Ohio [Mr. Brown]." p. 1678.

[15] Closed rules do not mean that the House has no influence over the substance of bills reported by Ways and Means. Chairman Mills has a reputation for keeping his ear close to the ground and for gauging House sentiment. House demands, if they are strong enough to attract wide support, are reflected in Ways and Means bills even though no floor amendments are allowed. In order to ease passage of the 1962 Revenue Act, for example, Mills reduced

Members of the Ways and Means Committee are induced to follow the norm of restrained partisanship when they mark up a bill because of the autonomy which the closed rule gives to the Committee. A Republican, for example, expressed the common view that,

> On our Committee we have a responsibility to the House, we have to do the best job we can. . . . The closed rule prevents amendments and changes so we have to perfect the bill. Other committees can bring a bill to the floor with provisions in it they know will be taken out on the floor. Ways and Means doesn't do this, we can't do this.

One Committee member explained that "there are congressmen who have been here for years and can't understand social security. The average congressman can't understand what we deal with and you just can't open it up on the floor. We try to report well-rounded packages of legislation, the best bills we can. We compromise a lot to get a good bill we can report out. You don't report controversies just for the sake of controversy."

A House vote on whether or not to debate Ways and Means bills under a closed rule is in a sense a vote of confidence in the Committee. The Committee is widely thought to be the master of its esoteric subject matter and almost every member has a stake in maintaining this reputation. The House expects the Committee to polish its bills to near perfection technically and, perhaps more important, to make a satisfactory adjustment of the competing demands which surround Ways and Means bills. This expectation partly explains why Ways and Means is noted for time-consuming diligence, and it also buttresses the Committee's adherence to the norm of restrained partisanship. The distinctiveness of Ways and Means was expressed by one member when he said, "the House is jealous of the Committee. Many members say our bills can't be amended because we know it all, we're the experts. They are jealous." One of his colleagues sounded the same note when he observed that "the House says here are a bunch of smart guys, we won't tamper too much with what they do. The Ways and Means Committee has a reputation of being a well-balanced, level-headed group and the House respects this. . . . You just can't open a tax bill on the floor. The House knows we won't pull any fast ones."

---

the amount of the controversial investment credit from 8 percent to 7 percent. *Congressional Quarterly Weekly Report,* March 30, 1962, p. 492.

II

If the Ways and Means Committee has been able to manage internal partisan conflict more successfully than the House Education and Labor Committee—and apparently it has—this is due in no small way to the leadership style of the chairman, Wilbur D. Mills (D., Ark.) .[16] With the exception of one member who denied that there is a leadership structure within Ways and Means (it is, he claimed, an "amalgamated mess"), members agree that Mills runs the Committee and runs it well.

Mills's fellow Democrats consider him "powerful," "prestigeful," "quite a guy," "clever," "fine," "subtle," "smart," "patient," "expert," "best mind on the Committee," "leader," "key man." Perhaps of greater significance for purposes of integration is that these views are shared by the Republican members. They say Mills is "very effective," "a good synthesizer," "leader," "real student," "master of tax affairs," "fair," "calm," "intelligent," "impartial," "able," "well educated," and "not arbitrary."

Mills promotes integration by treating everyone fairly. He is careful to protect the rights of the Republican members and he gives the Republicans, a former staff member claimed, "pride of authorship" in bills even though the minority members may ultimately oppose them on the floor. Constraints on participation, both in public hearings and in executive sessions, are very loose.[17] One high-ranking Republican said of Mills,

> We deal with things on which Republicans and Democrats are in basic, fundamental disagreement and when you have something like this you are bound to get disagreement and

---

[16] Compare this description of Mills with that of Graham Barden (D., N.C.), former chairman of Education and Labor, whose leadership tended to create rather than resolve internal conflicts. Munger and Fenno, *op. cit.*, pp. 122–24.

[17] During the hearings on the Trade Expansion Act of 1962, for example, Keogh (D., N.Y.) complained about the amount of time consumed by Curtis (R., Mo.). Mills replied that the Committee would sit until Curtis was through with his interrogation. Committee on Ways and Means, 87th Cong., 2d sess., *Hearings on H.R. 9900, Trade Expansion Act of 1962*, II, 740. On another occasion, Mills moderated an interchange between Representative Bruce Alger (R., Texas) and James B. Carey of the A.F.L.-C.I.O. over whether or not Carey had implied that Ways and Means, by failing to pass the King-Anderson health care bill, was responsible for the death or discomfort of the aged. Mills ruled that Carey did not have to answer Alger's question but he defended Alger's right to propound such a query. Alger took pride in Mills's defense of his rights. Committee on Ways and Means, 88th Cong., 2d sess., *Hearings on H.R. 3920, Medical Care for the Aged*, IV, 1880–83.

minority reports. I think the major reason things don't disintegrate is Mills. Chairman Mills is very fair and reasonable. I can visualize disintegration and bickering if some of the members now ever become chairman, quite frankly, but all the time I've been on the Committee the chairmen have been reasonable men.

Mills recalls that as a boy he used to hear his father talk about the Ways and Means Committee with William A. Oldfield, an Arkansas congressman who was a member of the Committee during the 64th–70th congresses. When Mills was elected to the House he knew that Ways and Means was a choice assignment and he made an early attempt to get on it. His first try failed largely because he did not lay the proper foundation with the House leadership, but he tried again and with the leadership's support succeeded. Mills's attitude toward the Committee helps explain why he leads it as he does, always sensitive to threats to the Committee's status and prestige; but it is also a source of pride for some of the members. "You hear some criticism of Wilbur," said a Republican, "but he has a high regard for the Committee. *He takes care of it, respects it, and acts to insure its effectiveness on the floor.*" This commitment to the good of the Committee is a subtle factor in Committee integration but its presence is undeniable, even if there is no precise way to measure its importance.

For Mills, the Committee's reputation is dependent upon House acceptance of its bills. He does not like to lose and he usually avoids becoming so committed to an issue that he risks losing a bill on the floor.[18] After waiting sixteen years to become chairman he lost part of the first major bill he brought to the floor; because of his bargaining skill and willingness to compromise, members feel, he has been beaten only once since then on a bill of any consequence.[19]

Part of the reason why Mills tries to accommodate different and sometimes conflicting political demands is the internal composition

---

[18] The most dramatic recent example of how a committee's subject matter can affect its behavior and success in the House was the issue of federal aid to education. See H. Douglas Price, "Schools, Scholarships, and Congressmen: The Kennedy Aid-to-Education Program," *The Centers of Power,* ed. Alan F. Westin (New York, 1964), pp. 53–105.

[19] The first bill Mills lost was a temporary unemployment compensation measure. *Congressional Record,* May 1, 1958, Vol. 104, pp. 7910–11. The second was a conference report to carry out the International Coffee Agreement, *Congressional Record,* August 18, 1964 (daily edition), pp. 19501–07.

of the Committee. Two or three of the Democratic members are more conservative than the rest and—before the Committee's party ratio was changed from 15–10 to 17–8 they could determine outcomes by voting with a solid Republican bloc. Conversely, one or two Republicans have been known to "go off the reservation" and vote with the Democrats.[20] Depending on the issue, Mills may have to contain Democratic defections or lure a Republican vote. His base on the Democratic side is large and firm on most issues; even if some Democrats do not attend he can get their proxies. Neither party, however, is completely monolithic on all issues. Levels of commitment vary and in a delicately balanced situation Mills proceeds cautiously to make sure that he has the votes when he needs them. Two staff members commented: "Mills really likes to get a consensus if he can and this is one of the reasons partisanship is relatively low. He lets things settle and tries for agreement. He's just like that." "It's surprising how much Mills gets his own way. He'll sit back very quiet and let the boys thrash it out, let them go at it with their paper swords. Then he'll say we ought to do this and usually that's the way it's done." Committee integration may be positively or negatively affected by the style, ability and personality of committee chairmen.

The influence of the chairman on integration may also vary with committee structure. For example, the chairman may be a crucial factor in a committee, such as Ways and Means, that does its work in full committee rather than in subcommittees; but he may be less important or have different effects in a committee that operates through relatively autonomous subcommittees (Appropriations).

III

Political socialization is a dynamic and continuous process by which a group perpetuates its norms, values and roles.[21] It is

---

[20] See the votes reported in Elizabeth J. Brenner, *The Trade Expansion Act of 1962*, Congressional Quarterly Special Report, pp. 29–30; also the close votes on key sections of the Revenue Act of 1964, *Congressional Quarterly Weekly Report*, August 23, 1963, pp. 1473–83.

[21] Compare this definition with that of Gabriel Almond who says by political socialization "we mean that all political systems tend to perpetuate their cultures and structures through time, and that they do this mainly by means of the socializing influences of the primary and secondary structures through which the young of the society pass in the process of maturation. ... Political socialization is the process of induction into the political culture." Gabriel A.

dynamic in that the content of what is passed on changes with new problems and demands; it is continuous in that it affects both newcomers and experienced members. To the new member socialization involves exposure to and inculcation with the norms of the group. To the experienced member it consists of the maintenance of his conformity to group norms or, if he resists, tension between his values and behavior and those of the group.

Socialization depends upon the attractiveness of the group and upon its ability to regulate behavior through the allocation of positive and negative incentives.[22] Objectively measured, Ways and Means is the most attractive committee assignment in the House. John C. Eberhart compared House committees from 1914 to 1941 and found that Ways and Means had the highest prestige.[23] Similarly, Warren Miller has compared committee assignments between the 80th and 88th Congresses and Ways and Means places first.[24]

Members are attracted to Ways and Means for a variety of reasons. Most frequently mentioned are its power and prestige. Ways and Means is "tops," "the guts of government," a "real blue-ribbon committee," a "choice one." One member, who was neither especially attracted to Ways and Means nor happy with the detailed nature of the Committee's work, said you just don't leave a "blue-ribbon" committee like Ways and Means. "You just go up from Ways and Means," a Democrat said, "you don't go to another committee—Appropriations, Rules, or Interstate. You go to Senator, Governor, that sort of thing. It's a springboard and many members have gone on from it." When asked if he ever tried to shift to a different committee another Democrat replied, "are you kidding! Why leave heaven to go to hell? There's no committee in Congress, including Appropriations, that's as important as Ways and Means. Why step downward once you have reached the top?"

Almond and James S. Coleman, *The Politics of the Developing Areas* (Princeton, 1960), p. 27.

[22] Barnard, *op. cit.*

[23] Cited in George B. Galloway, *Congress at the Crossroads* (New York, 1946), p. 90. For some critical comments on Eberhart's methodology see James A. Robinson, "Organizational and Constituency Backgrounds of the House Rules Committee," *The American Political Arena,* ed. Joseph R. Fiszman (Boston, 1962), p. 214.

[24] Warren E. Miller and Donald Stokes in a forthcoming volume on representation and Congress, to be published by Prentice-Hall in 1969.

Group identification is high on the Ways and Means Committee and the members usually refrain from behavior that is likely to weaken the Committee's position in the House. The Committee's attractiveness buttresses the norm that outlaws such behavior. Members may disagree and they may even quarrel among themselves but, as one Democrat said, "we fight our battles in executive session and not in public." A conservative Republican member who almost never agreed with anything supported by the Democrats declared that "we keep personal things to ourselves and we stick together when someone attacks the Committee." The Committee has been criticized by its own members but this happens very rarely.[25] Every member derives satisfaction from the Committee's reputation; they are predisposed by the Committee's attractiveness to follow the ground rules of partisan battle which place rigid constraints on the ways in which disagreement is manifested.

Socialization is also affected by the group's ability to offer the members positive incentives in return for approved modes of behavior. The Ways and Means Committee serves as the source of positive incentives in at least three important ways:[26] (1) affective relations inside the Committee, (2) influence in the House; and (3) relations with constituents.

(1) Unlike most other congressional committees (Senate Finance is another example), the Ways and Means Committee functions in executive sessions of the full committee, and not through subcommittees. Members meet in direct face-to-face contact for weeks at a time and this style of deliberation is accompanied by a fairly well defined set of interpersonal norms. Committee meetings are not supposed to be partisan battles; some acrimony does develop but on the whole the members feel that to be effective they must maintain decorum and act in a gentlemanly way. Bitter personal disputes

---

[25] The Committee was reluctantly criticized by a Republican member in 1955 for rushing through H.R. 1, the extension of the Reciprocal Trade Act, without giving the members time to study it or propose amendments. *Congressional Record,* February 18, 1955, Vol. 101, pp. 1743–44.

[26] March and Simon contend that the stronger the individual's identification with a group, the more likely his goals will conform to his perception of group norms. They identify five factors which affect group identification: (1) prestige; (2) perception of shared goals; (3) satisfaction of individual needs; (4) frequency of interaction; and (5) degree of competition between group and individual. In this paper I deal with the first three of these. James G. March and Herbert A. Simon, *Organizations* (New York, 1958), pp. 65–66.

erupt infrequently and even public conflicts which appear to be disruptive of interpersonal relations are often played out in a benign spirit. A Republican who found it difficult to follow these norms was "talked to" by a senior Republican and told that he was losing his effectiveness by being so adamant. If a member starts to berate another member his colleagues will try to restrain him. You "don't attack one man continually" on Ways and Means; "we spar a lot but it never gets serious." "We don't have knock-outs, maybe we are a little more clubby, more closely knit than others." Members believe that they are "responsible" men who "respect the other fellow" and who "get along pretty well with others."

These attitudes and norms help make the Committee a satisfying group to belong to. A Republican said,

> Relations with the Democrats are usually harmonious. It's like a fraternity where you have different clubs with different symbols and minor disagreements. There's a spirit of *camaraderie* that prevails. Oh, we have our differences now and then, and we jab back and forth, but it never really gets too serious. We are all concerned with how the Committee looks to outsiders and if there's a lot of bickering the Committee doesn't look good. Take Banking and Currency for example after Patman took over. He's arbitrary and the Committee's prestige has sunk way down. We know that to be an effective committee we must be reasonable.

In the words of a Democrat "everyone's a moderate ... they screen out those members who would play for publicity and make a lot of noise. . . ." Two Democrats attributed their appointments to Ways and Means to personal characteristics of their rivals as aspirants. One of these "went off half-cocked," was "controversial" and not "well-liked"; the other was "compulsive" and he would not be right for Ways and Means where members have to "contain" themselves. Another member said plainly, "we don't want any screwballs and since I've been a member we haven't had any screwballs. These men are pretty carefully selected, you know, so you don't get radicals."[27] "Comparing Ways and Means with my former committees, and with other committees I know of, there is

---

[27] The same man, a Democrat, explained his election to Ways and Means in these words: "No one wanted to go much farther north ... for fear of running into a radical liberal, and no one wanted to go much further south for fear of running into an extreme conservative, so they picked me. They wanted a moderate liberal and a liberal moderate and I fit the bill."

a spirit of cooperation between Republicans and Democrats. We are members of the 'club' now."

Personal traits are not the only consideration in the recruitment process to Ways and Means. Seniority, region, and policy orientation are important and, in many cases, decisive. When these criteria are not of overriding importance, or when more than one contestant meets them, a popular man who is "responsible" has an edge over someone who has made enemies, especially on the Democratic side where Ways and Means members are elected by a vote of all Democratic members of the House; and objective reasons can usually be found to rationalize affective predilections. These informal recruitment criteria and norms of behavior combine with the Committee's attractiveness to produce men who are inclined to follow group norms, to value harmony, and to promote integration. Members prefer to disagree amicably if they can; they feel more comfortable in a low-tension environment and they realize that to protect the Committee's status as the "queen committee" they must manage partisan dissension in a non-destructive way.

As indicated above, partisan considerations and policy orientation are important factors in determining contests over seats on the Ways and Means Committee. In 1963, for example, Phil Landrum of Georgia was denied a seat on Ways and Means largely because he was considered to be too conservative by his Democratic colleagues in the House. Landrum was elected to Ways and Means in 1965 after demonstrating more liberal inclinations by, among other things, guiding the poverty bill through the House.[28] Republicans, on the other hand, want men on Ways and Means who "all fall within pretty much the same general philosophical area" and who will "go down the line" for the party.

(2) Membership on the Ways and Means Committee makes one a member of the House elite. Ways and Means members share in the Committee's prestige and, at a more practical level, they are in a good position to accumulate political credits with their colleagues. All congressmen, at one time or another, are concerned with problems that relate to taxes, social security or trade. On swapping favors one Committee member explained,

---

[28] *Congressional Quarterly Weekly Report,* January 18, 1963, p. 46. Landrum's growing liberal tendencies are reflected in his scores on the federal role index: 86th Congress, 33 percent support for a larger role; 87th Congress, 61 percent; 88th Congress, 80 percent. *Congressional Quarterly Almanac,* XVI, 1960, p. 136; footnote 9, *supra.*

Hell, I'm always being approached by members. It's important, you know. I might go to a member of Public Works once in ten years but they seek my assistance all of the time. Same with all the members of Ways and Means.... When I need a favor I can always call on Republicans whom I have helped on Ways and Means bills.

Democrats on Ways and Means have a unique source of influence because of their control over assignments to other committees.[29] Committee assignments in a political system whose life revolves around committees are of major concern to every member of the House. The Ways and Means members normally enjoy—with the exception of assignments to the Rules Committee, which are of special interest to party leaders—a high degree of influence in making appointments. The committee-on-committees function increases their contacts with members from their zone. Newly elected congressmen are indebted to them from the first day they arrive and, as a member moves up the committee hierarchy, he is continually dependent on his representative on Ways and Means.[30] "They call you 'Mr.' and 'Sir' when you are on the Committee on Committees," one member said. House members "look up to me"; a third member said "*they* come to you and that's very important. Members are always coming to me for things and when I go to them, boy they remember."

In short, the members of Ways and Means stand above many of their peers in the House and they associate this preeminence with the Committee. They are, therefore, induced to follow the norms which insure the continuation of the Committee's stature: restrained partisanship, responsible law making, and reasonable behavior.

(3) Most members of the Ways and Means Committee find the

---

[29] On the Committee on Committees see Charles L. Clapp, *The Congressman: His Work as He Sees It* (Washington, 1963), pp. 183–212; also Nicholas A. Masters, "Committee Assignments in the House of Representatives," this REVIEW, Vol. 55 (June, 1961), pp. 345–57.

[30] A "latent function" of the Committee on Committees was evident on the 1963 tax bill, when Mills used the 15 members to help get the bill through the House. Ripley, *op. cit.*, p. 570. Members sometimes take soundings for Mills and act as an informal whip system of their own. As one member remarked, "If I can support it in Committee and on the floor then they [members from his zone] can support it too." When asked what he could do if they did not vote as he did on a Ways and Means bill he added, "Well, I suppose if it were [a senior member] I couldn't do very much, but if it were some new member who didn't have a prime committee yet I could do something."

Committee a good place from which to satisfy constituent demands. Not every member believes that he can serve his constituents better from Ways and Means than he could from any other House committee, but several do. Moreover, no member's district is so intimately dependent on a committee other than Ways and Means that he risks electoral defeat simply because of his committee assignment.[31] Few members would disagree with a newly appointed member, Dan Rostenkowski (D., Ill.), who told his constituents in a newsletter,

> This has been a wonderful year for me. In May I was selected to fill a vacancy on the House Ways and Means Committee. As this is the Committee on Committees, appointment must be made by a vote of the Democratic members of the House, and I am proud to say that I was unanimously chosen by my colleagues.... This is the most important committee in the House.... It is a most interesting assignment, but more important, it places me in a position whereby I can be more effective in assisting you with your needs, both personal and legislative.[32]

Intensive bargaining surrounds the myriad parts of a major Ways and Means bill and it is often possible for a member to promote or protect constituent interests by letting it be known that he will support a position unfavorable to the Administration. Executive department representatives may even try to lure Republican support, as evidenced by the late Howard Baker's success in getting one of his favorite proposals included in the Revenue Act of 1964.[33]

---

[31] Joel Broyhill, appointed to the Committee in 1964, was thought to be running a grave risk in leaving the District of Columbia Committee and the Post Office and Civil Service Committee because many of his Virginia constituents are government employees who work in the District. Broyhill met the issue head-on by stressing the importance and prestige of Ways and Means and he was re-elected, albeit with a somewhat smaller percentage of the vote than he received in 1962. *Washington Post*, October 3, 1964, p. B2. He was reappointed to the District Committee in 1965 without having to yield his seat on Ways and Means, notwithstanding the general rule that membership on the latter is "exclusive."

[32] Dan Rostenkowski, "Washington Report," July 20, 1964, p. 2. Congressman George M. Rhodes (D., Pa.), shortly after he was elected to Ways and Means, could take credit for two amendments to a social security bill which were of interest to his constituents. "A Report from Congressman George M. Rhodes," July 16, 1964, p. 1.

[33] For an explanation of this provision see Committee on Ways and Means, 88th Cong., 1st sess., H. Rept. No. 749, *Revenue Act of 1963*, pp. 45–47. It allowed the exclusion from gross income of a limited amount of capital gain received from the sale or exchange of a personal residence by a person 65 years old or over.

"You know, you can really do things for your constituents on the Committee. Boy, if you are a horse-trader you can really move. Exports, imports, that sort of thing."

Major legislation is not the only opportunity for serving one's constituents and friends. Ways and Means also processes so-called "members' bills," which are perhaps the best examples of bipartisan cooperation on the Committee. A member's bill is supposed to be a minor piece of legislation that ameliorates the impact of some small feature in the tax laws or makes some "technical" improvement in other laws that come under the Committee's jurisdiction; it is regarded as a "little" thing, of no special interest to anyone other than the Committee member who introduced it.[34]

From time to time during the course of a Congress, Committee members are asked to list in the order of their preference (or chance of passage) those bills which they would like the Committee to consider during "members' bill time." Every member is given the opportunity to call up a bill or bills, depending on how many times they go around the table. If he can get the unanimous consent of his colleagues, his bill will be reported to the House, called up on the House floor by unanimous consent or suspension of the rules, and usually passed without objection.

On April 30, 1964, Chairman Mills stood on the floor of the House and asked unanimous consent for the immediate consideration of twelve members' bills.[35] Eleven of these bills were passed by voice vote and one, H.R. 4198 introduced by Representative Shelley (D., Calif.), was defeated when another non-Ways and Means member, Matsunaga (D., Hawaii), objected. H.R. 4198 provided for the free importation of soluble and instant coffee and Matsunaga thought that before it was passed the Hawaiian coffee industry should be consulted. Mills had also intended to call up a bill introduced by Hale Boggs (D., La.), the third ranking

---

[34] Typical members' bills alter the tariff on brooms made of broom corn, provide a credit or refund of self-employment taxes in certain cases, allow the free importation of spectrometers for universities, provide tax-exempt status for non-profit nurses' professional registries, continue the suspension of duties for metal scrap, etc.

[35] *Congressional Record,* April 30, 1964 (daily ed.), pp. 9397–9410. Mills also tried to get S. Con. Res. 19 which expressed the sense of Congress that bourbon whiskey is a distinctive product of the United States and that no imported whiskey should be labeled "bourbon" passed at this time, but John Lindsay (R., N.Y.), objected on behalf of two female constituents whose income came from a small distillery in Mexico. Sober heads prevailed and the resolution passed the House later.

Democrat on Ways and Means, but another member of the Committee, Thomas B. Curtis (R., Mo.), prevented it by indicating to Mills that he would object.

Of the eleven bills passed at this time, four were introduced by non-members of Ways and Means. The Committee reported these bills as favors to them. Two of the remaining seven were introduced by Republican members of Ways and Means, and five by Democratic members.[36] All twelve were reported unanimously by the Committee and most were supported actively on the floor by the ranking Republican member, John Byrnes (Wis.).

A member's bill may be killed by another member of the Committee, as in the case of the Boggs bill, or it may be killed or postponed by other members of the House, as illustrated by Matsunaga's objection to H.R. 4198. Not every member's bill becomes law. But many do. If influence in the House is defined as the ability to accumulate credits and dispense them with skill then the members of the Ways and Means Committee, if they stick together, are in a good position to exert influence and satisfy the demands of their constituents and friends.[37] Favors that are "little" in the sum total of things are often large to individual congressmen, and when small favors like these are dispensed over a period of years they amount to a considerable fund of credit on which the Committee (and its Chairman) may draw if the need arises. Ways and Means reports and passes a relative handful of major bills; it processes dozens of noncontroversial members' bills. When the Committee "cashes in its chips" to pass a major bill the chips are members' bills and other favors which it performs for members of the House.

Members' bills are important benefits which members of both parties enjoy by virtue of their membership on the Committee. They help satisfy the members' need to meet some of the demands of their constituents; and they induce the members to cooperate with one another to this end. The continued success of members' bills depends on the Committee's relations with the House. Members'

---

[36] On December 18, 1963, the Committee similarly announced its intention to report 32 members' bills. Seven of them were introduced by non-members, 17 by Democratic members, and 8 by Republican members.

[37] For discussions of bargaining see Robert A. Dahl and Charles E. Lindblom, *Politics, Economics, and Welfare* (New York, 1963), chs. 12, 13; Lewis A. Froman, Jr., *People and Politics* (Englewood Cliffs, 1962), pp. 53–58; Robert L. Peabody, "Organization Theory and Legislative Behavior: Bargaining, Hierarchy and Change in the U. S. House of Representatives," a paper read at the annual meeting of the American Political Science Association, New York City, September 4–7, 1963.

bills are positive incentives which emanate from the Committee and by helping to promote the members' interests they promote integration.

IV

Committee integration is also affected by the hierarchy of status and role which exists within the group. Members of the Ways and Means Committee play different roles and if the Committee is to be well integrated these roles must be legitimized and ordered.[38] Two sets of roles are of special significance: chairman and ranking minority member, and experienced member-newcomer.

The relationship between the chairman and the ranking minority member is a potential source of conflict in the Committee. Mills, who was elected to the Committee in 1942, has been chairman since 1958. John Byrnes of Wisconsin has 18 years' experience on Ways and Means and has been the ranking Republican member since 1963.[39] Their roles set limits to the degree of cooperation between them and they frequently oppose one another on key policy matters, both within the Committee and on the House floor. There is, however, a good deal of cooperation and mutual respect between them. Both men realize that their positions may be reversed some day and they therefore cooperate on most procedural and some substantive matters.

When the Ways and Means Committee comes to the House floor with a major bill it is often the quintessence of party conflict in the House. But the easy fraternization between Mills and Byrnes even at the height of floor battles is indicative of the spirit within which the Committee has performed its day-to-day labors.

Mills and Byrnes have jointly sponsored legislation which is referred to Ways and Means and they have collaborated on certain kinds of bills on the floor.[40] One staff member described the two men in these words,

---

[38] Parsons and Shils, eds., *op. cit.*, p. 203; John C. Wahlke, Heinz Eulau, William Buchanan, and LeRoy C. Ferguson, *The Legislative System* (New York, 1962), pp. 7–28.

[39] Several people associated with the Committee stated that Mills and Byrnes played prominent leadership roles even before they formally became chairman and ranking minority member.

[40] See H.R. 12545 and 12546, 88th Cong., 2d sess., 1964. These bills concern the relative priority of federal tax liens over the interests of other creditors. In addition to their cooperation on members' bills see the debate on H.R. 11865, the 1964 Social Security Amendments, *Congressional Record,* July 29, 1964 (daily ed.), p. 16680.

Mills calls the shots, he runs the show. If a member would like a Committee meeting next Monday, for example, he'd have to get Mills to call it. Every once in a while Mills is questioned about hearings and witnesses but he's very good about it. He discusses these things with Byrnes. The hearings last fall [1963] on beer concentrate were Byrnes's doing. He wanted them, so he and Mills arranged a date. It's quite informal. Mills and Byrnes are good friends. *In many ways they are very similar. Both are dedicated and have no outside life —no hobbies, never take vacations. The Committee is their life. They take work home. They remind me of guys working in a factory who punch in and out, go home and wait for the next work day to begin.*

Members of both parties are "safe" on critical issues and they are, therefore, bound to be opposed on some things. The disintegrative effect of this built-in partisanship is tempered, however, by the tendency of newly elected partisans to accept subordinate roles within the Committee until they become familiar with the subject matter and are accustomed to Committee procedure.

The apprentice role is firmly established on Ways and Means and the new member who wants to be effective does not (even if he could) try to match wits with his more experienced colleagues. This is due in part to the Committee's complex subject matter. One veteran member said that "when I first went on the Committee I used to leave the meetings with a headache, truly a headache! The stuff was just over my head. I just kept plugging along and gradually you catch on. The things we deal with are so complex!" "Detail and technical, oh there's so much detail and it's so technical! You have to take work home and study. Everything is complicated now. Social security has become complicated, tax and tariff too." A junior Democrat added,

Leadership is pretty constant. The men who sit at the head of the table naturally lead the Committee. They are knowledgeable and have been around a long time. ... Now that doesn't mean that if I have a question I can't get my oar in. There's no problem about that. But leadership is as you go up the ladder. Neither _____ nor I will ever be fire-balls on the Committee; we are too old.

Or a junior Republican,

Byrnes and Curtis are real students, are experienced, and know more about it. They *should* lead the Committee. Yesterday, for example, I could have spoken on the Renegotiation Act but I am quite content to let Byrnes and Curtis handle it. They are the experts. I'd tell a new member to get familiar with the four or five major things the Committee deals with. To study hard.

"Jennings is a smart member and Martha Griffiths shows a lot of potential. But we are all learners and beginners, the older members are the ones we listen to." "You have to learn," a Republican said, "and I want to learn. It would be resented if I tried to talk too much or overdid it. . . . So keep your damn big mouth shut a while. If I tried to talk a lot it would be resented, while it wouldn't for an older member."

Newcomers to Ways and Means are expected to "attend religiously, study hard, and pay attention to what the experts are saying." And the "experts" are the experienced members. A new member may participate right away but it is a fundamentally different kind of activity from that of the senior members.[41] Junior members are neither muzzled nor immobilized; they exist in a state of animated quiescence until they have absorbed enough information to make meaningful contributions to the policy discussion.

Friendly and cooperative relations between the chairman and the ranking minority member, plus well established norms of deference governing the degree and kind of participation by senior and junior members, constitute a system of decision-making which is marked by restrained partisanship. During their apprentice period the behavior of new partisans is controlled by the impossibility of rapidly accumulating expertise in the Committee's subject matter. They are exposed to the norms of the group; they soon detect the Committee's leaders; and they learn how to become effective members.

The socialization process is not perfect on Ways and Means but in terms of its ability to negate the influence of divisive partisan factors it compares favorably in recent years[42] with some other committees, most notably the House Education and Labor Com-

---

[41] The role of apprentice on the Ways and Means Committee contrasts sharply with the Education and Labor Committee, where newcomers are expected to play a major part immediately. Munger and Fenno, *op. cit.,* p. 119.

[42] The importance of time and chairmen becomes clear when one compares the conflict-ridden way the Committee handled the excess profits tax in 1950 with its relatively pacific handling of both the 1962 and 1964 Revenue Acts. For the 1950 bill see Stephen K. Bailey and Howard D. Samuel, *Congress at Work* (New York, 1952), pp. 350–52.

mittee. It is doubtful if any amount of incentives derived from the Committee, or any number of years experience on the Committee, could result in the total integration of dedicated conservatives like James Utt or committed liberals like George Rhodes, but not even the most ideologically oriented members are immune from the group pressures to restrain partisanship, to articulate dissension in certain ways and not in others, and to contribute to the perpetuation of the Committee as the number one committee in the House.

* * *

The major differences in emphasis between Fenno's approach and the one adopted here are that I have stressed the influence of external House demands on the internal operations of the Committee, taken the role of chairman as an independent variable of prime importance to the Ways and Means Committee, considered socialization as a blend of attractiveness and inducements, and attempted a linkage between Parsons's focus on integration and Barnard's stress on inducements. Whatever the approach, it is clear that the inner life of congressional committees, a hitherto little explored part of the workings of Congress, deserves the attention of political scientists as a way of increasing our knowledge about legislative behavior and explaining why Congress accepts or rejects the recommendations of its "little legislatures."

V

THE FUNCTIONS OF INFORMAL GROUPS:
A STATE DELEGATION*

Alan Fiellin

SOCIAL SCIENTISTS have long recognized the value of the two approaches combined in the analysis reported in this paper—namely, functional analysis and the study of informal groups. Political scientists, however, have been slow to apply them *systematically* in their investigations of political institutions and behavior. Neither has as yet achieved a permanent place in the methodology of our discipline. For this latter reason, it will be worthwhile to examine briefly the meaning of these concepts before presenting the substantive analysis.

The relationship of political scientists to functional analysis is roughly that of M. Jourdain to prose; not fully conscious of his methodology, the analyst fails to use it systematically and thus fails to take full advantage of its potential. A quick review of the literature of political science would reveal many references to the functions of political behavior patterns and institutions, but self conscious systematic uses of the concept and approach would be hard to find. Moreover, owing to our traditional emphasis upon legal-constitutional and prescriptive analysis, many investigations have been limited to either the constitutionally prescribed functions[1] or functional prescriptions based upon the authors' values. Though both of these may be legitimate enterprises, they do not fully exploit functional analysis and without supplementation

---

* Reprinted from "The Functions of Informal Groups in Legislative Institutions," *Journal of Politics*, XXIV (February, 1962), 72–91. Copyright © 1962, Southern Political Science Association.

[1] For a discussion of the limitations of traditional frameworks see Gabriel Almond's introductory chapter, "A Functional Approach to Comparative Politics," in Gabriel Almond and James S. Coleman, *The Politics of the Developing Areas* (Princeton, New Jersey: Princeton University Press, 1960), especially pp. 3–4.

may lead to incomplete understanding and therefore superficial evaluation.[2]

Functional analysis is one way of viewing, understanding, or explaining behavior within a system. The observer asks what consequences a given behavior pattern has for the systems of which it is a part. For example, what are the functions and dysfunctions of boss-controlled political machines for the social, economic, and governmental systems of which they are a part,[3] or of seniority and the committee system for the legislative system, party system, and inclusive political system? The conclusions of such an analysis provide an understanding of the item as a functional unit of the institutions for which it is relevant.

Systematic functional analysis of social behavior requires more than the usual precision in the use of the term "function" and also requires that some distinctions between kinds of functions be made. The definition to be used here is that of Merton. "Functions are those observed consequences which make for the adaptation or adjustment of a given system."[4] As adapted to the present study, consequences make for the adaptation or adjustment of a given system when they (1) constitute positive and necessary contributions to the existence of the system, or (2) merely contribute to the achievement of participants' goals. Criterion 1 raises the issue and problems of the functional prerequisites of the systems considered. By supplementing this with the less demanding criterion 2, the problems involved in determining whether or not a particular function is vitally necessary are avoided. As the purpose of the analysis is to explain the existence of legislative informal groups, it seems justified to call attention to a variety of consequences without limiting attention to only those without which the various systems could not survive. Consequences which merely contribute to goal attainment are thus included not primarily for the purpose of avoid-

---

[2] A single example will clarify this point. The report of the Committee on Political Parties of the American Political Science Association, *Toward a More Responsible Two-Party System,* concentrates almost exclusively on the dysfunctions of United States parties and the functions which the authors feel they should perform (not actually do). A complete functional analysis in providing a more thorough understanding of the parties, would provide an appropriate basis for an evaluation of the net contribution of our parties to the political system and democracy.

[3] See the systematic analysis of Robert K. Merton in *Social Theory and Social Structure* (Glencoe, Illinois: The Free Press, 1957), pp. 71–82.

[4] Merton, *op. cit.,* p. 51.

ing problems but, more importantly, to permit a more complete explanation of informal groups.

The concept "dysfunction" is then used to refer to those consequences "which lessen the adaptation or adjustment of the system."[5] Merton points out that our analytical framework must also take into account the possibility of non-functional consequences—those which are irrelevant to the adaptation of adjustment of the system. It should be noted that a given behavior pattern may have all three kinds of consequences.

In addition to the above, there is the equally important distinction between manifest and latent functions. "Manifest functions are those objective consequences contributing to the adjustment or adaptation of the system which are intended and recognized by participants in the system; latent functions, correlatively, being those which are neither intended nor recognized."[6] The principal importance of this distinction is that it brings the frequently overlooked latent functions to the attention of the observer. Perceptive explorations of the latent functions of behavior patterns, because they go beyond the frequently common knowledge of manifest functions, are likely to result in new insights. A few examples will most adequately demonstrate this point—Veblen's analysis of conspicuous consumption,[7] the catharsis and legitimizing functions of congressional committee hearings, the social mobility function of political machines.

The framework to be used here thus consists of three categories—behavior patterns to which consequences are imputed, the general and specific consequences of those patterns, and units or systems for which the behavior has consequences. The behavior patterns to be analyzed are those of individuals in informal legislative groups. The general consequences will be described using the classifications developed above—manifest, latent; functional, dysfunctional, nonfunctional. Only where the distinction seems to be of theoretical importance and there are sufficient data, will functions be classified as manifest or latent. Specific consequences are the ways in which the pattern promotes adaptation and adjustment—for example, the communication channels of informal groups facilitate negotiation and coalition formation. The several systems for which the behavior

---

[5] *Ibid.*
[6] *Ibid.*
[7] *Ibid.*, p. 69.

analyzed in this case study has consequences will be specified in the following section which outlines the kinds and sources of data used for the functional analysis.[8]

NEW YORK DEMOCRATS AND INFORMAL GROUP BEHAVIOR

The analysis presented in the following pages is based upon part of a larger study of one informal group in the House of Representatives.[9] All of the members of the group are New York Democratic Representatives. The existence of an informal group within the delegation was not, however, inferred from the common membership of the Representatives in a state delegation.[10] Interview data on the interactions of the members were used to determine the existence and boundaries of a genuine interaction group. Thus the approximate correspondence of delegation and group boundaries was not assumed in the research design.[11]

Interviews in conjunction with participant-observation provided the data on the behavior patterns of the members.[12] These behavior

---

[8] For more extensive discussions of functional analysis and some inherent problems see Merton, *op. cit.,* Chap. 1; Ernest Nagel, *Logic Without Metaphysics* (Glencoe, Illinois: The Free Press, 1956), Chap. 10; Carl G. Hempel, "The Logic of Functional Analysis," in *Symposium on Sociological Theory,* ed. Llewellyn Gross (Evanston, Illinois: Row, Peterson and Co., 1959); Marion J. Levy, Jr., *The Structure of Society* (Princeton: Princeton University Press, 1952).

[9] Alan Fiellin, "The Behavior of a Legislative Group in the House of Representatives: A Case Study of New York Democrats" (Unpublished Ph.D. dissertation, Department of Government, New York University, 1960). The author wishes to express his special thanks to Professor Joseph Tanenhaus of New York University for his helpful supervision of this project.

[10] Cf. David Truman, *The Congressional Party: A Case Study* (New York: John Wiley and Sons, 1959), Chap. 7.

[11] A brief statement of the procedure followed and the results obtained will clarify this point. The members of the New York Democratic delegation in the 85th Congress were selected as the *initial* respondents for the interviews. It was thought likely that these respondents' frequent reference to Representatives outside the delegation would lead to the identification of an informal group consisting of both delegation and non-delegation members. This proved not to be the case. The seventeen members of the delegation constituted a rather uncohesive group; thirteen of these seventeen constituted the highly cohesive, relatively closed group of interactors. Each of these thirteen represented a district within New York City as did three of the others. Congressman Leo O'Brien of Albany was the only member of the delegation not from New York City.

[12] The collection of data was made possible by a Congressional Fellowship for which the author wants to thank the American Political Science Association and the donors to the program.

patterns are of two types—(1) those interactions (communication and organization for example) which are group behavior patterns, and (2) individual behavior patterns common to all members which are not, however, group behavior.

The empirical basis for both the analysis and the hypotheses which are developed (the latter are outlined in the conclusion) was supplemented with information on informal group activities found in the literature. Though not rich in systematic analyses of informal groups, books and articles by both political scientists and congressmen do contain many scattered references to their activities and functions.[13]

Despite the use of supplementary information, the limitations of a case study have not been entirely avoided. We know that the members of Congress form a variety of kinds of groups. These groups find their roots in a variety of common experiences—party membership, state and regional representation, religion, committee membership, similarity of views on the issues of the day, friendship, and so forth. Some are cohesive, some not. Some are relatively permanent, others ad hoc and temporary. In some, leadership roles are differentiated and clearly defined, while in others leadership is quite informal, perhaps shifting from one member to another. Some groups have only a few members, others are quite large. They also differ, undoubtedly, in the functions they perform. A classification scheme which could be used for distinguishing the functions different kinds of groups perform may eventually be developed. In the present exploratory study, no such attempt is made. Thus the extent to which the findings are appropriately generalized from this one group to all others is problematic.[14]

For purposes of this analysis an informal group is defined as an identifiable, self-conscious, relatively stable unit of interacting members whose relationships are not officially prescribed by statutes

---

[13] See especially the following: Stephen K. Bailey and Howard D. Samuel, *Congress at Work* (New York: Henry Holt and Co., 1952); David Truman, *The Governmental Process* (New York: Knopf, 1951) and *The Congressional Party* (New York: John Wiley and Sons, 1959); Jerry Voorhis, *Confessions of a Congressman* (Garden City, New York: Doubleday and Company, 1947).
    The literature does contain at least two systematic studies of interpersonal relations in state legislatures. See Garland Routt, "Interpersonal Relationships and the Legislative Process," *Annals*, CXCV (January, 1938), pp. 129–36; Samuel Patterson, "Patterns of Interpersonal Relations in a State Legislative Group," POQ, XXIII (Spring, 1959), pp. 101–09.
[14] For the complete analysis of the internal structure of the New York Democratic group see Fiellin, *op, cit.*, Chap. 3.

and rules. The justification for approaching the study of Congress with this conceptual tool rests upon the assumption that such units exist and have important consequences for the nature of the legislative process. That the use of the approach will prove valuable seems likely in the light of the success researchers in other fields of social and political science have had with this approach[15] and our knowledge that Congress is a relatively unstructured legislative institution.[16] David Truman has indicated the reasons for using this approach in studying Congress.

> Such a body is not properly conceived as a collection of individual men, unorganized and without internal cohesion. Nor is it any better accounted for exclusively in terms of the formal, legal structure of the legislature. *A legislative body has its own group life, sometimes as a unit, perhaps more often as a collection of subgroups or cliques.* It has its own operating structure, which may approximate or differ sharply from the formal organization of the chamber.[17]

The following is an initial attempt to be reasonably systematic in analyzing the consequences of informal groups in the House of Representatives. Some limitations of the analysis as previously explained, stem from primary reliance on data from a single case study. In addition, no attempt has been made to test rigorously hypotheses stating the functions of such groups. Rather the analysis is used for the purpose of generating hypotheses which may prove to be useful for future research.

In each of the following sections, one pattern of behavior is

---

[15] In the related fields of public administration and industrial management, the importance of informal groups as both facilitating and disturbing factors seems to be generally accepted. See Fritz J. Roethlisberger and William J. Dickson, *Management and the Worker* (Cambridge: Harvard University Press, 1939); Herbert A. Simon, *Administrative Behavior: A Study of Decision-Making Processes in Administrative Organization* (New York: Macmillan Co., 1947), pp. 147–49 and *passim;* Marshall E. and Gladys O. Dimock, *Public Administration* (New York: Rinehart and Co., 1953), pp. 104–06 and works cited therein. In the field of voting behavior see Bernard Berelson, Paul F. Lazarsfeld, and William N. McPhee, *Voting: A Study of Opinion Formation in a Presidential Campaign* (Chicago: University of Chicago Press, 1954), Chap. 6. For a thorough review of the literature in sociology and social-psychology as well as the report of an empirical study of opinion formation see Elihu Katz and Paul F. Lazarsfeld, *Personal Influence: The Part Played by People in the Flow of Mass Communications* (Glencoe, Illinois: The Free Press, 1955).

[16] The meaning of "unstructured" as used here is made more explicit in footnote 43, below.

[17] *The Governmental Process,* p. 343, emphasis added. Truman goes on to point out that this informal structure will have important consequences for the access of interest groups.

identified and explained and then the consequences of the pattern for relevant systems are suggested. The relevant systems for this analysis are (1) the members of the New York Democratic group, (2) the leadership of the group, (3) other members and groups in the House of Representatives, (4) the House itself as a legislative institution, (5) the electoral Democratic Party leaders of New York City and State, (6) New York City as the collective constituency represented by the group.

COMMUNICATION

From what is known about the behavior and functions of informal structures in other kinds of large scale organizations,[18] it is not surprising that the communication activities of the New York Democrats are functional for several units within the House. In fact, because of the absence of an effective hierarchical structure in the House, probably the most important functions of informal groups and relationships result from their use as communication networks.

The New York Democratic Congressmen

The communications network of the group performs three services for the individual members. It provides them with (1) "trustworthy" information on bills and legislative politics; (2) cues for making voting decisions;[19] and (3) adaptive norms, perceptions and rationalizations. All of these, since they are shared within the group, are socially supported. Providing social support for members' attitudes and behavior may thus be a latent function of informal groups.

It is a truism that legislators need information and advice. They

---

[18] Literature cited in footnote 15.

[19] For the data and statistical verification of this point see Fiellin, *op. cit.*, Chap. 5. Truman's study of state delegations and congressional committees is also relevant. *The Congressional Party*, Chap. 7. Duncan MacRae, on the basis of the results of scale analysis, also infers that face-to-face relationships affect roll call vote decisions. "Roll call votes are taken in sequence, sometimes with a considerable interval of time between them. That social controls have ample time to operate accounts, in part, for the higher degree of consistency in scaling obtainable with roll calls than with questionnaire data. One result of these social controls may be that those individuals who change position on the continuum do so in groups on the basis of face-to-face association." "Some Underlying Variables in Legislative Roll Call Votes," *Public Opinion Quarterly*, XVIII, no. 2 (Summer, 1954), p. 194. On patterns of advice giving and taking in the U.S. Senate see Donald Matthews, *U.S. Senators and Their World* (Chapel Hill: University of North Carolina Press, 1960), pp. 251–54.

must be informed on both the technical and political aspects of legislation in order to make those decisions which may determine their political futures.[20] Members of the House of Representatives, of course, receive information from many sources—committee hearings and reports, floor debate, personal staff, the Legislative Reference Service, interest groups, mass media, and so forth. In fact this profusion of information from so many sources probably complicates the problem of decision-making rather than facilitating its solution.[21] It is for this reason that communication within informal groups may be particularly valuable to the individual member. Information, advice, and voting cues come from trusted sources— those with similar or identical interests and views. Several interview respondents attested to the value of such information and suggested the reasons for its special quality.

> I can take the advice of other members of the group on what to do and how to vote because they not only have expert opinions, their districts are essentially similar to mine. They have the same kinds of problems and the same basic viewpoint.[22]

In the particular case of the New York Democrats and other informal legislative groups based on the similar constituencies of the members, the reliability of information and advice is built-in. The constituencies of the members are essentially similar and the electoral party organizations and interest groups upon which they rely are either the same or have similar views and expectations.[23]

---

[20] See David Truman, *The Governmental Process*, pp. 334–35; Roland Young, *The American Congress* (New York: Harper and Bros., 1958), pp. 78–79.

[21] "Literally tons of information are available to Congress to keep it informed about what is happening in its own bailiwick and elsewhere in the government. The trouble is that the data are not in a form that can be used easily. Members are supposed to keep up with the executive agencies by reading their annual reports. The latter are voluminous, and those who compile them tell Congress and the people to a considerable extent, only what they want known. But with the pressure of work already imposing a physical strain on many legislators, very few have time to read the reports." Estes Kefauver and Jack Levin, *A Twentieth-Century Congress* (New York: Duell, Sloan and Pearce, 1947), p. 203.

[22] Reconstructed from interview responses.

[23] For some groups of legislators, establishing "sameness" of party organization and "similarity" of constituencies and relevant interest groups would present some difficult problems and definition and require the use of precise indices. Refined measurement seemed unnecessary for this case study since all but one of the members of the delegation in the 85th Congress were from New York City. Though New York City congressional districts do vary in socioeconomic composition, the variations are relatively minor. For occupational

Most important of all, perhaps, is that the member in taking cues from the New York group cannot get into electoral difficulties as a result of deviation. There is security in numbers. If the member honors this maxim and follows the advice of his informal group colleagues, he cannot be singled out for an "incorrect" decision.[24]

A division of labor, corresponding to the committee structure of the House, develops in some groups and provides benefits for the individual. By virtue of his informal ties, the New York Democrat, for example, has ready access to committees of which he is not a member. Individual members may, and do, use group connections to check on the status and prospects of legislation in committees other than their own.[25] In the absence of personal ties with members of most House Committees, the task of quickly getting trustworthy information on the work of many committees would be most difficult.[26] The New York Democrat may save many hours of leg-work, reading, and anxious deliberation by holding a brief conversation with a likeminded colleague who knows the material and has previously sifted through it.

Members on first entering the House have much to learn. They must learn to make sense of this new world and understand their place in it—in short, become socialized in a new institution and

---

distributions within congressional districts see Duncan MacRae, Jr., *Dimensions of Congressional Voting* (Berkeley: University of California Press, 1958), Appendix B. All members of the group were, of course, within the jurisdiction of the same state party organization. The several county organizations involved, though independent and sometimes in conflict over local affairs, do frequently work together in city-wide affairs of concern to all and do seem to hold a common view of congressional politics. Certainly New York Democrats in the House tend strongly to identify themselves with the larger collective constituency, New York City.

[24] Cf. Bailey and Samuel, *op. cit.*, "In general, however, [Congressman Smith] was not inclined to compile a voting record that contrasted too sharply with the records of the other six members of the Mississippi delegation in the House." p. 131. "Often his decision followed hasty conferences with other members of the Mississippi delegation in the cloakroom outside of the Chamber." p. 132. On state delegation unity see also Bailey and Samuel, pp. 120–121; Voorhis, *op. cit.*, Chap. 7; Senator Tom Connally as told to Alfred Steinberg, *My Name is Tom Connally* (New York: Thomas Y. Crowell Co., 1954), p. 89.

[25] It is also quite possible that this access to other committees is used to secure action on members' own bills. Thus, access to committees may be used to exert influence as well as secure information.

[26] In the 86th Congress, 2d Session, there were New York Democrats on all House committees with the following exceptions: Armed Forces, Government Operations, House Administration, Un-American Activities, and Veterans Affairs. U.S. Congress, *Congressional Directory*, 85th Congress, 2nd Session, 1958, pp. 241–47.

role. By providing the new member with a social and political home away from home, by offering him viable conceptions of the national legislative process and his role in it, the group performs important functions for the individual. Since the "regular" New York Democrat is automatically a member of the group by virtue of his election, some of his difficult initial role problems are solved by his acceptance of the group and its "folkways."[27]

This function may be of greater than normal importance for the New York Democratic Representative because of his membership in what is pejoratively referred to as the "Tuesday to Thursday Club," *i.e.*, the "deviant" practice of too often restricting one's stay in Washington to these three days of the week.[28] Because of his membership in the group, however, this deviant behavior and the accompanying rationalization are socially sanctioned and supported.[29]

Though the group's provision and support of role conceptions and norms is in general an important function in a loosely structured situation,[30] that some conceptions in this case are deviant may be dysfunctional for the individual. This is true to the extent that these particular deviations reduce the members' influence.[31]

Other Informal Groups and the House as a Legislative Institution

The communication which occurs through the channels of informal groups is functional not only for the individual members, but also for the institution and its component groups as well. It would be nearly impossible for the members of Congress to perform

---

[27] Evidence of this function can also be found in the literature. "The other members [of the Ohio Republican delegation], all of whom were veterans, had been helpful in showing him [Congressman Ayers] the ropes of Congressional procedure." Bailey and Samuel, *op. cit.*, p. 121. "Through our Young Turks meetings [an informal House group], through my committee meetings, through contacts on the floor and elsewhere I was learning about Congress and about congressmen as they actually are—not as they are reported to be by the columnists or the humorists of the country." Voorhis, *op. cit.*, p. 31.

[28] See discussion below and Donald Matthews, *op. cit.*, pp. 94–95.

[29] For a complete discussion of this behavior and the reasons for it see Fiellin, *op. cit.*, pp. 24, 26 ff., 52 f., 147 ff., 163 ff.

[30] On the role problems of legislators and politicians see Edward A. Shils, "The Legislator and His Environment," *University of Chicago Law Review*, XVIII (1950–1951), pp. 571–84; William C. Mitchell, "Occupational Role Strains: The American Elective Public Official," *Administrative Science Quarterly*, III (September, 1958), pp. 210–28.

[31] See discussion below, pp. 86–87.

their legislative functions in the absence of such communication channels.[32] Committees, political parties, and floor debate solve only part of the communication problem of Congress. Informal groups supplement and fill in the remaining gaps. The following example of the operation of informal groups suggests that the functions of communication within and between such groups may lie especially in the area of forming coalitions, negotiating compromises, and developing legislative strategy.

An informal group of "Democratic Young Turks" was established during the 85th Congress.[33] The stated purpose of the group was to enhance the strength of Western and Northern Democratic "liberals" in Democratic Party and House politics. *Congressional Quarterly* expressed the view that the chief spokesman, Eugene McCarthy, was opposed to any formal organization as " . . . it might be construed as a direct challenge to Rayburn's leadership." The report goes on to state that nevertheless ". . . communication among the 80 signers of the program is effective even without a formal organization."[34] The relationship between this group and the New York Democrats, 14 of whom joined the "Young Turks," is instructive in demonstrating how a pre-existing informal group facilitated this communication.

Though much communication among the members took place in informal conversations on the floor of the Chamber and in the cloakrooms and dining rooms, the communication channels of informal groups were also used to disseminate messages quickly and effectively to all members. For example, Congressman Multer, the Democratic whip for New York State and a leader of the informal group, became an unofficial "whip" of the "Young Turks." In this way, liaison was established between the two informal House groups. The New York Democratic group "tied" its members to the outside legislative world while at the same time facilitating communication from outside groups to its members. Many messages were transmitted through these channels. At least in some of the "Young Turks'" meetings and conversations to plan program and strategy, one New York Democrat "represented" the entire group.

---

[32] In other legislatures which are highly organized by parties or other agencies, communication through informal groups may be less important.

[33] Eighty members of the House who had signed a manifesto were members. Information is from informal interviews and *Congressional Quarterly Weekly Report*, XV (February 22, 1957), 224–25.

[34] *Ibid.*, p. 225.

Though in this particular example the communication channels may have become more regularized than is customary, it does illustrate the kind of function which may be served by such groups. Until the business and politics of Congress becomes more completely structured by other kinds of organizations, one may expect informal groups to arise and facilitate a variety of essential kinds of communication.

New York Party and Public Officials

It was expected by the author that group channels would be used by both party and public officials in New York City and State to communicate their views on legislation. Available data, which may be incomplete, suggest that this is not the case. On the contrary, interview data indicate that the few messages members receive in which public officials state their views on pending legislation are sent directly to the individual members rather than being channeled through group leaders.

GROUP MEETINGS

It is not uncommon for members of informal legislative groups to meet together regularly—frequently for lunch or dinner. In the extent to which business is formally conducted and group decisions reached during these meetings, there is probably considerable variation from group to group. The following procedure is that normally followed by the New York Democratic delegation. That it is not an entirely unique case is evident from the descriptions of other group meetings found in the literature.[35]

Congressman Multer, the Assistant Whip for the New York Democrats, acts as the coordinator of these monthly meetings—setting the time and place and calling the members together. The manifest function of these meetings for the leaders is to discuss legislation and crystallize the position of the delegation. When a measure is scheduled for consideration in the House, Congressman Multer requests a summary of the bill and the pros and cons from that member of the delegation serving on the committee. At the next meeting of the group, Multer presents this information to-

---

[35] For information on the meetings of other legislative groups see Voorhis, *op. cit.*, pp. 30–31; Kefauver and Levin, *op. cit.*, pp. 89–90; Bailey and Samuel, *op. cit.*, pp. 108–09, 120–21, 125.

gether with his and the committee member's recommendations for group action. The measure is then discussed and an attempt is made to arrive at a group decision.

In arriving at group decisions, the delegation follows rules similar to those of the party caucus. When there is disagreement within the group, the members of the majority, through persuasion, attempt to bring about unanimity. "Members in the minority are told what the New York City interest is, they are informed of the party position as expressed in the platform, and the interests of their constituencies are analyzed."[36] But if individuals persist in their dissent because of contrary campaign pledges or the dictates of conscience, then, in the words of one member, "we don't try to stop them."

Bailey and Samuel, in discussing the meetings of the Ohio Republicans, present additional evidence of the informational function of regular group meetings.

> For the members themselves, the weekly luncheons usually provided some information of value; at least one of the fourteen Ohio Republicans was bound to be a member of the committee handling the current legislation. Finally, for the Republican leadership, it was helpful to get the fourteen Ohio Republicans around the same table. After the meetings, Representative J. Harry McGregor of the 17th District who served as the Ohio whip could estimate with fair accuracy how his fellow members would vote.[37]

Thus the manifest functions of these meetings for members and leaders are (1) dissemination of information, (2) exchange of views on pending legislation, and (3) at least for the New York Democrats, determination of the group's position.

An important latent function of these meetings results from the social, convivial nature of the occasion. It is well known that for many groups such affairs have the effects of developing *esprit de corps* and of reinforcing group identity. These in turn contribute to unity of action which is necessary for the realization of group goals. From very meagre information on the New York Democrats' dinner meetings, it seems probable that they also have this latent emotional function in addition to their manifest functions of information, discussion, and decision.

---

[36] Paraphrased interview response.
[37] Bailey and Samuel, *op. cit.,* p. 121.

BLOC VOTING

In contributing to the achievement of goals in the House, bloc voting is functional for the group members and leaders, the electoral party leaders, and the collective constituency, New York City. Its special contribution to goal attainment consists in providing the group with a measure of influence out of proportion to the number of its members.

Leaders especially are aware of the positive consequences of bloc behavior, whereas some of the rank-and-file seem to be totally unaware of any purpose served by the group's cohesive voting. These variations in awareness of the benefits of group cohesion can be explained in part by the greater involvement of leaders in House politics and their greater concern for the strategic problems of acquiring influence and achieving goals. As representatives of the group in negotiations concerning legislation, committee assignments, and so forth, the leaders of the delegation are made aware of the potential contribution of group unity to the achievement of desired ends.[38] Votes are one medium of exchange in political bargaining; the ability to "deliver" a large bloc of votes may contribute mightily in bringing negotiations to a successful conclusion.[39]

Two minor incidents which were brought to the attention of the author suggest specific ways bloc voting might be used to advantage in House politics. On one occasion, reportedly, it was suggested to the members of the delegation that all vote in the Democratic caucus in favor of the appointment of a *non*-New York Democrat to a committee vacancy. It was argued that unanimity on the part of the delegation on this vote would enhance its future bargaining position for favorable committee assignments for its own members.

The other example comes from the administrative assistant of a House Democrat. With great admiration, he spoke of the "smooth" operation of the New York Democrats. He had observed his "boss" rounding up votes for a bill in which the latter was interested. In doing so, the Representative contacted, among others, only one New

---

[38] Group leadership and its roles are discussed in Fiellin, *op. cit.*, pp. 58 ff.

[39] Connally in his autobiography calls attention to the function of clannishness within the Texas delegation. "Although we Texans were a smaller House group than the member's from New York, Pennsylvania, Illinois, or Ohio, as a rule the eighteen of us exerted a degree of influence far out of proportion to our numbers. For we generally voted together on a bill and this unity helped make up for the fact that we held no committee Chairmanships and that none of us was important except John Garner, then only fifth ranking man on the Ways and Means Committee." Connally, *op. cit.*, pp. 89–90.

York Democrat. He confidently relied upon this single contact as sufficient for obtaining the full support of the New York Democrats (17 votes) ; he was not disappointed by the final results.

Truman also describes an example which illustrates the advantages of bloc behavior.

> An excellent illustration of logrolling . . . occurred in connection with appropriations in 1950 for unemployment relief and farm parity payments. During that session the Farm Bureau's supporters in Congress had been in opposition to representatives from some of the Eastern cities on these two measures and on others. Neither had sufficient reliable votes on these bills to assure it a majority in the House. Under the leadership of Mayor LaGuardia of New York and President O'Neal of the Farm Bureau, an arrangement was made during the voting on parity payments in the House of Representatives. The votes of a number of urban congressmen on that measure were exchanged for those of certain representatives from farm areas on general relief appropriations.[40]

Such arrangements may of course be worked out in the absence of an appropriate informal group structure. Nevertheless, there is no doubt that such a structure facilitates the formation of coalitions, and that willingness to play the game increases the influence of stable groups. In contrast, individual members outside of the bloc structure will only in the case of very close votes have the necessary influence to enter into negotiations with sufficient leverage to expect a reasonably favorable *quid pro quo*.

These examples suggest how bloc behavior might be used by the leaders for their own success as well as the promotion of the interests of rank-and-file members, the group, the constituencies and interest groups.[41] They also provide additional evidence of the function of groups in facilitating legislative negotiations.

To appreciate fully the contribution of bloc voting to a member's legislative life and career it must be seen within the context of his

---

[40] *The Government Process*, p. 368.

[41] Truman's point regarding interest groups' relations with legislators is pertinent to the above analysis. "A group [interest group] is handicapped if its only connections are with a maverick or a newcomer. It is not enough for the legislator to be a member, in some sense, of the interest group or even to be in a position of formal power. He must 'belong' within the legislature as well." *The Governmental Process*, p. 345. Influence in legislative negotiations depends upon one's ability to "tie in" to appropriate informal networks at some point.

total situation in the legislature. New York Democrats who come to Congress rarely achieve great individual influence. For a variety of reasons, their approach to Congress typically limits the likelihood of their joining the "inner circle." Their membership in the "Tuesday to Thursday Club," short tenure as congressmen, and a tendency to limit personal contacts to other New York Democrats combine to make it less than likely that individual members will be accepted by their colleagues as "congressmen's congressmen." Since we expect our representatives to acquire influence in order to further constituency interests (ample evidence from interviews indicates that New York Democrats define this as a central role expectation), the individual New York Democrat without the group as a channel of participation and influence might have some difficulty in meeting his role expectations. From this perspective, bloc voting and the resulting collective influence can be viewed as a substitute for individual influence. The members' obligations (manifest function) to promote and defend the common interests of their constituencies (New York City) is thus fulfilled. Success in this should be functional also for the electoral party's goal of winning elections.

Collective action may also provide, probably latently, a defense and protection for the individual in his relationship with lobbyists. For much the same reason that the British backbencher is relatively free of pressures from outside groups, the rank-and-file New York Democrat may be less besieged by them than is usual for members of the House.

The psychological, cue-giving function of informal group membership as it relates to the re-election problems of members was previously mentioned in discussing the communication functions of the group. It is pertinent to refer again to this function because of its direct connection with bloc voting. Voorhis in his insightful autobiography poignantly calls attention to the psychological and electoral problems of members, which may be partially solved by informal group memberships.

> Everyone desires the inner warmth that comes from the knowledge that he has friends who can be counted upon. The members of the organized groups desire this. So do the congressmen. It is, again, a formula for re-election.

✻ ✻ ✻ ✻ ✻

Thus I have been able to understand why members sought a kind of political "home" in the bosom of some strong group, whose interests they would always protect and who could then be depended upon to go all out for the candidate for re-election whenever the need arose.[42]

In order fully to appreciate the importance of Voorhis' point for an understanding of the New York Democrats' group behavior in Congress, it is necessary to be aware of the ties between the congressional delegation and the electoral parties. Faithful membership in the delegation group is one way for the member to remain in good standing with party officials regarding his activities in Washington. In situations where party support is normally a *sine qua non* of re-election (and it probably is for most New York Democratic Congressmen) "belonging" is likely to be a high priority objective.

THE "TUESDAY TO THURSDAY CLUB"

A practice which has both manifest functions and latent dysfunctions for the individual is his membership in the Tuesday to Thursday Club—that is, spending only three or four days in Washington while the House is in session. It is likely that the commuting involved is not welcomed by all members. Evidence from interviews suggests that party leaders and constituents partly because of established tradition *expect* their congressmen to maintain close contact with them by making frequent trips home. Both for re-election and for "promotion" to higher political office, their time should be divided between Washington and New York. Thus the practice has manifest functions for the individual's political career.

Many members also take advantage of the economic opportunities by maintaining their previously established law practices and businesses. In this way, they supplement their incomes and maintain non-political careers to which they may return in the event of electoral defeat or political retirement.

Though functional for the member's New York political career, it seems probable that "Tuesday to Thursday Club" membership is dysfunctional for his congressional career. Frequent absence from "the Hill" earns the member a reputation as a parttime congressman. For many House colleagues, particularly those that count, this is a violation of the norm requiring that each member carry his share of the work load and spend nearly full-time in Washington while the House is in session. Some individuals (perhaps Con-

---

[42] Voorhis, *op. cit.*, p. 37.

gressman Celler, for example) may substantially overcome this handicap after long service and gain considerable influence both formally and informally. For most members, however, the deviation results in some reduction in prestige and influence with House colleagues.

CONCLUSION

The foregoing analysis of the functional meaning of some standardized behavior patterns of the members of one informal group in the House of Representatives suggests hypotheses for further research. Only those which may prove fruitful for the understanding of the functions of informal groups in general (as opposed to those whose meaning is limited to the particular characteristics of the New York Democrats) will be reformulated. Again the reader must be warned that these are suggested hypotheses, not firmly established propositions.

1. Informal groups arise in unstructured legislative situations.[43]

2. These groups perform manifest and latent functions (dysfunctions) for the members and the institutions.

3. Informal groups are the principal "socializing" agencies in such legislatures.

   a. Members learn role expectations and institutional norms within informal groups.

4. Informal groups may function to provide support for behavior adjudged to be deviant in the light of institutional norms.

5. Decisions of legislators depend, in part, on their informal group memberships.

6. Conscious bloc behavior is characteristic of informal groups under conditions of "sufficient" integration of the members and similarity of interests between them.

---

[43] This hypothesis asserts nothing about structured legislative situations. These terms, "structured" and "unstructured," will need to be more precisely defined. In the loose usage here, the distinction is being made between situations such as that of the British House of Commons, where much if not most of what transpires is determined by party and cabinet, and that of Congress, where no such all-important agencies exist. In the latter case, individuals are "forced" to be free, their behavior not having been "pre-determined" to the same extent, and they must "improvise" mechanisms to perform functions which party and cabinet perform in the British example.

    a. This bloc behavior is, by defination, manifestly related to political strategy and goal attainment.

7. Latent functions for the individuals and the group leadership result from the division of labor within these groups, e.g., access to a variety of committees in order to secure information and exercise influence.

8. Legislative functional requisites[44] are among the consequences of informal groups in legislatures.

    a. One function performed by informal groups is the exchange of political and technical information.

    b. Informal groups structure otherwise hopelessly confused legislative situations.

        b. 1. The politics of otherwise unstructured legislatures occur, for the most part, within and between these groups and through their channels, e.g. negotiation, compromise, and the formation, of coalitions.

        b. 2. "Generalized support" will be characteristic of the relationship between these groups.[45]

Applying this orientation to the House of Representatives, it is hypothesised that House politics is not unintelligibly complex, consisting only of the individual behavior of each of 435 isolated members. Rather, it is much more simply structured through a network of informal groups and relationships. This network provides channels for information exchange, political negotiation, and the formation of compromises—probably impossible tasks for 435

---

[44] Using Merton's explanation of this concept, "it is assumed that there are certain *functions* which are indispensable in the sense that, unless they are performed, the society (or group or individual [in this application it is the legislature]) will not persist." Merton, *op. cit.*, p. 33.

[45] This hypothesis has a theoretical basis in Talcott Parson's formulations on the American political system. See his " 'Voting' and the Equilibrium of the American Political System," in *American Voting Behavior,* eds. Eugene Burdick and Arthur Brodbeck (Glencoe: The Free Press, 1959), pp. 89–90. Professor Parsons suggests that generalized support of leadership on the part of the electorate (a relationship in which *specific* policy commitments are absent) is necessary for "the political integration of a complex social system." The hypothesis stated above suggests that in the absence of *vertical* generalized support in the House (probably characterized of the British House of Commons) one would expect *horizontal* generalized support (between groups and individuals) to develop. In other words, "logrolling" in which there is a specific and *explicit quid pro quo* will be relatively rare.

atomized units.[46] Just as this structure makes House politics understandable for the participants, so it is through this perspective that the observer may understand them. It is by locating and "mapping" such groups and their intra- and inter-relationships that the observer may simplify the task of understanding what seem to be hopelessly confused political institutions and processes.[47]

---

[46] Katz and Lazarsfeld point out that in a variety of areas of social behavior, a simplified model of atomized individuals is inappropriate and misleading. *Op. cit.*, Introduction; Part I, Chaps. 1–4. Many scholars are coming to realize that the same is true of Congress. In addition to the references cited throughout the paper, the works of Roland Young and Holbert Carroll contain references to the functions of informal relationships. Young writes, "In formulating policy Congress carries out its work through various types of units and alliances. Some of these units and alliances are recognized in the official rules; others are free-forming, as it were, operating within the legislative structure while not being a constituent part of the legal framework." *The American Congress* (New York: Harper and Bros., 1958), p. 47. Also see pp. 56, 157. Holbert N. Carroll, *The House of Representatives and Foreign Affairs* (Pittsburgh: The University of Pittsburgh Press, 1958), pp. 101, 237, 263.

[47] Truman's warning should be kept in mind. "It is important not to assume that these interactions produce an integrated, hierarchical structure. They may, but the life of the legislative group as of others may as easily involve a loosely allied collection of cliques." . . . "Party government is a form of legislative group life, but it is not the only or the most common form in the United States." *The Governmental Process*, p. 346.

VI

THE APPROPRIATIONS COMMITTEE AS A POLITICAL SYSTEM*

Richard F. Fenno, Jr.

STUDIES OF Congress by political scientists have produced a time-tested consensus on the very considerable power and autonomy of Congressional committees. Because of these two related characteristics, it makes empirical and analytical sense to treat the Congressional committee as a discrete unit for analysis. This paper conceives of the committee as a political system (or, more accurately as a political subsystem) faced with a number of basic problems which it must solve in order to achieve its goals and maintain itself. Generally speaking these functional problems pertain to the environmental and the internal relations of the committee. This study is concerned almost exclusively with the internal problems of the committee and particularly with the problem of self-integration.[1] It describes how one congressional committee—The Committee on Appropriations of the House of Representatives—has dealt with this problem in the period 1947–1961. Its purpose is to add to our understanding of appropriations politics in Congress and to suggest the usefulness of this type of analysis for studying the activities of any congressional committee.

---

* Reprinted from "The House Appropriations Committee as a Political System: The Problem of Integration," *American Political Science Review*, LVI (June, 1962), 310–24. Copyright © 1962, the American Political Science Association. The author wishes to acknowledge his indebtedness to the Committee on Political Behavior of the Social Science Research Council for the research grant which made possible this study, and the larger study of legislative behavior in the area of appropriations of which it is a part. This is a revised version of a paper read at the Annual Meeting of the American Political Science Association at St. Louis, September, 1961.
[1] On social systems, see: George Homans, *The Human Group* (New York, 1950); Robert K. Merton, *Social Theory and Social Structure* (Glencoe, 1957); Talcott Parsons and Edward Shils, *Toward A General Theory of Action* (Cambridge, 1951), pp. 190–234. Most helpful with reference to the political system has been David Easton, "An Approach to the Analysis of Political Systems," *World Politics* (April, 1957), pp. 383–400.

The necessity for integration in any social system arises from the differentiation among its various elements. Most importantly there is a differentiation among subgroups and among individual positions, together with the roles that flow therefrom.[2] A committee faces the problem, how shall these diverse elements be made to mesh together or function in support of one another? No political system (or subsystem) is perfectly integrated; yet no political system can survive without some minimum degree of integration among its differentiated parts. Committee integration is defined as the degree to which there is a working together or a meshing together or mutual support among its roles and subgroups. Conversely, it is also defined as the degree to which a committee is able to minimize conflict among its roles and its subgroups, by heading off or resolving the conflicts that arise.[3] A concomitant of integration is the existence of a fairly consistent set of norms, widely agreed upon and widely followed by the members. Another concomitant of integration is the existence of control mechanisms (*i.e.,* socialization and sanctioning mechanisms) capable of maintaining reasonable conformity to norms. In other words, the more highly integrated a committee, the smaller will be the gap between expected and actual behavior.

This study is concerned with integration both as a structural characteristic of, and as a functional problem for, the Appropriations Committee. First, certain basic characteristics of the Committee need description, to help explain the integration of its parts. Second comes a partial description of the degree to which and the ways in which the Committee achieves integration. No attempt is made to state this in quantitative terms, but the object is to examine the meshing together or the minimization of conflict among certain subgroups and among certain key roles. Also, important control mechanisms are described. The study concludes with some comments on the consequences of Committee integration for appropriations politics and on the usefulness of further Congressional committee analysis in terms of functional problems such as this one.

---

[2] On the idea of subgroups as used here, see Harry M. Johnson, *Sociology* (New York, 1960), ch. 3. On role, see specifically Theodore M. Newcomb, *Social Psychology* (New York, 1951), p. 280; see generally N. Gross, W. Mason and A. McEachern, *Explorations in Role Analysis: Studies of the School Superintendecy Role* (New York, 1958). On differentiation and its relation to integration, see Scott Greer, *Social Organization* (New York, 1955).

[3] The usage here follows most closely that of Robert Merton, *op. cit.*, pp. 26–29.

I

Five important characteristics of the Appropriations Committee which help explain Committee integration are (1) the existence of a well-articulated and deeply rooted consensus on Committee goals or tasks; (2) the nature of the Committee's subject matter; (3) the legislative orientation of its members; (4) the attractiveness of the Committee for its members; and (5) the stability of Committee membership.

Consensus

The Appropriations Committee sees its tasks as taking form within the broad guidelines set by its parent body, the House of Representatives. For it is the primary condition of the Committee's existence that it was created by the House for the purpose of assisting the House in the performance of House legislative tasks dealing with appropriations. Committee members agree that their fundamental duty is to serve the House in the manner and with the substantive results that the House prescribes. Given, however, the imprecision of House expectations and the permissiveness of House surveillance, the Committee must elaborate for itself a definition of tasks plus a supporting set of perceptions (of itself and of others) explicit enough to furnish day-to-day guidance.

The Committee's view begins with the pre-eminence of the House—often mistakenly attributed to the Constitution ("all bills for raising revenue," Art. I, sec. 7) but nevertheless firmly sanctioned by custom—in appropriations affairs.

It moves easily to the conviction that, as the efficient part of the House in this matter, the Constitution has endowed it with special obligations and special prerogatives. It ends in the view that the Committee on Appropriations, far from being merely one among many units in a complicated legislative-executive system, is *the* most important, most responsible unit in the whole appropriations process.[4] Hand in hand with the consensus on their primacy goes a

---

[4] This and all other generalizations about member attitudes and perceptions depend heavily on extensive interviews with Committee members. Semi-structured interviews, averaging 45 minutes in length were held with 45 of the 50 Committee members during the 86th Congress. Certain key questions, all open-ended, were asked of all respondents. The schedule was kept very flexible, however, in order to permit particular topics to be explored with those individuals best equipped to discuss them. In a few cases, where respondents encouraged it, notes were taken during the interviews. In most cases notes were not taken, but were transcribed immediately after the interview. Where unattributed quotations occur in the text, therefore, they are as nearly verbatim as the author's power of immediate recall could make them. These techniques were all used so as to improve *rapport* between interviewer and respondent.

consensus that all of their House-prescribed tasks can be fulfilled by superimposing upon them one, single, paramount task—*to guard the Federal Treasury*. Committee members state their goals in the essentially negative terms of guardianship—screening requests for money, checking against ill-advised expenditures, and protecting the taxpayer's dollar. In the language of the Committee's official history, the job of each member is, "constantly and courageously to protect the Federal Treasury against thousands of appeals and imperative demands for unnecessary, unwise, and excessive expenditures."[5]

To buttress its self-image as guardian of public funds the Committee elaborates a set of perceptions about other participants in the appropriations process to which most members hold most of the time. Each executive official, for example, is seen to be interested in the expansion of his own particular program. Each one asks, therefore, for more money than he really needs, in view of the total picture, to run an adequate program. This and other Committee perceptions—of the Budget Bureau, of the Senate, and of their fellow Representatives—help to shape and support the Committee members in their belief that most budget estimates can, should and must be reduced and that, since no one else can be relied upon, the House Committee must do the job. To the consensus on the main task of protecting the Treasury is added, therefore, a consensus on the instrumental task of *cutting whatever budget estimates are submitted*.

As an immediate goal, Committee members agree that they must strike a highly critical, aggressive posture toward budget requests, and that they should, on principle, reduce them. In the words of the Committee's veterans: "There has never been a budget submitted to the Congress that couldn't be cut." "There isn't a budget that can't be cut 10 per cent immediately." "I've been on the Committee for 17 years. No subcommittee of which I have been a member has ever reported out a bill without a cut in the budget. I'm proud of that record." The aim of budget-cutting is strongly internalized for the Committee member. "It's a tradition in the Appropriations Committee to cut." "You're grounded in it. . . . It's ingrained in you from the time you get on the Committee." For the purposes of a larger study, the appropriations case histories of 37 executive bureaus have been examined for a 12-year period,

---

[5] "History of the Committee on Appropriations," House Doc. 299, 77th Cong., 1st sess., 1941–1942, p. 11.

1947–1959.⁶ Of 443 separate bureau estimates, the Committee reduced 77.2 per cent (342) of them.

It is a mark of the intensity and self-consciousness of the Committee consensus on budget-cutting that it is couched in a distinctive vocabulary. The workaday lingo of the Committee member is replete with negative verbs, undesirable objects of attention, and effective instruments of action. Agency budgets are said to be filled with "fat," "padding," "grease," "pork," "oleaginous substance," "water," "oil," "cushions," "avoirdupois," "waste tissue," and "soft spots." The action verbs most commonly used are "cut," "carve," "slice," "prune," "whittle," "squeeze," "wring," "trim," "lop off," "chop," "slash," "pare," "shave," "fry," and "whack." The tools of the trade are appropriately referred to as "knife," "blade," "meat axe," "scalpel," "meat cleaver," "hatchet," "shears," "wringer," and "fine-tooth comb." Members are hailed by their fellows as being "pretty sharp with the knife." Agencies may "have the meat axe thrown at them." Executives are urged to put their agencies "on a fat boy's diet." Budgets are praised when they are "cut to the bone." And members agree that "You can always get a little more fat out of a piece of pork if you fry it a little longer and a little harder."

To the major task of protecting the Treasury and the instrumental task of cutting budget estimates, each Committee member adds, usually by way of exception, a third task—*serving the constituency to which he owes his election.* This creates no problem for him when, as is sometimes the case, he can serve his district best by cutting the budget requests of a federal agency whose program is in conflict with the demands of his constituency.⁶ᵃ Normally, however, members find that their most common role-conflict is between a Committee-oriented budget-reducing role and a constituency-oriented budget-increasing role. Committee ideology resolves the conflict by assigning top, long-run priority to the budget-cutting task and making of the constituency service a permissible, short-run exception. No member is expected to commit electoral suicide; but no member is expected to allow his district's desire for federal funds to dominate his Committee behavior.

---

⁶ The bureaus being studied are all concerned with domestic policy and are situated in the Agriculture, Interior, Labor, Commerce, Treasury, Justice and Health, Education and Welfare Departments. For a similar pattern of Committee decisions in foreign affairs, see Holbert Carroll, *The House of Representatives and Foreign Affairs* (Pittsburgh, 1958), ch. 9.

⁶ᵃ See, for example, Philip A. Foss, "The Grazing Fee Dilemma," Inter-University Case Program, No. 57 (University, Alabama, 1960).

Subject Matter

Appropriations Committee integration is facilitated by the subject matter with which the group deals. The Committee makes decisions on the same controversial issues as do the committees handling substantive legislation. But a money decision—however vitally it affects national policy—is, or at least seems to be, less directly a policy decision. Since they deal immediately with dollars and cents, it is easy for the members to hold to the idea that they are not dealing with programmatic questions, that theirs is a "business" rather than a "policy" committee. The subject matter, furthermore, keeps Committee members relatively free agents, which promotes intra-Committee maneuvering and, hence, conflict avoidance. Members do not commit themselves to their constituents in terms of precise money amounts, and no dollar sum is sacred—it can always be adjusted without conceding that a principle has been breached. By contrast, members of committees dealing directly with controversial issues are often pressured into taking concrete stands on these issues; consequently, they may come to their committee work with fixed and hardened attitudes. This leads to unavoidable, head-on intra-committee conflict and renders integrative mechanisms relatively ineffective.

The fact of an annual appropriations process means the Committee members repeat the same operations with respect to the same subject matters year after year—and frequently more than once in a given year. Substantive and procedural repetition promotes familiarity with key problems and provides ample opportunity to test and confirm the most satisfactory methods of dealing with them. And the absolute necessity that appropriations bills do ultimately pass gives urgency to the search for such methods. Furthermore, the House rule that no member of the Committee can serve on another standing committee is a deterrent against a fragmentation of Committee member activity which could be a source of difficulty in holding the group together. If a committee has developed (as this one has) a number of norms designed to foster integration, repeated and concentrated exposure to them increases the likelihood that they will be understood, accepted and followed.

Legislative Orientation

The recruitment of members for the Appropriations Committee produces a group of individuals with an orientation especially conducive to Committee integration. Those who make the selection pay special attention to the characteristics which Masters has described as those of the "responsible legislator"—approval of and conformity to the norms of the legislative process and of the House of Representatives.[7]

Key selectors speak of wanting, for the Appropriations Committee, "the kind of man you can deal with" or "a fellow who is well-balanced and won't go off half-cocked on things." A Northern liberal Democrat felt that he had been chosen over eight competitors because, "I had made a lot of friends and was known as a nice guy"—especially, he noted, among Southern Congressmen. Another Democrat explained, "I got the blessing of the Speaker and the leadership. It's personal friendships. I had done a lot of things for them in the past, and when I went to them and asked them, they gave it to me." A Republican chosen for the Committee in his first term recalled,

> The Chairman [Rep. Taber] I guess did some checking around in my area. After all, I was new and he didn't know me. People told me that they were called to see if I was—well, unstable or apt to go off on tangents . . . to see whether or not I had any preconceived notions about things and would not be flexible—whether I would oppose things even though it was obvious.

A key criterion in each of the cases mentioned was a demonstrable record of, or an assumed predisposition toward, legislative give-and-take.

The 106 Appropriations Committee members serving between 1947 and 1961 spent an average of 3.6 years on other House committees before coming to the Committee. Only 17 of the 106 were selected as first term Congressmen. A House apprenticeship (which Appropriations maintains more successfully than all committees save Ways and Means and Rules[8]) provides the time in which

---

[7] Nicholas A. Masters, "House Committee Assignments," *American Political Science Review,* Vol. 55 (June, 1961), pp. 345–357. [Chapter II of this volume.]

[8] In the period from 1947 through 1959, (80th to 86th Congress) 79 separate appointments were made to the Appropriations Committee, with 14 going to freshmen. The Committee filled, in other words, 17.7 per cent of its vacancies with freshmen. The Rules Committee had 26 vacancies and selected no freshmen at all. The Ways and Means Committee had 36 vacancies and selected 2 freshmen (5.6 per cent). All other Committees had a higher percentage of freshmen appointments. Armed Services ranked fourth, with 45 vacancies and 12 freshmen appointed, for a percentage of 26.7. Foreign affairs figures were 46 and 14, or 30.4 per cent; UnAmerican Activities figures were 22 and 7, or 31.8 per cent. cf. Masters, *op. cit.*

legislative reputations can be established by the member and an assessment of that reputation in terms of Appropriations Committee requirements can be made. Moreover, the mere fact that a member survives for a couple of terms is some indication of an electoral situation conducive to his "responsible" legislative behavior. The optimum bet for the Committee is a member from a sufficiently safe district to permit him freedom of maneuver inside the House without fear of reprisal at the polls.[9] The degree of responsiveness to House norms which the Committee selectors value may be the product of a safe district as well as an individual temperament.

Attractiveness

A fourth factor is the extraordinarily high degree of attractiveness which the Committee holds for its members—as measured by the low rate of departure from it. Committee members do not leave it for service on other committees. To the contrary, they are attracted to it from nearly every other committee.[10] Of the 106 members in the 1947–1961 period, only two men left the Committee voluntarily; and neither of them initiated the move.[11] Committee attractiveness is a measure of its capacity to satisfy individual member needs—for power, prestige, recognition, respect, self-esteem, friendship, etc. Such satisfaction in turn increases the likelihood that members will behave in such a way as to hold the group together.

The most frequently mentioned source of Committee attractiveness is its power—based on its control of financial resources. "Where the money is, that's where the power is," sums up the feeling of the members. They prize their ability to reward or punish so many other participants in the political process—executive officials, fellow Congressmen, constituents and other clientele groups. In the eyes of its own members, the Committee is either the most powerful in the House or it is on a par with Ways and Means or, less frequently, on a par with Ways and Means and Rules. The second

---

[9] In the 1960 elections, 41 out of the current 50 members received more than 55.1 per cent of the vote in their districts. By a common definition, that is, only 9 of the 50 came from marginal districts.

[10] The 106 members came to Appropriations from every committee except Ways and Means.

[11] One was personally requested by the Speaker to move to Ways and Means. The other was chosen by a caucus of regional Congressmen to be his party's representative on the Rules Committee. Of the 21 members who were forced off the Committee for lack of seniority during a change in party control, or who were defeated for reelection and later returned, 20 sought to regain Committee membership at the earliest opportunity.

important ingredient in member satisfaction is the government-wide scope of Committee activity. The ordinary Congressman may feel that he has too little knowledge of and too little control over his environment. Membership on this Committee compensates for this feeling of helplessness by the wider contacts, the greater amount of information, and the sense of being "in the middle of things" which are consequent, if not to subcommittee activity, at least to the full Committee's overview of the federal government.

Thirdly, Committee attractiveness is heightened by the group's recognizable and distinctive political style—one that is, moreover, highly valued in American political culture. The style is that of *hard work;* and the Committee's self-image is that of "the hardest working Committee in Congress." His willingness to work is the Committee member's badge of identification, and it is proudly worn. It colors his perceptions of others and their perceptions of him.[11a] It is a cherished axiom of all members that, "This Committee is no place for a man who doesn't work. They have to be hard working. It's a way of life. It isn't just a job; it's a way of life."

The mere existence of some identifiable and valued style or "way of life" is a cohesive force for a group. But the particular style of hard work is one which increases group morale and group identification twice over. Hard work means a long, dull, and tedious application to detail, via the technique of "dig, dig, dig, day after day behind closed doors"—in an estimated 460 subcommittee and full committee meetings a year. And virtually all of these meetings are in executive session. By adopting the style of hard work, the Committee discourages highly individualized forms of legislative behavior, which could be disruptive within the Committee. It rewards its members with power, but it is power based rather on work inside the Committee than on the political glamour of activities carried on in the limelight of the mass media. Prolonged

---

[11a] A sidelight on this attitude is displayed in a current feud between the House and Senate Appropriations Committees over the meeting place for their conference committees. The House Committee is trying to break the century-old custom that conferences to resolve differences on money bills are always held on the Senate side of the Capitol. House Committee members "complain that they often have to trudge back to the House two or three times to answer roll calls during a conference. They say they go over in a body to work, while Senators flit in and out. . . . The House Appropriations Committee feels that it does all the hard work listening to witnesses for months on each bill, only to have the Senate Committee sit as a court of appeals and, with little more than a cursory glance, restore most of the funds cut." *Washington Post,* April 24, 1962, p. 1.

daily work together encourages sentiments of mutual regard, sympathy and solidarity. This *esprit* is, in turn, functional for integration on the Committee. A Republican leader summed up,

> I think it's more closely knit than any other committee. Yet it's the biggest committee, and you'd think it would be the reverse. I know on my subcommittee, you sit together day after day. You get better acquainted. You have sympathy when other fellows go off to play golf. There's a lot of *esprit de corps* in the Committee.

The strong attraction which members have for the Committee increases the influence which the Committee and its norms exercise on all of them. It increases the susceptibility of the newcomer to Committee socialization and of the veteran to Committee sanctions applicable against deviant behavior.[12]

Membership Stability

Members of the Appropriations Committee are strongly attracted to it; they also have, which bears out their selection as "responsible legislators," a strong attraction for a career in the House of Representatives. The 50 members on the Committee in 1961 had served an average of 13.1 years in the House. These twin attractions produce a noteworthy stability of Committee membership. In the period from the 80th to the 87th Congress, 35.7 per cent of the Committee's membership remained constant. That is to say, 15 of the 42 members on the Committee in March, 1947, were still on the Committee in March, 1961.[13] The 50 members of the Committee in 1961 averaged 9.3 years of prior service on that Committee. In no single year during the last fourteen has the Committee had to absorb an influx of new members totalling more than one-quarter of its membership. At all times, in other words, at least three-fourths of the members have had previous Committee experience. This extraordinary stability of personnel extends into

---

[12] This proposition is spelled out at some length in J. Thibaut and H. Kelley, *The Social Psychology of Groups* (New York, 1959), p. 247, and in D. Cartwright and A Zander, *Group Dynamics: Research and Theory* (Evanston, 1953), p. 420.

[13] This figure is 9 per cent greater than the next most stable House Committee during this particular period. The top four, in order, were Appropriations (35.7%), Agriculture (26.7%), Armed Services (25%), Foreign Affairs (20.8%).

the staff as well. As of June 1961, its 15 professionals had served an average of 10.7 years with the Committee.[14]

The opportunity exists, therefore, for the development of a stable leadership group, a set of traditional norms for the regulation of internal Committee behavior, and informal techniques of personal accommodation. Time is provided in which new members can learn and internalize Committee norms before they attain high seniority rankings. The Committee does not suffer from the potentially disruptive consequences of rapid changeovers in its leadership group, nor of sudden impositions of new sets of norms governing internal Committee behavior.

II

If one considers the main activity of a political system to be decision-making, the acid test of its internal integration is its capacity to make collective decisions without flying apart in the process. Analysis of Committee integration should focus directly, therefore, upon its subgroups and the roles of its members. Two kinds of subgroups are of central importance—subcommittees and majority or minority party groups. The roles which are most relevant derive from: (1) positions which each member holds by virtue of his subgroup attachments, *e.g.*, as subcommittee member, majority (or minority) party member; (2) positions which relate to full Committee membership, *e.g.*, Committee member, and the seniority rankings of veteran, man of moderate experience, and newcomer;[15] (3) positions which relate to both subgroup and full Committee membership, *e.g.*, Chairman of the Committee, ranking minority member of the Committee, subcommittee chairman, ranking subcommittee member. Clusters of norms state the expectations about subgroup and role behavior. The description which follows treats the ways in which these norms and their associated behaviors mesh and clash. It treats, also, the internal control mechanisms by which behavior is brought into reasonable conformity with expectations.

---

[14] The Committee's permanent and well integrated professional staff (as distinguished from its temporary investigating staff) might be considered as part of the subsystem though it will not be treated in this paper.

[15] "Newcomers" are defined as men who have served no more than two terms on the Committee. "Men of moderate experience" are those with 3–5 terms of service. "Veterans" are those who have 6 or more terms of Committee service.

Subgroup Integration

The day-to-day work of the Committee is carried on in its sub-committees each of which is given jurisdiction over a number of related governmental units. The number of subcommittees is determined by the Committee Chairman, and has varied recently from a low of 9 in 1949 to a high of 15 in 1959. The present total of 14 reflects, as always, a set of strategic and personal judgments by the Chairman balanced against the limitations placed on him by Committee tradition and member wishes. The Chairman also determines subcommittee jurisdiction, appoints subcommittee chairmen and selects the majority party members of each group. The ranking minority member of the Committee exercises similar control over subcommittee assignments on his side of the aisle.

Each subcommittee holds hearings on the budget estimates of the agencies assigned to it, meets in executive session to decide what figures and what language to recommend to the full Committee (to "mark up" the bill), defends its recommendations before the full Committee, writes the Committee's report to the House, dominates the debate on the floor, and bargains for the House in conference committee. Within its jurisdiction, each subcommittee functions independently of the others and guards its autonomy jealously. The Chairman and ranking minority member of the full Committee have, as we shall see, certain opportunities to oversee and dip into the operations of all subcommittees. But their intervention is expected to be minimal. Moreover, they themselves operate importantly within the subcommittee framework by sitting as chairman or ranking minority member of the subcommittee in which they are most interested. Each subcommittee, under the guidance of its chairman, transacts its business in considerable isolation from every other one. One subcommittee chairman exclaimed,

> Why, you'd be branded an imposter if you went into one of those other subcommittee meetings. The only time I go is by appointment, by arrangement with the chairman at a special time. I'm as much a stranger in another subcommittee as I would be in the legislative Committee on Post Office and Civil Service. Each one does its work apart from all others.

All members of all subcommittees are expected to behave in similar fashion in the role of subcommittee member. Three main norms define this role; to the extent that they are observed, they promote harmony and reduce conflict among subcommittees.[16] Subcommittee autonomy gives to the House norm of *specialization* an intensified application on the Appropriations Committee. Each member is expected to play the role of specialist in the activities of one subcommittee. He will sit on from one to four subcommittees, but normally will specialize in the work, or a portion of the work, of only one. Except for the Chairman, ranking minority member and their confidants, a Committee member's time, energy, contacts and experience are devoted to his subcommittees. Specialization is, therefore, among the earliest and most compelling of the Committee norms to which a newcomer is exposed. Within the Committee, respect, deference and power are earned through subcommittee activity and, hence to a degree, through specialization. Specialization is valued further because it is well suited to the task of guarding the Treasury. Only by specializing, Committee members believe, can they unearth the volume of factual information necessary for the intelligent screening of budget requests. Since "the facts" are acquired only through industry an effective specialist will, perforce, adopt and promote the Committee's style of hard work.

Committee-wide acceptance of specialization is an integrative force in decision-making because it helps support a second norm— *reciprocity*. The stage at which a subcommittee makes its recommendations is a potential point of internal friction. Conflict among subcommittees (or between one subcommittee and the rest of the Committee) is minimized by the deference traditionally accorded to the recommendation of the subcommittee which has specialized in the area, has worked hard, and has "the facts." "It's a matter of 'You respect my work and I'll respect yours.' " "It's frowned upon if you offer an amendment in the full Committee if you aren't on the subcommittee. It's considered presumptuous to pose as an expert if you aren't on the subcommittee." Though records of full Committee decisions are not available, members agree that subcommittee recommendations are "very rarely changed," "almost

---

[16] A statement of expected behavior was taken to be a Committee norm when it was expressed by a substantial number of respondents (a dozen or so) who represented both parties, and varying degrees of experience. In nearly every case, moreover, no refutation of them was encountered, and ample confirmation of their existence can be found in the public record. Their articulation came most frequently from the veterans of the group.

always approved," "changed one time in fifty," "very seldom changed," etc.

No subcommittee is likely to keep the deference of the full Committee for long unless its recommendations have widespread support among its own members. To this end, a third norm—*subcommittee unity*—is expected to be observed by subcommittee members. Unity means a willingness to support (or not to oppose) the recommendations of one's own subcommittee. Reciprocity and unity are closely dependent upon one another. Reciprocity is difficult to maintain when subcommittees themselves are badly divided; and unity has little appeal unless reciprocity will subsequently be observed. The norm of reciprocity functions to minimize inter-subcommittee conflict. The norm of unity functions to minimize intra-subcommittee conflict. Both are deemed essential to subcommittee influence.

One payoff for the original selection of "responsible legislators" is their special willingness to compromise in pursuit of subcommittee unity. The impulse to this end is registered most strongly at the time when the subcommittee meets in executive session to mark up the bill. Two ranking minority members explained this aspect of markup procedure in their subcommittees:

> If there's agreement, we go right along. If there's a lot of controversy we put the item aside and go on. Then, after a day or two, we may have a list of ten controversial items. We give and take and pound them down till we get agreement.

> We have a unanimous agreement on everything. If a fellow enters an objection and we can't talk him out of it—and sometimes we can get him to go along—that's it. We put it in there.

Once the bargain is struck, the subcommittee is expected to "stick together."

It is, of course, easier to achieve unity among the five, seven, or nine members of a subcommittee than among the fifty members of the full Committee. But members are expected wherever possible to observe the norm of unity in the full Committee as well. That is, they should not only defer to the recommendations of the subcommittee involved, but they should support (or not oppose) that recommendation when it reaches the floor in the form of a Committee decision. On the floor, Committee members believe, their power and prestige depend largely on the degree to which the norms of reciprocity and unity continue to be observed. Members warn each other that if they go to the floor in disarray they will be "rolled," "jumped," or "run over" by the membership. It is a cardinal maxim among Committee members that "You can't turn an appropriations bill loose on the floor." Two senior subcommittee chairmen explain,

> We iron out our differences in Committee. We argue it out and usually have a meeting of the minds, a composite view of the Committee. . . . If we went on the floor in wide disagreement, they would say, 'If you can't agree after listening to the testimony and discussing it, how can we understand it? We'll just vote on the basis of who we like the best.'

> I tell them (the full Committee) we should have a united front. If there are any objections or changes, we ought to hear it now, and not wash our dirty linen out on the floor. If we don't have a bill that we can all agree on and support, we ought not to report it out. To do that is like throwing a piece of meat to a bunch of hungry animals.

One of the most functional Committee practices supporting the norm of unity is the tradition against minority reports in the subcommittee and in the full Committee. It is symptomatic of Committee integration that custom should proscribe the use of the most formal and irrevocable symbol of congressional committee disunity—the minority report. A few have been written—but only 9 out of a possible 141 during the 11 years, 1947–1957. That is to say, 95 per cent of all original appropriations bills in this period were reported out without dissent. The technique of "reserving" is the Committee member's equivalent for the registering of dissent. In subcommittee or Committee, when a member reserves, he goes on record informally by informing his colleagues that he reserves the right to disagree on a specified item later on in the proceedings. He may seek a change or support a change in that particular item in full Committee or on the floor. But he does not publicize his dissent. The subcommittee or the full Committee can then make an unopposed recommendation. The individual retains some freedom of maneuver without firm commitment. Often a member reserves on an appropriations item but takes no further action. A member explained how the procedure operates in subcommittee,

> If there's something I feel too strongly about, and just can't go along, I'll say, 'Mr. Chairman, we can have a unanimous

report, but I reserve the right to bring this up in full Committee. I feel duty bound to make a play for it and see if I can't sell it to the other members.' But if I don't say anything, or don't reserve this right, and then I bring it up in full Committee, they'll say, 'Who are you trying to embarrass? You're a member of the team, aren't you? That's not the way to get along.'

Disagreement cannot, of course, be eliminated from the Committee. But the Committee has accepted a method for ventilating it which produces a minimum of internal disruption. And members believe that the greater their internal unity, the greater the likelihood that their recommendations will pass the House.

The degree to which the role of the subcommittee member can be so played and subcommittee conflict thereby minimized depends upon the minimization of conflict between the majority and minority party subgroups. Nothing would be more disruptive to the Committee's work than bitter and extended partisan controversy. It is, therefore, important to Appropriations Committee integration that a fourth norm—*minimal partisanship*—should be observed by members of both party contingents. Nearly every respondent emphasized, with approval, that "very little" or "not much" partisanship prevailed on the Committee. One subcommittee chairman stated flatly, "My job is to keep down partisanship." A ranking minority member said, "You might think that we Republicans would defend the Administration and the budget, but we don't." Majority and minority party ratios are constant and do not change *i.e.,* in 1958) to reflect changes in the strength of the controlling party. The Committee operates with a completely non-partisan professional staff, which does not change in tune with shifts in party control. Requests for studies by the Committee's investigating staff must be made by the Chairman and ranking minority member of the full Committee and by the Chairman and ranking minority member of the subcommittee involved. Subcommittees can produce recommendations without dissent and the full Committee can adopt reports without dissent precisely because party conflict is (during the period 1947–1961) the exception rather than the rule.

The Committee is in no sense immune from the temperature of party conflict, but it does have a relatively high specific heat. Intense party strife or a strongly taken presidential position will get reflected in subcommittee and in Committee recommendations. Sharp divisions in party policy were carried, with disruptive impact, into some areas of Committee activity during the 80th Congress and subsequently, by way of reaction, into the 81st Congress.[17] During the Eisenhower years, extraordinary presidential pleas, especially concerning foreign aid, were given special heed by the Republican members of the Committee.[18] Partisanship is normally generated from the environment and not from within the Committee's party groups. Partisanship is, therefore, likely to be least evident in sub-committee activity, stronger in the full Committee, and most potent at the floor stage. Studies which have focussed on roll-call analysis have stressed the influence of party in legislative decision-making.[19] In the appropriations process, at any rate, the floor stage probably represents party influence at its maximum. Our examination, by interview, of decision-making at the subcommittee and full Committee level would stress the influence of Committee-oriented norms—the strength of which tends to vary inversely with that of party bonds. In the secrecy and intimacy of the subcom-mittee and full Committee hearing rooms, the member finds it easy to compromise on questions of more or less, to take money from one program and give it to another and, in general, to avoid yes-or-no type party stands. These decisions, taken in response to the integrative norms of the Committee are the most important ones in the entire appropriations process.

Role Integration

The roles of subcommittee member and party member are common to all.

Other more specific decision-making positions are allocated among the members. Different positions produce different roles, and in an integrated system, these too must fit together. Integration, in other words, must be achieved through the complementarity or reciprocity of roles as well as through a similarity of roles. This may mean a pattern in which expectations are so different that

---

[17] See, for example, the internal conflict on the subcommittee dealing with the Labor Department. 93 *Cong. Record,* pp. 2465–2562 passim; 94 *Cong. Record,* pp. 7605–7607.

[18] See, for example, the unusual minority report of Committee Republicans on the foreign aid appropriations bill in 1960. Their protest against Committee cuts in the budget estimates was the result of strenuous urging by the Eisenhower Administration. House Report No. 1798, *Mutual Security and Related Agency Appropriation Bill,* 1961, 86 Cong. 2d sess. 1960.

[19] David Truman, *The Congressional Party* (New York, 1959); Julius Turner, *Party and Constituency: Pressures on Congress* (Baltimore, 1951).

there is very little contact between individuals; or it may mean a pattern in which contacts require the working out of an involved system of exchange of obligations and rewards.[20] In either case, the desired result is the minimization of conflict among prominent Committee roles. Two crucial instances of role reciprocity on the Committee involve the seniority positions of old-timer and newcomer and the leadership positions of Chairman and ranking minority member, on both the full Committee and on each subcommittee.

The differentiation between senior and junior members is the broadest definition of who shall and who shall not actively participate in Committee decisions. Of a junior member, it will be said, "Oh, he doesn't count—what I mean is, he hasn't been on the Committee long enough." He is not expected to and ordinarily does not have much influence. His role is that of apprentice. He is expected to learn the business and the norms of the Committee by applying himself to its work. He is expected to acquiesce in an arrangement which gives most influence (except in affairs involving him locally) to the veterans of the group. Newcomers will be advised to "follow the chairman until you get your bearings. For the first two years, follow the chairman. He knows." "Work hard, keep quiet and attend the Committee sessions. We don't want to listen to some new person coming in here." And newcomers perceive their role in identical terms: "You have to sit in the back seat and edge up little by little." "You just go to subcommittee meetings and assimilate the routine. The new members are made to feel welcome, but you have a lot of rope-learning to do before you carry much weight."

At every stage of Committee work, this differentiation prevails. There is remarkable agreement on the radically different sets of expectations involved. During the hearings, the view of the elders is that, "Newcomers . . . don't know what the score is and they don't have enough information to ask intelligent questions." A newcomer described his behavior in typically similar terms: "I attended all the hearings and studied and collected information that I can use next year. I'm just marking time now." During

---

[20] The ideas of "reciprocity" and "complementarity," which are used interchangeably here, are discussed in Alvin Gouldner, "The Norm of Reciprocity," *American Sociological Review* (April, 1960). Most helpful in explaining the idea of a role system has been the work of J. Wahlke, H. Eulau, W. Buchanan, L. Ferguson. See their study, *The Legislative System* (New York, 1962), esp. Intro.

the crucial subcommittee markup, the newcomer will have little opportunity to speak—save in locally important matters. A subcommittee chairman stated the norm from his viewpoint this way: "When we get a compromise, nobody's going to break that up. If someone tries, we sit on him fast. We don't want young people who throw bricks or slow things down." And a newcomer reciprocated, describing his markup conduct: "I'm not provocative. I'm in there for information. They're the experts in the field. I go along." In full Committee, on the floor, and in conference committee, the Committee's senior members take the lead and the junior members are expected to follow. The apprentice role is common to all new members of the House. But it is wrong to assume that each Committee will give it the same emphasis. Some pay it scant heed.[21] The Appropriations Committee makes it a cornerstone of its internal structure.

Among the Committee's veterans, the key roles are those of Committee Chairman and ranking minority member, and their counterparts in every subcommittee. It is a measure of Committee integration and the low degree of partisanship that considerable reciprocity obtains between these roles. Their partisan status nevertheless sets limits to the degree of possible integration. The Chairman is given certain authority which he and only he can exercise. But save in times of extreme party controversy, the expectation is that consultation and cooperation between the chairman-ranking minority member shall lubricate the Committee's entire work. For example, by Committee tradition, its Chairman and ranking minority member are both *ex officio* voting members of each subcommittee and of every conference committee. The two of them thus have joint access at every stage of the internal process. A subcommittee chairman, too, is expected to discuss matters of scheduling and agenda with his opposite minority number. He is expected to work with him during the markup session and to give him (and, normally, only him) an opportunity to read and comment on the subcommittee report.[22] A ranking minority member described his subcommittee markup procedure approvingly:

> Frequently the chairman has a figure which he states. Sometimes he will have no figure, and he'll turn to me and say, '——, what do you think?' Maybe I'll have a figure. It's very

---

[21] For example, the Committee on Education and Labor, see footnote 26.

[22] See the exchange in 101 *Cong. Rec.*, pp. 3832, 3844, 3874.

flexible. Everyone has a chance to say what he thinks, and we'll move it around. Sometimes it takes a long time. . . . He's a rabid partisan on the floor, but he is a very fair man in the subcommittee.

Where influence is shared, an important exchange of rewards occurs. The chairman gains support for his leadership and the ranking minority member gains intra-Committee power. The Committee as a whole insures against the possibility of drastic change in its internal structure by giving to its key minority members a stake in its operation. Chairmen and ranking minority members will, in the course of time, exchange positions; and it is expected that such a switch will produce no form of retribution nor any drastic change in the functioning of the Committee. Reciprocity of roles, in this case, promotes continued integration. A ranking minority member testified to one successful arrangement when he took the floor in the 83rd Congress to say:

> The gentleman and I have been see sawing back and forth on this committee for some time. He was chairman in the 80th Congress. I had the privilege of serving as chairman in the 81st and 82nd Congresses. Now he is back in the saddle. I can say that he has never failed to give me his utmost cooperation, and I have tried to give him the same cooperation during his service as chairman of this Committee. We seldom disagree, but we have found out that we can disagree without being disagreeable. Consequently, we have unusual harmony on this committee.[23]

Reciprocity between chairmen and ranking minority members on the Appropriations Committee is to some incalculable degree a function of the stability of membership which allows a pair of particular individuals to work out the kind of personal accommodation described above. The close working relationship of Clarence Cannon and John Taber, whose service on the Committee totals 68 years and who have been changing places as Chairman and ranking minority member for 19 years, highlights and sustains a pattern of majority-minority reciprocity throughout the group.

Internal Control Mechanisms

The expectations which apply to subcommittee, to party, to veterans and to newcomers, to chairmen and to ranking minority mem-

---

[23] 99 *Cong. Rec.*, p. 4933.

bers prescribe highly integrative behaviors. We have concentrated on these expectations and have both illustrated and assumed the close correlation between expected and actual behavior. This does not mean that all the norms of the Committee have been canvassed. Nor does it mean that deviation from the integrative norms does not occur. It does. From what can be gathered, however, from piecing together a study of the public record on appropriations from 1947 to 1961 with interview materials, the Committee has been markedly successful in maintaining a stable internal structure over time. As might be expected, therefore, changes and threats of change have been generated more from the environment—when outsiders consider the Committee as unresponsive—than from inside the subsystem itself. One source of internal stability, and an added reason for assuming a correlation between expected and actual behavior, is the existence of what appear to be reasonably effective internal control mechanisms. Two of these are the socialization processes applied to newcomers and the sanctioning mechanisms applicable to all Committee members.

Socialization is in part a training in perception. Before members of a group can be expected to behave in accordance with its norms, they must learn to see and interpret the world around them with reasonable similarity. The socialization of the Committee newcomer during his term or two of apprenticeship serves to bring his perceptions and his attitudes sufficiently into line with those of the other members to serve as a basis for Committee integration. The Committee, as we have seen, is chosen from Congressmen whose political flexibility connotes an aptitude for learning new lessons of power. Furthermore, the high degree of satisfaction of its members with the group increases their susceptibility to its processes of learning and training.

For example, one half of the Committee's Democrats are Northerners and Westerners from urban constituencies, whose voting records are just as "liberal" on behalf of domestic social welfare programs as non-Committee Democrats from like constituencies. They come to the Committee favorably disposed toward the high level of federal spending necessary to support such programs, and with no sense of urgency about the Committee's tasks of guarding the Treasury or reducing budget estimates. Given the criteria governing their selection, however, they come without rigid preconceptions and with a built-in responsiveness to the socialization processes of any legislative group of which they are members. It is crucial to Committee integration that they learn to temper their potentially disruptive welfare-state ideology with a conservative's concern for saving money. They must change their perceptions and attitudes sufficiently to view the Committee's tasks in nearly the same terms as their more conservative Southern Democratic and Republican colleagues. What their elders perceive as reality (*i.e.,* the disposition of executives to ask for more money than is necessary) they, too, must see as reality. A subcommittee chairman explained:

> When you have sat on the Committee, you see that these bureaus are always asking for more money—always up, never down. They want to build up their organization. You reach the point—I have—where it sickens you, where you rebel against it. Year after year, they want more money. They say, 'Only $50,000 this year'; but you know the pattern. Next year they'll be back for $100,000, then $200,000. The younger members haven't been on the Committee long enough, haven't had the experience to know this.

The younger men, in this case the younger liberals, do learn from their Committee experience. Within one or two terms, they are differentiating between themselves and the "wild-eyed spenders" or the "free spenders" in the House. "Some of these guys would spend you through the roof," exclaimed one liberal of moderate seniority. Repeated exposure to Committee work and to fellow members has altered their perceptions and their attitudes in money matters. Half a dozen Northern Democrats of low or moderate seniority agreed with one of their number who said: "Yes, it's true. I can see it myself. I suppose I came here a flaming liberal; but as the years go by I get more conservative. You just hate like hell to spend all this money. . . . You come to the point where you say, 'By God, this is enough jobs.'" These men will remain more inclined toward spending than their Committee colleagues, but their perceptions and hence their attitudes have been brought close enough to the others to support a consensus on tasks. They are responsive to appeals on budget-cutting grounds that would not have registered earlier and which remain meaningless to liberals outside the Committee. In cases, therefore, where Committee selection does not and cannot initially produce individuals with a predisposition toward protecting the Treasury, the same result is achieved by socialization.

Socialization is a training in behavior as well as in perception. For the newcomer, conformity to norms in specific situations is insured through the appropriate application, by the Committee veterans, of rewards and punishments. For the Committee member who serves his apprenticeship creditably, the passage of time holds the promise that he will inherit a position of influence. He may, as an incentive, be given some small reward early in his Committee career. One man, in his second year, had been assigned the task of specializing in one particular program. However narrow the scope of his specialization, it had placed him on the road to influence within the Committee. He explained with evident pleasure:

> The first year, you let things go by. You can't participate. But you learn by watching the others operate. The next year, you know what you're interested in and when to step in. . . . For instance, I've become an expert on the——program. The chairman said to me, 'This is something you ought to get interested in.' I did; and now I'm the expert on the Committee. Whatever I say on that, the other members listen to me and do what I want.

At some later date, provided he continues to observe Committee norms, he will be granted additional influence, perhaps through a prominent floor role. A model Committee man of moderate seniority who had just attained to this stage of accomplishment, and who had suffered through several political campaigns back home fending off charges that he was a do-nothing Congressman, spoke about the rewards he was beginning to reap.

> When you perform well on the floor when you bring out a bill, and Members know that you know the bill, you develop prestige with other Members of Congress. They come over and ask you what you think, because they know you've studied it. You begin to get a reputation beyond your subcommittee. And you get inner satisfaction, too. You don't feel that you're down here doing nothing.

The first taste of influence which comes to men on this Committee is compensation for the frustrations of apprenticeship. Committee integration in general, and the meshing of roles between elders and newcomers in particular, rests on the fact that conformity to role expectations over time does guarantee to the young positive rewards—the very kind of rewards of power, prestige, and personal satisfaction which led most of them to seek Committee membership in the first place.

The important function of apprenticeship is that it provides the necessary time during which socialization can go forward. And teaching proceeds with the aid of punishments as well as rewards. Should a new member inadvertently or deliberately run afoul of Committee norms during his apprenticeship, he will find himself confronted with negative sanctions ranging in subtlety from "jaundiced eyes" to a changed subcommittee assignment. Several members, for example, recalled their earliest encounter with the norm of unity and the tradition against minority reports. One remembered his attempt to file a minority report. "The Chairman was pretty upset about it. It's just a tradition, I guess, not to have minority reports. I didn't know it was a tradition. When I said I was going to write a minority report, some eyebrows were raised. The Chairman said it just wasn't the thing to do. Nothing more was said about it. But it wasn't a very popular thing to do, I guess." He added that he had not filed one since.

Some younger members have congenital difficulty in observing the norms of the apprentice's role. In the 86th Congress, these types tended to come from the Republican minority. The minority newcomers (described by one of the men who selected them as "eight young, energetic, fighting conservatives") were a group of economy-minded individuals some of whom chafed against any barrier which kept them form immediate influence on Committee policy. Their reaction was quite different from that of the young Democrats, whose difficulty was in learning to become economy-minded, but who did not actively resent their lack of influence. One freshman, who felt that "The appropriations system is lousy, inadequate and old fashioned," recalled that he had spoken out in full Committee against the recommendations of a subcommittee of which he was not a member. Having failed, he continued to oppose the recommendation during floor debate. By speaking up, speaking in relation to the work of another subcommittee and by opposing a Committee recommendation, he had violated the particular norms of his apprentice role as well of the generally applicable norms of reciprocity and unity. He explained what he had learned, but remained only partially socialized:

> They want to wash their dirty linen in the Committee and they want no opposition afterward. They let me say my piece in Committee. . . . But I just couldn't keep quiet. I said some things on the floor, and I found out that's about all they would take. . . . If you don't get along with your Committee and have their support, you don't get anything accomplished around

here. . . . I'm trying to be a loyal, cooperative member of the Committee. You hate to be a stinker; but I'm still picking at the little things because I can't work on the big things. There's nothing for the new men to do, so they have to find places to needle in order to take some part in it.

Another freshman, who had deliberately violated apprenticeship norms by trying to ask "as many questions as the chairman" during subcommittee hearings, reported a story of unremitting counteraction against his deviation:

In the hearings, I have to wait sometimes nine or ten hours for a chance; and he hopes I'll get tired and stay home. I've had to wait till some pretty unreasonable hours. Once I've gotten the floor, though, I've been able to make a good case. Sometimes I've been the only person there. . . . He's all powerful. He's got all the power. He wouldn't think of taking me on a trip with him when he goes to hold hearings. Last year, he went to———. He wouldn't give me a nudge there. And in the hearings, when I'm questioning a witness, he'll keep butting in so that my case won't appear to be too rosy.

Carried on over a period of two years, this behavior resulted in considerable personal friction between a Committee elder and the newcomer. Other members of his subcommittee pointedly gave him a great lack of support for his non-conformity. "They tried to slow him down and tone him down a little," not because he and his subcommittee chairman disagreed, but on the grounds that the Committee has developed accepted ways of disagreeing which minimize, rather than exacerbate, interpersonal friction.

One internal threat to Committee integration comes from new members who from untutored perceptions, from ignorance of norms, or from dissatisfaction with the apprentice role may not act in accordance with Committee expectations. The seriousness of this threat is minimized, however, by the fact that the deviant newcomer does not possess sufficient resources to affect adversely the operation of the system. Even if he does not respond immediately to the application of sanctions, he can be held in check and subjected to an extended and (given the frequency of interaction among members) intensive period of socialization. The success of Committee socialization is indicated by the fact that whereas wholesale criticism of Committee operations was frequently voiced among junior members, it had disappeared among the men of moderate experience. And what these middle seniority members now accept as the facts of Committee life, the veterans vigorously assert and defend as the essentials of a smoothly functioning system. Satisfaction with the Committee's internal structure increases with length of Committee service.

An important reason for changing member attitudes is that those who have attained leadership positions have learned, as newcomers characteristically have not, that their conformity to Committee norms is the ultimate source of their influence inside the group. Freshman members do not as readily perceive the degree to which interpersonal influence is rooted in obedience to group norms. They seem to convert their own sense of powerlessness into the view that the Committee's leaders possess, by virtue of their positions, arbitrary, absolute, and awesome power. Typically, they say: "If you're a subcommittee chairman, it's your Committee." "The Chairman runs the show. He gets what he wants. He decides what he wants and gets it through." Older members of the Committee, however, view the power of the leaders as a highly contingent and revocable grant, tendered by the Committee for so long and only so long as their leaders abide by Committee expectations. In commenting on internal influence, their typical reaction is: "Of course, the Committee wouldn't follow him if it didn't want to. He has a great deal of respect. He's an able man, a hard-working man." "He knows the bill backwards and forwards. He works hard, awfully hard and the members know it." Committee leaders have an imposing set of formal prerogatives. But they can capitalize on them only if they command the respect, confidence and deference of their colleagues.

It is basic to Committee integration that members who have the greatest power to change the system evidence the least disposition to do so. Despite their institutional conservatism, however, Committee elders do occasionally violate the norms applicable to them and hence represent a potential threat to successful integration. Excessive deviation from Committee expectations by some leaders will bring counter-measures by other leaders. Thus, for example, the Chairman and his subcommittee chairmen exercise reciprocal controls over one another's behavior. The Chairman has the authority to appoint the chairman and members of each subcommittee and fix its jurisdiction. "He runs the Committee. He has a lot of power," agrees one subcommittee chairman. "But it's all done on the basis of personal friendship. If he tries to get too big, the members can whack him down by majority vote."

In the 84th Congress, Chairman Cannon attempted an unusually broad reorganization of subcommittee jurisdictions. The subcommittee chairman most adversely affected rallied his senior colleagues against the Chairman's action—on the ground that it was an excessive violation of role expectations and threatening to subcommittee autonomy. Faced with the prospect of a negative Committee vote, the Chairman was forced to act in closer conformity to the expectations of the other leaders. As one participant described the episode,

> Mr. Cannon, for reasons of his own, tried to bust up one of the subcommittees. We didn't like that. . . . He was breaking up the whole Committee. A couple of weeks later, a few of the senior members got together and worked out a compromise. By that time, he had seen a few things, so we went to him and talked to him and worked it out.

On the subcommittees, too, it is the veterans of both parties who will levy sanctions against an offending chairman. It is they who speak of "cutting down to size" and "trimming the whiskers" of leaders who become "too cocky," "too stubborn" or who "do things wrong too often." Committee integration is underwritten by the fact that no member high or low is permanently immune from the operation of its sanctioning mechanisms.

III

Data concerning internal committee activity can be organized and presented in various ways. One way is to use key functional problems like integration as the focal points for descriptive analysis. On the basis of our analysis (and without, for the time being, having devised any precise measure of integration), we are led to the summary observation that the House Appropriations Committee appears to be a well integrated, if not an extremely well integrated, committee. The question arises as to whether anything can be gained from this study other than a description of one property of one political subsystem. If it is reasonable to assume that the internal life of a congressional committee affects all legislative activity involving that committee, and if it is reasonable to assume that the analysis of a committee's internal relationships will produce useful knowledge about legislative behavior, some broader implications for this study are indicated.

In the first place, the success of the House Appropriations Committee in solving the problem of integration probably does have important consequences for the appropriations process. Some of the possible relationships can be stated as hypotheses and tested; others can be suggested as possible guides to understanding. All of them require further research. Of primary interest is the relationship between integration and the power of the Committee. There is little doubt about the fact of Committee power. Of the 443 separate case histories of bureau appropriations examined, the House accepted Committee recommendations in 387, or 87.4 per cent of them; and in 159, or 33.6 per cent of the cases, the House Committee's original recommendations on money amounts were the exact ones enacted into law. The hypothesis that the greater the degree of Committee unity the greater the probability that its recommendations will be accepted is being tested as part of a larger study.[24] House Committee integration may be a key factor in producing House victories in conference committee. This relationship, too, might be tested. Integration appears to help provide the House conferees with a feeling of confidence and superiority which is one of their important advantages in the mix of psychological factors affecting conference deliberations.

Another suggested consequence of high integration is that party groups have a relatively small influence upon appropriations decisions. It suggests, too, that Committee-oriented behavior should be duly emphasized in any analysis of Congressional oversight of administrative activity by this Committee. Successful integration promotes the achievement of the Committee's goals, and doubtless helps account for the fairly consistent production of budget-cutting decisions. Another consequence will be found in the strategies adopted by people seeking favorable Committee decisions. For example, the characteristic lines of contact from executive officials to the Committee will run to the chairman and the ranking minority member (and to the professional staff man) of the single subcommittee handling their agency's appropriations. The ways in which the Committee achieves integration may even affect the success or failure of a bureau in getting its appropriations. Committee members, for instance, will react more favorably toward an administrator who conforms to their self-image of the hard-working master-of-detail than to one who does not—and Committee response to individual administrators bulks large in their determinations.

Finally, the internal integration of this Committee helps to

---

[24] *Cf.* Dwaine Marvick, "Congressional Appropriations Politics," unpublished manuscript (Columbia, 1952).

explain the extraordinary stability, since 1920, of appropriations procedures—in the face of repeated proposals to change them through omnibus appropriations, legislative budgets, new budgetary forms, item veto, Treasury borrowing, etc. Integration is a stabilizing force, and the stability of the House Appropriations Committee has been a force for stabilization throughout the entire process. It was, for example, the disagreement between Cannon and Taber which led to the indecisiveness reflected in the short-lived experiment with a single appropriations bill.[25] One need only examine the conditions most likely to decrease Committee integration to ascertain some of the critical factors for producing changes in the appropriations process. A description of integration is also an excellent base-line from which to analyze changes in internal structure.

All of these are speculative propositions which call for further research. But they suggest, as a second implication, that committee integration does have important consequences for legislative activity and, hence, that it is a key variable in the study of legislative politics. It would seem, therefore, to be a fruitful focal point for the study of other congressional committees.[26] Comparative committee analysis could usefully be devoted to (1) the factors which tend to increase or decrease integration; (2) the degree to which

---

[25] See Dalmas Nelson, "The Omnibus Appropriations Act of 1950," *Journal of Politics* (May, 1953).

[26] This view has been confirmed by the results of interviews conducted by the author with members of the House Committee on Education and Labor, together with an examination of that Committee's activity in one policy area. They indicate very significant contrasts between the internal structure of that Committee and the Appropriations Committee—contrasts which center around their comparative success in meeting the problem of integration. The House Committee on Education and Labor appears to be a poorly integrated committee. Its internal structure is characterized by a great deal of subgroup conflict, relatively little role reciprocity, and minimally effective internal control mechanisms. External concerns, like those of party, constituency and clientele groups, are probably more effective in determining its decisions than is likely to be the case in a well-integrated committee. An analysis of the internal life of the Committee on Education and Labor, drawn partly from interviews with 19 members of that group, will appear in a forthcoming study, *Federal Aid to Education and National Politics*, by Professor Frank Munger and the author, to be published by Syracuse University Press. [See Chapter VIII of the present volume.] See also Nicholas R. Masters, *op. cit.*, note 7 above, pp. 354-355 [Reprinted as Chapter II of the present volume.] and Seymour Scher, "Congressional Committee Members as Independent Agency Overseers: A Case Study," *American Political Science Review*, Vol. 54 (December, 1960), pp. 911-920.

integration is achieved; and (3) the consequences of varying degrees of integration for committee behavior and influence. If analyses of committee integration are of any value, they should encourage the analysis and the classification of congressional committees along functional lines. And they should lead to the discussion of interrelated problems of committee survival. Functional classifications of committees (*i.e.*, well or poorly integrated) derived from a large number of descriptive analyses of several functional problems, may prove helpful in constructing more general propositions about the legislative process.

VII

THE AGRICULTURE COMMITTEE AND THE PROBLEM OF REPRESENTATION*

Charles O. Jones

STUDENTS OF American politics are told that our political system is fundamentally a *representative* democracy. Concepts of representation, since Burke, have commonly employed his distinction between action taken in response to instructions from constituents and action based on an independent appraisal of the national interest.[1] A very recent analysis has offered a refinement of this, by distinguishing three types: "delegate," "trustee" and "politico."[2] Theory and history alike tell us, however, that a representative does not invariably act in only one of these roles. There have been a number of empirical studies of representatives, few of which con-

---

* Reprinted from "Representation in Congress: The Case of the House Agriculture Committee," *American Political Science Review,* LV (June, 1961), 358–67. Copyright © 1961, The American Political Science Association. The author wishes to acknowledge the generosity of Congressman E. Y. Berry (R–South Dakota) in providing office space and other aids, as well as the helpful suggestions and comments of Leon D. Epstein and Ralph K. Huitt, University of Wisconsin; Samuel C. Patterson, State University of Iowa; and Wayne G. Rollins, Wellesley College.

[1] Some of the most useful studies of representation are: Charles Beard and J. D. Lewis, "Representative Government in Evolution," *American Political Science Review,* Vol. 26 (April, 1932), pp. 223–40; Francis M. Carney, "Concepts of Political Representation in the United States Today," unpublished Ph.D. dissertation, University of California, Los Angeles, 1956; Alfred de Grazia, *Public and Republic* (New York, 1951); John A. Fairlie, "The Nature of Political Representation," *American Political Science Review,* Vol. 34 (April and June, 1940), pp. 236–48 and 456–66; H. F. Gosnell, *Democracy, The Threshold of Freedom* (New York, 1948); James Hogan, *Election and Representation* (Oxford, 1945). For an extended bibliography see Charles O. Jones, "The Relationship of Congressional Committee Action to a Theory of Representation," unpublished Ph.D. dissertation, University of Wisconsin, 1960, pp. 413–28, from which materials for this article were drawn.

[2] Heinz Eulau *et al.,* "The Role of the Representative: Some Empirical Observations on the Theory of Edmund Burke," *American Political Science Review,* Vol. 53 (Sept., 1959), pp. 742–756.

centrate on specific policy fields;[3] and studies also of the play of interests in the enactment of specific legislation, but without a systematic account of the legislative committee members involved, acting in their representative capacities as they saw them. How then can we tell when to expect a representative to view his role in one way rather than another? The aim of this article is to shed a little light on some aspects of this broad question by means of a case study.

The subjects of the study were the members of the House Agriculture Committee and their action on the omnibus farm legislation (H. R. 12954 and S. 4071) in 1958 (85th Congress, second session).[4] Most of the data were obtained from interviews[5] with thirty of the thirty-four Committee members, but, in addition, the specific stands of members in subcommittees, the full committee, and on the House floor were traced, through the printed hearings and the *Congressional Record* of floor debates. Finally, other interested and knowledgeable people were interviewed, newspaper accounts were studied, and the characteristics of constituencies were examined.

For analytical purposes the most useful concept I developed, to account for the behavior of a representative, was one I shall call his "policy constituency." This may be defined as those interests within his geographical or legal constituency which he perceives to be affected by the policy under consideration. When he regards these interests as actively and homogeneously concerned, they are ordinarily sufficient to determine his public stand. When he sees them as weak, indifferent or divided, other factors come into play.

---

[3] Two studies which do concentrate on specific policies are: Lewis Dexter, "The Representative and His District," *Human Organization*, Vol. 16 (Spring, 1957), 2–13 [Reprinted as Chapter I of the present volume]; and L. E. Gleeck, "96 Congressmen Make up Their Minds," *Public Opinion Quarterly*, Vol. 4 (March, 1940), 3–24.

[4] I selected a committee which is more likely than most to be constituency-oriented. Commonly, representatives from farm areas are anxious to get on this committee to represent their constituency interests, though interviews with Republican members indicate that this generalization would now need modification since recent farm policies have not been notably successful. See the accompanying article by Nicholas A. Masters, "House Committee Assignments," *American Political Science Review*, Vol. 53 (June, 1961), pp. 345–357 [Reprinted as Chapter II of the present volume].

[5] Focused interviews were conducted in March, 1959. An interview guide was followed but it was kept flexible. I wrote as the respondents discussed the questions and typed the responses immediately after the interview. All respondents were guaranteed anonymity.

But he is affected too by the nature of the committee institution within which the policy is being formed.

I. THE HOUSE AGRICULTURE COMMITTEE AND ITS WORK

Organization

In 1958 a Republican President was again faced with a Democratic Congress in a congressional campaign year. The margin of control for Democrats in the House Agriculture Committee was a less-than-comfortable four votes; the split was 19 to 15. The margin in subcommittees was one vote in most cases.

Harold D. Cooley (D–North Carolina) was chairman in 1958, as he had been in every Democratic Congress since 1949. Members did not class him among the strong House committee chairmen, but respected him as fair and honest. W. R. Poage (D–Texas) was vice-chairman. The Agriculture Committee was the only House committee in 1958 to have a vice-chairman and one member suggested that this was due to the chairman's complete and admitted willingness to share the responsibility of leadership with the very forceful, knowledgeable, and capable "Bob" Poage.

The ranking minority member in 1958 was William S. Hill (R–Colorado). Like Cooley, he was not considered a strong leader and it became apparent that Charles Hoeven (R–Iowa) was recognized as the spokesman of the minority viewpoint. Hoeven has since become the ranking minority member.

The principal work units in the House Agriculture Committee are the subcommittees. In 1958 there were 18 subcommittees of two kinds—ten commodity subcommittees and eight special-action subcommittees. The former are more important since they consider legislation designed to solve the many crises for specific commodities. Usually a member is assigned to at least one commodity subcommittee of his choice. The chairman consults the ranking minority leader but has the last word on appointments. Actually few decisions have to be made, since most commodity subcommittees are permanent and their membership is continuing; only the new members need assignments. The size of subcommittees varies considerably (from 12 for tobacco to five for rice), giving the chairman some flexibility in case several members are interested in one commodity.

Finally, the House Agriculture Committee has been able to rely on a small expert staff consisting of a counsel, research director, majority and minority clerks, and five staff assistants.

Representing Agriculture

As might be expected, congressmen from constituencies with significant interests in farm policy make up the membership of the House Agriculture Committee. In 1958 there was but one exception to this rule—Victor Anfuso, Democrat from Brooklyn. Thirteen of the 19 Democrats came from areas where tobacco, cotton, peanuts, and rice are the principal commodities. Republican Committee members came from areas producing corn, hogs, small grain, wheat, and areas where the farming is diversified. Table I shows the geographical distribution of members.

Committee members may be classified by commodities of greatest interest to their constituencies, as in Table II. Commodities receiving price supports are grown in the constituencies of members of all six groups there listed. The *basic* commodities, so labeled by the Agricultural Adjustment Act of 1938, are corn, cotton, tobacco, rice, wheat, and peanuts; price supports have been mandatory for them. An increasing number of *non-basics* have also received price supports, *e.g.*, milk and wool. The "diversified" (mainly non-basics) group often find their interests conflicting with those of representatives in the other groups. They complain that their farmers are at a disadvantage since their non-basics either do not receive price supports or receive less support than the basics; the price supports for the few basics grown do not make up for the deprivation of profits attributable to acreage and marketing controls (the complaint of California cotton farmers); and they must pay higher prices for the basics as well as pay higher taxes.

TABLE I

*Geographical Representation on the House Agriculture Committee**

Land-Use Area	Democrats	Republicans	Totals
Northeast	1	3	4
Appalachian	5	—	5
Southeast	3	—	3
Mississippi Delta	2	—	2
Southern Plains	3	1	4
Corn Belt	2	3	5
Lake States	2	2	4
Northern Plains	—	3	3
Mountain	—	2	2
Pacific	1	1	2
Totals	19	15	34

* Based on the areas presented in Bureau of Census and Department of Agriculture, Bureau of Agricultural Economics, *Land Utilization, A Graphic Summary, 1950* (December, 1952), p. 5.

TABLE II

*Committee Members and Their Constituencies' Commodities**

1. *Corn and Livestock*
   Harrison (R-Nebraska)
   Harvey (R-Indiana)
   Hill (R-Colorado)†
   Hoeven (R-Iowa)
   Polk (D-Ohio)
   Simpson (R-Illinois)†
2. *Cotton and Rice*
   Abernethy (D-Mississippi)
   Albert (D-Oklahoma)
   Gathings (D-Arkansas)
   Grant (D-Alabama)
   Jones (D-Missouri)
   Poage (D-Texas)
   Thompson (D-Texas)
3. *Dairy, Livestock, Small Grains*
   Johnson (D-Wisconsin)
   Knutson (D-Minnesota)
   Quie (R-Minnesota)
   Tewes (R-Wisconsin)
   Williams (R-New York)†

4. *Diversified* (non-basics)
   Anfuso (D-New York)
   Dague (R-Pennsylvania)
   Dixon (R-Utah)
   Hagen (D-California)
   McIntire (R-Maine)
   Teague (R-California)
5. *Tobacco*
   Abbitt (D-Virginia)
   Bass (D-Tennessee)
   Cooley (D-North Carolina)
   Jennings (D-Virginia)
   McMillan (D-South Carolina)
   Matthews (D-Florida)
   Watts (D-Kentucky)
6. *Wheat*
   Belcher (R-Oklahoma)
   Krueger (R-North Dakota)†
   Smith (R-Kansas)

* Members were classified on the basis of their constituencies' principal commodities, as listed in the *Census of Agriculture*, Vol. I, 1956, and interviews with the members.
† These members were not interviewed. Simpson, Williams and Krueger clearly belong to the groups to which they have been assigned. Hill might also have been included in the wheat group.

Almost without exception the six groups show an alignment between commodity interests and party allegiance. The corn and livestock group has five Republicans and one Democrat; the cotton and rice group, seven Democrats; the dairy, livestock, small grains group, two Democrats and three Republicans; the diversified group, four Republicans and two Democrats; the tobacco group, seven Democrats; and the wheat group, three or four Republicans.[6] Consequently, different commodities will ordinarily be favored when different parties are in control. For example, cotton, rice, and tobacco usually receive more attention when the Democrats are a majority in the Committee.[7]

Committee organization has been strongly influenced by the commodity problems in agriculture. First, subcommittees are established to deal with currently critical commodity problems. Sec-

---

[6] Four, if Hill were also assigned to it. Anfuso is assigned to the diversified (non-basics) group because he does not fit elsewhere. The overlap between the corn and livestock, and the dairy, livestock, small grains group is explained by the fact that livestock production is important to both but corn is more important in one and dairy products in the other.

[7] Recent Democratic victories in the middle west have changed the pattern somewhat. There are more Democrats from corn, livestock, and dairy constituencies than previously.

ond, members are assigned to commodity subcommittees on the basis of their constituency interests. Table III shows the high correlation prevailing. Only one Democrat (Anfuso) was assigned to no commodity subcommittee representing producers in his constituency and he has no agricultural production at all in his Brooklyn district, though the poultry trade is important there.[8] Two Republicans (Harrison and Dixon) found themselves on subcommittees of little or no concern to their constituencies. Significantly both of these members were identified by other members as being supporters of Secretary Benson's recommendations.

Party considerations dictate that some members must be on subcommittees of no concern to their constituencies: there must be Republicans on the cotton subcommittee and Democrats on the wheat subcommittee. For the most part, members who have little interest in the proceedings are expected either to remain silent during hearings or not to attend.

The Work of the Committee—1958

In 1958 serious problems existed for cotton, rice, wheat, dairy products, and corn. These crises involved four of the six commodity groups shown in Table II, leaving the tobacco and diversified groups with little direct and positive interest in the legislation. The Committee decided to employ the "omnibus" procedure so as to get as much backing for the bill as possible. Apparently the leadership on both sides agreed to this, though some Republicans complained about such obvious "logrolling."

The work of the Committee proceeded according to plan with the cotton, dairy products, livestock and feed grains, and wheat subcommittees holding extensive hearings. The result was a 62-page bill (H. R. 12954) which included eight titles. In addition to titles designed to solve immediate crises, titles to extend certain popular programs were added so as to increase the bill's dubious chances of passage.[9]

The Committee voted on June 13 to report H. R. 12954 favorably, but on June 25, the Rules Committee's motion to debate

---

[8] Anfuso almost monopolized the Committee hearings on the extension of the Agricultural Trade Development and Assistance Act, since many New York City firms were testifying. His activity in these hearings provided unexpected evidence of constituency-representative relationships.

[9] The titles were: I—Foreign Trade; II—Rice; III—Cotton; IV—Wool; V—Wheat; VI—Milk; VII—Feed Grains; and VIII—Miscellaneous. Titles I and IV in particular were included because they were popular programs.

TABLE III

*Constituency Interests and Commodity Subcommittee Assignments**

Member†	Major Agricultural Interests In Constituency	Commodity Subcommittees
Democrats		
Poage	Cotton, Livestock, Peanuts	Cotton; Livestock & Feed Grains (C)
Grant	Cotton, Peanuts, Wood Products	Forests (C); Peanuts
Gathings	Cotton, Rice, Soybeans	Cotton (C); Rice; Soybeans-Oilseeds
McMillan	Cotton, Tobacco, Peanuts	Forests; Peanuts (C); Tobacco
Abernethy	Cotton	Cotton; Dairy Products (C); Soybeans-Oilseeds
Albert	Cotton, Livestock	Livestock and Feed Grains; Peanuts; Wheat (C)
Abbitt	Tobacco, Peanuts	Tobacco (C); Peanuts
Polk	Feed Grains, Livestock, Dairy	Dairy Products; Tobacco
Thompson	Rice, Cotton, Peanuts	Rice (C); Poultry-Eggs
Jones	Cotton, Livestock, Soybeans	Rice; Soybeans-Oilseeds (C); Wheat
Watts	Tobacco, Feed Grains, Seeds	Tobacco; Wheat
Hagen	Cotton, Alfalfa Seed, Potatoes, Fruit	Cotton; Soybeans-Oilseeds
Johnson	Dairy, Forests, Livestock	Dairy Products; Forests; Poultry-Eggs
Anfuso	None	Poultry-Eggs
Bass	Tobacco, Cotton	Tobacco; Wheat
Knutson	Wheat, Dairy, Feed Grains	Dairy Products
Jennings	Tobacco, Livestock	Livestock and Feed Grains; Tobacco; Wheat
Matthews	Tobacco, Peanuts, Vegetables	Livestock and Feed Grains; Tobacco
Republicans		
Hoeven	Feed Grains, Livestock	Livestock and Feed Grains; Soybeans-Oilseeds
Simpson	Feed Grains, Livestock	Cotton; Livestock and Feed Grains; Soybeans-Oilseeds; Tobacco
Dague	Tobacco, Truck Farming, Poultry, Dairy	Tobacco; Wheat
Harvey	Feed Grains, Livestock	Livestock & Feed Grains; Soybeans-Oilseeds
Belcher	Wheat	Cotton; Peanuts; Wheat
McIntire	Forests, Poultry, Potatoes	Forests; Poultry-Eggs; Tobacco
Williams	Dairy, Truck Farming	Dairy Products; Rice
Harrison	Feed Grains, Livestock	Peanuts; Poultry-Eggs
Dixon	Wheat, Potatoes, Small Grain, Sugar Beets	Forests; Poultry-Eggs
Smith	Wheat	Peanuts; Wheat
Krueger	Wheat, Small Grains	Rice; Wheat
Teague	Vegetables, Fruit, Small Grains, Cotton	Cotton; Forests
Tewes	Dairy, Tobacco, Livestock	Dairy Products; Tobacco
Quie	Dairy, Feed Grains, Livestock	Dairy Products; Tobacco

* The major interests were deduced from the *Census of Agriculture, 1954,* Vol. 1, 1956, and from interviews with members.
† Members listed according to committee rank. Chairman Cooley, whose principal interests were tobacco, cotton and poultry, and William Hill, whose principal interests were wheat, feed grains, and sugar beets, were *ex officio* members of all subcommittees by virtue of their positions as chairman and ranking minority member, respectively.

the bill (H. Res. 609) was lost in the House, thereby defeating the bill.[10] Shortly afterword, on June 27, the Senate passed its farm bill (S. 4071) and sent it to the House. The House Agriculture Committee amended S. 4071 to bring it into line with their previously defeated bill and reported it on August 4. On August 6, Chairman Cooley moved that the House suspend the rules and pass S. 4071 as amended. The motion received a simple majority, but not the two-thirds vote required for such a motion, and so S. 4071 was also defeated. The House Agriculture Committee made a final attempt to modify their amendments to S. 4071, and on August 14 Chairman Cooley once again moved that the House suspend the rules and pass the bill as amended. This time S. 4071 was accepted after a short debate by a voice vote, and on August 28 it was signed into law by the President. (P.L. 85-835).

In general, H. R. 12954 solved the cotton, rice, and feed grain problems to the satisfaction of Committee representatives from those areas and they were apparently willing to trade their support. Their modifications of S. 4071 were attempts to bring that bill closer to the provisions of H. R. 12954 for these commodities. The wheat and dairy titles in H. R. 12954 had little support outside the groups representing those interests. Though the Secretary of Agriculture and the American Farm Bureau Federation had objections to all titles in H. R. 12954, their most serious protests were directed against the dairy and wheat titles. Cotton and rice representatives were willing to drop these objectionable titles when the bill reached the House floor in order to save the sections of the bill they wanted most. Neither wheat nor dairy was included in S. 4071.[11]

S. 4071 was more in line with the Secretary of Agriculture's recommendations for fewer controls and lower supports.[12] Its ultimate passage, even with the modifications to bring it closer to H. R. 12954, was generally conceded to have been a victory for the Eisenhower Administration.

---

[10] The reported vote in Committee was 21–10. The House vote on H. Res. 609 was 171–214.

[11] The dairy situation illustrates the in-fighting. Evidently the cotton and rice Democrats were opposed to any dairy legislation. Hearings were held but only after long delays. The Secretary of Agriculture's objections to the "self-help" bill proposed by dairy representatives were given the spotlight of a full committee hearing rather than a less sensational subcommittee hearing. The title which resulted was developed at the last minute and had little support, even among the national dairy groups.

[12] See *The Congressional Digest*, Vol. 37 (March, 1958), pp. 75–7, for details of the Administration's recommendations.

II. MEMBER DISCUSSION AND EVALUATION

The vote on the rule to debate H. R. 12954 was split along party lines (Democrats for, Republicans against) with the major exception of urban Democrats. Of the 59 Democrats who indicated opposition (either by voting against, pairing against, or answering the *Congressional Quarterly* poll), 47 were from metropolitan or mid-urban districts. Several Committee members charged that the opponents of H. R. 12954 had tried to identify it as a "consumers' tax" bill in order to win the support of the urban representatives. The Committee vote, also split along party lines, is indicated in Table IV.

TABLE IV

House Agriculture Committee Vote on House Resolution 609*

Democrats		Republicans	
Yea	*Nay*	*Yea*	*Nay*
Cooley	Hagen	Harvey	Hill
Poage		Smith	Hoeven
Grant		Quie	Simpson
Gathings			Dague
Abernethy			Belcher
Albert			Harrison
Abbitt			Dixon
Polk			Krueger
Thompson			Teague
Jones			Tewes
Watts			
Johnson	Not Voting		Not Voting
Anfuso	or Paired		or Paired
Bass	———		———
Knutson	McMillan		McIntire
Jennings	(paired for)		(paired against)
Matthews			Williams

	Totals		
	Yea	*Nay*	*Not Voting or Paired*
Democrats	18	1	1
Republicans	3	11	2
Committee	21	12	3

* Compiled from data in the *Congressional Quarterly Almanac*, 85th Cong., 2d sess., 1958, pp. 392–3. Members are listed according to committee rank.

Opinion of the Legislation

Members were asked in interviews for their opinions of the legislation, both H. R. 12954 and S. 4071. Two conclusions emerged. First, there was little unqualified opinion in support of either bill.

Of the 30 members interviewed in regard to H. R. 12954, three considered it good, five said that most of it was good, fifteen were equivocal (some sections good, some sections bad); and seven considered it poor. Of the 28 who were interviewed in regard to S. 4071, four labeled it good, eight thought it "mostly good", fourteen were equivocal, and only two considered it bad. Table V distributes the opinions by commodity group.

Several comments are appropriate. The commodity groups can be classified into the principal beneficiaries of H. R. 12954 (corn and livestock, cotton and rice) who enjoyed broad support; the champions of controversial titles who were also directly and positively affected (dairy, wheat); and the onlookers who were not involved or only indirectly affected (diversified, tobacco). Examined in this way the most favorable opinions were offered by those most affected: six of the eight "good" or "mostly good" responses came from representatives of the main beneficiaries. The middle category, concerned with controversial titles, tended to be suspicious of the

TABLE V

Member Opinion of the Legislation, by Commodity Group*

Commodity Interest	H. R. 12954				S. 4071			
	Good	Mostly Good	Equivocal	Bad	Good	Mostly Good	Equivocal	Bad
Corn and Livestock								
Democrats†			1					
Republicans		1	1	1	1	2		
Cotton and Rice								
Democrats	3	2	2		1		6	
Dairy, Livestock, Small Grains								
Democrats			2					2
Republicans				2		2		
Diversified								
Democrats#			1	1		1		
Republicans		1	2	1	2	1	1	
Tobacco								
Democrats		1	6			1	6	
Wheat								
Republicans				2		1	1	
Totals	3	5	15	7	4	8	14	2

* In answer to the question, "Did you consider H. R. 12954 (S. 4071) a good bill, a bad bill, something in between, or just what?"
† Polk not interviewed on S. 4071.
# Anfuso not interviewed on S. 4071.

bill. Both dairy and wheat members suggested that their titles would be sacrificed once the bill got to the floor.

Though it might be expected that Democratic tobacco represen-tatives would actively support a bill from a Democratic committee, they were equivocal about H. R. 12954. On the basis of such com-ments as, "Frankly, I didn't think it would help very much," indi-cations were that the tobacco representatives did little more than vote for the rule to debate. Nothing in either bill was of primary concern to their constituencies.

The diversified group offered very little favorable comment on H. R. 12954 and only one of them, a Democrat, voted for the bill on the floor. Once again, the bill gave very little direct, positive benefit to the group's constituencies though, as will appear, it soon became evident that they did have a constituency interest in the bill.

Opinion on the second bill shows a party split. Though the Republicans had less direct constituency interest in the bill (ex-cept for the corn and livestock group which considered it "good" or "mostly good"), nine of eleven committee Republicans considered the bill "good" or "mostly good." The Democrats were more quali-fied, with many of the cotton and rice group stating, "It was the best we could get." The tobacco group was no more enthusiastic about S. 4071 than they had been about H. R. 12954. Republicans obviously considered this a better bill because it was not a clear-cut victory for Democratic commodities. Though Republican com-modities had not fared too well, the Democrats were not able to write the legislation with a free hand. Republicans from diversified farming areas were much more satisfied with S. 4071 since it re-duced controls and price supports.

Second, the members' opinions, not only of the bill as a whole but also of specific titles, were influenced by their constituencies' interests. When asked what they liked most and least about the bills, members whose constituencies were directly affected replied that they liked best those sections which were designed to solve commodity problems in their own constituencies. On H. R. 12954, four from the cotton and rice group mentioned those titles, one from corn and livestock, both members from wheat, and two from dairy. The same held true for S. 4071.

Members were reluctant to say what sections they liked least. Some spoke in general terms, mentioning the over-all cost, the politics involved, the issues not faced, etc. Only the dairy title drew much critical comment. Ten members (six Democrats and four

Republicans) suggested that the dairy title was not good legislation and was harmful to the bill. The most numerous response for S. 4071 was that no sections were "least liked."

As a follow-up question, members were asked which sections had beneficial or adverse effects on their constituencies. Once again, the replies supported the conclusion. In discussing H. R. 12954 all groups directly affected by the bill mentioned most often, as being beneficial, those titles of greatest interest to their respective constituencies. The most frequent response from the two least affected groups (diversified, tobacco) was that no section was beneficial. For S. 4071, those most affected were the cotton and rice and corn and livestock members. They all mentioned the titles of interest to their constituencies as most beneficial. Other groups either chose some section which was of tangential importance or stated that none was beneficial. Hardly any member admitted that any sections adversely affected his constituency.

Concepts of Representation

Members were also asked to discuss what they relied on in their action on the first bill (H. R. 12954)—independent judgment, constituency wishes, a combination of factors, or something else. The results are summarized in the following conclusions.

First, a majority of members stated that in making up their minds they relied on independent judgment or a combination of factors (22 of 27 interviewed on this question). There was no important difference between Republicans and Democrats on this question. (See Table VI.)

Second, analysis by commodity groups reveals that those groups least positively affected by the legislation most often responded that they relied on "independent judgment." But the record shows that the diversified group did act to benefit constituency interests.

The members' replies must be weighed after taking into consideration both the importance of the legislation to their constituencies and the effect of their action for their constituencies. Of the ten who said that they followed independent judgment, four were from the tobacco group and three from the diversified. One other member from the diversified group said he supported his party in this instance but usually relied on independent judgment.

Despite these replies, two observations are pertinent: (a) all tobacco representatives who relied on independent judgment nevertheless voted in support of their party[13] and (b) the voting action (against the bill) of the diversified group tended to favor the best interests of their farmers—as they themselves described these in-

TABLE VI

Bases Asserted for Action on H. R. 12954*

Commodity Groups	Independent Judgment	Constituency Wishes	Combination	Other (Party)
Corn and Livestock†				
Republicans	1		2	
Cotton and Rice				
Democrats	1	2	3	1
Dairy, Livestock, Small Grains				
Democrats			2	
Republicans	1		1	
Diversified #				
Democrats	1			
Republicans	2		1	1°
Tobacco**				
Democrats	4		2	
Wheat				
Republicans		1	1	
Totals	10	3	12	2

* In answer to the question, "What did you rely on in your action on H. R. 12954— (1) independent judgment, (2) the wishes of your constituency, (3) perhaps a combination of these, or (4) something else?"
† Polk not included.
# Anfuso not included.
° Usually relied on independent judgment.
** Cooley not included.

terests. As one member put it: "Benson is an asset to me. I agree with him and there is nothing political involved because his philosophy is good for my farmers." All of the diversified group who responded "independent judgment" indicated that a continued program of high supports and controls for *basic* commodities was bad for their farmers, who grow principally non-basics.

The other three members who mentioned independent judgment were from the corn and livestock group (an admitted Administration and American Farm Bureau Federation supporter—he thought

---

[13] Some tobacco representatives noted the importance of the wheat and feed grain titles for their constituencies. They thought these might eventually affect their livestock farmers (using the slogan, "cheap feed means cheap livestock"). Many of their farmers relied on wheat as an alternative crop.

their programs would be best for his constituency in the long run);
the cotton and rice group (a generally inactive member who "didn't
have too much information from my constituency"); and a dairy
Republican who said, "I only had this chance to vote against the
cotton deal."

Third, those groups most directly and positively affected by the
legislation relied on a "combination" or on "constituency wishes."
Replies of these members indicated they were well aware of the
problems involved in representing *all* interests in their legal constituency on such a piece of legislation.

Nine of the twelve responses indicating a reliance on a combination of factors came from members whose constituency interests
were directly affected by the legislation. Some of the most detailed
analyses of the process of representation were offered by senior
members who replied that representation on policy was not a simple choice between independent judgment on the one hand and
constituency wishes on the other. Typical of the extended remarks
are the following:

> I understand the problems of that area [his district]. I know
> what is best for the farm section. And I think that the majority
> in my area reflect my views.

> I am in close contact with them at all times. I meet with
> them, ask their opinions on all matters. I don't use polls. I
> know the people. I vote my convictions and hope that they
> [constituents] will follow these. They expect this—unless a real
> organized group is excited about something. They generally
> expect that you have more information than they do.

> I am sent here as a representative of 600,000 people. They
> are supposed to be voting on all the legislation. I try to follow
> my constituents—to ignore them would be a breach of trust—
> but I use my judgment often because they are misinformed. I
> know that they would vote as I do if they had the facts that
> I have. A lot of people expect you to use your judgment.

> Under our form of government you have to rely on a com-
> bination. If I know the views of the constituents I will vote
> these views—as a representative, I must—but when I don't know
> I substitute my best judgment. There is not one case in a
> hundred where I do know their views fully. I figure if they
> knew what I know . . . they would understand my vote. Most
> of us vote what we believe is sound, based on the information
> and our judgment. This can be changed if the people express

themselves clearly enough. This, however, is improbable and doesn't happen very often.

Even the junior members in these groups had definite ideas about how their constituencies were affected:

> I thought that it was a good bill and then I thought that I could go ahead in view of the referendum and support the bill. If there weren't a referendum [included in the bill], I would have checked [with the constituency] but I felt I could go ahead. On some legislation I hear from the people and rely on their judgment . . . [after probing for specifics]. On labor legislation I rely on groups in my area since I don't know too much about it.

> I depend on a combination. I should educate them; they don't really care how you vote. I make up my mind and then temper it with what the people want. After all, I think as they do.

One member who relied on constituency wishes was frank in explaining his position:

> I vote for what I think will be the best economic interests of my people. Throughout the years I have gained an idea of what those best interests are. This is the way representative government should work.

Fourth, an analysis of members' extended discussions coupled with an examination of their interest and activity on the legislation reveals the importance of a concept of "constituency" in the action of members.

Those who purported to rely on independent judgment were of three types: members who had no commodities to represent on the legislation but opposed the bill—an action evidently in the best interests of their constituencies; members in the tobacco group who supported their party but had no direct interest in the legislation (though some expressed indirect interest); and members who had a constituency interest in the bill but said they relied on independent judgment in their actions, though this did not seem the case in fact.

Those relying on a combination of factors argued that defining constituency interests was no simple, straightforward interpretation. In their subcommittee work on the bill, however, these members—

the most active of all who worked on the bill—evinced a shrewd conception of their constituencies' commodity interests.

Clearly, more evidence than the self-explained motivation for voting is relevant in appraising a representative's action and in interpreting his conception of representation: his work in subcommittee on acceptable compromises, *e.g.*, or his interrogation of witnesses in hearings, or his part in the Committee's executive sessions. The data gathered here from such successive stages of action as these tend to confirm Eulau's typology of "delegates," "trustees" and "politicos," and his suggestion that a representative might act in more than one of these roles.[14]

Knowing the Constituency

In order to discover some of the relationships and means of communication between the representative and his constituency, members were asked how they knew their constituency wishes on H. R. 12954. Table VII summarizes the responses. The most im-

TABLE VII
Methods for Determining Constituency Wishes*

Method	Democrats† Mentioning	Republicans Mentioning	Totals
Just know it (live there, sense it)	8	5	13
Meetings	6	3	9
Correspondence	4	3	7
Questionnaire	1	2	3
Newspaper	—	2	2
Testimony	1	1	2
Advisory Committee (to advise on agricultural policy)	—	1	1
Telephone calls	—	1	1
Visitors	1	—	1

* In answer to the questions, "How did you find out what your constituency wishes were on this bill?" and "Are there other ways you use to tap opinion and get information about your constituency's agricultural interests? What are these?"
† Does not include Cooley, Polk, or Anfuso.

portant method, members said, was a type of individual "sounding-board" procedure. Some of those mentioning "intuition" or "sixth sense" observed that their own identity with the culture or mood of the district made it natural that they would know their neighbors' wishes. Responses which typified the members' analyses were:

You are in a position to know, of course, on a lot of things. I live there—there are many things I just know. I don't have

---

[14] Above, note 2.

to ask anybody. There are very few bills where I have to guess. If I did, I wouldn't be here as the representative.

I am a native of ——. I get letters—though I don't get very much mail. I have sent out questionnaires but I don't now. It is just the fact that I know and I can judge their needs.

Some of the members pointed out that they were farmers and reasoned that this gave them a special ability to know the needs of fellow farmers. Others indicated that their familiarity with the district through campaigns or frequent visits made it possible for them to know. Either way, they were identifying a "policy constituency."

Though such responses suggest that the representative has a concept of his constituency interests on legislation, there is still no reliable evidence as to how he develops it. But whether he gets it by divination, intuition or instruction, it appears to dominate his behavior as a representative where its outline is sharp.

III. CONCLUSIONS

The conclusions suggested by this case study can be set forth somewhat more systematically as follows:

1. If a policy measure is seen to affect substantial interests in a representative's legal constituency, then he will rely on his perception of the interests affected (his "policy constituency") when he acts at the working level (usually the subcommittee) in regard to this measure.

A. Institutional arrangements affect his ability to represent his policy constituency. The House Agriculture Committee is organized to allow a maximum of constituency-oriented representation.

B. The representative has a "sense" of constituency interests drawn from first-hand experience in the "legal" constituency and this "sense" influences his perception of a policy constituency.

C. Party allegiance is an important modifying factor.

(1) The legislative majority party may demand a vote in support of its policies. The legislative minority party may demand a vote in opposition to the majority's policies. The Administration may press for support for its stands.

(2) Representatives, whether or not affected by the legislation, tend to support their party's position more as the action

moves beyond the basic working level, and most at the final vote.

2. If a measure is seen to have little or no direct effect on interests in a representative's legal constituency, then he will tend more readily to look to his political party for a cue when he acts in regard to this measure.

A. The representative will tend the more to suggest that he relies on "independent judgment," the less his constituency's interests are seen to be directly or positively affected by a policy.

B. He will vote in support of his political party but will not actively support the policy in other ways if his constituency interests are not perceived to be affected.

A final comment suggests a further and more tentative generalization. In this case study it became necessary to reconcile actions of certain members who seemed motivated by different forces at different action points. Table IV shows that 11 Republicans voted or paired against the rule to debate H. R. 12954. Of these, seven were from constituencies which had a direct, positive interest in the legislation. Four of the seven were particularly active in effecting compromises in titles of major concern to their constituencies. They were apparently satisfied with the respective titles, yet had no difficulty in rationalizing opposition to the entire bill on the House floor. Further, while members of the diversified group apparently did little to obstruct the work on H. R. 12954 at the subcommittee level (thereby following an apparent norm for Agriculture Committee members), it nevertheless became obvious that some of them worked actively to defeat the bill on the House floor.[15]

An adequate concept of representation should account for a total action pattern, not merely a final vote. The representative on the House Agriculture Committee can view his composite role retrospectively as one in which he has taken several separate actions to make up a total pattern in regard to the omnibus farm legislation. He also can recognize that on different occasions he felt differing demands upon him in his several capacities, as a member of a party, a representative of a constituency, a member of a committee, of a Congress, of interest groups, etc. He was able to reconcile,

---

[15] Minority party members are more likely to feel conflicting demands since the majority party's commodities will probably be favored. Some majority party members will find, however, that they are not as directly concerned with the legislation and so will be less actively involved at all stages of action.

compromise or avoid some of the inherent conflicts in these demands, at least in part, because of the multiple action points. Examples of such reconciliations in this case study justify a final hypothesis which merits separate study:

3. If a representative has a multiplicity of conflicting demands upon him in any series of actions on policy, he can satisfy many of them, over a period of time, because of the multiplicity of action points at successive stages in the legislative process.

VIII

CONGRESSMEN AND THE MAKING
OF MILITARY POLICY*

Lewis Anthony Dexter

ROLE CONCEPTIONS OF CONGRESSMEN

This report is concerned with the way in which congressmen, especially those assigned to committees dealing with military matters, interpret their role and status, and what they assert and affirm about their exercise of influence over military policy and military men.

The conceptions held by a group of men about their role, status, responsibility, and influence presumably have some sort of relationship to what they actually do—but there is no reason for supposing that the relationship is direct and unequivocal.[1] Men may, con-

---

* This paper was based upon 100 interviews, chiefly with members of congressional committees having military responsibility and other leading congressmen, and with a few committee staff members, administrative assistants, and legislative liaison personnel from the Department of Defense. The majority of these interviews were undertaken under contract with the Center for International Studies, Massachusetts Institute of Technology, under a Carnegie Corporation grant; others were for the Advisory Committee on Civil Defense, National Research Council. The writer had previously conducted 400 interviews with congressmen, lobbyists, and prominent constituents on foreign trade issues, often touching on "defense essentiality." This other study appears in part in R. Bauer, I. Pool, and L. Dexter, *American Business and Public Policy* (New York: Atherton Press, 1963). See also, "The Representative and His District," reprinted as Chapter I of this volume. An emphatic disclaimer must be made of any responsibility of anyone but myself for any views or findings stated or implied herein.

[1] This point probably ought to be a perfectly obvious one, but I was delayed in interpreting the results of interviews conducted in 1955–57 because it took me five years fully to see that I was not reporting on how congressmen affect military policy but simply on *how congressmen define* their role and responsibility in regard to military policy.

Were this simply a personal error of my own, it would hardly be worth commenting upon, but I suspect that whether relying upon documents or interviews, a good many reports about politics, especially about Congress, fall into a similar error—role definition, attitude, or orientation, is interpreted as though

sciously or unconsciously,[2] emphasize or underemphasize their influence and importance; they may emphasize one aspect of their activity and underemphasize another. Tentatively, it seems reasonable to suppose that the way in which men define situations has some effect on how they behave in those situations; this point (that men's definitions of situations tend to have real and significant consequences) presumably is just as important in studying the congressional work-roles as in studying any other social behavior.

MILITARY POLICY IS NOT CONSIDERED

Congressmen interviewed generally indicate that they have little tendency to raise or consider questions of military policy *in terms of its meaning for some national or international political objective or goal.* By military policy is meant specific decisions about interpreting or handling weapons, personnel, appropriations, missions, organization, administration. In fact, during the 1946–57 period, few examples could be found where congressional committees created any impression of seriously evaluating decisions about weapons, appropriations, personnel, missions, organization, or administration in terms of national or international goals or objectives. The great difficulty in making this statement is the obvious fact that here, as elsewhere in politics, there is a rhetoric of justification which purports to explain what was decided in terms of high and serious considerations quite regardless of the relevance of these considera-

---

it threw *direct* light on the substantive exercise of influence or formation of policy. An extreme, but obvious, parallel is this: a whole series of interviews with quarrelling husbands and wives would not necessarily tell us what happens when spouses disagree. What it would tell us—and an extremely important thing to know—is how husbands and wives of certain sorts interpret their roles, responsibilities, etc. But it is important to know, too, what such sources do not *by themselves* yield.

[2] I am certain that all the congressmen (not necessarily all the staff assistants or Department of Defense personnel) I interviewed were "sincere" in expressing the definition of their stated role—of course a different situation or a different interviewing technique might have stimulated other, contradictory, but equally sincere definitions of role. There has been so little experimentation on the conscious modification of interview technique in the interviewing of elite personnel that one simply has to guess as to how "representative" of the range of alternative roles which an individual may assume the particular responses in a given interview are. I would guess—partly on the basis of other interviews on other subjects with some of the same informants, partly on the basis of direct personal acquaintance with some of them and personal acquaintance with many who have worked with a number of them, and partly on "intuition"—that the responses I use are representative.

tions to the decision-making process. I have not come across any major example where the rhetoric of justification seems to reflect much predecision policy analysis; nor have I found any other evidence during the 1946–57 period where there seems to have been much congressional concern with the over-all policy implications of military decisions.

On the other hand, instances where Congress has *appeared* to concern itself with over-all military policy seem generally to fall into one of the following categories: (1) Those where Congress feels it is able to judge between clamoring claimants—usually different military services—and give one or another of them a larger slice of the available pie. (2) Where congressmen are concerned with some local situation, usually an employment situation. Congressional support, especially support in the House of Representatives, of what Huntington has called "strategic monism,"[3] consisted largely of the congressional assumption of a judicial role, tempered by the pressure of various local contractor and employment interests—all within a framework of verbal "toughness." This is stance rather than a policy.

Congressmen also occasionally wish to mollify widespread personnel complaints (*e.g.* those emanating from the National Guard mobilization in 1961). And, of course, congressmen have personal concerns of their own (*e.g.*, personal loyalty to the Marine Corps). And, naturally, they always have straight constituent interests to defend (*e.g.*, preserving specific military installations in local areas).[4]

---

[3] Samuel P. Huntington, "Radicalism and Conservatism in National Defense Policy," *Journal of International Affairs*, VIII (1954), 206–33. This exceptionally brilliant analysis of the politics of national defense differs from the present report in one significant respect—it works back from the consequences of significant decisions to presumed ideologies and therefore takes seriously the justifications given in more or less formal statements for the record as to the reasons why a position has been taken. This may be a perfectly valid approach to political behavior, but in the instant case, at least, it seems to the writer that it misleads, much as the effort to categorize office-holders in terms of what they happen on some particular issue to say about "home rule" would mislead. Unfortunately, in terms of the available data and the present state of political science knowledge, there is no clear reason for choosing between Huntington's approach and others.

[4] R. H. Dawson, "Congressional Innovation and Intervention in Defense Policy: Legislative Authorization of Weapons Systems," *American Political Science Review*, LXVI (1962), 42–57 (reprinted as Chapter X of the present volume), reports a congressional effort (in 1959 and following years) to assume more systematic responsibility. Unfortunately, my study and interviews were entirely confined to the pre-1959 period; however, I strongly suspect that what Dawson reports could be interpreted more precisely in terms of the role which

POLICY ANALYSIS: MILITARY VERSUS CIVILIAN

The attitudes and responses to military policy-making of members of the congressional committees concerned with military policy contrasted with those of members of committees concerned with foreign economic policy. Also, members not on key committees in either field showed a similar difference between these fields. In general, the broad aspects of military policy are not considered. In the tax field, members of Ways and Means often consider the presumptive effect of particular tax legislation upon national economic policy, but military decisions are generally treated by the relevant committees as independent of broader policy decisions.

This need not be the case, for it has not always been the case. In the 1930's, available evidence suggests, Ross Collins of Mississippi, for many years a member, sometime chairman, of the Subcommittee on Military Appropriations of the House Appropriations Committee, did in fact stimulate research and development in tank warfare—and he did a great deal to keep the possibilities of tank warfare before the informed public.[5] In fact, Collins' impact in the United States may be compared with that of the military

---

Congress from time to time does assume as an arbiter between technologists, discussed below; in the absence of such arbitrament and of such local pressures (as to which congressmen typically do regard themselves as experts) the episode would not have occurred.

I suspect, also, that Dawson in a sense is dealing with the congressmen's public and overt picture of themselves—the kind of picture which is likely to be presented in reports and speeches—whereas I am dealing with the private picture (the covert culture) of Congress. There is nothing which of necessity makes a man's private picture of himself or a covert culture "truer" than the public picture; both must be taken into account, and, if they are different, may suggest further investigation.

However, it is possibly relevant that in 1955–56, a distinguished scholar, familiar with congressional action on military matters in recent years, initially challenged emphatically my point that Congress in fact had very little influence on military policy. He stated that he had a list of some fourteen areas in which Congress had been influential. But after he reconsidered the point, he stated he had to agree that Congress had either given a little more or a little less than the Department of Defense asked or decided between competing technologists, but had not, in fact, undertaken any initiative.

[5] On Collins, see Frank C. Hanaghen, "The U.S. Army," *Harper's Magazine* (December, 1940), esp. pp. 9–13, and Ross A. Collins, "Do We Want a Mass Army?" *Reader's Digest* (June, 1941), pp. 1–9. It is greatly to be hoped that, with the present emphasis on oral history and on congressional behavior, some foundation will have the imagination and initiative, while some of the participants are still alive, to undertake interviews which would permit testing more accurately such matters as the assertions made in the text about Collins.

critics Fuller and Liddell-Hart in Britain and the military officer, de Gaulle, in France. (It may now be largely forgotten that de Gaulle's first claim to fame was as a theorist of mobile warfare.)

In addition, in two particular areas, the Subcommittee on Military Operations of the House Government Operations Committee during the 1950's played a similar part. For a number of years, serious thinking about *civil* defense, its mission, purpose, and meaning, has been kept alive by that subcommittee, especially by its chairman, Chet Holifield (D.-Calif.); it is probably no exaggeration to say that if it were not for the pressure of the Holifield subcommittee on the administration, the whole subject of civil defense would have lapsed into a patronage "boondoggle." Despite the word "civil," "civil defense" is in fact an item in military policy[6]—but it is quite possible that it was very psychologically important for congressional activity that civil defense was called "civil" and until 1961 had a "civil" administration. If so, this would be crucial in terms of the rest of our argument.[7] Other congressmen were probably more willing to accept Congressman Holifield's leadership here because civil defense seemed civilian; they did not think that they were infringing on military technology.[8]

Particularly under the chairmanship of Congressman Riehlman (R.-N.Y.), but during the entire decade of the fifties, the same subcommittee has also been actively concerned with, and has probably stimulated, intelligent action about the optimal use of scientists in defense research, a matter which is at least on the fringes of military policy.

---

[6] The well-known writings of Herman Kahn make this point from one standpoint. From another—emphasis on "Defense Means Protection"—I make the same point in an article by that title, published in the *American Scholar*, XXIV (Summer, 1955), 299–308.

[7] The argument that congressmen are timid about invading the area of the military specialist; see below.

[8] Of course, this fact has been by no means an unalloyed benefit to civil defense. Some of those who advocated the action which actually took place in 1961—the transfer of civil defense to the Department of Defense—supported it partly because they thought a military identification would provide it with more prestige. However, part of the objective which advocates of the transfer had in mind was not achieved when the Thomas Subcommittee of the House Appropriations Committee, the subcommittee dealing with independent offices, which was accustomed to deal very harshly with civil defense budget requests, succeeded in keeping responsibility for the civil defense budget. Supporters of civil defense had hoped that the responsibility would be transferred to the Military Appropriations Subcommittee which is inclined to be much more generous and less critical.

Congress has in the past and perhaps has now some influence on military policy. But it is purely negative, probably as a consequence of dogmatic doctrines. Probably Congress made the adequate fortification of Guam by the Franklin Roosevelt Administration impossible, and perhaps that failure to fortify Guam encouraged Japanese militarists.[9]

THE ARMED SERVICES COMMITTEE "IS PRIMARILY A REAL ESTATE COMMITTEE"

In general, it was necessary to avoid the phrase "policy" in interviews on military policy; it was too ambiguous, although it was not too ambiguous in 1953–56 interviews with congressmen on foreign economic "policy." At that time, it was rarely necessary to explain to congressmen what was meant when we came to discuss policy implications; congressional thinking about the tariff and reciprocal trade have been structured in terms of policy by a history of discussion and communications within and outside Congress.[10]

One congressman, who was probably more concerned about the apparent absence of concern with military policy in the Congress than any other member of a relevant committee with whom I talked, said:

> If I were talking to a new member of [my committee], I'd say that the main problem is to pinpoint responsibility at the White House and the boards [the various councils and committees concerned with national security] for policy determination. You can't really tell who does determine it; it moves into DOD [Department of Defense] and each of the three services, and you have a feeling [that], as relates to appropriations, there is not any unity. The capable men in each area are just trying to push for more for their services which is natural, but it means they think more in terms of how to spend more and more money than they do in terms of really thinking out a strategy that would more successfully justify these great appropriations.
> In our hearings, I tried for purposes of communication to do some research to determine this matter of policy. What were

---

[9] Similarly, it is possible that the efforts of a congressman like Kastenmeier (D.-Wis.) to have the Congress, as a national policy, renounce chemical warfare, may indirectly have inhibiting effects upon support for chemical warfare.

[10] In fact, in these interviews, because I was chiefly (though not exclusively) interested in communications, I often found it necessary to steer informants away (sometimes quite sharply as with the late Senator George of Georgia) from discussion of policy toward consideration of communications.

they thinking of? Did they anticipate [this or that] . . . ? What had they in mind to accomplish?

Then, of course, you wonder about what actually the policy of the Congress is. . . . It's never been clear to me what direction there is in the matter. . . . Policy is supposed to be wrapped up [by the Joint Chiefs] under certain restrictions, but you wonder sometimes if the chairman of the Joint Chiefs knows what is going on in the minds of other chiefs . . . .

After our lengthy hearings, I wonder to what extent members of Congress . . . bring together sufficient staff to get a real perspective. *Most questions even in what are called policy hearings are directed really towards production. This is true equally of off-the-record hearings.* People are asked questions about specific manpower requirements, et cetera, not about general policy.

It does look as though the congressional committees operate in a vacuum. It comes right back to the tragic lack of time for reflection and study on the part of members of the Congress. *So maybe they don't get clear in their minds what policy is.*

. . . I believe there should be some serious policy thinking on the ideological side. It should relate the military to State and USIA . . . .

So far as I know you are the only person in my [more than eight years of] *service in Congress, or outside, who has been making any effort to delve into these problems.* I called on several people in various government departments, DOD, the committee staff, et cetera, to try to help me to frame questions to get at these policy issues [but did not get much help]. Symington's subcommittee is concerned with program and production—not too much with big policy issues.

I can see enormous possibilities in a very careful study of the problem. Could we move into new types of weapons and a future type of defense? How can we become more potent ideologically? [The military] lack direction. We [the Congress] must assume responsibility for policy determination.

More typical was the response of a much more influential member of the House Committee on Armed Services—who, when I tried to explain that I was trying to find out what Congress did do or could do on policy said:

What the hell is the point of that? What would you do with it? I don't see that any public service could be performed by it. You can't find anything particular to say. In fact, how do we [members] know what should be considered? We mostly reflect what the military people recommend; military policy is made by the Department of Defense.

Our committee is a real estate committee.

How do we check the military recommendations? I don't know. We just ask a lot of questions—questions that are not resolved. It's most difficult to make inquiries. Take bases. DOD says we need such-and-such bases. Well, we want to know why such-and-such a size. But we don't mostly know how to evaluate the answers; we aren't equipped to do so. So 95 per cent of the legislation is what DOD recommends. It's only when you come to personnel problems, size of army, that sort of thing, that you find us doing more—and that's naturally because that affects the lives of every voter.

And perhaps the most experienced staff man on military matters on the Hill, when I told him I was studying the Armed Services Committee, repeated again and again, to be sure the idea was properly communicated, "Our committee is a real estate committee. Don't forget that. *If you study our committee, you are studying real estate transactions.*" By that, he meant that the *location of installations and related transfer, purchase, and sale of properties is the main concern of the House Armed Services Committee.*

One of the major reasons why the congressional committees involved concern themselves with accountable and avoidable waste marginal issues in the appropriations field, personnel problems, and other such peripheral matters is the fear of lack of competence.[10a]

THE TYRANNY OF INFORMATION AND IDEAS: "WHO ARE WE TO SAY 'NO'?"

Congress is today better equipped to evaluate, assay, and sometimes develop and integrate ideas than it is to invent them or stimulate their invention. But if Congress is to function smoothly, there must *somewhere* be people who invent and transmit competing ideas. That is to say, generally speaking, Congress can readily check and balance when there are within the politically alert public, sets of ideas and interests which check and balance each other, thus creating a situation within which the Congress is able to *sift, winnow, and judge.*

But if there is no check and balance *outside* the Congress, then the Congress will find it difficult to perform the legislative functions

---

[10a] I discuss the general phenomenon of the increasing fear by the non-expert of the expert as a function of our schooling and university systems in my book, tentatively titled, "On the Sociology of Stupidity," to be published by Basic Books, 1964.

of investigation, inquiry, check, and balance. So far as congressmen are aware (or were aware in 1955–57), there is no such climate of controversy, opinion, and interest pertaining to military policy as such—outside the armed services themselves. The people for the most part certainly believe in a "strong National Defense," but beyond that, the members of Congress receive little or no articulate information on military policy from them. Most congressmen on relevant committees reported in interviews that, so far as constituent views and attitudes on military policy are concerned, there were none! This situation contrasts more or less sharply with other policy fields regarding which congressmen may hear a good deal from constituents; the members are well aware of the difference.

In regard to other matters of legislative concern, there are persons known to congressmen who have articulate views and to whom the congressmen can turn for ideas, suggestions, ammunition, and moral backing. The latter point is very important; few congressmen want to challenge the experts in a highly specialized field without first having their own experts to back them.[11]

In any case, members of Congress share the views which they generally attribute to their constituents: they hesitate to question the *basic* proposals of the military; that is, they regard the military as *experts*, not only on matters of organization and command, but on types of war plans, etc. Said one member of a relevant committee, better prepared by previous experience than most committee members, "The whole problem is that we are not military experts, and we have to rely upon what the military people tell us. We try to get them to cut out the window dressing, but it's hard."[12] He repeated

---

[11] The point is not so much to be guided by the specific advice of a particular expert; it is, rather, not to stick one's neck out by finding oneself opposed to all those who are "respectable" and "informed." A few seeming experts who take a minority view are all that are sometimes needed to embolden those who latently sympathize with them.

[12] Significantly, in the course of these interviews, no member said anything (except for reference to civil defense theorists) which indicated an awareness that there is within the scientific community considerable controversy about war plans. However, I know that three or four of the members I talked with do have some knowledge of the sort of argument one would find in the *Bulletin of Atomic Scientists,* but only one of them mentioned the matter in the framework of our interviews. In terms of the orientation of this article—*the social psychology of the occupational interfaces between* congressmen and military specialists—the omission did not need to be challenged; it would be interesting to replicate my interviews today to see if there is more spontaneous mention of the scientific discussion.

several times in the course of our talks the rhetorical question: "Who are we to say 'no' to the military people?" Members do not feel this respect for foreign policy experts from the State Department or for tax experts from the Treasury or for economists from relevant agencies.

MILITARY SPECIALISTS EXERCISE A MONOPOLY ON THE PRESENTATION OF ALTERNATIVES

In terms of the feeling just described, most congressmen and members of the relevant committees usually, if not always, *do* follow the recommendations of the military when these are clearly and explicitly propounded. However, members of Congress do not, in fact, want to know the military's specific war plans for security reasons,[13] and in many cases, they are not at all concerned with the nature of the war plans. In general, they seemed to be assuming that there are only two possible kinds of war—either (1) a thermonuclear war, or (2) a Korean-type war. They appear to have no idea that other possibilities (of other kinds of war) are worth investigating.

The military exercises a monopoly or quasi-monopoly on presentation of alternatives, with the result that congressmen have no reason to be aware of the gamut of possibilities open to them. When the generals very largely determine the explanations they hear, and the choices they are forced to make, congressmen have little opportunity to move into an area of reflection broader than that of the generals—unless they have the time and ability to innovate.[14]

The problem for congressmen is, then, to get alternatives posed for them. The issue is not confined to the military field; it is, impressionistically speaking, probably true in all areas in which the legislative branch is faced with specialists whose occupational prestige is such that members of the legislature are apt to feel that they are sticking their necks out by contradicting them. In other words, military men often belong to a category of technological specialists who can to a considerable degree get their own way by

---

[13] That is, they are afraid they will be inhibited and restrained and embarrassed by having access to more confidential security information than they desire to know.

[14] In an area not one of military policy as we have defined the term, but closely related thereto, Congressman John W. McCormack (D.-Mass.) has, according to members of his staff, manifested such innovative tendencies: He has, they report, played a creative part in pressuring the Department of Defense to rationalize purchasing procedures.

posing the questions for the legislature; public health specialists are another such category.[15]

"How the Hell Do We Know What Should Be Considered?"

How do the members of the relevant committees reach their decisions and evaluate the proposals made by the military? The answer seems to be that usually no such evaluation is made. In answer to the question, "Aside from your common sense and whatever help the staff can supply you, is there any way to check on the military experts?" members said:

> No. The most effective way is for a congressman to have a good knowledge of the installations in his district which unfortunately I do not have.
>
> * * *
>
> The problem as I see it is that even if we put into effect policy legislation, the executive department can circumvent it if it wants to. [This member stated that he probably attends more committee and subcommittee meetings than any other member; he was referred to by several committee colleagues as "an expert."]
>
> * * *
>
> Lord knows we need some help; I hope you can find something which tells us what to listen to.
>
> * * *
>
> How the hell do we know what should be considered anyway? We mostly reflect what the military men tell us. [This was from a member widely regarded as one of the two or three ablest men on relevant committees.]

Such acceptance of the leadership of the military, so far as the House is concerned, seems to be more characteristic of the Armed Services Committee than of the Appropriations Subcommittee on Defense. Almost all members agreed with the following point:

> We don't have a hell of a lot before our [Armed Services] committee. There's really much scarcity of policy legislation. . . . Maybe we have given to much authority to the

---

[15] Of course, this is a report from the standpoint of the legislature; most military men and public health experts will probably feel that they do not get their own way; and sometimes the legislature may say "no" to them, or say more often "a little less" or "a little later," but generally the legislature does concede to them the formulation of the issues.

Secretary of Defense and the Joint Chiefs of Staff. Congress itself has promulgated legislation which says to them "use your own judgment." . . . So policy is found in Appropriations more than anywhere else. Yes, the question of jurisdiction on these matters keeps people sore. Vinson stays at loggerheads with Cannon about it [Vinson (D.-Ga.), Chairman, Armed Services, Cannon (D.-Mo.), Chairman, Appropriations]

And, from another member of Armed Services:

Our committee accepts reports of the Department of Defense more completely than does Appropriations. We never question opinions about personnel, et cetera. [This is not absolutely correct, but more or less so.] We kid Appropriations members about this, say we aren't military experts, but they are, et cetera.

The foregoing comments apply to the House rather than the Senate. Although there are differences in the personalities of the members of the two House committees, the significant contrast seems to arise out of the functional differences between them. Armed Services is a *legislative* committee, and, as such, deals chiefly with the basic issues only once—when they are enacted into legislation. The Appropriations Committee, on the other hand, considers issues *annually,* and, as one member of Armed Services said:

Right. Appropriations *is* more important. We are over-all men and deal with the over-all things. Now, you must qualify that to this extent; this may not be true from the standpoint of the armed services themselves. We do deal with things that might not seem very important to civilians but are tremendously important to the military—like how many general officers can there be? [A Senate committee staff member indicated that they have more personal visits on personnel matters, promotions, pensions, etc., than on any other matter.][16]

But in the conventional course of events, the Appropriations Committee is concerned mainly not so much with *legislation* as with avoiding *accountable waste.* As to getting into the *policy* field, there its members have no clear viewpoint of whether they should or should not. Thus, by and large, when Appropriations Committee members do get into a policy question, it is either by accident or

---

[16] The parallel with school committees in cities and towns—which in some instances spend more time discussing routes and who is entitled to bus rides than considering educational matters—is interesting.

because some external event has attracted attention to it, or because of the personal interest of particular members.[17]

"We Need More Interservice Squabbling"

Several fairly senior members, when asked, "What are the major characteristics of a good committee member?" replied, in effect, "Be suspicious of the military! We need guys who won't let them put anything over on us."

For instance, one member said:

> Well, now, I'm sure you can supply [better] words to what I'm saying. . . . There's no way on earth to prevent military leaders from pulling the wool over our eyes. But we should keep check. . . . You have to watch their requests; many times they're made for political expedience. You've got to trust what military leaders tell you, but you can't turn them loose on things. . . . I'm not one of those who think the military are all bad, but we need a close check on them. Unfortunately you cannot have such a check unless you have well-staffed standing committees with tremendous expenditure.

Another [one of the two most impressive members of the relevant committees in 1956]:

> Congress can preserve a republican form of government and avoid a dictator by this sort of control [which Appropriations supplies]. . . . They frequently forget man is a human being; [yet] they're always talking about morale until I'm sick of the word. . . . A very important ability [on Appropriations] is to resist the blandishments and glitter of stars and rank. I make a rule never to accept any social invitation involving a top-ranking military man. . . . [Then you have] to be thick-skinned. It's hard to say "no." The services may not attack you directly, but indirectly. . . .

But since the military is supposed to be "trying to put something over on us" [the Congress and the people], what then? Again and again, the members said, in effect: "What we need is more inter-

---

[17] But the tremendous workload of the committee, plus the quite inadequate staff assistance, means that, at present, its most conscientious and penetrating members would have to make a very conscious decision to let millions of dollars of avoidable, accountable, or quasi-accountable, waste go unchecked, if they were to allow themselves the time to think through military policy problems! For anyone, and particularly for the kind of man who is likely to gravitate to the Appropriations Committee, this would be a most difficult decision.

service squabbling. *When the military falls out, then and only then can the Congress find out."*

One of the more influential staff men, a trusted advisor of one of the most influential men on the Hill, said, for example:

> Looking at these things, as I must, from the big end of the funnel, it seems to me that if everything goes smoothly, nobody ever knows what's going on, neither Congress nor anybody else. But when some one of the forces gets into trouble or gets riled up, then we hear about it and learn a lot. [Of course] we don't know whether the roots are in the military services themselves or start with the DOD civilians or with the military contractors; I just don't know and I wouldn't want to be [identifiably] quoted, but I'd like to know whether Boeing has stirred things up chiefly on these B-52s. Naturally, Senator Jackson [D.-Wash.] openly says . . . he'd like to see some more jobs there.
>
> I would say there is no secret that [in 1956] SAC has priority in people and things—*all over*. And the big squabbles arise when it [or somebody else] gets hurt. . . . But if nobody gets badly hurt, all the services will sit there as calm as can be, and Congress will hear nothing about it. . . .
>
> This old stuff of roles and missions is the central thing in our investigations, and always there you're cutting or threatening to cut flesh, nerve, muscle; and everybody wants to be seated at the table where such a threat is made. The reason for all the sensitivity is the simple possibility of a change in roles and missions.
>
> Fights get to Congress and lead Congress to know what's going on. . . .
>
> If somebody comes to you and wants you to investigate such-and-such a condition, you'll learn only what they in the services want you to learn, *unless there is interservice rivalry.* Then you can find out from the Air Force or vice versa and from Strategic Air Command about Air Defense or vice versa. That is, each service, then [when there's a fight], is ready to say "those dirty dogs are doing so-and-so" and you learn something.

A staff member is quoted here because he expressed, as it happened, more articulately and systematically what many members clearly indicated or implied. Said a member who had actually campaigned on the basis of membership on a committee related to the armed services:

> The thing I was least aware of before my service [here on the committee] was the interservice rivalry. Of course, my community tends towards one particular service; I'm not objecting to this [interservice rivalry]. I think a spirited competition is a very healthy thing.

This emphasis on competition and on the healthiness of it seems to imply what the staff member just quoted actually said; in a couple of instances, it came very close to the old saying, "When thieves fall out, honest men have their day." The atmosphere of not trusting the armed services was widespread in the Congress. Not that they think the military witnesses and leaders are thieves, of course, but in the words of another member:

> I suppose I'm unique among congressmen; I have a strong native bias against the military, as witness that word "garbage" which I just used as applied to what I hear from the Pentagon, but for refined intellectual reasons I'm more convinced than most that we have to have an intelligent defense policy and defend it, so I refrain from criticism except on special points. I find myself, that is, a strong supporter of an institution which I distrust profoundly.[18]

The belief that other members have a higher opinion than oneself has of the military seems fairly common, so I raised the question, "Do you really think that's unique? It seems to me to be standard."

> Oh, well, I think a lot of 'em would say "We've got to have the——s but we hate 'em"; mine is a more refined, permanent, philosophical distrust!

"The Military Is the Real Corruptor of Congress"

Another sophisticated member, recalling the then current excitement about the efforts by oil and gas interests to bribe a senator, said:

> Relatively, if they were really to study "corruption," all that [oil business] is peanuts in my judgment; the people who are really trying to bribe and pressure Congress are from the Department of Defense. They learn you want to go somewhere, and they call you up and say, "How about travelling on one of our planes?" And it just so happens there is riding along with you a pleasant, agreeable officer from the service which gives you the ride; he does not argue with you at all, but he does call your attention to things from their standpoint.

The member then pointed out that this kind of contact is designed to give the armed services the opportunity to determine what issues

---

[18] This member shared with several others the illusion that this was a unique point of view; in fact, it was the commonest one.

the congressman thinks about. He averred that, collectively, such contacts are far more "corrupting" than oil industry efforts because they do more to shape the way Congress looks at military questions than any mere bribe. His kind of awareness, however—that all the military services *may share* a common set of assumptions or views which it would be profitable to question, or *may omit* from consideration some important point which, in terms of over-all national interest, should be taken into account—is not commonly found among members of the committees directly concerned with military issues.

In fact, congressmen frequently assume the validity of the terms in which interservice disputes are raised because they know of no other way of getting at the issues. In any event, it is a common enough human tendency to accept the framework within which an argument is conducted; but in the Congress this tendency is considerably enhanced by the feeling that the Armed Services Committee is a *"quasi-judicial* committee."[19] Perhaps the judicial role is often a desirable model for congressmen to adopt; it might in fact increase impartiality and a readiness to change one's mind on due cause being presented. On the Armed Services Committee, it leads to the notion that that committee has two chief responsibilities: (1) to listen to the requests of the various services and say "yes" or "no"; or (2) in more complex issues, to decide which of the "litigants"—Army, Navy, Air Force, Marines, or subservices—shall get the most of what is wanted in the way of missions, money, prestige, and power.[20]

---

[19] This notion of being engaged in a judicial process is common enough on congressional committees, naturally so in a body which contains many lawyers, some would-be judges, and some would-be members of regulatory commissions. Committee chairmen may operate on the notion that they conduct hearings with the neutrality which a judge shows in court. At the time of this investigation such chairmen as former Senator Millikin (R.-Colo., Senate Finance) or the former chairman of the House Interior Committee, now Senator Engle (D.-Calif.), who had clearly-known views on controversial legislation, endeavored to portray themselves as impartially engaged in a judicial activity while conducting hearings on such legislation.

[20] Of course, on many matters, the committees could have great importance because of their latent power (the degree to which the executive branch calculates upon their acceptance or rejection of proposals may be as important as the actual approval or disapproval they articulate) rather than because of what they actually do. Hypothetically, it should be pointed out that committees would "rubber-stamp" all suggestions from a department if the department always guessed correctly what the committees would approve and submitted no other suggestions.

But this notion appears to have the grave weakness that it assumes that through the operation of some form of invisible hand, the "litigants" will necessarily present the basic issues of public policy with which the Congress ought to be concerned. It also assumes that the interservice hostility, thus not diminished, will not interfere with genuine cooperation between the armed forces where this is desirable.

WHAT IS "TECHNICAL" AND WHAT IS "NON-TECHNICAL"?

"You Have to Gnaw and Gnaw to Get Anything Out of the Service"

Even more basic, possibly, than the points already made in explaining or "justifying" congressional reluctance to tackle military policy problems is the little word technical. Congressmen tend to regard as "technical" such questions for "professional" military men as the nature of war plans. But they regard as "non-technical" and fit subjects for their consideration such matters as the way in which oil is stored at overseas installations or how service credit shall be allocated for ROTC or military academy training—problems of the type which at some universities would be thankfully left as a "technical" matter for registrars to decide.[21] Similarly, Congress will evaluate or try to evaluate the efficiency of given types of rifles or waste in the procurement of military overcoats. However—with the partial exceptions of the Subcommittee on Military Operations when Riehlman (R.-N.Y.) was chairman and the Senate Foreign Relations Committee in 1959–60—they have recently shown little interest in stimulating the invention and development of newer types of weapons or innovations in "grand strategy."[22] The historic distinction between *grand* strategy—war plans involving, for instance, such

---

[21] Officers might or might not receive longevity pay credit for their years in the military academies or in the ROTC; Congress in this case has tended to support reservists against the claims to special considerations from West Pointers, etc.

[22] The Foreign Relations Committee may seem an unlikely candidate here, but the truth was well-expressed by a sophisticated and experienced staff member of another committee who said, "I think you'll find out that jurisdiction is nine-tenths assertion" among congressional committees. If several influential members of the Interior Committee desired to do so, no doubt they could study basic military policy because of their responsibilities for public lands, conservation, etc., which provides an entering wedge; the only difficulty would be that, if they did this, they would not have time to do something else which they might wish to do.

matters as the desirability and feasibility of *massive* retaliation versus *measured* retaliation—and *specific* strategies is quite unfamiliar in the Congress. This explains in part why questions about military policy are often regarded as suggesting that congressmen concern themselves with *technical* military issues. In other words, many congressmen assume that there is some sort of over-all approach to military policy which need not be questioned, or which is axiomatic. In any case, questions of over-all policy are not raised by many witnesses or "litigants" (in general, it would be against the interest of *most* of the vociferous litigants who approach Congress to query prevailing assumptions). But a contrast is provided by congressmen who have recently been able and eager to consider basic policy in fields such as full employment or international trade.

A number of members made the point that the Constitution gives the President special authority over military matters because he is designated as Commander-in-Chief. This, again, seems to assume that questions about military policy must necessarily deal with specific war plans and to ignore the area of grand strategy. In any case, it might equally well be argued that the American constitutional system is supposed to operate through competition between the branches of government, that is to say, check-and-balance, and that there is also constitutional warrant for assumption by Congress of responsibility in military matters.

One reason cited by several congressmen for hesitation about "interfering" with the executive branch on military matters is that efforts to do so during the Civil War resulted (actually or supposedly) in difficulty and trouble. Southern members, who are, of course, in senior positions when the Democratic party is in the majority, seem to be particularly influenced by this contention. Perhaps Senator Truman of Missouri, through his establishment of and leadership in a committee concerned with investigating defense mobilization, contracting difficulties, etc., and because of his own intense historical sense, called attention to or enhanced the importance of this point of view.

The question is, could Congress learn to think about military policy without getting into the war plans area? This is, of course, a standard problem of legislative-executive relationship, generalist-specialist tension, and, for that matter, top administrator-middle administrator difficulty. The president of a university, and the board of trustees under some circumstances, may properly be concerned with the curriculum but not with the content of the comprehensive examination; they may set policy within which future comprehensive examinations may be established, but they should never handle complaints about current comprehensives. Senator Truman's position (which he probably saw no reason to change when he became President) was that the Congress could not, psychologically, make the judicious sort of distinction here described, and therefore should stay out of the field altogether.[23]

Under present practice, it is probably true to say, as one active and influential congressman did, that "On these matters, you have to be a——bulldog and gnaw and gnaw and gnaw to get any [information out] of the services." (He added, "the whole damn trouble with Congress is they let people file things.") "You've got to be a policeman and keep hounding and hounding . . . to get a job done."

POWER-SEEKING POLITICIANS VERSUS TECHNOLOGISTS?

One commonly held conception about politics is that politicians seek power actively and aggressively. Whatever other conclusions may be derived from the present report, it seems apparent that congressmen on relevant committees could readily enough strive for greater power in military affairs with a reasonable chance of obtaining it. *In fact, they think that the satisfactions they obtain by not seeking power are greater than those they would get by trying to maximize it.* Among the factors which may explain such "restraint" are (1) traditions of institutional organization including "separation of powers"; and (2) the notion in Congress that professional and technical matters should be left to professional and technical men. On the basis of the present study we cannot say whether these traditions and notions are "rationalizations" of some other motivation (such as the discomfort conceivably involved in systematic thinking about the potentialities of modern war—former Civil Defense Administrator Petersen, also a politician, spoke of himself as one "who [has] been looking into hell for three years") or are independent causal factors. The writer's best guess is that they are, to a considerable extent, causal factors, the weight and

---

[23] The Congress does not ordinarily get into specific administration; however, I have several times heard the assertion that under Senator McCarran's chairmanship, the Judiciary Committee did get into specifics of immigration administration. In some state legislatures, ways and means committees deal on a continuing basis with administrative matters, although of course state governments do not anticipate the same military crises the Congress must envisage.

significance of which are very much increased by other motivations, such as the one just mentioned, and by simple fear that a civilian who fights a technical man will be made to look ridiculous before his public.[24]

---

[24] For another discussion of self-restraint where some interpretations would predict an aggressive seeking of power, see Lewis A. Dexter, "Where the Elephant Fears to Dance Among the Chickens. Business in Politics? The Case of Dupont," *Human Organization*, XIX (1960–61), 188–94, republished with some modifications in Bauer, Pool, and Dexter, *op. cit.*

PART THREE

Leadership and the Legislative Process

IX

THE PARTY WHIP ORGANIZATIONS IN THE UNITED STATES HOUSE OF REPRESENTATIVES*

Randall B. Ripley

IN THE literature on political parties in the United States Congress two points are usually stressed. First, it is said that the political party label lacks a precise programmatic content because "party government" in the British sense is absent in the American Congress.[1] Second, however, it is contended that the party label is the single most important and reliable attribute in predicting the voting behavior of a Senator or Representative.[2]

---

* Reprinted from *The American Political Science Review*, Vol. LVII, No. 3, September, 1964.

The research for this article was conducted while the author was an intern in the Office of the Democratic Whip in the United States House of Representatives, from April to September, 1963. The research was financially sponsored by a Brookings Institution Research Fellowship. In addition to the printed sources this article is based on interviews and correspondence with members and former members of the House, employees of the House, and various staff members; and on files of the Office of the Democratic Whip.

I am especially indebted to Congressman Hale Boggs and his Administrative Assistant, D. B. Hardeman, for cooperating in many ways in the research for this article. I am also grateful to John Bibby, Lewis A. Froman, Jr., Theodore Lowi, Robert Peabody, and H. Douglas Price, as well as Hardeman, for their careful critiques of an earlier draft.

The findings and conclusions are those of the author and do not purport to represent the views of the Brookings Institution, its trustees, officers, or other staff members.

[1] See Austin Ranney and Willmoore Kendall, *Democracy and the American Party System* (New York, 1956), p. 399; E. E. Schattschneider, *Party Government* (New York, 1942); and the Committee on Political Parties of the American Political Science Association, "Toward a More Responsible Two-Party System," *APSA Review* Vol. 44 (Sept., 1950).

[2] See David B. Truman, "The State Delegations and the Structure of Party Voting in the U. S. House of Representatives," *APSA Review*, Vol. 50 (Dec., 1956), p. 1023; Truman, *The Congressional Party* (New York, 1959), pp. vi-vii; Julius Turner, *Party and Constituency: Pressures on Congress* (Baltimore,

Between these two contentions lies a sizeable area of unexplored territory. If party is the best predictive device in analyzing voting behavior in Congress then, despite the lack of "party government," the party machinery in both houses must have effects that deserve study. Professor Huitt has suggested the necessity and importance of this kind of study: "... the preoccupation with reform has obscured the fact that we have no really adequate model of party leadership as it exists in Congress, and that none can be constructed because we lack simple descriptions of many of the basic working parts of the present system."[3] Huitt himself and a few others have filled some of these gaps.[4]

An important office of party leadership that has received no sustained treatment is that of whip. Only two moderately long articles have been specifically devoted to it, and neither analyzes the relation of the whips to rule by the majority party.[5] Other works on Congress mention the whips, but only in passing.[6]

1951); and Avery Leiserson, *Parties and Politics* (New York, 1958), p. 379 (appendix).

[3] Ralph Huitt, "Democratic Party Leadership in the Senate," *APSA Review* Vol. 55 (1961), p. 334; see also Robert L. Peabody and Nelson Polsby, *New Perspectives on the House of Representatives* (Chicago, 1963), pp. 269–270.

[4] See Huitt, *op. cit.;* Malcolm E. Jewell, "The Senate Republican Policy Committee and Foreign Policy," *Western Political Quarterly,* Vol. 12 (Dec., 1959), pp. 966–980; Hugh A. Bone, "An Introduction to the Senate Policy Committees," *APSA Review* Vol. 50 (June, 1956), pp. 339–359; George Galloway, "Leadership in the House of Representatives," *Western Political Quarterly,* Vol. 12 (1959), pp. 417–441; and James A. Robinson, *The House Rules Committee* (Indianapolis, 1963). Paul Hasbrouck, *Party Government in the House of Representatives* (New York, 1927), is an older treatment of some parts of the House leadership.

[5] These are "Whips' Effectiveness Tested on Close 1961 House Votes," *Congressional Quarterly,* Weekly Report #24 (June 16, 1961), pp. 992–998; and Alfred Steinberg, "Shepherds of Capitol Hill," *Nation's Business,* Jan., 1952, pp. 31–33. The first article presents roll call data and infers "effectiveness" from them; but no direct link between the data and the whips is established. The second is a popular treatment of the role and importance of the whips.

A short article for a small audience (University of Oklahoma alumni) but with some general interest is Carl Albert, "Oklahoma and the Democratic Whip," *Sooner Magazine,* July, 1955, pp. 18–19.

[6] See Clem Miller, *Member of the House* (New York, 1962), pp. 52–54; DeAlva S. Alexander, *History and Procedure of the House of Representatives* (Boston, 1916), pp. 104–106; George Brown, *The Leadership of Congress* (Indianapolis, 1922), p. 222; Truman, *The Congressional Party,* pp. 227 ff.; Neil MacNeil, *Forge of Democracy* (New York, 1963), pp. 97–100; George Galloway, *History of the United States House of Representatives,* H. Doc. 246, 87th Cong., 1st sess. (1961), pp. 102–103; Floyd M. Riddick, *Congressional Procedure* (Boston, 1941), pp. 75–77; and Riddick, *The United States Congress: Organization and Procedure* (Manassas, Va., 1949), pp. 101–102.

This article proposes to (1) recount briefly the 20th Century history of the whips in the House of Representatives, (2) describe the whip organizations in the House, (3) analyze the role played by the House Democratic whip organization in the Second Session of the 87th Congress (1962) and the First Session of the 88th Congress (1963), and (4) suggest the broader importance of the whips in the House.

I

Champ Clark, Speaker of the House for eight years (1911–19), called the whips "the right hands of the two leaders," and described the principal duty of a whip as "to have his fellow political members in the House when needed."[7] His comments are still accurate, although the functions performed by the whips have become more diversified in recent years. The whips are (1) responsible for the presence of their fellow party members, but they must also (2) transmit certain information to them, (3) ascertain how they will vote on selected important pieces of legislation, and (4) guide pressure to change the minds of the recalcitrant and stiffen the wills of the wavering.

Most of these functions have been performed at least haphazardly in the House since 1789, although the name "whip" was not formally applied to a party official in the House until the end of the 19th Century.[8] Throughout most of the 19th Century members functioning as whips were in evidence only in connection with important legislation and only when the division between the parties was close enough to necessitate a device that would help gain a high degree of party regularity.[9] Many of these whips were

---

[7] Champ Clark, *My Quarter Century of American Politics* (New York, 1920), Vol. 2, p. 337.

[8] The name "whip" derives from the British fox-hunting term "whipper-in," used to describe the man responsible for keeping the hounds from leaving the pack. It was first applied to the British Parliament about 1770. For a description of the British whips see Roland Young, *The British Parliament* (London, 1962), pp. 75–77; also Eric Alexander, Viscount Chilston, *Chief Whip* (London, 1961).

For a brief description of the whip in the United States Senate see a speech by J. Hamilton Lewis, long-time Democratic Senate whip, *Congressional Record*, Vol. 80, pt. 7, pp. 7044–7046 (1936).

[9] See MacNeil, *op. cit.*, pp. 97–100; and Alexander, *op. cit.*, p. 104. See also David S. Barry, *Forty Years in Washington* (Boston, 1924), pp. 100 ff. for comments on one Republican whip in the late 19th Century, Omar Conger of Michigan.

volunteers for a given floor fight only.[10] Both parties began to designate their whips formally for an entire Congress around the turn of this century. Table I lists them and summarizes their House careers.

TABLE I

Party Whips in the House

Name, State, Years of service as whip	House career		
	Years before becoming whip	Years as whip	Years after being whip
Democrats			
Oscar W. Underwood, Alabama, 1900–01	5	1	14
James T. Lloyd, Mo., 1901–08	4	8	8
Thomas M. Bell, Ga., (1913–15?)†	?	?	?
William A. Oldfield, Ark., 1921–28	12	8	—
John McDuffie, Alabama, 1929–33	10	4	2
Arthur Greenwood, Indiana, 1933–35	10	2	4
Patrick Boland, Pa., 1935–42	4	7	—
Robert Ramspeck, Ga., 1942–45	12	3	—
John Sparkman, Alabama, 1946	9	1	—
John McCormack, Mass., 1947–49; 1953–55	18	4	13*
Percy Priest, Tenn., 1949–53	8	4	4
Carl Albert, Okla., 1955–62	8	7	2*
Hale Boggs, La., 1962–	17	2*	
Republicans			
James A. Tawney, Minn., 1897–1905	4	8	6
James E. Watson, Indiana, 1905–09	8	4	—
John W. Dwight, N.Y., 1909–13	6	4	—
Charles Burke, S.D., 1913–15	12	2	—
Charles M. Hamilton, N.Y., 1915–19	2	4	—
Harold Knutson, Minn., 1919–23	2	4	26
Albert H. Vestal, Indiana, 1923–31	6	8	—
Carl G. Bachmann, W.Va., 1931–33	6	2	—
Harry L. Englebright, Cal., 1933–43	6	11	—
Leslie C. Arends, Ill., 1944–	9	20*	

* As of the end of 1963.
† Bell served in the House from 1905 until 1931.

The Republicans. The exact method of Tawney's initial appointment as Republican whip in 1897 is obscure. Speaker Cannon ended it by appointing him Chairman of the Appropriations Committee in 1905, although he had never previously served on

---

[10] Clark, *op. cit.*, p. 338, says he was acting as volunteer whip as late as 1909. Important Republicans who acted as volunteer whips in the late 19th Century were Thomas Reed of Maine and James Wilson of Iowa.

that Committee. Watson, who succeeded Tawney,[11] resigned from the House in 1908 to run for the governorship of Indiana; he later served 16 years in the Senate. Though he had left the House, Cannon consulted him as a personal assistant in the 1910 rules fight.[12] The third Republican whip, Dwight, began to organize a more extensive system and develop modern techniques—particularly the use of a systematic poll prior to an important vote.[13]

During Wilson's presidency Burke and Hamilton were understandably less active than Dwight had been. In 1919, with the Republicans again in control of the House, the post of whip resumed its importance to them. In that year, reflecting other changes in party practice after 1910, the power of appointing the Republican whip was transferred from the Speaker (or Minority Leader, depending on electoral fortunes) to the Republican Committee on Committees.[14] The Republican Conference (caucus) could ratify or reject the Committee's recommendation. Except in 1919 itself the normal practice has been for the Conference automatically to adopt it.[15]

---

[11] DeAlva S. Alexander, *op. cit.,* note 6 above, p. 105, states that Watson was, in 1899 (his second term), the first whip chosen by party caucus; and he indicates that Tawney succeeded Watson. Alexander's assertion is repeated by MacNeil, p. 97; Galloway, *History,* p. 102; Steinberg, *op. cit.;* and in a speech by Representative Guy Hardy of Colorado in 1928, which is cited in Cannon's *Precedents,* Vol. 8, p. 958 (1936).

This view is mistaken. Tawney was the first whip and was succeeded by Watson in 1905; see the *New York Times,* Dec. 3, 1905, 3:2; the *Washington Post,* Dec. 3, 1905, 2:2 and Dec. 13, 1905, 4:6; Edward T. Taylor, *A History of the Committee on Appropriations, House of Representatives,* H. Doc. 299, 77th Cong., 1st sess. (1941), p. 51; and Charles W. Thompson, *Party Leaders of the Time* (New York, 1906), pp. 153, 195.

The exact date of Tawney's appointment as whip is as obscure as his method of appointment. Taylor, *loc. cit.,* gives the date as 1897 and says that Speaker Reed made the choice. Thompson, *op. cit.,* refers to Tawney as being whip in 1902, although he does not indicate how long he had then been so. Before 1920 the documentation for the identity of party whips was almost non-existent. I have therefore given footnote references identifying the whips before that date.

[12] Kenneth W. Hechler, *Insurgency* (New York, 1940), p. 70.

[13] See MacNeil and Alexander; also the *New York Times,* Jan. 20, 1928, and the *Washington Star,* March 14, 1809, 1:8; March 22, 1909, 1:5; and April 4, 1911, 4:2.

[14] Cannon's *Precedents,* Vol. 8, p. 961.

[15] In 1919 the old-guard Republicans dominated the Party Conference, to the dismay of more progressive members. Fights over many issues, including the choice of the new whip, occurred in the Conference. See the *New York Times,* March 12, 1919, 1:4. Knutson, the winner, received 118 votes out of 182 cast.

Knutson, who later became Chairman of the Committee on Ways and Means, was whip for four years.[16] He was followed in turn by Vestal, Bachmann, Englebright, and Arends. The last three in particular developed, expanded, and solidified the organizational structure of the Republican whip.

The Democrats. The first Democratic whip, Underwood, later became floor leader in the House, and still later, the same in the Senate. Underwood offered the resolution at the 1900 Democratic Caucus—going into a campaign year—which formally created the posts of whip and assistant whip. The Minority Leader then announced Underwood's appointment as whip.[17] The method of appointment for Democratic whips has never changed. The floor leader, aided by Democratic Speakers, has appointed all the Democratic whips.

Lloyd succeeded Underwood and served until he resigned to become Chairman of the Democratic Congressional Campaign Committee in the crucial election years of 1908, 1910, and 1912.[18] The identity of the Democratic whip in the period from 1909 until 1921 is obscure. Bell was the whip during at least the 63rd Congress (1913–15). He may have been whip for the entire 12 years,

---

[16] The only reference to Burke as whip I could find was on the floor plan of the Capitol in the *Congressional Directory* for the 63d Congress. For Hamilton see the *Washington Star*, April 1, 1917, 1:2. Hamilton also returned a form to the office of the *Biographical Directory of Congress* in 1928 in which he indicated that he was the Republican whip in the 64th and 65th Congresses. Knutson listed his tenure as whip as the 66th and 67th Congresses, on a similar form. Vestal became whip in 1923, not in 1925 as the *Biographical Directory* states. The files of the *Biographical Directory* indicate that his service as whip began in 1923; so does his obituary in the *Anderson* (Ind.) *Daily Bulletin*, April 2, 1932.

[17] See the *Washington Post*, Jan. 10, 1900, 4:5; and the *New York Times*, Jan. 10, 1900, 1:6. Sydney P. Epes of Virginia, who died two months later, was named assistant whip.

[18] Lloyd's service as whip is mentioned in the following places: *Congressional Record*, Vol. 90, pt. 3, p. 3420 (1944); the *Hannibal* (Mo.) *Courier-Post*, April 4, 1944; and the *Canton* (Mo.) *Press-News*, April 4 (?), 1944. James E. Watson, in his memoirs, *As I Knew Them* (Indianapolis, 1936), p. 295, mentions Claude Swanson of Virginia as a Democratic whip. I have found no other substantiation for this, however. Lloyd was the designated Democratic whip during the entire time Watson was the Republican whip. I wish to thank Professor Clarence Berdahl for bringing Lloyd's service to my notice. See Berdahl's articles, "Some Notes on Party Membership in Congress," *APSA Review*, Vol. 43 (1949), pp. 309–321, 492–508, 721–734, for a treatment of many important facets of party history.

or there may have been others, as yet unidentified, who served part of that period.[19]

Oldfield was whip for eight years, serving until his death. McDuffie followed him for four years, resigning after an unsuccessful race for Speaker against Henry Rainey in the 1933 Democratic Caucus. Greenwood also ceased to be whip after an intraparty struggle which resulted in the election of Joseph Byrns to the Speakership. He was replaced by Boland, an important Byrns supporter. Greenwood and Boland built the modern Democratic whip organization in the House in the course of coping with the exigencies of New Deal legislation.

The party whip organizations were initially the product of the close, hardfought party battles of the late 19th Century. By the late 1920s and the beginning of the party battles that predated the New Deal struggles the whips became even more prominent in the House. Both parties were eager to maintain disciplined lines either for or against far-reaching legislation. The top-heavy Democratic majorities of the 1930's began to be plagued by dissenting Southerners and Westerners; defection increased the need for machinery aimed at a high degree of party unity in voting. Republicans desired to produce a united opposition, and needed discipline to participate effectively in their recurrent coalitions with Southern Democrats. By 1963 the Democratic whip had a reasonable expectation of succeeding to the floor leadership and even the Speakership.[20]

Gradually the House began to recognize not only the importance of the individuals serving as whips but also the importance of the whips as institutions. From 1911 until the present the Republican

---

[19] The *Congressional Directory* floor plan of the Capitol for the 63d Congress shows Bell as whip. His obituary in the March 20, 1941, *Gainesville* (Ga.) *News* speaks of him as Democratic whip "for a term or two." Berdahl thinks that Bell was whip from 1909 until 1919; I have not been able to substantiate this. Bascom N. Timmons, in his *Garner of Texas* (New York, 1948), pp. 59–60, 61, 64, 74, indicates that John N. Garner was Democratic whip, probably during the 1909–1913 period. I have been unable to find other evidence for this.

[20] This expectation was not a guarantee, however. In 1962 all of the leaders advanced one place after the death of Speaker Rayburn. This provides some precedent but does not establish a pattern. For evidence that Albert's tenure as whip helped lead to his election as Majority Leader see Polsby, in Peabody and Polsby, *op. cit.*, pp. 246–247. It is customary, especially on the Democratic side, for the floor leader to become Speaker when that office falls vacant.

whip has had an office in the Capitol, unless he chose to operate from his congressional office. The Democratic whip had an office in the Capitol in the 63d Congress (1913–15) and has had an office there continuously since 1919.[21] Since 1913 the House has provided for at least limited staff help to be appointed by the whips.[22] The sum was to be used for a messenger for each whip until 1947, when provision was also made for two clerks. In 1953 the party whips were given administrative assistants.[23] By 1963 the office of each whip had a budget of about $40,000.[24]

II

The whip organizations of the parties grew in size and complexity through the years of this century. By 1963, on both sides they were large, formal organizations that performed a variety of tasks.

The Republican Organization.   John Dwight in 1909–1913 was apparently the first Republican whip to have assistants.[25] There is no evidence that any Republican until Carl Bachmann in 1931 again used assistant whips. Bachmann organized the Republican whip system on essentially the same basis that is still in use. He divided the country into two divisions and appointed Joseph Martin of Massachusetts to be in charge of the Eastern division and Harry Englebright of California to be in charge of the Western division.

---

[21] This statement is based on the floor plans of the Capitol in the *Congressional Directory* for each session. The record may be somewhat incomplete.

[22] This information comes from a perusal of the Legislative Appropriations Acts in the *U. S. Statutes-at-Large.* The title "whip" was first used in the 1913 legislation.

[23] When the Republicans captured the House in the 1952 elections John McCormack was slated to move from Majority Leader to minority whip. He asked Speaker Martin, Majority Leader Halleck, and Minority Leader Rayburn if he might keep one of his long-time employees as Administrative Assistant. He and the Republican whip, Les Arends, then agreed that they both would have Administrative Assistants.

[24] The value of the party whip organizations was widely enough recognized in the House by the late 1950s for a portion of the Democratic membership to imitate the political parties and establish a third whip organization. In 1957 a loose alliance of liberal Democrats was formed in the House under the leadership of Representative Eugene McCarthy of Minnesota. This group immediately established a whip organization, which functioned at least sporadically. In 1959 both the Democratic Study Group and its whip organization were formally established. The Secretary of the DSG also serves as its whip.

[25] See the speech by Majority Floor Leader John Q. Tilson of Connecticut, *Cong. Rec.,* Vol. 69, pt. 2, p. 1757 (1928).

He also designated a "key man" in each state with Republican members. When a poll of the Republican members was necessary Bachmann asked Martin and Englebright to get reports from the key men about their state delegations.[26] When Englebright became Republican whip in 1933 he retained the pattern of assistant whips (increasing them to three in number) and "key men" in the state delegations.

The Republican whip from 1944 to the present, Les Arends of Illinois, formalized and expanded the key man system. By 1963 he had a deputy whip, three regional whips, and 12 assistant whips. After the chief whip is chosen he has a free hand in appointing all of his assistants. The Republican organization in the First Session of the 88th Congress is summarized in Table II.

TABLE II

Republican Whip Organization, 1963
Whip: Leslie C. Arends, Illinois
Deputy Whip: Charles Hoeven, Iowa

Regional and Assistant Whips

Name and State	*States in Zone*	*No. of GOP Members*
Regional Whip: Katherine St. George, New York		
William Bates, Mass.	Conn., Mass., N.J., Me., N.H., Vt.	19
Carleton King, N.Y.	New York	21
William Curtin, Pa.	Pa.	14
Regional Whip: Jackson Betts, Ohio		
Elford Cederberg, Mich.	Michigan	11
Jackson Betts, Ohio	Ohio	18
William Van Pelt, Wisc.	Wisc., Minn., Iowa	16
Robert Michel, Ill.	Illinois	14
Richard Roudebush, Ind.	Indiana, Ky., Tenn.	12
Regional Whip: Catherine May, Wash.		
Walter Norblad, Ore.	Ore., Colo., Mont., Utah, Wash., Wyo.	13
Hjalmar Nygaard, N.D.	N.D., S.D., Nebr., Kans., Okla.	13
John Baldwin, Cal.	California	14
William Cramer, Fla.	Fla., Ariz., Md., N.C., Tex., Va., W.Va.	12

The Republican whip organization performs the four functions already mentioned, involving attendance, information, polling, and

---

[26] Letter from Carl G. Bachmann to the author, August 15, 1963.

pressure. The Republican whip keeps records of Republican members' voting on teller votes as well as on roll calls. This the Democratic whip does only informally and sporadically, without notes or records being kept.

The Republicans have developed a different pattern of leadership succession. Joe Martin had been an assistant whip before becoming Minority Leader and then Speaker, but no whip has yet become the Republican floor leader. Similarly, when a Republican Speaker has been forced to become Minority Leader the Republican whip has kept his job, rather than surrendering it to the former Majority Leader. Thus Arends remained as whip in both 1949 and 1955 while Halleck lost any formal leadership title.[27] So long as Arends is content to continue indefinitely as whip, without contesting for the Speakership, the succession ladder simply bypasses him. This may be a temporary accident of personality; the test will come after his retirement, when it is seen whether his successor proves to be an aspirant for the Speakership or whether the post has become permanently neutralized.

The Democratic Organization. On the Democratic side Underwood had an assistant whip in 1900. But in the 1921–1928 period Oldfield had no assistant whips. John McDuffie (1929–1933) had two assistants. The great expansion in the whip organization, which had come in 1931 in the Republican Party, came in 1933 for the Democrats under Arthur Greenwood. He organized a system of 15 assistant whips, each responsible for the Democrats in a specific zone. The zones were identical with those established for the Democratic Steering Committee, which was also created in 1933.[28] The Steering Committee withered quickly but the whip zones remained. The initial 15 zones were similar in composition to the present 18 zones.

Greenwood's successor, Pat Boland of Pennsylvania, worked diligently to perfect the functioning of the organization. During his 7-year tenure the press and other Democratic leaders began to take public notice of his operations.[29]

---

[27] In 1949 Halleck expected Martin to appoint him Deputy Minority Leader and so did not desire to be whip. In 1955 Halleck saw no need to disturb the 11-year tenure of Arends as whip merely for the sake of a title.

[28] Letter from Clarence Cannon to the author, September 23, 1963; Cannon's *Precedents*, Vol. 8, pp. 961–962 (1936); and E. Pendleton Herring, "First Session of the Seventy-Third Congress," *APSA Review*, Vol. 28 (Feb., 1934), p. 69.

[29] See the statement by John McCormack after Boland's death, *Cong. Rec.*, Vol. 88, pt. 3, p. 4318, 77th Cong., 2d sess. (1942). See also the *Washington*

The Democratic deputy whip, who is especially active on the floor in checking attendance and voting, is appointed by the whip.[30] The Democratic assistant whips are either appointed by the dean of the delegations for which they are responsible or they are elected by members of those delegations.[31] Table III summarizes the Democratic whip organization in the First Session of the 88th Congress.

TABLE III

Democratic Whip Organization, 1963
Whip: Hale Boggs, Louisiana
Deputy Whip: John Moss, Calif.

Assistant Whips

Name and State	States in Zone	No. of Dems.	Method of Selection
Torbert Macdonald, Mass.	Mass., Conn., R.I.	14	Election
Abraham Multer, N.Y.	N.Y.	20	Election
George Rhodes, Pa.	Pa.	13	Election
Peter Rodino, N.J.	N.J., Del., Md.	14	Election
Thomas Downing, Va.	Va., N.C.	17	Appointed
John Flynt, Ga.	Ga., S.C.	16	Appointed
James O'Hara, Mich.	Mich., Minn., Wisc.	16	Election
Winfield Denton, Ind.	Indiana	4	Election
Harley Staggers, W.Va.	W.Va., Ohio	10	Election
Robert Everett, Tenn.	Tenn., Ark., Ky.	15	Election
Gillis Long, La.	La., Miss.	13	Election
Don Fuqua, Fla.	Fla., Alabama	18	Election
Frank Karsten, Mo.	Mo., Iowa	9	Election
Dan Rostenkowski, Ill.	Illinois	12	Appointed
Jack Brooks, Tex.	Texas	21	Appointed
Ed Edmondson, Okla.	Oklahoma	5	Election
Thomas Morris, N.M.	N.M., Ariz., Alaska, Colo., Ida., Hawaii, Mont., Nev., Ore., Wash.	17	Appointed
John McFall, Calif.	California	23	Appointed

Star, August 18, 1935, D-2:6 and June 4, 1936, A-10:1; the *Washington Post,* August 25, 1935, III-3:2; and the *Scranton Times,* May 18, 1942.

[30] The post of deputy whip as a formal leadership position was created in 1955 for Hale Boggs of Louisiana, the present whip. John Moss of California became deputy whip in 1962. Boland had a "principal assistant" or "chief assistant" whip, Thomas Ford of California. See the *Washington Star,* August 18, 1935, D-2:6, and *Cong. Rec.,* Vol. 88, pt. 3, p. 4320, 77th Cong., 2d sess. (1942).

[31] Boland apparently appointed his own assistant whips. In 1939 he threatened to "fire" some of them for disloyalty to the President's program. *New York Times,* August 22, 1939, 20:3.

The assistant whips may develop some independent weight in their state delegations. See the chapter by Alan Fiellin in Peabody and Polsby, *op. cit.,* p. 70.

The assistant whips are responsible for a small number of Democrats, averaging between 14 and 15. The whips, or staff members designated by them, make the regular contacts with all of the Democratic members' offices. When the Democratic leadership in the House wishes to transmit information to all Democrats—or elicit information from them—the chief whip's office contacts the 18 assistants. In this way all Democrats can be alerted to come to the floor in 15 to 20 minutes. The leadership can ascertain the sentiments of virtually every Democrat in the House on a given bill in a day or two.[32]

III

The purpose of this section is to analyze the functioning of the Democratic whip organization in the Second Session of the 87th Congress (1962) and the First Session of the 88th (1963)[33], years of great activity for it. The Democratic whip organization, be it remembered, has worked as an arm of the majority party in the House ever since 1933, except for two two-year periods (1947–49 and 1953–55). In the 1930s, as noted above, Boland had greatly expanded its use. Rayburn, on the other hand, who was a strong leader and had never been whip himself, used it less than the weaker Speakers of the 1930s. For example, the whip who served for the longest period under Rayburn, Carl Albert, employed his top staff member on congressional business rather than on whip business.[34]

---

[32] In the Democratic Study Group the Secretary and whip since its founding has been Frank Thompson of New Jersey. He was elected initially and has continued to be re-elected every two years by the full membership of the DSG, which totaled 126 in 1963. He has appointed four regional whips, each of whom has either four or five regional subwhips reporting to him. The subwhips are responsible for calling from four to six other DSG members.

The DSG whip organization takes no polls on legislation, since the group was formed on the basis of ideological congeniality. The organization distributes information on pending legislation and works for maximum attendance, particularly on teller votes on amendments in Committee of the Whole.

[33] One primary fact determined the time span here studied—the availability of files.

[34] This is not to suggest that Albert was not important as whip. Rayburn consulted him, but the whip organization as a whole was used less than in 1962–1963. It should be noted that when Albert became whip he replaced Percy Priest, who decided not to continue as whip in 1955 because he had become Chairman of the Committee on Interstate and Foreign Commerce. *Cong. Rec.*, Vol. 101, pt. 1, pp. 191–192 (1955).

But in 1962 and 1963 the new Speaker, John McCormack, began to use the whip organization for a greater number of formal polls. McCormack had been whip, as had the new Majority Leader, Albert. Hale Boggs, the new whip, had been deputy whip under Albert. Thus the three top Democrats in the House all appreciated the potentialities of the whip organization—both formal and informal. These three men, joined by D. B. Hardeman, Administrative Assistant to Boggs, and the deputy whip, John Moss, functioned as a small, close-knit group dedicated to attaining the most favorable voting outcomes on Administration bills. This group—not, conspicuously, including the chairman of the Rules Committee—met with White House and Departmental officials on legislative matters throughout 1962 and 1963.

The Office of the Democratic Whip was composed of four people —Boggs, Hardeman, a secretary, and an intern—during the entire period studied. The office had a contact—generally a staff member —in the office of each of the 18 assistant whips. Information on poll requests was transmitted by telephone between the whip's office and the offices of the assistant whips. Occasionally the whip's office made contact with all Democratic members of the House directly, either on substantive legislative matters or on attendance needs.[35] The whip's office, located in the Capitol, served as a meeting place for White House and Departmental congressional liaison officials interested in the success of a particular bill.

The whip during these two years was Hale Boggs of Louisiana, a loyal Administration supporter on most matters. The deputy whip, John Moss of California, was even more consistently loyal.[36] The assistant whips, the primary direct contacts with rank and file Democratic members, varied considerably in their voting loyalty to the Administration. Table IV shows the support they gave the Administration on the 17 votes chosen for analysis here,[37] together with the support given by all Democrats in each whip zone on these

---

[35] An unusual instance of this occurred in the drive for adjournment in October, 1962, when the leadership was having difficulty in keeping a quorum in Washington. The whip's office called or sent telegrams to all missing Democrats from east of the Mississippi at their homes, asking them to return. A similar situation, even more acute, developed in 1963 after President Kennedy's assassination, as the House struggled until Christmas eve to pass a foreign aid appropriations bill acceptable to President Johnson.

[36] For the 87th Congress *Congressional Quarterly* reports that Boggs had a 73 per cent and Moss a 91 per cent Kennedy Support Score.

[37] See footnote 40, *infra,* for a listing of the votes chosen.

same votes. In general, the assistant whips tend to be more loyal to the Administration than all Democrats, and variations in their individual loyalty tend to reflect the normal variations by zone.[38]

TABLE IV

Voting of Democratic Assistant Whips and
Members of Their Zones, 1962–1963

Part I: Per Cent Support of Administration on 17 Key Roll Calls

States in Whip Zone	1962		1963	
	Assist-ant Whip	All Zone Members	Assist-ant Whip	All Zone Members
	(%)	(%)	(%)	(%)
Mass., Conn., R.I.	100	95	100	97
N.Y.	100	95	100	97
Pa.	100	98	90	95
N.J., Del., Md.	100	92	100	99
*Va., N.C.	43	53	60	56
Ga., S.C.	86	62	89	74
Mich., Wisc., Minn.	100	97	100	97
Ind.	100	96	100	97
W.Va., Ohio	57	83	100	93
Tenn., Ky., Ark.	71	81	90	90
*Miss., La.	86	41	100	53
*Alabama, Fla.	67	62	78	70
Mo., Iowa	100	80	100	81
*Illinois	100	98	100	98
*Texas	29	51	100	70
Okla. (Kan. & Mont. in 1962)	100	78	90	90
Wash., Ore., Alaska, Hawaii, Ariz., N.M., Utah, Colo., Ida., Nev. (Mont. in 1963)	67	86	100	92
California	100	98	100	97
Average	84	79	94	85

---

[38] This evidence that assistant whips were more loyal (hence, more liberal) should be compared with Duncan MacRae's suggestion that elected party leaders tend to take middle-of-the-road positions on issues. MacRae, *Dimensions of Congressional Voting* (Berkeley and Los Angeles, 1958), ch. 4.

The *Congressional Quarterly* study of the whips, *op. cit.,* p. 994, concludes that in terms of Democratic party support for the first half of the 1961 session "The performance of the whips was matched roughly by that of the membership as whole . . ." David Truman, *The Congressional Party,* p. 227, attributes some of the influence of the principal whips in the House to "their individual positions in the voting structure of the party." Donald Matthews, *U. S. Senators and Their World* (Chapel Hill, 1960), suggests that the Senate whips tend to fall off in party-line voting.

Part II: Per Cent Support of Specific Legislation

Year and Legislation	Support by all Assistant Whips	Support by all Democrats
1962:	(%)	(%)
Urban Affairs	61	55
Tax Bill	94	86
Debt Limit	89	84
Farm Bill	78	81
Trade Expansion Act	89	83
Public Works	89	82
U.N. Bonds	87	81
1963:		
Rules Committee	83	81
Public Works Appropriation	94	86
Medical Student Loans	95	87
Feed Grains Program	93	88
Debt Limit (May)	100	87
Area Redevelopment	83	77
Debt Limit (August)	100	93
Tax Bill	100	90
Debt Limit (November)	100	85
Cotton Bill	93	79

* Assistant whip changed during the two-year period.

The problem of "disloyal" assistant whips is troublesome. The power to appoint and replace them rests exclusively with the Democratic delegations involved. But even if the whip had the power to remove assistant whips the roll-call voting record of the assistants would not be an infallible test. For example, in 1962 one assistant whip supported the Administration only rarely and yet did an excellent job as assistant whip, not only in reporting accurately but also in indicating the weak point of each member through which he might be induced to change his mind and support the Administration on a given bill. Loyalty is less important than accuracy and thoroughness. The Democratic assistant whips are expected to perform the functions involving attendance, information, and polling but they have a great deal of discretion in deciding whether they also wish to pressure their zone members to vote the Administration position.[39]

---

[39] The Republicans, starting with a base of greater party agreement on issues, look on their assistant whips as definite agents of the leadership. The method of appointment for Republican assistant whips—by the chief whip himself—insures some accountability to the leadership. On the Democratic side Boggs

An analysis of how the Democratic whip organization performed these four main functions in dealing with the major legislation the House acted on in 1962 and 1963 will form the bulk of this section. "Major legislation" here indicates those measures on which the House leadership decided a poll should be taken, on which the poll was taken and completed, and on which the House acted either favorably or unfavorably by roll-call vote. This definition includes seven bills in 1962 and ten in 1963.[40] The 17 votes include 14

---

obviously cannot assume that the assistant whip appointed by Howard Smith will be an avid Administration supporter.

Boggs summarized the job of assistant whip in a telegram to the *Shreveport* (La.) *Times* in the fall of 1963: "The assistant whips keep members in their zones informed as to which bills will be scheduled for a vote and when. On a request from the House leadership, they ascertain how each member in their zone will vote on a specific measure, and report the results to the leadership. When important bills are being considered by the House, they try to make sure that the members from their zone are present for key votes. The assistant whips are responsible solely to their party colleagues in their zones. The executive branch has absolutely no voice in either selecting or removing assistant whips."

[40] The specific issues in 1962 were: (1) final passage of the resolution disapproving the reorganization plan which would have created an Urban Affairs Department, (2) final passage of the 1962 Revenue Act, (3) final passage of an increase in the national debt limit, (4) recommittal motion of the feedgrains section of the farm bill, (5) recommittal motion substituting a one-year extension of reciprocal trade for the Trade Expansion Act, (6) recommittal motion on the accelerated public works bill, and (7) final passage of the bill authorizing the President to purchase U. N. bonds.

The specific issues in 1963 were: (1) adoption of the resolution permanently enlarging the Rules Committee, (2) passage of an amendment to a supplemental appropriations bill adding $450 million to the accelerated public works program, (3) recommittal motion deleting medical student loan provisions from the Health Professions Educational Assistance Act, (4) final passage of an increase in the national debt limit, (5) final passage of a bill authorizing a voluntary feed-grains acreage diversion program for 1964–1965, (6) final passage of Area Redevelopment Act amendments, (7) final passage of a second debt-limit extension, (8) recommittal motion on the tax bill making a tax cut dependent on reduced governmental spending, (9) final passage of a third debt-limit extension, and (10) final passage of the cotton bill.

The recommittal motion on the 1963 tax bill did not fully meet the stated criteria, because part of the poll on the recommittal motion was taken through the Democratic members of the Committee on Ways and Means. The 15 zones used by these men when acting as the Democratic Committee on Committees were also employed in this poll and the results were channeled first to Chairman Mills and then to the whip's office. Aside from this significant deviation, however—a display of Mills's independent power—the whip's office performed its normal functions during this struggle. Since the bill was one of the most important to the Administration and the House leadership in 1963, an accurate picture of the whip system could hardly be given without including it here.

A few examples in the text will come from whip operations on bills other than the 17 listed above.

which the Administration won (11 by close margins) and three which the Administration lost (two by close margins).[41]

The first function of the whip organization is to insure maximum Democratic attendance on the floor when critical votes are taken. Getting this is a matter both of keeping the members in Washington and getting them to the House chamber when the vote comes. To this end, the whip's office uses a variation of a poll called an attendance check. In this procedure the assistant whips simply ask the members if they will be in town "next Wednesday" or "next Wednesday and next Thursday." Answers to these questions tell the whip which members should be asked to change their plans and stay in town. Or, if the leadership has a choice in scheduling it can estimate on which one of two or three days the attendance and absence situation will work most in the Administration's favor.

On the day of a vote on the floor the whip's office checks its attendance poll against the absentees on the first quorum call of the day to indicate what members need to be called or may need pairs. The whip's office is particularly anxious to arrange live pairs—whereby an anti-Administration vote actually present is nullified by an absent pro-Administration vote. As the time of the vote or votes approaches, whip calls go out from the whip's office, specifying what is being voted on and indicating that the Speaker, Majority Leader, and whip desire the member's presence on the floor.[42]

The whip's office goes to great lengths to guarantee the presence of members on crucial votes. In April, 1963, votes on a medical student loan provision and on the feed-grains program were scheduled for the same week. The whip's office called one Democratic member who was on the West Coast to make a long-scheduled speech and arranged for her to fly back for the votes. It reached another member touring his district with the Argentine Ambassador and asked him to return to Washington. In the May, 1963, fight over

---

[41] The three lost were Urban Affairs and the farm bill in 1962 and the Area Redevelopment Act amendments in 1963. The phrase "close margin" means roll calls on which a change of 25 votes or less would alter the result. Urban Affairs, the recommittal motion on the trade bill, and U. N. bonds were not "close" in 1962. Only the medical student loan provisions was not "close" in 1963. Nine of the 17 voting results could have been changed by a shift of 15 or fewer votes.

[42] The Majority Manager of Telephones on the floor also instructs his operators to call each member's office when a vote is near but the operators do not specify what is at issue.

increasing the limit on the national debt the whip's office was instrumental in arranging for two Democrats to attend the session in wheel chairs. Occasionally, faulty timing lost a vote. In the June, 1963, vote on the Area Redevelopment Act amendments, a member was told that the vote would be taken about two hours later than it actually came. Consequently he was at the Washington Airport when his vote was needed.

The promotion of optimum attendance can also involve some selectivity. On the day of the Area Redevelopment vote in 1963 the Air Force was scheduled to take 19 members to an air show in Paris. The whip's office called the Air Force to get assurances that the plane would not leave until one hour after the final vote on the bill. Then it got word to the six Democratic members known to be friendly to the bill who were also scheduled to go on the trip and let them know this, so as to insure their presence on the floor.

In the August, 1963, debt-limit fight the whip's office was especially active in working on attendance. Democrats friendly to the bill and not answering the quorum call on the day before the vote received telegrams from Boggs urging them, in the Speaker's name, "to make every effort to be present Thursday ..." for the vote. On the day of the vote the whip's office called the offices of 15 Democratic members who had not answered the quorum call that morning. Despite the previous stress on attendance seven of these members had absented themselves without informing the leadership.

In late August, 1963, there was a long, bitter floor fight over the foreign aid authorization bill. The whip organization made a concerted effort to get all Democrats to the floor and keep them there; a series of teller votes was anticipated on Wednesday and Thursday. On Tuesday a meeting held in the whip's office was attended by all but one of the assistant whips (or their representatives), the Democratic House leadership, Executive liaison personnel, Undersecretary of State Harriman and AID Administrator Bell. Harriman and Bell explained the provisions of the bill and the necessity of defeating crippling amendments. The leadership stressed that all assistant whips should be on the floor during the entire voting period (which consumed 10 to 12 hours) and should keep track of the members from their zones. The appeal was effective to the extent that all 18 assistant whips were on the floor during both days of teller votes. Yet two early votes were lost because of absentees and thus a whip call directed at friendly assistant whips (15 of the 18 on this issue) stressed the necessity of winning the first teller vote on the next day.

The attendance in voting on the tax bill in 1963 was almost perfect. On the most important vote (on the Republican recommittal motion) only one Democrat was unexpectedly absent. The other four Democratic absentees had been identified for several days; three of them were in the hospital. Special efforts were made to get everyone else. For example, two Democrats flew back from a conference abroad specifically for the vote.

No statistical measure can judge *precisely* the effect of the Democratic whip organization on attendance for roll call votes. Yet some inferences can be drawn from a few figures.[43] On the 17 bills in these two sessions on which the whip organization was fully active total Democratic voting attendance was 94 per cent. This can be compared with the Democratic attendance on all roll calls: 83 per cent in 1962 and 84 per cent in 1963.[44] This higher attendance was partially a function of the importance of the bills. Yet the specific instances recounted above suggest that the whip organization had some marginal effect in producing a high voting turnout.

The second function of the whip's office is providing information to Democratic members on pending measures. At the most mechanical level the whip's office is responsible for informing all Democrats what is scheduled for floor action week by week. But the office also provides information more directly related to legislation which is highly important to the Administration and to the House leadership. In May, 1963, during the struggle over the increase in the debt limit the whip organization distributed sheets of information on what the defeat of such an increase would mean to the country and to all Democratic members. A more neutral communication was sent to all Democrats directly from the whip's office with reference to the June, 1963, Area Redevelopment amendments. The content of this letter was an outline explanation of the provisions of the bill. A similar letter

---

[43] The *Congressional Quarterly* study of the first half of 1961, *op. cit.*, pp. 993–994, documents the high voting turnout in that session and suggests the whip organizations might be part of the cause.

[44] The assistant whips had attendance records much like those of all Democrats on all roll calls, but on the 17 key votes they did somewhat better than the rank and file. In 1962 the assistant whips voted 83.4 per cent of the time on all roll calls and 84.7 per cent in 1963. But on the 17 key votes their voting attendance rose to 96 per cent.

—signed by Albert and Boggs—was sent in connection with the cotton bill late in the 1963 session.

In 1963, prior to the passage of the foreign aid authorization bill, an effort at informing the assistant whips on specific features of the program was made at the meeting described above. As a result of the meeting, AID prepared two memoranda which were then distributed to the assistant whips through the whip's office.

Before the voting on the tax bill in 1963 the whip's office was instrumental in helping Chairman Mills distribute a short summary of the bill to all Democratic members. It was accompanied by a brief letter urging support for final passage and defeat of the recommittal motion because "this bill is essential to our national well-being." The letter was signed by Mills, the Speaker, Albert, and Boggs.

The third function of the whip's office is to ascertain how the Democratic members of the House will vote on certain pieces of legislation central to the Administration's program.[45] The principal device used to get this information is the poll. The whip's office does not take a poll until the leadership decides one is needed. This comes usually some time after the bill has been reported from the committee and before it is scheduled for floor action. Ordinarily, then, the poll must be completed within a period lasting from two days to two weeks. Naturally the longer time periods produce greater accuracy in results. Likewise, the more clear and specific the question asked of the members the more accurate the result. If the legislation is extremely complex a simple response for or against the bill may hide important feelings about amendments. The most effective assistant whips probe the sentiments of their membership about specific provisions. If a current of opinion develops against a certain feature, the legislation may be changed

---

[45] The Democratic whip's office also relays to the leadership whatever information it receives about Republican voting probabilities. Such information may come from lobbyists, Executive officials, or personal contacts between Democratic and Republican members. The Republican and Democratic whips' offices do not, of course, trade information.

Information on Republican voting tends to be quite unreliable when it reaches the Democratic whip's office. For example, during the debt-limit fight in May, 1963, it was supposed that at least eight to 10 Republicans would vote for the increase. Only one did. When the Administration lost the Area Redevelopment bill in June, 1963, the whip's office had received information that 21 Republicans would vote for the bill. Only 15 did. During the 1963 struggle over enlarging the Rules Committee six Republicans who finally voted with the Democratic leadership had been written off as lost to Halleck and Judge Smith.

in time to save it from defeat. In 1963 a poll was started on a bill extending the Export-Import Bank and allowing it to continue direct or "backdoor" borrowing from the Treasury. The initial poll results revealed a strong feeling against backdoor financing and the Banking and Currency Committee changed the bill to eliminate it.

The question the assistant whips are to ask members is precisely framed, since ambiguous questions produce ambiguous answers. It is not always on the final passage of the legislation. Often it is on the recommittal motion to be offered by the Republicans, if the "instructions" in this motion can be discovered in advance of the vote. At other times a specific amendment is the subject of a poll.

The results of the poll are supplemented by and checked with officials from the White House and the Executive Department involved, and occasionally group lobbyists provide some information. Without a sensitive and knowledgeable interpreter of the poll data the results could be highly misleading. Fortunately for the Democratic leadership such an interpreter was in charge of the office during the period studied. He could tell when a report from a member was of dubious validity and when it could be accepted at face value.[46] He had a "feel" for contacting the proper members.

How accurate were the final poll results which were submitted to the leadership? Accuracy is important because decisions about provisions in the bill, scheduling the bill for floor action, and attempts to change Democratic votes are based partially on these results. To judge the accuracy of the whip poll the final complete poll presented to the leadership usually two days before the vote —which still left time for any of the actions indicated above—was checked, individual by individual, against the final roll call embodying the issue on which the poll had been taken. The results are summarized in Table V, to show the percentage of members

---

[46] There are several reasons for a member's making an inaccurate report of his position. He might want to avoid leadership pressure by not alerting anyone to his opposition. He might be annoyed at the inconvenience of repeatedly reporting his position. Finally, he might use the report of opposition as a bargaining device. For example, on the poll on the debt limit increase in May, 1963, a loyal Administration supporter from the midwest reported "doubtful" and, at the same time, indicated his eagerness for final Treasury confirmation that a new Internal Revenue Service installation would be located in his district.

TABLE V

Accuracy of Democratic Whip Polls, 1962–1963

	Per cent Correct	Number Correct	Number Incorrect	Number Unknown
1962:	(%)			
Urban Affairs	87	226	15	19
Tax Bill	81	212	26	23
Debt Limit	90.5	237	18	7
Farm Bill	82.5	216	36	10
Trade Expansion	92	241	15	6
Public Works	87.5	228	23	10
U.N. Bonds	87	227	24	10
1963:				
Rules Committee	97	247	2	8
Public Works Approp.	91	233	8	15
Medical Student Loans	94	240	0	16
Feed Grains	84	214	16	26
Debt Limit (May)	93	239	9	8
Area Redevelopment	91	232	17	6
Debt Limit (August)	85	218	32	6
Tax Bill*	96	246	6	4
Debt Limit (Nov.)	92	235	19	2
Cotton Bill	84	214	34	8

* Not formally a whip organization poll. See footnote 40, *supra.*

reported correctly by the poll and also the number reported correctly and incorrectly and the number whose positions could not be ascertained. Evidently the whip's office increased in accuracy in 1963 as compared with 1962. Apparently the refinement of techniques and the lessons of experience were put to good use.

Probably the most important use for the poll results is in helping the leadership determine where to apply pressure. Meetings of the Speaker, Majority Leader, whip, Administrative Assistant to the whip, deputy whip, White House and Departmental liaison officials, and the relevant Committee Chairman begin during a period between three weeks and three days before a bill comes to the floor. At these meetings a division of labor is made, on the basis of the whip poll. Thus a more thorough and accurate poll produces fewer wasted contacts and enhances the probability that the contacts that are made will be with members who may be persuaded.

This fourth function of the whip's office—that of directing pressure—is, in some ways, the most important of the four. The goal of the office is, after all, to produce votes for the President's program. There is no precise systematic or statistical way of charting the effectiveness of this whip-guided pressure, since the ultimate test would compare what happened with what might otherwise have happened.[47] But an indication of some incidents involving the legislation studied in this article will give a sample of the work done and its effectiveness.

The whip's office was effective in 1962 in identifying the trouble spots on the tax bill of that year. One particularly dangerous area was the New York delegation, which was finally brought into line, with the loss of only three votes. Several Southern delegations were initially opposed to the bill but a caucus of the North Carolina delegation, together with the effective work of the assistant whip for Texas, helped hold Southern losses on the bill to 15 votes. At the last minute, during the floor debate, the secretary in the whip's office discovered that some of the members from a midwestern state might be wavering in their support for the bill. This message was transmitted to Boggs on the floor and he proceeded to escort one of the delegation's members to the Speaker's office where both the Speaker and the President (on the telephone) convinced him that he should support the bill.

During the 1962 prelude to the vote on increasing the national debt limit the whip's office was instrumental in enlisting Francis Walter of Pennsylvania to use some of his credit with the Southerners to convince one major Southern delegation to vote for the bill. As a result, only three Democrats from that state voted nay.

During the week of June 25, 1962, the whip poll began to show that the Republican motion to recommit the trade bill with instructions to continue the reciprocal trade agreements program for another year might attract as many as 80 Democratic votes. Frantic activity on the part of the President, Chairman Mills of the Ways and Means Committee, Secretaries Goldberg and Hodges and Undersecretaries Wirtz and Price, the Speaker, Majority Leader,

---

[47] Conceivably, some inferences might be drawn from a comparison of the winning percentage on roll calls used by *Congressional Quarterly* in computing its Presidential Support Index with the Administration's record of success on the key votes analyzed here. The question could be put whether the President won a greater percentage of the time when the Democratic whip organization was fully engaged in the battle. On the 17 key votes the President won 14 times— 82 per cent support—as against an overall 85 per cent winning record (on 60 roll calls) in 1962. From this it might be argued that the whip organization made no material difference, since the winning percentages are about the same. But it might also be argued that since the roll calls used here represent the "toughest" of the more numerous roll calls chosen by *Congressional Quarterly* the winning percentage is higher than could be expected without concentrated whip activity.

whip, and others on Tuesday and Wednesday of that week reduced the eventual Democratic losses on the recommittal motion on Thursday to 44.

During the 1963 Rules Committee fight, after the whip poll was relatively complete, the Speaker, Majority Leader, and whip each took a list of doubtful members to call. Of the 17 called about their vote seven finally voted with the leadership.

The events leading up to the passage of the debt-limit increase in May, 1963, provide another illustration of the use made of the information supplied by the whip poll. At a meeting five days before the vote the results of the poll were discussed. During this meeting the Speaker, Majority Leader, and Larry O'Brien of the White House called and talked to several members about either their opposition or their possible absence. Those members still considered doubtful or open to persuasion were divided among the leadership for further work. Chairman Mills asked that the latest whip poll be given to him the day before the vote so that postponement of the bill could still be announced if it appeared that defeat were likely. A week before the final vote the Speaker had seen an early version of the poll and, on the basis of that, persuaded six members reporting doubtful to commit themselves to voting for the bill. By the time of the floor action the poll indicated that the vote would be extremely close. Armed with that information the leadership secured promises from 13 Democrats who were planning to vote against the legislation that they would vote for it if their votes were needed to change defeat into victory.[48]

The passage of the second debt-limit increase of 1963, in August, was the occasion for a substantial amount of whip-directed activity. The Secretary of the Treasury persuaded one Southern Democrat to vote for the increase after the whip poll had shown him to be vacillating. The Speaker contacted 15 wavering Democrats directly and, as a result, persuaded 10 of them to vote for the bill. Chairman Mills was especially effective in getting Southerners to vote for the bill. Again, as in May, the leadership had ten "pocket votes," that is, men who preferred to vote nay but would vote aye if necessary to pass the bill.[49]

---

[48] Three of the 13 voted with the leadership even though they were not ultimately needed. The other 10 voted nay but remained on the floor after voting, ready to change their votes if necessary.

[49] Seven of these 10, largely at the urging of Mills, voted aye even though not needed. Mills was anxious to have a respectably large margin of victory. He was trying to set a precedent for November, when another debt limit increase would be necessary.

In summary, the whip's office performs its four functions in such a way as to enhance the chances of Democratic victories on floor votes in the House. No absolute figures can be given on votes won that would otherwise be lost. Yet the weight of evidence is that the efforts to insure a maximum attendance, to inform the Democratic membership of undesirable effects on the country if an Administration proposal is defeated, to ascertain voting expectations with great accuracy in advance, and to direct pressure to the precise spots where it will do the most good, result in some small, yet definite, net gains for the Democratic majority in the House.

IV

David Truman has commented that "the persistent reality of party in the functioning of the [House] chamber is unmistakable."[50] Julius Turner stated that "Party pressure seems to be more effective than any other pressure on congressional voting."[51] Yet neither they nor any other commentators on Congress using primarily statistical indices based on roll call votes have been able to be more specific about the nature of party activity in the House. The indices describe the *results* of the activity. But the *activity itself*—the "reality" of Truman or the "pressure" of Turner—cannot be caught by indices of votes.

The whip organizations are at the core of party activity in the House, particularly on the Democratic side. Thus the data here presented on the whip organizations are also data on parties in the House. They can be analyzed to provide a considerable range of generalizations about party activity in the House. Some of the generalizations which follow are quite speculative and demand much more research. Others come closer to being fully supported by the data on the whips.

1. The Democratic whip organization has become the focus of a corporate or collegial leadership in the House. Truman concluded that the evidence provided by record votes shows no collegial leadership,[52] although he indicated that the individual elective leaders in each party showed somewhat more unity. But observation of the Democratic whip organization suggests that the pattern of leadership in 1962 and 1963 was for the Speaker, Majority Leader, whip, deputy whip, and relevant committee chairman to

---

[50] Truman, "The State Delegations . . . ," *op. cit.*, p. 1045.
[51] Turner, *op. cit.*, p. 23.
[52] Truman, *The Congressional Party*, p. 245.

work closely together in the effort to pass a given piece of legislation. To expect a greater degree of corporate leadership—including *all* major committee chairmen on every separate piece of major legislation—is unrealistic. Each chairman has time to be concerned only about the legislation produced by his committee. The major missing participant during the period of this study, whom one would expect to find in a collegial leadership because he has a legitimate interest in all major legislation, is the Chairman of the Committee on Rules.[53]

2. Truman found that the voting structure of the parties in Congress "was focused upon one or a pair of positions: the Floor Leaders, joined at times, particularly on the Democratic side, by the Whips and, among the House Democrats, impliedly by the Speaker."[54] For House Democrats the operation of the whip organization helps explain why this focus is not mere coincidence. Even if the assistant whips do not uniformly "pressure" the members of their zones they do inform them of the voting preferences of the Speaker, Majority Leader, and whip. This information, as universally distributed to all Democrats, is one of the "triggers" which Bauer, Pool, and Dexter discuss.[55]

3. Truman suggests that the majority party has a natural basis for greater coherence than the minority party.[56] The Democratic whip organization, coordinated with the leadership offered by the President, helped the House Democrats to cohere on the major votes in 1962–1963. Similarly, the whip organization is an important institutional device for helping the House leadership perform a mediating role between the President and the rank and file Democratic membership. The elected legislative leaders of the President's party have a stake in his success in the House. The whip organization has a similar stake and also provides machinery for improving the President's chances.[57]

---

[53] Truman's reference to "the ambiguity surrounding the term 'the leadership' " (*ibid.*, p. 282) is also to the point here. "The leadership" is a fairly precise term when used in connection with a specific piece of legislation. It always includes the Speaker, Majority Leader, whip, and Committee Chairman. It may include the deputy whip, a Subcommittee Chairman, or a senior Committee member who is going to act as floor manager of the bill.

[54] *Ibid.*, p. 285.

[55] Raymond Bauer, Ithiel de Sola Pool, and Lewis A. Dexter, *American Business and Public Policy* (New York, 1963), p. 466.

[56] Truman, *The Congressional Party*, p. 278.

[57] See *ibid.*, ch. 8.

4. An important function of the Democratic whip organization is the carrying and recording of various bargains struck between party members on legislative matters. Within whip zones and even between whip zones both explicit and implicit bargains[58] are made between individual members. The whip organization then provides a framework for channeling the information on the bargains to a more central location—either the whip's office or the relevant Committee Chairman or one of the leaders individually. The transmission of information is incomplete but it is more complete than totally unorganized gossip.

5. The operations of the Democratic whip organization, especially of the sort noted in points 2 and 4 above, suggest that information can be as important and as effective as "pressure" of the classic mold. Information about legislation and about the intentions of individual legislators can be used to cue voting behavior favorable to the President and the leadership.[59]

6. The growth in the strength, complexity, and importance of both party whip organizations in this century suggests a growing sense of party solidarity within the House. The whip organizations now involve 16 Republicans and 20 Democrats directly. These 36 men and women have made a commitment of time—which members of the House must necessarily hoard—to work for their respective parties within the House. Unless they felt that party work was worth doing, a sufficient number of such commitments, of a desirable calibre, might not be forthcoming.

7. The history of the party whip organizations suggests that the importance of the whip partly depends on the mode of leadership exercised by the Speaker or Minority Leader, and secondarily on the role of the Rules Committee Chairman. Strong, solitary leaders like Rayburn have relied less on the whip than leaders who seek and need the active help of others. Leaders with fewer resources, like McCormack and Halleck, necessarily rely more on others in the leadership circle—including the whip and his organization.

---

[58] On implicit bargaining see Lewis A. Froman, Jr., *People and Politics* (Englewood Cliffs, N. J., 1962), pp. 55–56.

[59] Again this coincides with the findings of Bauer, Pool, and Dexter, *op. cit.* The importance of information is highlighted by Charles Clapp, *The Congressman* (Washington, Brookings Institution, 1963). He reports, p. 302, that criticism of both party whip organizations by House members centers "around the failure to perform the informing function." Lewis Anthony Dexter, in Peabody and Polsby, *op. cit.*, pp. 312 ff., discusses "the tyranny of information" in another context.

8. The contrast between the place of the Democratic whip organization and the Republican whip organization in 1962–1963 provides material for broader generalizations about the differences between the two parties in the House. The Democratic whip in these years was firmly lodged in a three-man leadership circle. His influence was great and his prospects for eventual advancement to Majority Leader were good. The Republican whip, however, would never obtain another leadership post. In addition, he had to work not only with the Minority Leader but also subject to the decisions of the 35-man Republican Policy Committee, of which he was but one member.[60] The majority leadership appeared to be substantially more compact than the minority leadership.

9. At the same time several features of the two party whip organizations suggest that the customary characterization of the Democratic Party in the House as a loose coalition of disparate groups without much central allegiance and of the Republican Party in the House as a closely-knit body of men dedicated to common principles may be at least partially correct. The Democratic assistant whips are regarded primarily as informing agents rather than as pressuring agents, although individual assistant whips may on occasion choose to pressure their zone members. The Democratic whip's office keeps no systematic voting records with which to confront the less loyal members. The Republican assistant whips, however, are expected to work for a solid Republican vote in accord with the dictates of the Policy Committee. The Republican whip's office keeps voting records, even on teller votes, so that the whip may berate the goats and praise the sheep when the occasion demands. The method of selection of the assistant whips is also an important difference. The Democratic whip is presented with assistants he may not want. The Republican whip picks his own assistants.[61]

---

[60] See the forthcoming book by Charles Jones on the House Republican Policy Committee.

[61] The voting records of the 1963 Republican and Democratic assistant whips over the previous two years indicate that each party organization had a similar number of "mavericks." Five Democratic assistant whips had a mean Larger Federal Role Support Score 22.6% lower than the mean Support Score of all 16 assistant whips who had been members of the 87th Congress. Five Republican regional and assistant whips had a mean Larger Federal Role Support Score 23% higher than the mean Support Score of all 14 regional and assistant whips who had been members of the 87th Congress. The Support Scores for individual members come from *Congressional Quarterly Almanac* for 1962.

Both the Republican and Democratic assistant whips had served, on the average, slightly more than nine years in the House by the end of 1963.

In short, the data suggest that a change is necessary in the typical description of the House which attributes, in the words of Professor Bone, "no consistently great influence in policy directing or in establishing party accountability for legislative program" to the party machinery.[62] As important pieces of party machinery the whip organizations possess such influence. How great and how consistent the influence, are still open questions. This article has attempted to provide some tentative answers to those questions.

---

[62] Hugh Bone, *American Politics and the Party System* (New York, 1955), p. 597.

X

COMMITTEE ASSIGNMENTS*

Nicholas A. Masters

ANY ATTEMPT to understand the legislative process, or to reckon how well it fulfills its purported functions, calls for a careful consideration of the relationships among congressmen. The beginning weeks of the first session of every congress are dominated by the internal politics of one phase of those relationships, the assignment of members to committees. Since congressmen devote most of their energies—constituents' errands apart—to the committees on which they serve, the political stakes in securing a suitable assignment are high. Competition for the more coveted posts is intense in both houses; compromises and adjustments are necessary. Members contest with each other over particularly desirable assignments; less frequently, one member challenges the entire body, as when Senator Wayne Morse fought for his committee assignments in 1953.[1]

The processes and patterns of committee assignments have been only generally discussed by political scientists and journalists. Perhaps the reason for this is too ready an acceptance of the supposition that these assignments are made primarily on the basis of seniority. Continuous service, it is true, insures a member of his place on a committee once he is assigned, but seniority may have very little to do with transfers to other committees, and it has virtually nothing to do with the assignment of freshman members. On what basis, then, are assignments made? Surely, not on the basis of simple random selection.

A recent student sees the committee assignment process as analogous to working out a "giant jig saw puzzle" in which the

* Reprinted from *American Political Science Review*, LV (June, 1961), 345–57. Copyright © 1961, The American Political Science Association. This study was made possible by the support of the Ford Foundation and Wayne State University. Neither of them, of course, is responsible for any errors of fact or interpretation.

[1] Ralph K. Huitt, "The Morse Committee Assignment Controversy: A Study in Senate Norms," *American Political Science Review*, LI (June, 1957), 313–329.

committees-on-committees observe certain limitations. These committees

> . . . must, of course, be guided by the number of vacancies and by the number of applications for transfer. Care is taken to attain geographical distribution, if not balance. Attention is paid to group desires and to the experience and training of individual legislators. And balance among the various factions of the party is sought. Beyond these more or less objective factors, being in the good graces of the party leader is certainly important in getting on major committees.[2]

This statement leaves significant questions unanswered. What, for example, is meant by geographical distribution or balance? Is every section or region represented in each party on each committee? Or does the committee's subject matter jurisdiction guide the type of geographical representation the committee-on-committees considers? Is the number of assignments allotted to a state party delegation on particular committees restricted? Do state party delegations develop a "vested interest" in certain committees and attempt to maintain continuous representation on them? What groups actively seek representation for their interests on the various committees by campaigning for an individual congressman to fill a vacancy? How influential are they? The study of committee assignments should also throw light on party factionalism, the differences between the parties in performing this organizational task, and the importance attached to the professional and group backgrounds of legislators.

As a step toward answers to these questions this study looks into the formal and informal processes of committee assignments in the House of Representatives.

The special hazards of this study deserve mention. No attempt was made to sample the House. The information derived from each Congressman must be used with caution, for legislators view events from a variety of perspectives. And finally, in all likelihood, some

---

[2] George Goodwin, Jr. "The Seniority System in Congress," *American Political Science Review,* LIII (June, 1959), 412–436.

[3] Data have been derived from unstructured interviews with members and staffs of the various committees, personal letters and similar papers, official documents of various types, and personal observations. I interviewed members of the committees-on-committees, deans of state delegations, and other members affected by the decisions. The survey covered the 80th through the 86th Congresses, with special attention to the 86th.

of the subtleties and nuances of the process have escaped observation. Despite these limitations, relatively crude techniques of analysis can yield significant results. For what sometimes frustrates our understanding of the most unique part of the American legislative process—the committee system—is the lack of organized data and the failure to analyse readily available data.

I. THE COMMITTEES-ON-COMMITTEES

In one of the more notable features of the reorganization of Congress in 1911, each party created a committee-on-committees to distribute committee assignments, on the theory, still asserted, that a party committee offers at least an opportunity for all party members to receive suitable assignments. Such a committee would go a long way toward eliminating the arbitrary judgments of the Speaker who, in the past, had used committee assignments as rewards and punishments, to help insure his control of pending legislation.

Though both parties use a committee for this purpose, their methods of selecting its members differ. Each committee therefore needs separate treatment, with comparisons from time to time.

Democrats

By custom the Democratic members of the House Ways and Means Committee, together with the Speaker and Majority Floor Leader (or the Minority Floor Leader when Democrats are in the minority), have constituted the committee-on-committees since 1911. This arrangement is evidently an outgrowth of the former practice of selecting the chairman of Ways and Means as the Majority Floor Leader. Because the Democratic members serve in this dual capacity, and although they are formally designated by the Democratic caucus, they are in fact self-perpetuating. The Speaker and Majority Floor Leader participate extensively in the Committee's deliberations and, of course, have considerable influence on the decisions.

The method of organizing the work of the Committee-on-committees in the 86th Congress was typical. Each member of the Committee was assigned a geographical zone within which his own district lies. (See Table I) All zones except two were geographically contiguous. Requests for committee assignments coming from members were handled by their respective zone committeeman.

For example, Representative Aime Forand from Rhode Island was responsible for the assignment and re-assignment requests of all Democratic representatives from districts within his zone, which includes, in addition to his own state, Connecticut, Maine, Massachusetts and Vermont. As can be seen from Table I, each zone representative served an average of approximately 18 members.

Although committee deliberations are closed, the procedure followed is well known among most House members. Each zone representative, speaking in order of seniority, nominates candidates from his zone for the various committee vacancies, usually with supporting arguments. Thereupon the Committee votes on each of the vacancies, and the nominee receiving the highest number of votes is designated to fill it.

The volume of work before the Committee varies, depending chiefly on the changes resulting from the preceding election. Almost always, however, there are more applications than vacancies; in the 86th Congress 124 applications were made for 75 places to be filled. The major committees were naturally most in demand; applications exceeded vacancies for all committees except District of Columbia, House Administration, Merchant Marine and Fisheries, Post Office and Civil Service, and Science and Astronautics—all regarded as lesser committees. Applicants usually list their order of preference, taking into account not only their personal desires but also advice from other members and their own assessments of where they stand the best chance to land at least an acceptable assignment. Without encouragement from above, an applicant, however much he might prefer to be on the Appropriations Committee, say, would hardly bother (or venture) to ask for what he realizes he has virtually no chance of getting.

Much more than committee structure and manner of procedure is involved in making assignments. Animating and guiding these formal mechanisms are the norms and customs observed when assignments are sought. The pervasive seniority rule, for example, works in a manner not commonly appreciated. Members seeking assignments, and particularly freshmen, channel their requests through the "dean" or senior member of their state party delegation. In negotiations between the Committee-on-committees and the applicants he plays a crucially important role in securing assignments. It is his special responsibility to see that his members receive adequate representation on the various committees. In performing this task, he tries to protect or maintain the delegation's place on

TABLE I

House Democratic Committee-on-Committees and Zone Assignments, 86th Congress

Committee Member	Zone	Dems. in State Del.	Freshmen	Committee Member	Zone	Dems. in State Del.	Freshmen
Mills (Ark.)	Ark.	6	(1)	Herlong (Fla.)	Fla.	7	(0)
	Del.	1	(1)		Ga.	10	(0)
	Kans.	3	(2)			—	—
	Okla.	5	(0)			17	(0)
		—	—	Ikard (Texas)	Texas	21	(1)
		15	(4)		N. Mex.	2	(1)
Forand (R.I.)	R.I.	2	(0)			—	—
	Conn.	6	(6)			23	(2)
	Me.	2	(1)				
	Mass.	8	(1)	Frazier (Tenn.)	Tenn.	7	(0)
	Vt.	1	(1)		N.C.	11	(1)
		—	—			—	—
		19	(9)			18	(1)
King (Calif.)	Calif.	16	(4)	Machrowicz	Mich.	7	(1)
	Alas.	1	(1)	(Mich.)	Ind.	8	(6)
	Ariz.	1	(0)		Ohio	9	(3)
	Nev.	1	(0)			—	—
	Utah	1	(1)			24	(10)
		—	—	Metcalf (Mont.)	Mont.	2	(0)
		20	(6)		Colo.	3	(1)
O'Brien (Ill.)	Ill.	14	(4)		Idaho	1	(0)
	Wis.	5	(2)		Nebr.	2	(2)
		—	—		N. Dak.	1	(1)
		19	(6)		Ore.	3	(0)
					S. Dak.	1	(0)
Boggs (La.)	La.	8	(1)		Wash.	1	(0)
	Ala.	9	(0)			—	—
	Miss.	6	(0)			14	(4)
		—	—				
		23	(1)	Green (Pa.)	Pa.	16	(4)
Keogh (N.Y.)	N.Y.	19	(2)		N.J.	5	(2)
		—	—			—	—
		19	(2)			21	(6)
Harrison (Va.)	Va.	8	(1)	Watts (Ky.)	Ky.	7	(2)
	S.C.	6	(0)		Md.	7	(3)
		—	—		W. Va.	5	(2)
		14	(1)			—	—
						19	(7)
Karsten (Mo.)	Mo.	10	(0)	Total		283	(63)
	Iowa	4	(3)				
	Minn.	4	(1)				
		—	—				
		18	(4)				

a major committee when a vacancy occurs and the seat has previously been held by a member of the delegation; he consults with, and advises, the members of his delegation seeking assignments as to what their chances are, and which committee assignments he will support for them. The dean's decisions must be made in consideration of the needs of his state, the qualifications of his own members, and the necessity for adjusting the requests among his members to prevent duplication on committees. It falls to his lot also to discourage and dissuade members who have unrealistic designs on the major committees—Appropriations, Rules, and Ways and Means.

The importance of the deans of the state delegations may be illustrated negatively. Connecticut, for the first time since 1936, elected six freshman Democrats in 1958. Since the entire delegation was composed of freshmen, no senior member could serve as the dean and apparently there was no time or forethought to form an agreement to become part of an area delegation. So when the committee assignments were made, only one of the six, Chester Bowles, felt that he had been given as good representation as he was entitled to. Bowles got the assignment of his choice, Foreign Affairs. Frank Kowalski was assigned to Armed Services because of his extensive military experience although it was not an assignment he wanted. The remaining four were given committee places they did not prefer, namely Science and Astronautics, Education and Labor, Government Operations, and a dual appointment to the District of Columbia and Post Office and Civil Service Committees. Several dissatisfied Connecticut congressmen complained, two of them quite bitterly, that their committee positions would not help them to be reelected—that they had received the "left over" assignments. These assignments had not been made from any desire to penalize them, but apparently because they were orphans with no dean or senior member to fight for their preferences or look after their interests.

If the Democratic Committee-on-committees is judged as a system of collective responsibility among men of equal status, then it is clear that the use of members of a permanent standing committee for this purpose has had almost the opposite effect. Each member does not carry equal weight on the committee. The status and rank of each Democratic member of Ways and Means are carried over to the Committee-on-committees. The ranking Democrat serves as chairman and the status of the other ranking members is unquestionably enhanced by the fact that they also serve as Ways and Means subcommittee chairmen when the Democrats are in the majority. These are the senior members in an institution that respects seniority.

Ways and Means members have had considerable congressional experience prior to their assignment. For the period 1913 to 1958, only five of 86 assignments to this Committee were given to congressmen without any seniority; and each of these five had had previous, but interrupted, congressional service. On the average, members have served at least three consecutive terms prior to being placed on the Committee, and the average is closer to five terms if computations are based simply on prior, rather than continuous, service before selection. The stability of the Committee's membership is also increased by the fact that, although a congressman may sometimes shrink from its responsibilities, only one member has ever left the Committee by his own request. What turnover there is results from death, resignation, or loss of party control, rather than from transfers or election defeat.

For a key functioning unit of the Democratic party's legislative apparatus, so much continuity in the Committee-on-committees makes it ill-designed for flexibility and responsiveness to electoral changes and public opinion trends. Rather, it is more analogous to a firmly entrenched bureaucracy, not completely immune but well insulated, and capable of considerable resistance to any pressures placed upon it.

Republicans

The Republican Committee-on-committees is specially set up for its function and is responsible for no other. It is composed of one member from each state having Republican representation in the House; thereby, a lone Republican from any state is automatically included. Each state delegation determines its member on the Committee. This method might be thought to provide an opportunity to select a new member for each new Congress, but the normal pattern, on the contrary, is for the senior member of the delegation, usually the dean, to assume membership on the Committee and hold it as long as he desires or remains in Congress. Table II shows the membership of the Republican Committee-on-committees for the 86th Congress.

The point is sometimes argued that the Republicans make it possible for each state delegation to assume a greater share of the organizational responsibility than the Democratic committee assignment process allows, and consequently that the decentralized

TABLE II
House Republican Committee-on-Committees, 86th Congress

State	Member	Votes	State	Member	Votes
Arizona	John J. Rhodes	1	New Jersey	Frank C. Osmers	9
California	James Utt	14	New York	Mrs. K. St. George	24
Colorado	J. Edgar Chenoweth	1	North Carolina	Chas. R. Jonas	1
Florida	William C. Cramer	1	North Dakota	Don L. Short	1
Idaho	Hamer Budge	1	Ohio	Clarence J. Brown	14
Illinois	Leo E. Allen	11	Oklahoma	Page Belcher	1
Indiana	E. Ross Adair	3	Oregon	Walter Norblad	1
Iowa	Charles B. Hoeven	4	Pennsylvania	Richard Simpson	14
Kansas	Edward H. Rees	3	South Dakota	E. Y. Berry	1
Kentucky	Eugene Siler	1	Tennessee	Howard H. Baker	2
Maine	Clifford G. McIntire	1	Texas	Bruce Alger	1
Massachusetts	William H. Bates	6	Utah	Henry A. Dixon	1
Michigan	Clare E. Hoffman	11	Virginia	Joel T. Broyhill	2
Minnesota	H. Carl Anderson	5	Washington	Jack Westland	6
Missouri	Thomas B. Curtis	1	West Virginia	Arch A. Moore	1
Nebraska	Phil Weaver	2	Wisconsin	John W. Byrnes	5
New Hampshire	Perkins Bass	2	Wyoming	E. Keith Thomson	1
			Total—153		

Subcommittee Appointed by Minority Leader

State	Member	Votes	Seniority
California	James Utt	14	4 consecutive terms
Idaho	Hamer H. Budge	1	5 consecutive terms
Illinois	Leo E. Allen	11	14 consecutive terms
Michigan	Clare E. Hoffman	11	13 consecutive terms
New Jersey	Frank C. Osmers	9	7 non-consecutive terms
New York	Katharine St. George	24	7 consecutive terms
North Carolina	Charles Raper Jonas	1	4 consecutive terms
Ohio	Clarence J. Brown	14	11 consecutive terms
Pennsylvania	Richard M. Simpson	14	7 consecutive terms
	Total—99		

Republican method is much more responsible to electoral changes. Actual Republican practice tends to contradict this argument. For the Republicans allow each representative on the Committee-on-committees to cast as many votes as there are Republicans in his delegation. This concentrates the power over committee assignments in the hands of the senior members from the large state delegations. In the 86th Congress, members from seven states—California, Illinois, Michigan, New Jersey, New York, Ohio, and Pennsylvania—controlled 97 of the 153 committee votes.

Not to mask the realities of power, the Republican committee assignments are handled by a Subcommittee which, in the 86th Congress for example, was composed of the senior members from these seven states and two others, with one vote each, evidently added to give a voice to large geographical areas (intermountain and southern) that would otherwise have gone entirely unrepresented. Together the Subcommittee members controlled about two-thirds of the full committee's votes. None of them had served less than four terms in Congress. By custom the Subcommittee is appointed by the Minority Leader (or Speaker, as the case may be) on the authority granted by a resolution of the full Committee. The resolution leaves the membership of the Subcommittee apparently at the discretion of the party leader, but the example just given shows how far he is hemmed in by the practice of appointing the same members from the larger delegations each time a new Congress convenes. The change in the minority leadership in the 86th Congress had no discernible effect on this part of the organizational process.

The Subcommittee receives and considers *all* applications for assignment and transfer, and the full Committee invariably accepts all of its recommendations. Subcommittee sessions are informal and each member is free to speak for or against any assignment. Information on newly elected members is obtained from the Republican Congressional Campaign Committee and the party leaders pride themselves on having extensive knowledge not only of the professional and personal backgrounds of their colleagues, but also of the constituencies they represent. Members of the full Committee who are not on the Subcommittee are entitled to participate in the determinations if they desire, but they seldom do.

Republicans from small states sometimes object that as a result of the system of proportional voting and large-state domination of the Subcommittee they have no real voice in committee assignments and are often overlooked for assignments to the better committees. Along the same line they complain that the Republican procedure allows no mechanism whereby the small state delegations can combine their voting power in the Committee-on-committees. The critics point to the Democratic practice of letting smaller state delegations select a joint dean in order to be able to negotiate for committee assignments from a position of strength.

Actually, the principal difference between Republican and Democratic practice in formal organization is that the Republicans have built into their system a voting formula that rewards heavy Republican areas; the Democrats offer no comparable leverage to the large delegations. Nor is it likely the Democrats would even consider such a plan as long as the seniority system prevails. For it would only lessen the power of the Southern Democrats by putting more control over committee assignments into the hands of the larger northern, midwestern, and western delegations, with their very different traditions and interests.

There is little to distinguish the manner and procedure followed by an individual Republican or Democratic congressman in securing an assignment. Republican freshman members also work through the deans of the state delegations, but the deans, unlike their Democratic counterparts, are usually members of the Committee-on-committees.

Despite these differences the arrangements in both parties for handling committee assignments have one basic feature in common. Both committees-on-committees are so constituted as to be virtually immune to immediate pressures brought about by electoral changes. This is no accident. Its justification rests on a number of considerations congenial to the norms and customs of the entire body. If junior or freshman members had the responsibility for making committee assignments they would immediately be thrust into difficult and delicate positions, particularly in deciding on transfer requests from senior members. Such decisions might well be controversial enough to damage permanently a junior member's career within the legislature and possibly outside of it. In private as well as public life, organizations seldom allow the newcomer—unfamiliar with the subtleties and the institutional trappings of the process—to make important personnel decisions; and committee assignments are party personnel decisions of the most crucial importance. Senior members simply would not willingly tolerate decisions made in this way. If forced to do so, the pressures, roadblocks and penalties they could evoke might be so severe and difficult to overcome that order in the whole legislative process might be endangered. The system has evolved as it has for these reasons, as well as for more positive benefits, such as the desire to rely on the more knowledgeable judgments of those with greater experience in the legislature.

Finally, the system is intended to give the process a tone of moderation and detachment. Members with seniority are less threatened by an election two years hence, being less subject to the vicissitudes of a competitive district. After years of experience in a collective body, senior members are readier to recognise the need for compromise and adjustment if work is to be done. Although competitive ambitions among members may be intense, prolonged debate over committee assignments would delay the conduct of legislative business which is already too long delayed by the employment of existing institutional and parliamentary devices.

The Role of Party Leaders

The role of the party leaders in making committee assignments is difficult to define; no simple definition fits all the realities. Generally speaking, the leadership of each party in the House is formidable and independent to a great degree, though the leaders' power varies with their personal relations with the other members. David Truman explains the dependence of the rank-and-file upon the party leaders as follows:

> The machinery of the House and of its parties is normally available to the ordinary member only, so to speak, on its own terms, because the source of its strength is also the source of its disabilities, namely, numbers. In a House of 435 or in a body roughly half that size, as one of the parties, there is a tendency . . . for the real and formal leadership closely to coincide. A formal, standardized system of communication and control is indispensable to the conduct of affairs in a body of that size. . . . This standardization of the communication structure implies that initiative tends to be centralized or at least that there are central controls on the flow of business. These the rank-and-file member cannot command or, as sometimes happens in the Senate, supplant. Hence, excepting some aspects of his own voting decisions, the independence of the ordinary member is restricted.[4]

The Democratic and Republican leaders not only play the principal role in the selection of the members of their respective committees-on-committees, but their personal judgments also tend to become the norm for major committee assignments. In practice, the leadership of both parties is directly involved in assignments to all the major committees, though the leaders do not usually concern themselves with applicants to lesser ones.

The party leaders use their power over committee assignments variously, to reward members who have been loyal and cooperative, and to reinforce the strength of their own positions by rewarding members whose loyalty may be suspected but whose strength may no longer be safely disregarded. Party leaders working with the com-

---

[4] *The Congressional Party: A Case Study* (New York, 1959), p. 195.

mittee-on-committees have in a number of instances offered important committee positions to members with demonstrated followings who were regarded as prospective threats. Such offers are made for the obvious purpose of securing cooperation, and so are frequently labelled as "sell-outs" or "the buying-off process" by some discontented members. Value judgments on particular cases will vary with individual viewpoints, but it must be recognized that Congress is not the only place where adjustments in the power structure are designed to accommodate or to absorb potentially strong rivals.

A specific example may be offered from the 86th Congress. Prior to the opening of the first session a group of liberal Democrats announced their intention to mobilize forces in the House in order to bring about the passage of legislation they favored. While the movement was underway—letters were being sent to the new Democratic members, as well as to incumbents sympathetic to their cause—Speaker Rayburn intervened, promising to use his influence to prevent the Rules Committee from blocking their bills. The Speaker, working with Chairman Wilbur Mills of the Ways and Means Committee and Majority Leader John McCormack, in order to demonstrate his willingness to cooperate with the group, offered one of their leaders, Lee Metcalf of Montana, an appointment to the Ways and Means Committee. Contrary to expectations, Metcalf said he did not want the assignment; he contended that he preferred to be on Interior and Insular Affairs—important for Montana. The leaders insisted, however, that he had a responsibility to his party to accept the post, and he finally did. Metcalf was the logical choice in a move to head off a possible revolt, because his previous behavior had satisfied the party leaders that he was a "responsible" legislator—a concept that warrants further examination presently.

II. CRITERIA FOR COMMITTEE ASSIGNMENTS

The committees-on-committees have rules to govern them in assigning members to the twenty permanent standing committees. The Legislative Reorganization Act of 1946 limited members of the House to service on a single committee, but this provision has since been amended as follows: (1) Three committees are *exclusive*—namely, Appropriations, Rules, and Ways and Means. A member who serves on any of these can serve on no other committee. An occasional exception is made, however. (2) Ten committees are *semi-exclusive;* members may serve on any one of them and any one of the seven non-exclusive committees. The ten are: Agriculture, Armed Services, Banking and Currency, Education and Labor, Foreign Affairs, Interstate and Foreign Commerce, Judiciary, Post Office and Civil Service, Public Works, and Science and Astronautics. (3) Seven committees are *non-exclusive.* A member may serve on any two of these seven, or any one of them and any one of the ten semi-exclusive committees. The seven are: District of Columbia, Government Operations, House Administration, Interior and Insular Affairs, Merchant Marine and Fisheries, Un-American Activities, and Veterans Affairs.

The 1946 Act also fixes the total membership of each committee, although changes can be and are made for the duration of a Congress by means of a House resolution. Party ratios on the Rules and Ways and Means committees are fixed by agreement among the party leaders, while the ratios on other committees ordinarily reflect the House division.[5]

Beyond these ground rules, experience has developed other criteria used in determining committee assignments. In discussing them here, the exclusive committees are treated separately first, because of the special attention given to filling vacancies on them. I will then turn to the variables that affect assignments to all of the committees.

Assignments to Major Committees

The three exclusive committees, Appropriations, Rules, and Ways and Means are regarded by all in both parties as being of special importance. Other committees—among them Agriculture, Armed Services, and Public Works—deal with issues that affect vital congressional and national interests, but none can lay con-

---

[5] In the 87th Congress a serious conflict arose over the Rules Committee ratio. There was newspaper talk of "purging" the ranking Democratic member, William Colmer from Mississippi, who had supported the Dixiecrat presidential candidacy of Mississippi's Governor Barnett in the 1960 campaign, and who regularly voted with Chairman Howard Smith in the coalition of southern Democrats and conservative Republicans that controlled the Rules Committee. But Speaker Rayburn, in order to break the "stranglehold" the coalition would have over the impending legislation of the Kennedy Administration, advocated instead an increase in the Committee's size. The conflict was resolved in Rayburn's favor by a narrow margin with the entire House participating in the vote. The subsequent appointments, however, were made along the lines suggested in this article.

tinuous claim to the power and prestige of the top three. As one Congressman stated, "If you get appointed to one of the top three, you have 'arrived.' "

Although the manner of attaining positions on these committees varies, each nominee must fit a bill of particulars. In practice, as indicated earlier, these lesser leaders are selected by the party leaders in consultation with the members of the committee-on-committees, rather than the other way around. A nominee's name may be first brought up by the party leaders, a committee member, or even by someone not involved in the mechanics, but whatever the technical circumstances surrounding the introduction of his name, if the nominee is assigned, he bears the party leaders' stamp of approval. This is true in both parties.

The principal factors involved in selecting members for a major committee may be grouped under three broad headings: (1) legislative responsibility, (2) type of district represented, and (3) geographical area represented.

(1) Legislative Responsibility. The most crucial test is whether a candidate is a "responsible" legislator, as the leaders of both parties use that term. What does a member have to be or do—or avoid—in order to be regarded as a responsible legislator?

According to the party leaders and the members of the committees-on-committees, a responsible legislator is one whose ability, attitudes, and relationships with his colleagues serve to enhance the prestige and importance of the House of Representatives. He has a basic and fundamental respect for the legislative process and understands and appreciates its formal and informal rules. He has the respect of his fellow legislators, and particularly the respect of the party leaders. He does not attempt to manipulate every situation for his own personal advantage. In the consideration of issues, he is careful to protect the rights of others; he is careful to clear matters that require clearance; and he is especially careful about details. He understands the pressures on the members with whom he cannot always agree and avoids pushing an issue to the point where his opponents may suffer personal embarrassment. On specific issues, no matter how firm his convictions and no matter how great the pressures upon him, he demonstrates a willingness to compromise. He is moderate, not so much in the sense of his voting record and his personal ideology, but rather in the sense of a moderate approach; he is not to be found on the uncompromising extremes of the political spectrum. Although the notions of those interviewed were somewhat vague on this point, a responsible legislator is apparently one who does not believe that the Congress is the proper place to initiate drastic and rapid changes in the direction of public policy. On the contrary, he is more inclined to be a gradualist, and to see public policy as a sort of "synthesis of opposing viewpoints." In short, a responsible legislator is politically pliant, but not without conviction.

A legislator can demonstrate his responsibility in many ways: how he manages a major bill; what he contributes in committee work; the sort of testimony he presents before other committees; the nature of his remarks on the floor—all these are tests of his responsibility. If he behaves properly in these settings and refrains from criticizing the party leadership—and gets reelected at home—his chances of being selected for a major committee post are very good. In the interviews, both Democrats and Republicans emphasized repeatedly the attention paid to the past performance of major committee applicants. For the major committees are "closed corporations," and their membership is composed only of those who have served their "apprenticeships" on lesser committees for considerable periods of time. Even in an instance in which party leaders feel compelled to appoint a member of a dissident wing of the party in order to gain greater cooperation, they will tend to select the member who most closely conforms to the norms of responsibility.

When the question was raised how Southern Democrats, who might be regarded as uncompromising on many questions, yet were appointed to major committees, the interviewees immediately pointed out how the Southerners differ from many of their "uncompromising" northern colleagues: they never denounce the legislative process as ill suited for public policy formation, they are never frustrated by its intricacies; rather, they master its techniques and use them skillfully and artfully to support their positions. "After all," one Congressman commented,

the Southerner usually joins this body free from the pressures many of the rest of us face and is usually eager to make his mark. Membership in Congress is the highest political office he is likely to attain and he will devote full time to the legislature. Other members often entertain higher political ambitions or may have to devote the majority of their time to keeping things running smoothly in their districts.

(2) Type of District Represented. It would be rare indeed for a member to earn regard as "responsible" in only one or two terms. No freshman has been assigned to the Rules Committee since the Legislative Reorganization Act was passed and only 14 have been assigned to the larger Appropriations Committee and two to the Ways and Means Committee (Table III). So the con-

TABLE III

Committee Assignments to Freshmen, House of Representatives, 80th–86th Congresses

Committee	Number of Freshman Assignments	
	Repub.	Dem.
Exclusive Committees:		
Appropriations	8	6
Rules	0	0
Ways and Means	2	0
Semi-Exclusive Committees:		
Agriculture	13	11
Armed Services	1	11
Banking and Currency	15	20
Education and Labor	17	27
Foreign Affairs	4	10
Interstate and Foreign Commerce	8	10
Judiciary	15	14
Post Office and Civil Service*	22	35
Public Works	20	20
Science and Astronautics†	0	8
Non-Exclusive Committees:		
District of Columbia	13	8
Government Operations	24	26
House Administration	11	19
Interior and Insular Affairs	17	28
Merchant Marine and Fisheries	24	26
Un-American Activities	6	1
Veterans' Affairs	33	30
Totals	253	310

* Reams of Ohio, Independent, assigned to Post Office and Civil Service in 82d Congress.
† Created by 86th Congress.
Data from *Congressional Directory,* 1st Session of each Congress. Includes only Representatives with *no* previous service at any time. Some Representatives received double assignments, so totals shown are higher than the total of freshmen in each Congress.

cept of responsibility is connected with an element beyond the member's personality, an element that takes into account the nature of his district. The members of the committees-on-committees have something more in mind here than simply a particular member's ability to be reelected. Long tenure by itself is an obvious objective fact, and common sense proof that a district is "safe"; but this is not enough. It is not necessarily to the point either

that the member's district may be safe for the incumbent but
not for any one else. The essence of the criterion lies in the
terms on which the member is returned rather than in the fact
of his return alone. The committee-on-committees wants to feel
that his district will not only reelect him but also allow him to
operate as a free agent, enabling him to make controversial decisions
on major policy questions without constant fear of reprisals at
the polls. His district must not be one that forces him to take
definite, uncompromising positions, for this would jeopardize his
usefulness in committee work. In the terminology of Eulau, Wahlke
et al., the district should be one that elects its member as a "trustee"
or a "politico" and not as a "delegate."[6] This requirement is of
special importance in considering assignments to the Rules Committee; many members would not relish being on this committee
despite its power, simply because it is inevitably involved in practically every issue before the Congress.

A related reason for the "safe" district requirement is based
on the idea that important committee posts should belong to the
professional, the veteran politician who has earned his way up
the ladder—the "politico" in preference to the "trustee." A politician from a safe district has fought and won enough political
battles to nail down a district and thus help his party maintain
control of the House. In short, he is a sure vote in the battle for
control and he should receive the rewards of the system.

Members of the committees-on-committees felt no compulsion
to explain away or camouflage this requirement. On the contrary,
they argue that a realistic appraisal of the factors operating in our
political system reveals that if a member sits on a congressional
committee in which compromises must continually be made on
matters of major policy, he cannot come from a district that does
not allow him flexibility.

(3) Geographical Area.   A legislator who is responsible and
who comes from a district that allows him considerable independence on issues still has no guarantee that he will be selected to fill
a major committee vacancy. He simply has a better chance than
others. A third factor serves to narrow the range of choice. For
both party committees tend to follow the practice of selecting a

---

[6] "The Role of the Representative: Some Empirical Observations on the
Theory of Edmund Burke," *American Political Science Review,* LIII (Sept.
1959), 742–756.

member from the same state party delegation as the member who vacated the seat, in order not to disturb the existing geographical balance. For example, upon the death or defeat of three members of the Ways and Means Committee, the Kentucky, Michigan, and Pennsylvania Democratic delegations asserted a prescriptive right to have members from their respective delegations chosen to fill the vacancies. Moreover, this practice sometimes extends to other committees. The Ohio Republican delegation, for example, insists that it should have one of its members on the Public Works Committee at all times.

Along this line, each party attempts to have every section of the nation represented on the Appropriations and Ways and Means committees. These are the only two committees, however, on which geographical balance is regarded as especially important. Actually the only geographical rule applied to all committee assignments provides that no state party delegation shall have more than one representative on any committee, except for the largest state delegations where strict application of the rule would be impossible.

General Criteria for All Committee Assignments

The most important single factor in distributing assignments to all other committees is whether a particular place will help to insure the reelection of the member in question. So although it might abstractly seem desirable and logical to place an urban congressman on the Agriculture Committee to protect consumer interests, there is little operative political warrant for such an assignment. Not only do congressmen from urban areas usually refrain from applying for such vacancies when they occur, but the committees-on-committees also insist that members coming from predominantly agricultural areas have first call on them in order that they may use the assignments to protect their tenure in office. Both parties take it for granted that wheat, cotton and tobacco areas should have the majority of representation on the committee. The leaders know from previous experience that assignment of an urban congressman to the Agriculture Committee would only make him "fair game" for each of the farm lobbies.

The same general reasoning applies to other committees as well. Assignments to Public Works, Interior and Insular Affairs or Merchant Marine and Fisheries are usually based on the ecological make-up of the members' districts, so as to allow them to serve their constituent interests and protect their incumbency. For example, South Dakota Democrat George McGovern's application for transfer to the Agriculture Committee from the Education and Labor Committee was approved primarily on the grounds that his former assignment handicapped his effectiveness in providing service to his constituents and was a disadvantage to him since it had become a major campaign issue in his farm district.

When two or more members stake a claim to the same assignment, on the ground that it is essential to their electoral success, both party committees usually, if not invariably, will give preference to the member with longer service. Members have often maneuvered for a position on a particular committee long before a vacancy existed, and sometimes even long before other applicants were first elected. But open importunity may be self-defeating, for no one likes a pest.

Some Special Cases

The assignment of members to the Education and Labor Committee—with jurisdiction over the explosive issues of school aid, segregation and labor-management relations—has called for the most careful attention to the constituencies of applicants. As the party committees have seen it in recent years, this assignment is no place for a neutral when there are so many belligerents around. Their assignments have produced a standoff between antagonists,[7] and a suggestion during the 86th Congress, dropped in the end, for a partition of the Committee as an alternative to the prospective accession of Adam Clayton Powell of New York to its chairmanship upon the retirement of Graham Barden of North Carolina. Apart from the Southerners and a handful of others from districts safe enough to allow them comfortable independence, Democrats have felt that only members who can afford politically to take an outright pro-labor position—*i.e.*, who get union support for election—should be assigned to this committee.

Members from farm or middle-class suburban districts are discouraged from applying. Service on this committee by a member whose district is relatively free of labor-management or segregation conflicts would only result in raising issues in his district that could prove embarrassing and even politically fatal to the member.

---

[7] *Cf.* Seymour Scher, "Congressional Committee Members as Independent Agency Overseers: A Case Study," *American Political Science Review*, LIV (Dec. 1960), 911–920.

Republicans appear to have concluded, too, that it is impossible to take a moderate position on labor-management issues. They also dissuade members from applying for this committee when it might impair their chances for reelection. Republican assignees, however, are more likely to take a pro-management or non-labor view for the obvious reason that fewer Republicans receive overt political support from organized labor; more have close ties with management groups.

For the Democratic Committee-on-committees, a special issue affects assignments to what has been commonly described as an unimportant committee, the District of Columbia Committee. Southern legislators attach a great deal of importance to their efforts to maintain representation on that committee and to control it. The objective is to block home rule for the District, with all the implications of extensive Negro participation in District political affairs.

More generally, southern congressmen have a more or less collective understanding that in order to maximize their influence on the legislative process they need to spread their strength over all the committees. This involves maneuvering for positions on the "housekeeping" committees. Although *a priori* calculations might seem to argue that dispersing members over twenty committees would weaken rather than strengthen southern control of the House, in actual practice the seniority rule vindicates their strategy. Collectively, congressmen from the South build up more seniority than any other sectional contingent and reap their rewards in committee and sub-committee chairmanships when the Democrats are in the majority.

Organized Interest Group Participation

All members of the committees-on-committees recognized that organized groups outside Congress take a hand in the assignment process from time to time. The influence of such groups is thought to be important, but little evidence is available on its nature and extent. Sometimes, though not often, organized groups formally endorse a nominee for a committee vacancy. For example, Representative Harold B. McSween (Dem., La.), when applying for assignment to the Agriculture Committee, had letters of endorsement from American Farm Bureau representatives placed in his application file. Democrats attempt to placate organized labor by placing pro-labor representatives on the Education and Labor Committee, while Republicans attempt to satisfy the National Association of Manufacturers by appointing pro-business members to the same Committee. The most widely publicized groups connected with assignments to the Ways and Means committee are spokesmen for the oil interests. Democratic members and staff personnel frequently mentioned in interviews that a nominee's acceptability for assignment to this committee often hinged on whether he demonstrated a willingness to oppose any attempts to reduce the oil depletion tax allowance.

Nevertheless, organized groups, with occasional exceptions, appear to refrain from direct intervention in committee assignments; overt intrusion is apt to be resented and so be self-defeating. Rather, they have certain "expectations" about the type of person who should be selected for the vacancies on committees which affect their interests. Each group usually counts several members "friendly" or responsive to their needs. Organized interests do not often concern themselves too much with the selection of a particular member of the "friendly" group so long as one of them is eventually chosen.

Other Considerations

The proposition is sometimes advanced that geographical balance is a deliberate objective in distributing assignments to all committees. If so, it has a low priority. There is no evidence of systematic effort to provide each section with representation on the various committees proportional to its representation in the House. The Appropriations and Ways and Means committees may be considered as exceptions, but even here a much more pressing consideration is representation for the large tax-paying states. An examination of the membership of the Interior and Insular Affairs Committee clearly shows that geographical balance is not necessarily a primary goal for all committees. Of the 19 Democratic members of this committee in the 86th Congress, 17 were from districts west of the Mississippi, and of the twelve Republican members six were from western states. Both committees-on-committees will, indeed, listen sympathetically to an applicant who argues that his section of the nation has no representation on the committee of his choice, but this argument is not a compelling reason for making the assignment. Ordinarily, applications are based on district and state delegation, not regional, considerations. Republican New Englanders, for instance, do not approach committee assignments

from the viewpoint that each committee should have a New Eng-
lander on it. A notable exception to this generalization sets the
Southern Democrats apart; as stated earlier, they regularly try
to have Southern representation on all committees.

Party factionalism is a more serious concern than geographical
balance. Republicans and Democrats alike, who were responsible
for making committee assignments, vigorously denied the existence
of factions within their parties; but readily admitted that their
respective groups harbored members with widely divergent viewpoints. Occasional alignments emerge, they acknowledged, but these
are regarded as fleeting in character. They asserted that no committee's party representation should be composed exclusively of
members who view political issues from the same perspective and
claimed to have made a reasonable effort to see that divergent
viewpoints within each party find expression on each committee.
We have already noted, however, that members on the extremes
of the political spectrum are usually passed over for vacancies in
the major committees; and a member's location on the spectrum
is assessed by the party leadership and the committee-on-committees.
It is a matter of opinion, therefore, how well founded is the frequent
claim that party representation on each committee is balanced
ideologically.

Unfavorable assignments, of little political value to the recipients,
are sometimes deliberately given by the powers that be as a mark
of disapproval, or for reasons that might be described as "for the
good of the order." In one recent instance Dale Alford, Democrat
from Arkansas, was said to have been assigned to the Post Office
and Civil Service Committee because some members of the Committee-on-committees felt that he had violated the "rules of the
game" in his campaign that displaced former Representative Brooks
Hays, a widely respected member, in the wake of the Little Rock
controversy. Two years later, after he had voted with the leadership
to "pack" the Rules Committee, he was given a place on the Appropriations Committee. Also, there was surprising agreement among
those interviewed that the original Democratic transfers to the newly
created Science and Astronautics Committee—not taken seriously in
the House at its founding—were made in order to provide the trans-
ferees with sinecures, and so to remove some of the less qualified
members from the other committees. The transfer offers were made
attractive to senior members by promises that they would receive
subcommittee chairmanships, which would provide them oppor-

tunities to build their niches within the legislative bureaucracy.

The professional background of an individual legislator is seldom in and of itself the controlling factor in his assignment. However, some general rules relating to the professional backgrounds of legislators are followed by both parties. Almost without exception, lawyers only are appointed to the Judiciary Committee. Members with outstanding experience in international relations or with extensive military service are regarded as excellent choices for the Foreign Affairs and Armed Services committees respectively. Other things being equal, former bankers and financiers may be given a slight edge over competing applicants for such committees as Appropriations, Ways and Means, and Banking and Currency. The same holds true for farmers who apply for the Agriculture Committee and for members closely identified with the labor movement who apply for the Education and Labor Committee. But all agreed that holding elective office, particularly a state legislative office, outweighed any other type of professional experience as a qualification for any committee assignment. Holding elective office is regarded as a profession by members of the committees, and they feel that the rewards of the system should go to the professionals. Although the patterns of committee assignments tend to document the importance of professional background, it would be a mistake to assume that the committees-on-committees seek out applicants on this ground. Normally, the reverse is true. Applicants tend to apply for assignments where they think their professional skills can be used to best advantage.

The manner in which a congressman campaigns for a committee is an important factor in the outcome. For example, a member seeking an assignment often solicits the support of members already on the committee. Another technique is to obtain the support of influential political leaders, such as endorsements from the governor, senators, or members of the state legislature. If an individual is comparatively unknown in national politics, he may attempt to familiarize the members of the Committee-on-committees with his background and training as it relates to the type of service he can give on the committee he desires. All these tactics, properly employed, can go a long way toward helping a member get favorable consideration by his party. He must be careful, however, to avoid giving the impression of exerting undue political pressure on the members of the Committee-on-committees. For example, if the committee tells him that a vacancy has already been promised to another, he is *expected* to accept this decision. Attempts to challenge either committee's decisions are generally regarded as serious departures from the norms of conduct in the House.

Religious considerations are not ignored in judging the qualifications of applicants. Most Democratic members interviewed conceded that it was important, when possible, to have at least one Roman Catholic on the major committees, and particularly on the Ways and Means and Education and Labor Committees. Republicans, on the other hand, contended that religious factors had no bearing on their assignments.

Racial and ethnic factors also enter into the calculations occasionally. For example, the Democratic committee-on-committees thought it made sense to appoint Charles Diggs, Democrat and Negro from the 13th District in Michigan, to the House Foreign Affairs Committee because of his race and because of the emerging prominence of Africa in international affairs. In his letter of application to the Committee, Diggs argued on these grounds. Republicans denied considering racial factors as they denied the relevance of religion.

Finally, a few committee assignments are made virtually at random. Usually a handful of lesser places are left over after the committees-on-committees have argued and settled all the applications. These may be handed out more or less indiscriminately to freshman members. At least two circumstances contribute to this result. One occurs when members fail to make their preferences known or to attract any advance support for their applications. This may stem simply from a freshman member's innocence of the process, or, as in the case of the Connecticut Democratic delegation, from the absence of any senior spokesman in their behalf. A second arises when the committee-on-committees members, along with the party leadership, have too many prior commitments to give serious consideration to each applicant's stated preference. These commitments may extend to members who are obviously less qualified than those who were passed over.

III. SUMMARY AND CONCLUSION

Committee assignments in the House of Representatives involve all the complexities of an organization whose members "are not automatons but reasoning men and women acting in a setting in which they are subject to a bewildering barrage of conflicting or, at the least, inconsistent, demands—from within their constituencies. . . ."[8] Caution is consequently in order in formulating generalizations to describe the assignment process. In this study I have not tried to go beyond an assessment of the factors taken into account at the time the assignments were made, by those who made them. Whether the behavior, then or later, of those who were assigned is consistent with the reasons given for the assignments, or vindicated expectations expressed, is outside the scope of my endeavor.

From the data, several conclusions can be advanced as hypotheses for future studies:

(1) Despite some important differences in the formal structure, both the Democratic and Republican committee assignments are handled by small groups composed of senior members appointed and greatly influenced by the party leaders.

(2) Party leaders, working in conjunction with their committees-on-committees, use assignments to major committees to bargain with the leaders of party groups or factions, in order to preserve and fortify their leadership positions and conciliate potential rivals, as well as to reward members who have cooperated.

(3) Assignment to the major committees is restricted, with some exceptions, to members who have served two or more terms, who are "responsible" legislators, and who represent districts which do not require them to take inflexible positions on controversial issues.

(4) Although a number of factors enter into committee assignments—geography, group support, professional background, etc.—the most important single consideration—unless it can be taken for granted—is to provide each member with an assignment that will help to insure his re-election. Stated differently, the most impressive argument in any applicant's favor is that the assignment he seeks will give him an opportunity to provide the kind of service to his constituents that will sustain and attract voter interest and support. In distributing assignments the party acts as a mutual benefit and improvement society, and this for the obvious reason that control of the House depends on the re-election of party members.

(5) With minor differences, both parties apply the same criteria for making committee assignments. This does not necessarily imply

---

[8] Truman, *op. cit.*, p. 279.

that there are no differences between Republican and Democratic assignees. It does show that both parties tend to emphasize factors beyond the ideological commitments of the members, and that calculations of party advantage lead them both to substantially the same criteria.

XI

THE DECISION TO ENLARGE
THE COMMITTEE ON RULES:
AN ANALYSIS OF THE 1961 VOTE*

Milton C. Cummings, Jr.
Robert L. Peabody

ON JANUARY 31, 1961, after an intense two-hour session, the United States House of Representatives, by a vote of 217 to 212, adopted House Resolution 127:

> *Resolved,* That during the Eighty-seventh Congress the Committee on Rules shall be composed of fifteen members.[1]

Simply phrased and innocuous in wording, this resolution was no routine exercise of congressional powers under the constitutional provision that "Each House may determine the Rules of its Proceedings . . . ." At stake in this action to increase the size of the Committee on Rules from twelve to fifteen members were the power and prestige of the newly elected President, John F. Kennedy, the Speaker of the House, Sam Rayburn of Texas, and the Chairman of the Committee on Rules, Howard W. Smith of Virginia. At stake, also, was the crucial issue of who was to control the powers lodged in the Committee on Rules: Rayburn and through him the President as head of the majority party, or the Chairman of the Rules Committee, acting independently and representing the views of the conservative southern Democratic-Republican voting alignment.

---

* This study was made possible by the support of The Brookings Institution. We are also indebted to numerous readers for helpful comments on early drafts of the manuscript. For any errors of interpretation or fact that remain, we alone are responsible.

[1] *Congressional Record,* January 31, 1961, p. 1502. This resolution temporarily amended Rule X, Clause 1 (p), of the House of Representatives, which sets the size of the Committee on Rules at twelve members. Lewis Deschler, *Constitution, Jefferson's Manual,* and *Rules of the House of Representatives of the United States,* House Document 479, 86th Cong., 2nd sess., 1961, p. 325. All references to the *Congressional Record* are to the unbound daily edition unless otherwise noted.

The outcome of this contest for control of the Committee on Rules had important implications for the way in which the House would conduct its business during the remainder of the Eighty-seventh Congress. As the key coordinating committee of a 435-member legislative body, the committee possesses extraordinary powers. It not only acts as the traffic controller for legislation, it also determines time limits on debate and the kind and number of amendments that may be offered from the floor.

> It may kill a bill by refusal to recommend a rule; it may expedite legislation by recommending appropriate rules; it may limit debate drastically; it may limit the amendments to be offered to bills; it may, in effect, determine the form of the question to be voted on by the House. The committee may even control the substance of the measures submitted to the House by declining to grant a rule until the legislative committee modifies the bill to meet its wishes.[2]

Furthermore, unless unanimous consent is obtained, a special rule must be granted by the Committee on Rules before House conferees can meet with Senate conferees to discuss disagreements between the two houses on legislation. The committee also may recommend to the House the creation of select committees and direct them to make investigations.

The purpose of this study of the 1961 House Rules controversy is threefold: first, to outline the events leading up to the crucial vote on the floor of the House; second, to analyze the vote itself, particularly the behavior of the sixty-four Democrats and twenty-two Republicans who bolted party lines; and, finally, to speculate briefly on some of the broader questions that were raised by the decision which the House made.[3]

---

[2] V. O. Key, Jr., *Politics, Parties and Pressure Groups* (4th ed.; New York: Thomas Y. Crowell, 1958), p. 719. See James A. Robinson, "The Role of the Rules Committee in Arranging the Program of the U.S. House of Representatives," *Western Political Quarterly*, XXII (September 1959), 653–69; and James A. Robinson, "The Role of the Rules Committee in Regulating Debate in the U.S. House of Representatives," *Midwest Journal of Political Science*, V (February, 1961), 59–69, for an extensive analysis of the actions of the Committee on Rules in the 76th–84th Congresses.

[3] At this point, a word of disclaimer is in order. In the subsequent analysis, we are less concerned with explaining why *individual* representatives voted the way they did than in establishing generalizations about the way groups of congressmen behaved in the *aggregate*—as, for example, the southern Democrats who broke with their party leadership. We gained our initial impressions about the 1961 House Rules controversy from observation of the floor fight and the

I. THE GROWTH OF DISSATISFACTION

During the early years of the American Republic, the House Committee on Rules operated as a select committee set up at the beginning of each Congress with authorization to report a system of rules and no other important function.[4] As the House increased in size, the powers and privileges of the Rules Committee grew. In 1858, the Speaker became a member of the committee; and in 1880, the committee was made a standing body of five members with the power to issue special orders. In subsequent years, the Speaker, as chairman of the committee, increasingly made it a device by which his party could control legislation. By 1910, opposition to the power which Republican Speaker Joseph Cannon of Illinois had acquired was sufficiently strong that insurgent Republicans combined with minority-party Democrats to remove the Speaker from his *ex officio* status as a member of the committee.[5]

---

open meetings of the Committee on Rules and from the coverage by the mass media. The core of the analysis, however, rests upon a detailed examination of the vote using data concerning the characteristics of the congressmen and the constituencies they represent. These findings then served as a basis for informal discussion with more than twenty congressmen and congressional staff members. For their assistance and insights, we extend our thanks.

[4] For a brief history of the Committee on Rules, see George B. Galloway (revised by Walter Kravitz), "A Short History of the Development of the House Committee on Rules" (Washington, D.C.: Library of Congress, Legislative Reference Service, Mimeographed, 1961). See also, Floyd M. Riddick, *Congressional Procedure* (Boston: Chapman & Grimes, 1941), pp. 79–83.

[5] The 1961 House Rules controversy presents an intriguing contrast to the overthrow of Speaker Cannon. On March 19, 1910, a "coalition" of insurgent Republicans led by George Norris of Nebraska and minority-party Democrats headed by Champ Clark of Missouri adopted a resolution which removed the Speaker from the Rules Committee, enlarged the committee's membership from five to ten (six from the majority party and four from the minority party), and assigned to the House as a whole the selection of its members. *Congressional Record*, 61st Cong., 2nd sess., 1910, XLV, Part 4, 3425–36; and Charles R. Atkinson, *The Committee on Rules and the Overthrow of Speaker Cannon* (New York: Columbia University, 1911). Three years later, a future Speaker of the House, Sam Rayburn, became a member of the Sixty-third Congress. Almost fifty-one years after the 1910 revolt, the power which had been used by Speaker Cannon to prevent bills opposed by the Taft Administration from reaching the floor was partially restored to Speaker Rayburn in order that the Kennedy legislative program might reach the floor of the House. See Arthur Krock, "A Curious Interplay of Reform and Reaction," *New York Times*, January 26, 1961, p. 28. Of course, few of Cannon's formal powers were restored to Speaker Rayburn, despite the fact that at least one congressman proposed putting the Speaker back on the Committee on Rules. *Congressional Record*, August 26, 1960, p. 16699. In both cases, however, the Committee on Rules was enlarged to prevent certain bills from being blocked in the committee. See also George B. Galloway, "Leadership in the House of Representatives," *Western Political Quarterly*, XII (June, 1959), 438–41.

While the size of the committee has fluctuated between ten and fourteen members since 1910, the majority party has maintained an approximately two-to-one advantage in membership. Thus, when the Democratic party controlled the House, as in the Eighty-fourth, Eighty-fifth, and Eighty-sixth Congresses, the Committee on Rules was composed of eight Democrats and four Republicans. In periods when the majority party was united, it was able to dominate the committee and thereby to control the order and rules governing legislation brought to the floor. From 1910 until 1937, except for occasional independent action by its chairman, the Committee on Rules functioned as a responsible instrument of the majority party leadership. But by 1937, a bipartisan coalition of dissident Democrats and conservative Republicans who were united in their opposition to President Roosevelt's legislative program had come to dominate the committee, and the House Democratic leadership was forced to use the discharge petition to get the bill that became the Wages and Hours Act of 1938 to the floor.[6]

Although Chairman John J. O'Connor was defeated in 1938, other members of the Rules Committee, including Smith of Virginia, survived Roosevelt's attempted "purge." Between 1939 and 1961, except for the Republican Eightieth and Eighty-third Congresses, the Committee on Rules tended to be dominated by a bipartisan conservative bloc, despite Rayburn's occasional successful use of personal influence with its members to work his will. One major attempt to restrict the formal powers of the Committee on Rules, the twenty-one-day rule, proved successful in getting bills to the floor of the House, but this rule was short-lived.[7]

During each succeeding Congress, controversy over the activity of the committee continued. The issue became most sharply drawn in the Eighty-sixth Congress, when the largest Democratic majority in the House since 1937 attempted to enact a legislative record on which to campaign in the 1960 elections. On January 3, 1959, Ray-

---

[6] Robinson, "The Role of the Rules Committee in Arranging the Program . . . ," *op. cit.,* p. 659.

[7] On January 3, 1949, the Eighty-first Congress adopted the "twenty-one-day rule," a procedure by which the chairman of a legislative committee which had reported a bill favorably and requested a rule from the Committee on Rules could bring the bill directly to the House floor if the Rules Committee failed to grant the rule within twenty-one calendar days of the request. Following Republican gains in the 1950 mid-term elections, Congress repealed the "twenty-one-day rule" on the opening day of the Eighty-second Congress. *Congressional Record,* 81st Cong., 1st sess., 1949, XCV, Part 1, 10–11; 82d Cong., 1st sess., 1951, XCVII, Part 1, 9–19. See also Galloway, "Leadership in the House . . . ," *op. cit.,* p. 440–41.

burn promised the leaders of the Democratic Study Group, a loose organization of some 100 to 120 liberally oriented Democratic representatives, that "legislation which has been duly considered and reported by legislative committees will be brought before the House for consideration within a reasonable time."[8] Three days later, however, House Republicans chose Charles Halleck of Indiana to replace Joseph Martin of Massachusetts as Minority Floor Leader. Martin had alternated as Minority Floor Leader and Speaker with Rayburn since 1940; and, by working through Martin, Rayburn had occasionally been able to pick up one or two votes from Republican moderates on the Rules Committee in order to get legislation to the floor.[9]

During the Eighty-sixth Congress, the two ranking majority members of the Committee on Rules, Chairman Smith of Virginia and William M. Colmer of Mississippi, consistently aligned themselves with the four Republican members of the committee, Leo E. Allen of Illinois, Clarence J. Brown of Ohio, B. Carroll Reece of Tennessee, and Hamer H. Budge of Idaho. Table I illustrates the ideological split that existed between the pro-Rayburn "moderates" and "liberals" and the anti-Rayburn "conservatives" on the Rules Committee, both before and after the decision to enlarge its membership. Whether one uses a "liberal" rating scale such as that compiled by Americans for Democratic Action, or a "conservative" index compiled by the business-orientated Civic Affairs Associates, the same basic voting pattern on the Committee on Rules is revealed.[10] The table indicates that, except on civil rights legislation, the voting record of Smith and Colmer on major issues was almost identical

---

[8] *Congressional Quarterly Weekly Report,* XVII (January 9, 1959), 45.

[9] To fill two vacancies formerly held by moderate Republicans on the Committee on Rules, Halleck appointed two conservative Republicans—B. Carroll Reece of Tennessee, who had had previous service on the committee, and Hamer H. Budge of Idaho.

[10] Interest group rating scales, as congressmen are among the first to point out, have a number of limitations. Not only are they usually restricted to a few selected issues in one or two sessions of Congress, but the issues and particular votes are sometimes chosen so as to demonstrate a pattern of voting sympathetic or opposed to the interest group's ends. Other rating scales, such as the AFL-CIO Committee on Political Education scale or the "conservative" Americans for Constitutional Action voting records, could have been used to demonstrate approximately the same gross distinctions. The Americans for Democratic Action scale, which is used in Table I and elsewhere in this study, was selected because it was based on nine issues in the most recent session of Congress (1960), several of which would again confront House members in the first session of the Eighty-seventh Congress. The derivation of the ADA and CAA (Civic Affairs Associates) indices are discussed in more detail in Table I, notes * and †.

with that of the committee's four Republican members during the Eighty-sixth Congress. It also suggests the combination of five "liberal" and three southern Democratic "swing" votes that made up the Rayburn majority following enlargement of the committee on January 31, 1961. Finally, Table I indicates clearly that the four new Republicans appointed to the committee in 1961 were apt to vote just as "conservatively" as the Republicans they replaced.

TABLE I

Members of the Rules Committee and Their Records on ADA and CAA Approved Measures During the Eighty-sixth Congress

	RULES COMMITTEE MEMBERS			
Members, 86th Congress	*Votes Approved by: ADA* CAA†* *(Per cent)*		*New Members, 87th Congress*	*Votes Approved by: ADA CAA* *(Per cent)*
Democrats				
Pro-Rayburn				
Madden (Ind., 1)	100	0		
Delaney (N.Y., 7)	100	0		
Bolling (Mo., 5)	100	0		
O'Neill (Mass., 11)	100	14		
			Sisk (Calif., 12)	100 0
			Elliott (Ala., 7)	75 15
Trimble (Ark., 3)	67	21		
Thornberry (Tex., 10)	67	36		
Anti-Rayburn				
Smith (Va., 8) Chairman	0	93		
Colmer (Miss., 6)	0	69		
Republicans‡				
Allen (Ill., 16)	11	100	St. George (N.Y., 28)	13 100
Brown (Ohio, 7)	11	93		
Reece (Tenn., 1)	11	93	Avery (Kansas, 1)	22 100
Budge (Ida., 2)	0	100	Smith (Calif., 20)	0 93
			Hoffman (Ill., 14)	0 93

* For a detailed description of the roll calls on which the ADA (Americans for Democratic Action) "liberalism-conservatism" index is based, see *Congressional Quarterly Weekly Report*, XVIII (October 7, 1960), 1655–66. The percentages indicate the degree to which each member voted in accordance with the ADA's position on nine selected issues during the second session of the Eighty-sixth Congress (1960), including an increase in the minimum wage, federal aid for school construction, a depressed areas bill, appropriations for the mutual security program, and the Civil Rights Act of 1960. See note 10 for the limitations of such rating scales.

† The CAA (Civic Affairs Associates) index is based on fourteen selected issues during the Eighty-sixth Congress (1959–60), including federal employee salary increases, a minimum wage, school construction, distressed areas, and the 1959 labor reform bill (Landrum-Griffin Act). The percentages indicate the degree to which each member supported the Civic Affairs Associates' orientation in favor of the private enterprise system as against "bureaucratic planning under a government enterprise system." *Ibid.*, pp. 1655–66, esp. p. 1656.

‡ Representative Allen retired, and Representative Budge was defeated for re-election in 1960. On March 28, 1961, Representative Avery was named to the Committee on Rules to replace Congressman B. Carroll Reece, who died March 19, 1961.

By a six-to-six tie vote, the conservative members of the committee were able to block, delay, or force revision of a number of social welfare measures in the Eighty-sixth Congress.[11] Under the leadership of Speaker Rayburn and Majority Floor Leader John McCormack, however, liberal Democratic members were able to use Calendar Wednesday proceedings to pass the aid to distressed areas bill, and, through threatened use of the discharge petition, to force release of what was to become the Civil Rights Act of 1960.[12] When Congress recessed for the 1960 nominating conventions, both political parties adopted platform planks critical of existing congressional procedures.[13] Shortly thereafter, criticism of the control exercised by the House Committee on Rules reached a high point during the post-convention August session, when the committee refused to grant a special rule allowing House conferees to meet with Senate conferees on the education bill.[14]

---

[11] For a detailed analysis of the events of the second session of the Eighty-sixth Congress, see Ivan Hinderaker, "From the 86th to the 87th Congress: Controversy over 'Majority Rule,' " *American Government Annual, 1961–62* (New York: Holt, Rinehart & Winston, 1961), pp. 76–98, esp. pp. 90–94. The activity of the Democratic Study Group in the House Rules controversy is given extended coverage in National Committee for an Effective Congress, *Congressional Report,* X, No. 1 (March 4, 1961), 1–5.

[12] Members of the House of Representatives who wish to circumvent or override the decisions of the Committee on Rules have recourse to a number of procedures: principally, unanimous consent, suspension of the rules, Calendar Wednesday proceedings, and the discharge petition. For a brief summary of each of these procedures, see *Congressional Quarterly Weekly Report,* XVIII (December 30, 1960), 1994. Some of the dilatory motions which can be used against Calendar Wednesday proceedings are demonstrated in the debate on the distressed areas bill, *Congressional Record,* May 4, 1960, pp. 8737–44. But see the remarks of Congressman Thomas B. Curtis, *Congressional Record,* July 25, 1961, p. 12466.

[13] The Democratic party platform urged that "the rules of the House of Representatives . . . be so amended as to make sure that bills reported by legislative committee reach the floor for consideration without undue delay." *The Rights of Man,* Democratic Platform, Report of the Committee on Resolutions and Platforms as adopted by the Democratic National Convention, Los Angeles, California, July 12, 1960, p. 47. Congressmen Chester Bowles and Chet Holifield, both leaders in the Democratic Study Group, were key members of the Democratic Platform Committee. The Republican platform specially criticized the Senate's Rule XXII. *Building a Better America,* Republican Platform, Adopted by the Republican National Convention, Chicago, Illinois, July 27, 1960, p. 29.

[14] On August 26, 1960, eleven Democratic representatives made or inserted statements critical of the House Committee on Rules. *Congressional Record,* August 26, 1960, pp. 16698–706. During the floor debate preceding the roll-call vote on the Rayburn resolution, Chairman Smith accused these representatives of opening the assault on the Committee on Rules. *Congressional Record,* January 31, 1961, p. 1505.

Maneuvering Before the Floor Fight[15]

In the November, 1960, elections, the Democratic party captured the White House and maintained control of both houses of Congress; but the Republicans made a net gain of twenty-one House seats, thus apparently diminishing the possibilities of a change in the House rules. In November, Democratic Chairman Smith announced his opposition to any change. Subsequently, he met with Republican Floor Leader Halleck to discuss plans for maintaining the status quo.[16]

When Speaker Rayburn returned to Washington three days before the Eighty-seventh Congress convened, he was convinced that some change had to be made, but he had not yet decided on which alternative to pursue.[17] After presenting Smith with an opportunity to introduce a resolution enlarging the Committee on Rules from twelve to fifteen members, which Smith refused, Rayburn met with the leaders of the Democratic Study Group. Representatives Chet Holifield of California, Frank Thompson, Jr. of New Jersey, and John Blatnik of Minnesota, reported back to other Democratic Study Group members on January 2, 1961, that while Rayburn was committed to some change, they were not free to say what that change would be. The next day press reports confirmed the rumor that Rayburn's plan would be to ask the Democratic Committee on Committees (Democratic members of the Ways and Means Committee) to remove Representative Colmer of Mississippi from the Rules Committee and to replace him with another, less recalcitrant, Democrat.[18] Colmer was one of the five southern Democratic Repre-

---

[15] For a concise résumé of the events of this period, with pertinent newspaper citations, see Walter Kravitz, "The Rules Committee Controversy in the 87th Congress: A Brief Résumé" (Washington, D.C.: Library of Congress, Legislative Reference Service, Mimeographed, 1961).

[16] *Washington Post,* November 12, 1960, p. A 9; *New York Times,* November 15, 1960, p. 35; Tom Wicker, "Coalition Chiefs Confer in House," *New York Times,* November 29, 1960, p. 30.

[17] The events of this period can be only partially reconstructed. What follows is a composite view based for the most part on newspaper accounts and unstructured interviews conducted in July and August of 1961 with over twenty key participants. Interviews, from fifteen minutes to over two hours in length, were confined for the most part to Rules Committee members and the majority and minority party leadership. In order to maintain the confidential nature of the information received, specific sources have not been cited for some statements of interpretation in the brief résumé which follows.

[18] Richard L. Lyons, "Rayburn Plans Purge of Colmer," *Washington Post,* January 3, 1961, p. A 2; John D. Morris, "Congress to Open Today; Rayburn Moving to Curb Conservative Rules Bloc," *New York Times,* January 3, 1961, p. 1.

sentatives who had publicly opposed the Kennedy-Johnson ticket during the 1960 presidential campaign.[19] Meanwhile, seven Republicans, headed by Thomas B. Curtis of Missouri and John V. Lindsay of New York, issued a manifesto deploring any coalition between Republicans and southern Democrats as contrary to the best interests of the country and the Republican party.[20]

On January 3, the 262-member Democratic majority elected Sam Rayburn to his ninth term as Speaker. Moments later, the House routinely adopted Chairman Smith's resolution that the rules of the Eighty-seventh Congress be the same as those governing the House of Representatives in the previous Congress.[21] A week later, however, Rayburn returned to his plan to enlarge the Committee on Rules, presumably on the urging of Representatives Carl Vinson of Georgia, Paul Kilday of Texas, and other southern moderates. While to some observers, Rayburn's plan to remove Colmer had been a tactical maneuver from the beginning, others felt that Rayburn backed down because such a plan would have alienated too many southerners.

On January 18, Rayburn's proposal to enlarge the committee was formally endorsed by the House Democratic caucus by a voice vote.[22] At this meeting, Chairman Smith agreed to bring the resolution to the floor when his committee was reconstituted the following week. The next day, urged on by Rules Committee member Clarence

---

[19] Other southern Democrats who openly opposed their party's presidential ticket were Jamie L. Whitten, John Bell Williams, and Arthur Winstead of Mississippi, and Otto E. Passman of Louisiana. In addition to posing problems of what to do with these representatives as far as committee assignments were concerned, the suggested ouster of Colmer raised the question of New York Representative Adam C. Powell's failure to support the Democratic ticket in 1956 without retribution. However, Colmer's removal from the Rules Committee had the advantage of being regarded as an internal party matter, thus probably preventing an open floor fight.

[20] This resolution was presented to the House Republican Policy Committee on January 2, 1961, and signed by Representatives Curtis of Missouri, Lindsay and Seymour Halpern of New York, Florence P. Dwyer and William T. Cahill of New Jersey, Perkins Bass of New Hampshire, and Silvio O. Conte of Massachusetts. All seven subsequently voted for the Rayburn resolution enlarging the Rules Committee.

[21] *Congressional Record*, January 3, 1961, pp. 21–22, 24.

[22] For the most part, Speaker Rayburn, "working things out in his own way," ignored those Democratic Study Group supporters who urged him to take advantage of certain parliamentary or party rules which might have facilitated the change. For example, the Speaker did not request a two-thirds binding caucus vote, although judging from the final roll-call vote, he probably could have obtained the approximately 175 votes necessary.

Brown, the Republican House Policy Committee unanimously rejected the enlargement plan, and on January 23, the Republican conference supported that decision with few dissents. Two days before the floor vote scheduled for Thursday, January 26, the Committee on Rules voted six to two to report the enlargement resolution. Only Smith and Colmer opposed House Resolution 127; the incumbent Republican members did not attend.

Postponement of the Vote

The day before the scheduled vote, Democratic leaders decided to postpone the vote until Tuesday, January 31. While the publicly voiced reason for postponing the vote was that "some members are unable to be here,"[23] this decision was at least tacit admission that Rayburn and McCormack lacked the necessary votes to get the enlargement resolution passed on the twenty-sixth. Minority Leader Halleck offered his own interpretation of the decision: "The New Frontier is having trouble with its first roundup."[24] That same evening, at his first press conference, President Kennedy announced his position on nationwide television. While declaring that any rules change was an internal House matter, he also said that he hoped a "small group of men" would "not attempt to prevent the members from finally letting their judgments be known."[25] Concurrently, members of the President's cabinet, notably Attorney General Robert Kennedy, Secretary of the Interior Stewart Udall, and the President's legislative liaison staff headed by Lawrence O'Brien, contacted individual congressmen by telephone and in person to solicit support for the resolution.[26]

---

[23] *Congressional Record,* January 25, 1961, p. 1169.

[24] *New York Times,* January 26, 1961, p. 18.

[25] Question 11, Transcript of the President's press conference, *New York Times,* January 26, 1961, p. 10.

[26] The impact of these Administration pressures, which were widely reported in the press, cannot be evaluated with certainty. Some observers claim that White House intervention turned what was a toss-up vote on Thursday into a five-vote victory on Tuesday. Not all of this Administration activity accomplished the desired objective, however, for some congressmen reacted unfavorably to what they felt were unfair pressure tactics. See the statement inserted in the *Congressional Record* by North Carolina's Representative Scott, January 31, 1961, pp. 1515–16, and the criticism of Secretary Udall's activities by Representative Lennon, also of North Carolina, reprinted in the *Congressional Record,* February 28, 1961, pp. 2615–18. One member of the majority-party whip system placed a different interpretation on the subsequent discussions of who was responsible for the resolution's success, remarking somewhat dourly, "They (the Administration) get the credit if we win, and we get the blame if we can't round up the votes!"

Over the weekend, party and interest group pressure increased. The vote-aligning techniques of the regular party whip system headed by Carl Albert of Oklahoma, abetted by an informal whip system led by Richard Bolling of Missouri and Frank Thompson of New Jersey, continued to counteract earlier activity by Chairman Smith. On Saturday, at least one attempt was made to effect a compromise. Rayburn might have been willing to call off the vote if he could have obtained Smith's written guarantee that the Rules Committee would not block any Kennedy legislative proposal during the coming session. But Smith would not go this far. Instead, he promised only to "interpose no obstacles in the Committee on Rules to the five major bills that the President has publicly announced as his program for this session."[27]

As the roll call vote neared, coverage of the issue by the mass media was intensified. On the eve of Kennedy's inauguration, *CBS Reports* devoted an hour television program to "The Keeper of the Rules: Congressman Smith and the New Frontier."[28] According to John D. Morris, of *The New York Times,* the power and prestige of "two tough and skillful septuagenarians" rode on the outcome.[29] Chalmers M. Roberts of the *Washington Post* reported that the President feared a possible "disastrous blow" to his Administration's prestige on his twelfth day in office.[30]

On Tuesday, January 31, the day of the vote, one of the largest crowds ever to attend a congressional debate competed for seats in the gallery. Shortly after twelve o'clock, Rayburn mounted the Speaker's rostrum to preside over the most critical fight of his career. One hour of debate, thirty minutes allocated to each party, preceded the vote.[31] The Republican leadership and Democratic Chairman Smith condemned the resolution as an attempt "to pack

---

[27] Letter from Howard W. Smith addressed to Representatives Carl Vinson and Francis E. Walter and sent to all members of the House of Representatives, dated January 28, 1961, *Congressional Record,* January 31, 1961, p. 1505. Vinson and Walter had called on Smith to suggest possible compromises after first meeting with Speaker Rayburn. The five legislative proposals at the top of President Kennedy's priority list of domestic legislation dealt with redevelopment of depressed areas, an increased minimum wage with broader coverage, expansion of housing programs, aid to education, and health insurance for the aged through social security payments.

[28] The transcript of this program, featuring interviews with Representatives Smith of Virginia, Bolling of Missouri, and Brown of Ohio, is reprinted in the *Congressional Record,* January 31, 1961, pp. 1422-27.

[29] *New York Times,* January 30, 1961, p. 12.

[30] *Washington Post,* January 30, 1961. p 1.

[31] *Congressional Record,* January 31, 1961, pp. 1502-19.

or purge" the Committee on Rules. "I will cooperate with the Democratic leadership of the House of Representatives," Smith stated, "just as long and just as far as my conscience will permit me to go. . . ." But, he continued, "when I am asked to pledge aid to the passage of any resolution or bill in this House that I am conscientiously opposed to, I would not yield my conscience and my right to vote in this House to any person or any Member or under any conditions."[32]

Speaker Rayburn, climaxing the debate in one of his rare statements from the floor, urged adoption of the enlargement proposal in order to facilitate passage of President Kennedy's legislative program:

> I think this House should be allowed on great measures to work its will, and it cannot work its will if the Committee on Rules is so constituted as not to allow the House to pass on those things. . . .
> Let us move this program. Let us be sure we can move it and the only way we can be sure that this program will move when great committees report bills, the only way it can move, in my opinion, my beloved colleagues, is to adopt this resolution today.[33]

On the roll-call vote, the House adopted the enlargement resolution, 217 to 212. Twenty-two Republicans joined 195 Democrats voting for the resolution; against it were 64 Democrats and 148 Republicans. The next day, the new Democratic committee assignments, made by Speaker Rayburn and approved by the Democratic Committee on Committees, included the appointments of Representatives Carl Elliott of Alabama and B. F. Sisk of California to the Committee on Rules.[34]

---

[32] *Ibid.*, pp. 1504–5.

[33] *Ibid.*, pp. 1508–10. Speaking or submitting statements in favor of the resolution were Democratic Representatives Trimble, Kilday, Walter, McCormack, Yates, Blatnik, Ryan, Pucinski, Thompson of New Jersey, Moorhead, and Addonzio; and Republican representatives Curtis of Missouri, Lindsay, Conte, and Halpern.

[34] Richard L. Lyons, "Committee Seats Filled with Eye to Rules Vote," *Washington Post*, February 2, 1961, p. 1 A. The following Monday, the House formally approved these majority committee assignments. *Congressional Record*, February 6, 1961, pp. 1704–5. The balance of Republican minority committee assignments were formally agreed to on February 13, 1961, including the appointments of Katherine St. George of New York, H. Allen Smith of California, and Elmer J. Hoffman of Illinois, to the Committee on Rules. *Congressional Record*, February 13, 1961, p. 2007.

II. ANALYSIS OF THE VOTE

Party Lines Predominate Outside the South

The dramatic outcome of the vote prompted a flood of explanations in the public press. Some observers attributed Rayburn's victory to the White House or to key cabinet members, such as Attorney General Robert F. Kennedy or Secretary of the Interior Stewart Udall. For others, it was the "pragmatic liberals" of the House, both inside and outside the Democratic Study Group, who deserved the major credit or blame. Still others stressed the importance of personal and political loyalty owed to Rayburn. Yet another characteristic of the vote, and one that encompasses all of these interpretations, deserves further emphasis. The decision to enlarge the House Committee on Rules was primarily a party-line vote. As Table II illustrates, three-fourths of the House Democrats supported the Rayburn resolution, and nearly seven-eighths of the Republicans opposed it. Among congressmen from districts above the Mason-Dixon Line, every Democrat who voted supported the Speaker, and these northern Democrats were joined by all but two of their border-state colleagues. Republicans from the North were slightly less cohesive, but in all only twenty-two GOP congressmen supported the Democratic leadership. In thirty-one of the thirty-nine non-southern states, the House delegation divided along party lines —with all Democrats supporting the Rayburn resolution and all Republicans opposing it.

In the South, of course, it was different. Here the Democratic lines splintered sharply, and Rayburn was opposed by nearly two-thirds

TABLE II

The Vote to Enlarge the Rules Committee by Democratic and Republican Congressmen from the North, Border States, and South

Region	Democrats			Republicans		
	Votes Against (Number)	Votes For (Number)	Proportion For (Per Cent)	Votes Against (Number)	Votes For (Number)	Proportion For (Per Cent)
North and West	0	129	100	137	20	13
Border States*	2	30	94	4	2	33
South†	62	36	37	7	0	0
TOTAL‡	64	195	75	148	22	13

* The border states are Kentucky, Maryland, Missouri, Oklahoma, and West Virginia.
† "South" here includes the eleven states of the former Confederacy: Alabama, Arkansas, Florida, Georgia, Louisiana, Mississippi, North Carolina, South Carolina, Tennessee, Texas, and Virginia.
‡ These totals do not include paired votes.

of his southern Democratic colleagues. However, the Speaker did get a vital thirty-six votes from the South without which the enlargement proposal would have surely failed. In a contest so close, virtually every vote was critical; but in the subsequent analysis, attention will be focused on the twenty-two Republicans and thirty-six southern Democrats whose votes, when added to those of the Democrats from the North and West, enabled the Rayburn resolution to prevail.

The Vote of the Southern Democrats

Political observers are sometimes tempted to speak of southern Democrats as a unit, both in reports of legislative conflict in the House and election returns in general. Yet, as V. O. Key observed more than a decade ago: "The politics of the South is incredibly complex. Its variety, its nuances, its subtleties range across the political spectrum."[35] Few House roll calls reveal the nuances and subtleties of southern congressional politics better than the decision to enlarge the Committee on Rules. In that one vote were etched most of the basic lines of political cleavage that exist within the South today—state delegation versus state delegation, rural congressmen versus urban congressmen, black belt representatives versus House members from districts where the Negro population is relatively small, economic liberals versus economic conservatives, and committee chairmen versus those southerners with less formal authority and seniority in the House.

The amount of support which southern congressmen gave to the Rules Committee enlargement varied widely from state to state. All but a handful of the southern votes for the Rayburn resolution came from five states—Alabama, Tennessee, Louisiana, Arkansas, and, above all, the Speaker's own state of Texas. At the other extreme, Mississippi and South Carolina cast a solid bloc of twelve votes against the resolution. In every southern congressional delegation save these two, there were votes both for and against the proposal.[36]

---

[35] V. O. Key, Jr., *Southern Politics in State and Nation* (New York: Knopf, 1949), p. ix.

[36] Interviews with several congressmen and their staffs, while not reflecting a systematic sampling, suggested that state delegation solidarity was used as a rallying point in support of Rayburn in Texas and as a means of defensive protection in southern state delegations opposing the enlargement resolution, the most notable example being North Carolina. The percentage

A clearer picture of the resolution's sources of strength and weak‑ness in the South emerges if one probes beneath the differences among state delegations to examine the relationship between key characteristics of an individual district and the way its representa‑tive voted on this crucial issue. As one would suspect, urban rep‑resentatives in the South, confronted with the attendant problems of industrialization and urban growth, were more likely to support enlargement of the Rules Committee than rural congressmen.[37] An even more clear-cut index, however, was the Negro percentage of the population in the congressman's district. In general, the hypothesis that southern representatives from districts with large Negro populations would be less likely to support the Rules Com‑mittee change than those who came from districts with relatively small Negro populations was sustained. As Table III suggests, the bulk of the support for Rayburn came from districts where preoc‑cupation with the race issue was likely to be less intense—those dis‑tricts where less than one-fifth of the population were Negroes. Approximately two-thirds of the thirty-two representatives from these districts voted for enlargement. In contrast, of sixty-six con‑gressmen from districts where the Negro population exceeded one in five, only fifteen voted for House Resolution 127. Nonetheless, the irregularities in the data presented in Table III indicate that there was no simple linear relationship between the percentage of Negroes in a district and the vote against the Rayburn resolution.

of southern Democratic House delegations voting in favor of the Rayburn proposal were: Texas, 70 per cent; Arkansas, 67 per cent; Louisiana, 63 per cent; Tennessee, 57 per cent; Alabama, 44 per cent; Georgia, 20 per cent; Florida, 14 per cent; Virginia, 12 per cent; North Carolina, 9 per cent; Mississippi, 0 per cent; and South Carolina, 0 per cent. Speaker Rayburn did not vote on the resolution. All seven southern Republican congressmen, two from Tennessee, two from Virginia, and one each from Florida, North Carolina, and Texas, voted against the Rules Committee enlargement resolu‑tion. For an extended analysis of roll-call votes in which state delegation solidarity operated as a significant alternative cue-mechanism to party mem‑bership, see David B. Truman, "The State Delegations and the Structure of Party Voting in the United States House of Representatives," *American Politi‑cal Science Review*, L (December, 1956), 1023–45.

[37] Fifty-five per cent of the twenty-nine representatives from the most urban districts of the South (Types III and IV according to the *Congressional Quarterly*'s method of classification) voted for the Rayburn resolution; where‑as only eighteen of sixty-four southern congressmen from more rural districts (Types I and II), or approximately 28 per cent, supported the proposal This analysis is based on data presented in the *Congressional Quarterly Al‑manac*, XII (1956), 790–91.

They also suggest that other factors than the race issue had an important bearing on the outcome of the vote.[38]

TABLE III

Southern Democratic Representatives: Votes to Enlarge the Rules Committee and Percentage of Negroes in their Districts

	Southern Democratic Representatives			
Negroes in District* (Per Cent)	Districts (Number)	Members Against Enlargement (Number)	Members For Enlargement (Number)	Members For Enlargement (Per Cent)
0–9.9	17	8	9	53
10–19.9	15	3	12	80
20–29.9	28	22	6	21
30–39.9	19	14	5	26
40–49.9	16	12	4	25
50.0 and over	3	3	0	0
TOTAL	98	62	36	37

* Figures for the percentage of Negroes in each district's total population are based on the 1950 census. The figures appear in the *Congressional Quarterly Almanac*, XII (1956), 796–97.

In the eyes of many northerners, southern Democrats are often equated with conservative Democrats—anti-labor, staunch defenders of fiscal responsibility, and resolute opponents of costly social welfare programs. Yet the fact is that the South's representatives are by no means so monolithic in their orientation. In the legislative session immediately preceding the 1960 elections, as in previous sessions of Congress, the support given to increased federal expenditures and expanded social welfare programs, or, to use the vernacular of American politics, the "liberalism" of southern House members, varied extensively.

The data presented in Table IV also make it clear that the voting records of southern Democrats were distinctly weighted in the conservative direction. Using a simple "liberalism-conservatism" rating such as that compiled by Americans for Democratic Action on nine roll-call votes in 1960, the median score for ninety-three

---

[38] Despite some radio and newspaper coverage in the South which gave the contrary impression, many southern congressmen were well aware of the limitations of the Committee on Rules as an effective roadblock to civil rights legislation even if the new Administration were to move more aggressively in this field. If northern Republicans join with northern and borderstate liberals on the Rules Committee, they were and are able to outvote the South on civil rights measures. Furthermore, both Thornberry of Texas and Trimble of Arkansas have occasionally voted to report a civil rights bill, reserving the right to vote against it on the floor.

southern Democrats re-elected to the Eighty-seventh Congress was only 29 per cent.[39] However, these congressmen ranged along the political spectrum from sixteen representatives who almost never supported ADA-approved legislation to the one Democratic congressman from Florida voting for enlargement, Dante B. Fascell of Miami, who was in agreement with the ADA position (and, incidentally, the position of most northern Democrats) on eight issues out of nine.

TABLE IV

Southern Democrats: Percentage of ADA-Approved Votes and Votes on the Resolution to Enlarge the Committee on Rules

Percentage ADA-Approved Votes*	Southern House Members† (Number)	Southern Members Against Enlargement (Number)	Southern Members For Enlargement (Number)	Southern Members For Enlargement (Per Cent)
0–9.9	16	16	0	0
10–19.9	16	15	1	6
20–29.9	16	11	5	31
30–39.9	8	4	4	50
40–49.9	9	3	6	67
50–59.9	13	7	6	46
60–69.9	7	1	6	86
70–79.9	7	0	7	100
80 and over	1	0	1	100
TOTAL	93	57	36	39

* The ADA liberalism index in this table is identical to that in Table I.
† These totals exclude freshmen representatives elected in 1960.

Furthermore, the data in Table IV indicate that liberal southern Democrats like Fascell were generally more likely than their conservative colleagues to support the Rayburn resolution. Yet it also appears that this relationship between the congressmen's support for liberal legislation and support for enlargement of the Rules Committee was curvilinear, rather than linear. The southern Democrats with ADA liberalism scores between 20 and 59.9 per cent varied considerably in how they voted on the Rayburn resolution. In fact, those with ADA liberalism scores of 50–59.9 per cent were slightly less likely to support the Speaker than those with ADA scores between 30 and 49.9 per cent. This lack of progression in the data suggests that for congressmen with moderately liberal voting records, factors other than their "liberalism" or "conservatism" probably weighed heavily. Conversely, among the southern congressmen whose voting records were either strongly "liberal" or

---

[39] See note *, Table I, *supra,* for the derivation of this index.

strongly "conservative," there was little doubt as to how they would vote—the "liberals" for the enlargement plan, and the "conservatives" against it. Only one[40] of thirty-two southern Democrats with a rating below 20 per cent supported Rayburn; and all but one[41] of the fifteen southern Democrats whose liberalism score exceeded 60 per cent backed the change.

Consider, for example, the case of Representative Pat Jennings, the one Virginian who opposed Judge Smith. Congressman Jennings' district was the "Fighting Ninth," long a center of insurgency against the Old Dominion's dominant Byrd machine. He also had the highest liberalism rating among his Virginia colleagues, 44 per cent. Rayburn picked up a few votes from southern conservatives, principally colleagues from Texas or committee chairmen, but the bulk of his support came from the more liberal representatives of the South.

Not all southern "liberals" supported Rayburn and the Kennedy administration, however. Among those southern House members who voted frequently for liberal domestic legislation, those from districts in which the Negro population was unusually high were less likely to vote for the enlargement proposal. Table V demonstrates findings derived from aggregate analysis of the data presented in Tables III and IV. Ten of the twelve southern Democrats with ADA liberalism scores of 40 to 59.9 per cent who also come from districts with relatively small Negro populations—the median for southern House districts in 1950 was 27 per cent—supported the change in the Rules Committee's composition. Not one of their six colleagues with similar records of support for liberal domestic programs who came from districts with Negro populations larger than 30 per cent supported Rayburn. Among the most liberal southern Democrats in the House—those with ADA scores of 60 per cent or higher—only one representative from a district with a large Negro population opposed the Speaker. The congressman in question, George Huddleston, Jr., of Birmingham, Alabama, at first declared himself for the Speaker, but later decided to vote against enlargement after extensive constituency pressures.

From the foregoing analyses it is clear that there was a demonstrable relationship between the nature of the southern representa-

---

[40] The late Overton Brooks (La.-4), then Chairman of the House Science and Astronautics Committee.

[41] Representative George Huddleston, Jr. (Ala.-9).

TABLE V

Southern Democrats: Percentage of Negroes in Home Districts, Voting Records, and Votes to Enlarge the Committee on Rules

Percentage ADA-Approved Votes	Southern Democratic Vote on Enlargement*								
	District Population under 20 Per Cent Negro			District Population 20–29.9 Per Cent Negro			District Population over 30 Per Cent Negro		
	Against	For	Per Cent For	Against	For	Per Cent For	Against	For	Per Cent For
0–19.9	4	0	0	13	0	0	14	1	7
20–39.9	3	4	57	6	2	25	6	3	33
40–59.9	2	10	83	2	2	50	6	0	0
Over 60	0	7	100	0	2	100	1	5	83

* These totals exclude freshmen representatives elected in 1960.

tives' constituencies and past voting records and their reaction to the Rayburn proposal to enlarge the Committee on Rules. The lower the Negro percentage of the total population in his district, the more likely a southern Democrat was to support the Speaker. And the more liberal his past voting record, the more likely he was to support the move to enlarge the Committee on Rules. But there also were some important exceptions to this general pattern—exceptions that point to the operation of other, special factors during the final maneuvering before the roll-call vote.

The vote of the South's committee chairmen in the House underscore this remark. Conservative southern Democrats who were the chairmen of important House committees were much more likely to back the Speaker than southern conservatives who were not committee chairmen. Four, or half, of the southern House committee chairmen with ADA liberalism scores of under 30 per cent in 1960 went along with Rayburn; whereas only one in every twenty of the southern Democrats with equally conservative voting records who were not committee chairmen supported Rayburn. Among the more liberal southern Democrats, by contrast, committee chairmen supported Rayburn by the same two-to-one ratio as the other representatives.

It was, moreover, among the chairmen of the House's most important committees that the Speaker's support was greatest. All but two of the heads of the major committees supported Rayburn. One exception was Smith himself. The other, Chairman of the Committee on Agriculture Harold D. Cooley of North Carolina, received a personal telephone call from the President requesting his support shortly before the showdown. It failed. But even so, in the supreme test of his legislative career, Rayburn had the support of a substantial number of the most authoritative leaders of the South—among them Carl Vinson of Georgia, and Oren Harris and Wilbur D. Mills of Arkansas—as well as unanimous backing from northern and border state committee chairmen, including the conservative head of the House Appropriations Committee, Clarence Cannon of Missouri.

Undoubtedly, some southern Democrats, particularly those who had served with Rayburn on the Hill for many years, surmounted constituency pressures because of a sense of personal loyalty to the Speaker. As Representative John L. Pilcher, one of two Georgians who voted for the Rayburn proposal, explained his vote in a letter to his friends:

> To have voted against Sam Rayburn, who will go down in history as one of the greatest Americans, and our own "Old War Horse" Carl Vinson, who has been here since Woodrow Wilson and knows more about the defense of our country than any man in Congress, I would have had to align myself with 150 Republicans who will take pleasure in seeing President Kennedy's program fail. I would also have been forced to vote against my conscience, and I am 62 years of age, and have held public office for 41 years, I cannot do that now. I may be wrong; only time will tell.[42]

But Rayburn needed more than party and personal loyalty to gain enough votes to offset the two-thirds of the southern Democrats who went along with the outlook and voting inclinations of another respected veteran of the House, Judge Smith of Virginia. In order to pass the Rules Committee proposal, some additional votes were required.

The Twenty-Two Republican Dissenters

The Rayburn resolution was supported by nearly all of the northern and border state Democrats and by more than a third of the Democrats from the South. But it also received twenty-two votes from the Republican side of the aisle. Although these twenty-two Republicans were but a small fraction of the total Republican House strength (seven of every eight GOP congressmen opposed the Rayburn resolution) , they had a decisive effect on the roll call's outcome. Barring additional support for Rayburn from southern Demo-

---

[42] Letter to his constituents from Representative John L. Pilcher (Ga.-2), quoted in the *Washington Post*, February 2, 1961, p. A 2.

crats,[43] three more Republican "nay" votes were all that would have been required to kill the Administration-backed resolution. Yet Minority Leader Charles Halleck was unable to get them from these Republicans, mainly, it appears, because most of these twenty-two congressmen were a special type of Republican. With several notable exceptions, these Republican dissenters differed markedly from most of their party cohorts—in the areas they represented, in their support for domestic social welfare legislation, and in the enthusiasm which President Kennedy's candidacy had evoked in their home districts.

The regional concentration of the Republicans who backed the Rayburn proposal underscores this point. Eighteen of the twenty-two came from urban and industrial districts in states along the Atlantic seaboard, including three from New York City, two from Pittsburgh, and one from Washington's Maryland suburbs. Republican support for the Rules Committee change was particularly strong in New Jersey and New England. Seven of ten GOP representatives from Massachusetts, New Hampshire, and Connecticut, and four of the eight New Jersey Republicans crossed party lines to support Speaker Rayburn.[44]

Three other dissenters—Ayres of Ohio, Curtis of Missouri, and Baldwin of California—also represented urban or suburban industrial constituencies. Yet in the region where the GOP had traditionally been strongest, there was little indication of dissatisfaction with the *status quo*. Throughout the farm belt, once the heartland of Republican insurgency and the region that spawned George Norris, leader in the revolt of 1910, only one Republican—O'Konski of Wisconsin—supported the change. Republican insurgency in the Rules Committee fight of 1961 came primarily from the eastern urban wing of the party.

It also stemmed primarily from the party's liberal wing. A simple index of liberalism similar to that used in the analysis of the southern Democrats will demonstrate this point. As the data presented in Table VI indicate, the higher a Republican congressman's liber-

---

[43] It was frequently asserted on Capitol Hill that Rayburn had two or more votes among southern Democrats that he could have tapped had he needed them. While observers differed as to who these representatives were, there was some agreement that he probably could have commanded at least one more vote from Texas and one from Mississippi.

[44] In addition, former Republican Speaker Joseph Martin of Massachusetts was paired in favor of enlargement of the Committee on Rules, thus canceling one Republican opposition vote.

alism score had been on nine selected issues in the 1960 legislative session, the more likely he was to support enlargement of the Committee on Rules in 1961. Of the GOP representatives with liberalism scores of 60 per cent or higher, seven out of eight supported the Rayburn resolution. At the other extreme, among conservative Republicans who opposed the ADA position more than 80 per cent of the time, not one voted for enlargement.

For the most part, it was the liberal Republicans who backed the Rules Committee change. But, as the data in Table VI indicate, there were some notable exceptions. The more conservative voting records of four of the Republicans who supported Rayburn—Ayres of Ohio, Bass of New Hampshire, Bates of Massachusetts, and Curtis of Missouri—suggested that these congressmen would probably vote against much of the President's domestic program. One of the four, Congressman Curtis, made his position explicit in the debate immediately before the vote:

> . . . [W]hichever party obtains the responsibility to organize the Congress should have the necessary power to meet that responsibility. . . . I intend to oppose most of the legislation I have heard Mr. Kennedy is going to send up to the House for consideration. I intend to be on the floor to do the best I can to defeat the measures on the merits.[45]

TABLE VI

House Republicans: Percentage of ADA-Approved Votes and Votes on the Resolution to Enlarge the Committee on Rules

Percentage ADA-Approved Votes*	Republican House Members			
	Total† (Number)	Vote Against Enlargement (Number)	Vote For Enlargement (Number)	Proportion For Enlargement (Per Cent)
0–9.9	15	15	0	0
10–19.9	30	30	0	0
20–29.9	34	32	2	6
30–39.9	18	16	2	11
40–49.9	8	6	2	25
50–59.9	11	7	4	36
60–69.9	4	1	3	75
70–79.9	2	0	2	100
80 and over	2	0	2	100
TOTAL	124	107	17	14

* The ADA liberalism index in this table is identical to that in Table I.
† These totals exclude freshmen representatives elected in 1960 and paired votes.

---

[45] *Congressional Record*, January 31, 1961, p. 1504. Curtis was the only dissenting Republican who was allowed floor time during the debate.

Still different considerations may have affected the vote of some of the other GOP dissenters. One possibility is that urban Republicans from economically distressed areas would be less satisfied with the existing House rules. Republicans who supported the Rayburn resolution were in fact more likely to have areas with substantial unemployment in their districts than those who did not, but the data on which this finding is based, while suggestive, cannot be considered conclusive.[46]

An equally plausible hypothesis is that Republican House members who were elected by a narrow margin in the 1960 elections might be especially likely to trim their sails in a liberal direction in order to broaden their base of support. Yet, in fact, this was not the case. Republicans who supported the Rayburn resolution were only slightly more likely to hold marginal House seats than those who did not.[47] Furthermore, of the twenty-nine Republican repre-

---

[46] Some fourteen of fifty-seven Republican representatives (approximately 25 per cent) from districts bordering on or within "areas of substantial labor surplus" voted for enlargement of the Rules Committee. These findings must be interpreted with considerable caution, however, because the boundary lines of congressional districts seldom coincide with the geographical areas set forth by the Bureau of Employment Security, United States Department of Labor, in its bimonthly survey, *Area Labor Market Trends.* Furthermore, it may be that these urban representatives were predisposed to vote for a change in the rules, with the extent of unemployment in their respective districts only one of a number of factors. In Democratic districts bordering on or in areas in which surplus labor was 6 per cent or greater, eighty out of ninety-two representatives voted for enlargement. As of January, 1961, 76 of the nation's 150 major areas were classified as areas of substantial labor surplus, the largest number since the low point of the 1957–58 recession. *Area Labor Market Trends* (January, 1961), p. 2.

[47] Sixteen per cent (four in twenty-five) of the Republican congressmen elected with between 50.1 and 52.4 of the two-party congressional vote supported the Rayburn resolution. The comparable figures for the Republican congressmen who were elected with larger margins of victory were: 10 per cent of those elected with 52.5–54.9 per cent of the vote (twenty cases); 14 per cent of those elected with 55–59.9 per cent of the vote (sixty-six cases); 11 per cent of those elected with 60–69.9 per cent of the vote (fifty-two cases); and 14 per cent of those elected with 70 per cent or more of the vote (seven cases). In contrast, support for the Administration-supported resolution was strongest among Democratic congressmen from marginal seats, again a reflection of the sectional cleavage within the Democratic party and the fact that most uncontested seats were in the South. With the exception of five North Carolina dissenters, support for the resolution was unanimous among the seventy-six Democratic representatives receiving less than 60 per cent of the two-party vote in their districts in 1960 (93 per cent). The comparable figures for the Democratic congressmen who were elected with larger margins of victory were: 89 per cent of those elected with 60–69.9 per cent of the vote (fifty-three cases); 78 per cent of those elected with 70–94.9 per cent of the vote (sixty cases); and but 43 per cent of those elected with 95 per cent or more of the vote (seventy cases).

sentatives who won seats previously held by Democrats, only four voted for enlargement.[48]

What is noteworthy about the districts these congressmen represented, however, is that they were all keenly fought at the presidential level. In more than half of them, Kennedy polled more votes than Nixon. The data which underpin this point appear in Table VII, in which the vote of Republican congressmen on the Rules Committee issue is related to President Kennedy's popular vote in their district in 1960. The import of the data is clear: the larger the Kennedy vote in a Republican congressman's district, the more likely the Republican was to support the Administration-backed measure to enlarge the Committee on Rules. Republican congressmen who supported the Rayburn resolution, in short, represented districts

TABLE VII

*Republican Congressmen: Kennedy's Percentage of the Presidential Vote in Their Districts in 1960 and Congressmen's Vote on the Motion to Enlarge the Committee on Rules**

| Kennedy Percentage in Congressional District, 1960 | Total (Number) | Republican House Members | | |
		Vote Against Enlargement (Number)	Vote For Enlargement (Number)	Vote For Enlargement (Per Cent)
0–44.9	99	98	1	1
45–47.4	29	25	4	14
47.5–49.9	17	13	4	24
50–52.4	12	6	6	50
52.5 and over	13	6	7	54
TOTAL	170	148	22	13

* Data compiled from "Complete Returns of the 1960 Elections by Congressional District," Part II of the *Congressional Quarterly Weekly Report*, XIX, No. 10 (March 10, 1961), 3–45. Paired votes are excluded from this analysis.

where the Democratic presidential ticket had had considerable appeal.[49]

---

[48] The eight Democratic representatives who won seats formerly held by Republicans, three from New York, one in New Jersey, and four from western states, all voted in favor of the resolution.

[49] Comparable data for Democratic congressmen are less clear-cut. Outside the South, of course, the Rayburn resolution received all but two votes. Among the southern congressmen, the Kennedy-backed resolution received its greatest support in districts where the Kennedy-Johnson ticket received between 50 and 59.9 per cent of the two-party vote. Among these representatives, 54 per cent supported the enlargement resolution (thirty-eight cases). Only 17 per cent of the southern congressmen voted for the resolution in districts in which the Kennedy-Johnson ticket had less than 50 per cent of the vote (twenty-nine cases). In districts where the Democratic ticket received 60 per cent or more of the two-party vote, 36 per cent of the southern Democratic

These Republican mavericks—more conservative than the northern Democrats, yet more liberal than their Republican colleagues—occupied a crucial position in the American political system. Thirteen of the twenty-two represented districts Nixon lost to Kennedy, districts which a Republican presidential nominee would probably have to carry in order for their party to regain control of the White House. Although they themselves had fared well at the hands of the electorate, the Kennedy vote in their districts made it clear that they came from closely contested political territory. In their public statements during the rules fight, one major theme predominated. If the Republicans supported Chairman Smith as a bloc, the public image of the GOP as an "obstructionist party" in alliance with the conservative southern Democrats would be reinforced. As Representative Lindsay of New York expressed it, the action of the House Republican leadership placed "the Republican minority in the position of seeming to coalesce with southern Democrats, a posture which in the long run is contrary to the principles and best interests of the Republican party."[50] By opposing their leadership, these twenty-two representatives provided the indispensable minimum of Republican support that enabled the Rayburn resolution to pass.

III. SUMMARY AND CONCLUSIONS

The decision to enlarge the House Committee on Rules was supported by nearly all of the Democratic congressmen outside the South, and by a third of the southern Democrats and an eighth of the Republicans. Among southern Democrats, the move drew its greatest support from committee chairmen and from congressmen with moderate to liberal voting records. It drew least support from southerners representing rural districts and districts with large Negro populations. The House delegations of Alabama, Tennessee, Louisiana, Arkansas, and, above all, Speaker Rayburn's own state of Texas provided the bulk of the southern votes for the change.

Among Republicans, what support there was for the Rayburn resolution came primarily from the more liberal Republicans of the

---

congressmen supported the Rules Committee enlargement (thirty-four cases). Analysis is further complicated by the presence of third-party slates in Mississippi, Alabama, and Louisiana.

[50] Lindsay made his statement after the Republican Party Policy Committee took the unprecedented action of releasing its decision to the press, prior to the meeting of the Republican Conference. *New York Times,* January 20, 1961, p. 16.

eastern seaboard, although a handful of GOP congressmen who did not belong to the party's eastern or liberal wings also voted for the measure. Nearly all of these Republican dissenters, however, represented districts where Kennedy polled a sizable vote for President. More than half came from districts which President Kennedy carried in 1960. With this support, the Rayburn resolution was carried by the slender margin of five votes.

This victory, however, should not obscure the fact that other courses of action designed to achieve the Speaker's aim of expediting the President's legislative program were also open to Rayburn. Several of these alternatives, in fact, received serious consideration before they were rejected by the House Democratic leadership at the beginning of the session. Although compelling practical arguments could be advanced against each of them, the range of legislative tactics that might have been employed was broad. The Speaker could, of course, have done nothing about the Rules Committee, planning to rely instead on bargaining with its members and the use of existing devices for bypassing the committee—such as the Calendar Wednesday procedure. He could have again resorted to a "twenty-one-day rule," modification of the discharge petition, or some other technique designed to provide a majority of the members of the House with a means of getting bills to the floor. He could have sought a compromise with Smith, based on Smith's agreement to grant a rule for certain specified key measures of the President's legislative program. He could have pushed his proposal to remove Representative Colmer from the committee through the Democratic party caucus. Or he could have attempted to persuade the House to make a basic change in the committee's powers.

Looming behind these various tactical choices open to the Speaker were larger questions of principle, for the enlargement struggle refocused attention on the basic issue of what the function of the Committee on Rules should be. Here again, a number of lines of speculation are possible—speculation that concerns both the committee's composition and its powers. Should the committee be an instrument of the House majority leadership? If so, should it be composed solely of members of the majority party, and should the Speaker himself be a member? Alternatively, should the committee be as nearly representative as possible of the total membership of the House—a microcosm of the whole? Or should the committee over-represent groups who are in a minority in the House, thus making the agreement of concurrent majorities a necessary prerequisite for action in the American governmental system?

Given these basic considerations, Rayburn's choice of tactics is instructive as to the workings of the House of Representatives. For Rayburn's decision for the floor fight that led to enlargement of the committee in effect enabled the Speaker to avoid a final resolution of these underlying issues. By making this choice, Rayburn opted for the positive course of action that created the minimum disturbance possible in the *status quo*. No attack was made on the committee's jurisdiction or powers. No member was unseated, nor was party discipline applied. Even the resolution to enlarge the committee was worded so as to apply to the Eighty-seventh Congress only. The enlargement resolution, as the Speaker himself said after abandoning his proposal to purge Colmer, was "the way to embarrass nobody if they didn't want to be embarrassed."[51]

The House Rules fight of 1961 thus resembled every previous battle over the powers of the Rules Committee in which some action was taken—each of which had been resolved by a change in the committee's membership or by providing a mechanism whereby a majority of the members of the House could bypass the committee. Like those previous battles, the House Rules fight of 1961 left the Committee on Rules with extensive powers to block the progress of some bills and to expedite the passage of others. The committee thus retained powers which even those committee members normally sympathetic to the House leadership might feel prompted to exercise independently on certain issues. It also held powers over which the conservatives might regain control if but one of the moderates and liberals was unable to attend meetings of the committee. Particularly toward the end of the session, the discretionary powers of the chairman would once again loom large.

Moreover, even before Rayburn's fatal illness made it necessary to select a new Speaker, it was clear that the enlargement decision itself was tentative, not permanent. When the Eighty-eighth Congress convened in January, 1963, the issue of the committee's size would be up for decision again. Whether the composition of the Committee on Rules would remain responsive to the wishes of the Democratic majority leadership in the House for long was thus an open question. It was also a question that, to a considerable extent, depended

---

[51] *New York Times*, January 1, 1961, p. 1.

upon the outcome of the mid-term elections of 1962. For only the election returns would determine the number and relative strength of congressmen who opposed or favored the policy predilections that frequently prevailed in the House Committee on Rules between 1937 and 1960.

IV. EPILOGUE

What should be the relationship between the formal leadership of the House of Representatives, the over four-hundred House members, and the Committee on Rules, the principal scheduling committee of the House? Since the classic confrontation between Speaker Sam Rayburn and Chairman Howard W. Smith in 1961, in the main the Committee on Rules has operated as an instrument of the majority leadership rather than as an agent of a conservative bipartisan majority. A number of factors—rule modifications, changes in committee composition, and continuing Democratic majorities—have helped to maintain the leadership's tenuous control over the committee.

In the 1962 midterm elections, House Democrats made the best showing by a party in control of the White House since 1934—a net loss of only four seats. In January, 1963 the House voted 235 to 196 in favor of a rules change which "permanently" increased the size of the Committee on Rules to fifteen members.[52] Throughout the 87th and 88th Congress the House leadership could generally count upon a solid eight of these votes—all the Democrats save for Smith and William Colmer of Mississippi.

In the presidential election of 1964, Democrats gained their largest majority in the House since the mid-1930's, 295 seats to 140 for the Republican minority. Capitalizing on these numbers, the Democrats passed several additional rules changes on the opening day of the 89th Congress which further limited the powers of the Committee on Rules. By reinstituting the so-called twenty-one day rule, the Speaker was given the right to recognize the Chairman or another member of a committee to bring a measure to the floor after a resolution providing for such action had been pending in the Rules Committee for twenty-one calendar days. Further the House ma-

---

[52] For a description of this contest and evaluation of the functions performed by the Committee on Rules, see Robert L. Peabody, "The Enlarged Rules Committee," *New Perspectives on the House of Representatives* 1st ed. (Chicago: Rand McNally & Co., 1963), pp. 129–164.

jority leadership was given the power to send legislation directly to a conference committee of the two houses without a special rule after differing versions of a bill had passed the House and the Senate.

The twenty-one day rule was short lived. It was rescinded at the opening of the 90th Congress following Republican gains in the midterm election of 1966. But two further factors have helped the Democratic party leadership maintain its control. One was the defeat of the venerable Chairman of the Committee on Rules, Smith of Virginia, in a Democratic primary in 1966. His successor as Chairman, Colmer of Mississippi, was just as conservative, but new members added at the opening of the 90th Congress converted the eight to seven split on the committee into a more stable nine to six Democratic majority.

Throughout this period, individual members occasionally exercised their right to leave the fold and vote against the wishes of the party leadership. For example, in March, 1968, one northern and one western member broke from the rest of their Democratic colleagues and voted with Colmer and the five Republican members to stretch out Committee hearings on a civil rights bill. But such actions were atypical. Most of the time the Speaker could count on a majority to vote in his interests, defeating a bill, delaying another, and bringing still others to the floor with a rule best calculated to expedite passage. Thus, the Committee on Rules continues to exercise substantial control over legislation. Since 1961 that control has largely been in the interests of a majority of the majority Democrats in Congress.

XII

THE HOUSE OF REPRESENTATIVES AND FEDERAL AID TO EDUCATION*

Richard F. Fenno, Jr.

THE RESOLUTION of conflict and the building of consensus are among the major functions which Congress performs for American society. The process by which House and Senate majorities are created and authoritative congressional decisions are made helps to resolve society-wide conflicts and increase society-wide agreement on public policy. One area, however, in which Congress has tried and failed to perform these normal functions is that of federal aid to elementary and secondary schools. For ninety-two years, this issue of "general" federal aid to education has commanded congressional attention; since 1945 alone, its committees have recorded 6.5 million words of testimony on seventy-seven different legislative proposals.[1] Yet no general aid bill has ever been enacted into law. By failing to take positive action, Congress repeatedly reconfirms an existing policy consensus in opposition to general federal aid. But, at the same time, the persistence of sharp, closely fought controversy in and out of Congress testifies to the root instability of that consensus. Conflict remains widespread, deep, and unresolved.

To speak of Congress' inability to promote a new consensus on federal aid policy is to focus attention on the House of Representatives. Since 1945, federal aid bills have never lacked a Senate majority, either in the Committee on Labor and Public Welfare or on the

---

* This article has been drawn largely from Chapters 5 and 6 by the author in Frank J. Munger and Richard F. Fenno, Jr., *National Politics in Federal Aid to Education*. Copyright © 1962 by Syracuse University Press (No. 3, "Economics and Politics & Public Education Series"). The material is used here by special permission of the publisher. A special debt of gratitude is owed to Frank Munger for his assistance and stimulation at all phases of the larger project.

[1] For purposes of this study, the meaning of federal aid to education is restricted to general aid to elementary and secondary schools. A much more extensive analysis of the issues and interest groups involved and of decision-making units (for instance, the executive branch and the Senate) will be found in *ibid*.

floor. The Senate has passed each bill debated in the postwar years—in 1948, 1949, 1960, and 1961. When the body has not acted, it has been for external reasons, not because federal aid stood in any danger of defeat. By contrast, however, majorities have been extremely hard to achieve at those points in the House where they must be produced—in the Committee on Education and Labor, the Committee on Rules, and on the floor. In the late 1940's and early 1950's the Education and Labor Committee held hearings but failed to report out a bill. In the more recent past the committee has reported out a bill six times. In three of those instances the Rules Committee refused to send the bill to the House floor. Two other bills which received Rules Committee approval were subsequently defeated on the floor. On the single occasion when a federal aid bill did pass in the House, it was stopped by the Rules Committee on its way to conference. See Figure 1.

On the record, the House of Representatives has not performed conflict-resolving and consensus-building functions in the area of federal aid to education. This study presents a summary analysis of the House record from 1945 to 1962. Legislative case histories typically focus upon a single bill and relate in depth the story of how that bill became a law. This analysis, in contrast, treats many bills over a considerable span of time and attempts to explain why none of them has ever become law. Doubtless, one explanation lies in the incredible complexity and sensitivity of the problems which comprise "the" issue of federal aid—problems involving control of the educational system, aid to non-public (especially parochial) schools, and the survival of segregated schools. Some readers may conclude that it is simply impossible for any legislative body to resolve such a tangle of criss-crossing conflicts. However, the Senate has performed quite normally in dealing with the same issues. The vastly different outcome of House action can best be understood by examining the issues of federal aid as they are processed by the particular individuals and institutions of the House.

THE COMMITTEE ON EDUCATION AND LABOR

The most powerful institutions of the House are its committees, where all demands for House decisions begin their journeys—and where most of these projected journeys end. In doing its work, each House committee participates in the conflict-resolution and consensus-building functions of the parent chamber. The conflicts which are resolved in committee are the ones most likely to be

Figure I
House Action on General Federal Aid to Education Bills
1945–1962

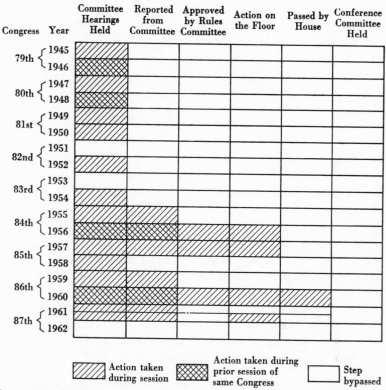

Congress	Year	Committee Hearings Held	Reported from Committee	Approved by Rules Committee	Action on the Floor	Passed by House	Conference Committee Held

Action taken during session

Action taken during prior session of same Congress

Step bypassed

Source: Frank Munger and Richard Fenno, *National Politics and Federal Aid to Education* (Syracuse, N.Y.: Syracuse University Press, 1962), p. 9.

resolved on the floor. If the committee majority supporting a policy agreement is cohesive and stable, the House as a whole is more likely to produce a stable legislative consensus. In the area of federal aid policy, the pattern of House activity has been fixed, to a considerable degree, by the pattern of activity in its Committee on Education and Labor.

Nearly all congressmen agree that this committee is probably the one in which it is most difficult to achieve a consensus and the one most susceptible to prolonged conflict. In the words of a leading Democratic proponent of federal aid:

It's a very discouraging committee. You can't get a resolution praising God through that committee without having a

three-day battle over it. . . . It's about the most difficult committee around. Our executive sessions are the most exciting
things you ever saw.[2]

A Republican opponent of federal aid uses a different perspective
but arrives at a similar conclusion:

We work by trying to split the Democrats on the committee.
And actually we don't have to work very hard. They'll split
off by themselves. . . [n]ot on the big issues on the final votes,
but on amendments and in the committee. They'll shout at
each other, stand up and bang their fists on the table and
stomp out.

The most basic fact about the House Committee on Education and
Labor is that, unlike its counterpart in the Senate, it exhibits an
almost classic incapacity as a consensus-building institution.

Jurisdiction

Most of the committee's internal problems are consequences of
the fact that within its jurisdiction fall a high proportion of the
most controversial, the most partisan, and the most publicized issues of American domestic politics. The committee, activated in
1947, cut its legislative teeth on the Taft-Hartley Bill and has been
a domestic political battleground ever since. All committee members agreed with two of their colleagues—the first a Republican, the
second a Democrat—whose explanations follow:

This is where the basic philosophies of the two parties really
come out strongly. It's a clash of philosophies. You don't get
that on Merchant Marine and Fisheries. Oh, what battles! You
should see the battles we have in executive session.

This is probably the most partisan committee in the House
because this is where the fundamental philosophical battles
are fought. . . . The things that identify the administration's
domestic program come out of our committee. You take mini-

---

[2] All unattributed quotations in this article are taken from interviews held
with twenty-one members of the House Committee on Education and Labor,
one member of the Senate Committee on Labor and Public Welfare, and with
staff members of both committees. The interviews were held in Washington in
June, 1961. They were semi-structured interviews, and questions were open-
ended. Notes were not taken during the interview but were transcribed
immediately afterward. The quotations are as nearly verbatim as the author's
power of immediate recall could make them. In all cases, the respondents
were told that their comments would not be attributed to them.

mum wage. That's a black and white proposition there. And all of our issues are fundamental, philosophical questions. You don't get that on Space or Foreign Affairs.

If a committee is to function as a consensus-building institution, there must be considerable opportunity for compromise and mutual accommodation of views. Conditions must be maintained in which the legislative techniques of give and take, bargaining, are possible. It is the chief consequence of nationwide partisan and philosophical controversies that they seriously limit the development of such internal conditions. A former Republican member reflected on his experience in the 1950's:

> Some of us were unalterably opposed to federal aid, and some on the other side were just as unalterably in favor of it. . . . There weren't many minds changed by discussion. Everybody had a fixed position when he came there, and nobody changed that opinion that I know of.

A Democrat, speaking of the situation in 1961, agreed, "The lines are drawn pretty tight on this committee, and there isn't much flexibility."

Issues involving the degree and direction of federal participation in such fields as labor-management relations, minimum wage, and education are among those which few legislators can avoid in their election campaigns. Several Republicans recalled debating their opponents on the federal aid issue in 1960; and they recalled, too, having taken a firm stand against all federal aid or a stand, following Vice President Nixon, in support of school construction aid only. Most committee Democrats, on the other hand, campaigned along with their standard-bearer, Senator Kennedy, in favor of both a construction and a teachers' salary aid program. Since they have assumed more or less unequivocal positions on federal aid before their constituents, members come to their committee work committed in advance and are denied the freedom to maneuver so basic to the production of legislative agreement. They have come from their election campaigns trained, positioned, and girded for head-on, showdown committee conflict.

In another way, too, the jurisdiction of the committee has hampered consensus-building in the field of federal aid. When the committee was established in 1946, its main focus was considered to be the field of labor. The great majority of committee members were oriented toward labor problems and professed only minor interest in education. Though there has been a tendency for some members to specialize in educational matters, such members still remain in the minority on the committee. Since the 1946 decision that the field of education did not warrant a separate committee, many large educational programs of the national government have been placed under the jurisdiction of other House committees.[3] Thus, the decision to combine education and labor has weakened and fragmented the efforts on behalf of federal aid by members of Congress and by supporting interest groups.

Educational controversy has also been infected with the by-products of labor controversy. Internal conflict would doubtless be harsh in a single education committee, but the tradition of charge and countercharge accompanying labor-management legislation has certainly made it more difficult to build a consensus among the same people in the area of education. There is, of course, an affinity of philosophy between the supporters of organized labor and the supporters of federal aid to education; the record of the AFL-CIO on behalf of federal aid is substantial. However, the Democratic membership of the committee has been chosen so as to maximize unity on labor matters, and concern for unity on federal aid to education has been secondary. The result is that while a Catholic Democrat and a non-Catholic Democrat or a Democrat with many Negro constituents and a Democrat with few Negro constituents can reach agreement on labor matters, they may be pulled in many directions when confronted with the divisive religious and racial issues involved in federal aid.

The passage of time has increased the heat of the federal aid controversy and has done very little to reduce committee conflict. There was a period in the 1940's when information was scarce, when a variety of new approaches was being explored, when there was no legacy of controversy, and when, therefore, some attitudes had not crystallized. Now, however, each successive layer of legislative struggle compresses the participants into positions of increasing inflexibility. Committee hearings, for example, function to add current data to support old positions and to add current reaffirmations of support or opposition to the store of old political intelligence. They may serve to promote communication between the interest group spokesmen and their own membership, but they have ceased

---

[3] See Robert M. Rosenzweig, "The Congress—How It Deals With Educational Issues," *Higher Education*, XVII (April, 1961), 8–11.

to promote, if they ever did, the communication between proponents and opponents. One member described the federal aid hearings
in this way:

> They don't do any good, and nobody listens to them any-
> way. The same people say the same things every year; only the
> statistics change. But the lines are hard and fast on this issue,
> and nobody changes his mind on or off the committee. It's a
> formality. . . . The teachers' groups and these other organiza-
> tions can prove to their members that they are getting their
> money's worth for their dues. That's all. They don't change
> anything.

Hearings may serve to inform newcomers, but they do not convert
anyone. One freshman said, "I tried to keep an open mind. I went
in there and listened with the attitude, 'let's see if you can convince
me I'm wrong.' And the more I heard, the more convinced I was
that I was right." In the hearing rooms and out, committee members
tend, they say, to maintain communications with only one set of
interest groups and one set of lobbyists—those with whom they
already agree. The only people who may have something new to
present, who may represent a potential for change, and who are,
therefore, listened to by both sides, are the spokesmen for the
President and his administration.

Membership

Conflict within the Committee on Education and Labor is, ultimately, not a conflict among issues but among individual members.
The selection of committee members is, therefore, critical in
determining the degree, if not the main lines, of internal conflict.
The net result has been that the members of the House committee
come from among those in their respective parties who already are
in the widest disagreement on the issues of federal aid. The people
who control assignments to the committee exercise considerable
care. On the Republican side, new House members are ordinarily
discouraged from applying for this committee unless their convictions are firm, their talents for combat considerable, and their districts reasonably safe.[4] Those who cannot be dissuaded and those
who must be solicited tend to lean toward the more conservative

---

[4] See Nicholas A. Masters, "House Committee Assignments," *American Political Science Review*, LV (June, 1961), 354–55. Reprinted as Chapter II of the
present volume.

wing of their party. A rather senior Republican said that he advises anyone who desires a political career to stay off the Committee— unless he is deeply committed. Of himself, he said:

> My people didn't vote for me. They voted for what I stood for, my principles. I was elected as a conservative, and that's a wonderful thing. . . . It's an awfully unpopular committee. I take a terrible pounding. But my future is behind me, and I don't give a good God damn.

"I'm the kind of person," echoed an equally conservative freshman member, "who jumps right into these hot spots. So I figured if this was the most controversial committee in the House, I'd like to get on it." When the leadership has to fill a slot with a member who has not applied, it may try to ascertain his views beforehand. One member explained:

> Halleck called a friend of mine in ——— and said, "What kind of a guy is this ———? We're thinking of putting him on Education and Labor, but we need someone who'll stand up, someone we can count on who won't waver in his views." My friend replied, "You don't have to worry about ———."

On the Democratic side, too, members are strongly issue-oriented, personally contentious, and vigorously committed. They tend to represent the more liberal elements of their party. Party leaders produce this result both by encouraging the appointment of labor-oriented congressmen and by discouraging the appointment of southerners. To an individual representing a manufacturing or mining constituency, a place on the committee dealing with labor matters will have positive electoral advantages. Many Democratic members (fifteen of nineteen in 1961) received financial assistance from the trade unions, and all of these are dependent upon labor support at the polls.[5] Union lobbyists sometimes actively intercede with the Democratic committee selectors on behalf of congressmen known to be sympathetic to them. On the other hand, no more than four (and usually fewer) southern Democrats have ever been placed on the committee at one time—despite the pleas of the southern committee members. No pretense is made at representativeness on this score; in 1961, 38 per cent of all Democratic congressmen (99

---

[5] *Congressional Quarterly*, XVII (April 10, 1959), 509–15; *Congressional Quarterly*, XVIII (November 11, 1960), 1857.

of 263) came from the eleven southern states, but only 11 per cent
(two of nineteen) of the committee members did.

Despite the most careful attention to their appointment, the
Democratic members of the committee constitute an extraordinarily
heterogeneous group. They are personally much more predisposed
to intraparty conflicts than are the Republicans. Moreover, if there
is a unifying bond among most of them, it is a bond on the issues
of labor, not education. The Republicans on the committee in 1961,
however, were all male, non-southern, non-border-state, and Protes-
tant—whatever their differences. They were all white, and not one
of them represented a constituency with a non-white population of
10 per cent or over. Though 17 per cent of the Roman Catholic
House members were Republicans, of these, none was on the committee. The 1961 Democratic members, by contrast, included two
women, two southerners, two border-state members, seven Roman
Catholics, and two Jews. The chairman was a Negro, and four Democrats represented constituencies with non-white populations of over
10 per cent.[6] These demographic differences are overlaid with vast
differences in personality and political style. Together they make
consensus-building on the Democratic side especially hazardous,
particularly on the issues of school integration and private school
assistance.

The combined result of Republican and Democratic appointment
practices, which is most significant for this study, is not only that
they guarantee sharp ideological and partisan division on the committee, but that they intensify internal committee division. The
Congressional Quarterly selected ten roll-call votes in 1961 to distinguish those House members who supported a larger federal role
in the nation's economic and social life (*i.e.*, liberals) and those
House members who opposed a larger federal role (*i.e.*, conservatives).[7] A majority of committee Democrats (twelve of nineteen)
voted on every occasion to expand government activity, and a
majority of committee Republicans (seven of twelve) voted on every
occasion in opposition to this expansion. Moreover, if the voting
percentages are scaled, every Democratic committee member voted

---

[6] Data on the non-white population by congressional districts are taken
from United States Bureau of the Census, *Congressional District Data Book*
(Washington, D.C.: Government Printing Office, 1961).
[7] The roll-call votes used and the records of each Representative are listed
in *Congressional Quarterly*, XIX (October 20, 1961), 1751–63.

more often for an expanded federal role than did any of the Republicans.

These ideological and partisan differences inside the committee are significantly greater than differences on the same issues in the House as a whole. Whereas average percentages among House Democrats were 78 per cent in favor of a larger federal role and 21 per cent against, committee Democrats averaged 91 per cent in favor and 8 per cent against. House Republicans averaged 12 per cent in favor and 87 per cent opposed, whereas committee Republicans averaged 7 per cent in favor and 93 per cent opposed. See Table I.

TABLE I

Ideological Representativeness of Committee on Education and Labor, 1961

	Votes For Expanded Federal Role (10 Roll Calls)	Votes Against Expanded Federal Role (10 Roll Calls)	Index of Ideological Representativeness*
	(Mean Percentage)		
All House Democrats	78	21	+57
House Education and Labor Committee Democrats	91	8	+83
All House Republicans	12	87	−75
House Education and Labor Committee Republicans	7	93	−86

Source: *Congressional Quarterly*, XIX (October 20, 1961), 1751–63.
* The Index of Ideological Representativeness constitutes the difference between the mean percentage of votes in favor of an expanded federal role and the mean percentage of those opposed.

Given the considerable degree of inflexibility within party groups, the ratio of Democrats to Republicans has assumed considerable importance. During the years of Republican control, it was certain that no bill would emerge from the committee. During the years of Democratic majorities, a coalition of Republicans plus southern Democrats could prevent committee action. Until the Eighty-sixth Congress in January, 1959, the Republicans plus the southern Democrats constituted a majority—hence a controlling influence whenever they could agree. In 1959, following the sweeping Democratic congressional victory of the previous November, the liberal Democrats and their interest-group allies succeeded in breaking the long-standing coalition majority. They persuaded Speaker Rayburn to recommend a new party ratio of twenty Democrats to ten Republicans instead of the previous seventeen Democrats to thirteen Republicans. Under the previous arrangements, thirteen Republicans plus Chairman Barden and Phil Landrum (Ga.) could create a tie vote. A third, a more liberal southerner, Carl Elliott of Alabama, one of the committee's few education specialists, was placed in a strategic position at the ideological center of the committee and in the eye of most internal storms. Six new Democrats, all supported by organized labor, were given committee membership in 1959; those southerners who applied were turned down. This membership change constitutes one of the landmarks of the federal aid controversy in Congress.

Procedures

The resolution of internal strife and the formation of legislative consensus are affected greatly by the way in which a committee organizes itself for decision-making. The style of decision-making best suited to the ends of this committee would be one which would emphasize mutual accommodation within the group and develop procedures for cooperation and compromise. Frequently, informal and traditional techniques of accommodation will develop on committees—between majority and minority party leaders, between legislatively experienced members and those who are legislatively inexperienced, between the experts in a particular subject matter and non-experts. The Committee on Education and Labor has not adopted this style of decision-making to any important degree. Its style tends to be fiercely competitive; the techniques are those of naked power, and the decision goes to whoever can command a simple majority in a showdown vote. The rules of the game are the formal rules of the House, untempered by private committee traditions or informal understandings. Committee members have no sense of the committee as an entity worth worrying about. Sentiments of mutual regard and group solidarity are few. Group morale is not high. The committee's decision-making procedures do nothing to lower tension or to increase cohesion inside the group.

Democrats and Republicans find it difficult to overcome their mutual suspicions sufficiently to establish even minimally harmonious working relationships. Throughout 1961, the committee chairman and the ranking minority member, whose cooperation should provide the major lubricant of decision-making, conducted a ridiculous public feud over the amount of room space allotted to their respective staffs.[8] A marked lack of communication seems to exist at all other levels of the committee as well.

Though it is doubtless true that, in the words of one Republican, "Some of our guys hate Democrats more than anything," it often appears that some Democrats hate some other Democrats with a similar passion. Democrats freely admit their natural propensity to fight one another, and a Republican remarked, "There's never that kind of fighting between Democrats and F.epublicans. They don't expect to convert us. It's like the old situation where they hate the heretic more than they do the infidel." In federal aid decisions, the injection of the segregation issue—splitting northerner from southerner and moderate from liberal—and the parochial school issue—splitting urban Catholic and rural non-Catholic—exacerbates the normal problems of consensus-building on the Democratic side. Republicans, less beset by racial and religious differences and in the minority during all but four years since World War II, have tended to cohere much more frequently—though President Eisenhower's support for federal aid split the group in the late 1950's.

One of the most common House traditions that functions to check conflicts on many committees is the informal norm of apprenticeship, which prescribes that committee newcomers should defer to those senior men more experienced in the work of the committee. Accordingly, the freshman is to attend meetings, do his homework, say very little, and participate minimally in the making of the group's decisions. The Education and Labor Committee gives virtually no service to this tradition. The committee's young men, who happen to be extraordinarily bright, able, and disputatious, are expected to carry a major share of the decision-making burdens. A freshman Republican put this in the strongest language possible:

> There isn't any bigger myth than the idea that new people can't do anything. After all this talk about seniority, I was surprised. You know you aren't going to be the committee chairman, and you know you aren't going to get to sponsor a major piece of legislation, but other than that you can participate as much as you want. You can even get to take leadership on a bill in committee. . . . Every time a bill comes out, the young members are asked to take five minutes or ten minutes

---

[8] Their battle was reported in the Capitol Hill newspaper, *Roll Call* during March, April, September, and December, 1961. There is, predictably, almost no contact between majority and minority staff members on the committee.

to speak on the floor. They ask us; we don't have to ask. So it's just the opposite from what the myth and fiction of seniority would have you believe.

A first-year Democrat spoke for his colleagues when he said:

> I was amazed. I was hesitant to do all the things they asked me to do—being a newcomer. I'm the only lawyer on that sub-committee . . . and in drafting the law they relied on me a great deal. A new man has no restrictions at all.

The weakness of seniority traditions is also evident in the fact that very senior members are sometimes denied the sponsorship of a bill or the chairmanship of a subcommittee to which their rank would otherwise entitle them. Chairman Barden refused to give top Democrat Adam Clayton Powell the chairmanship he wanted, and Powell, when he became chairman, rendered this kind of treatment to high-ranking Phil Landrum of Georgia.[9] Operation without the stabilizing influence of these traditions encourages decision-making by free-for-all.

Another force which often countervails against an every-man-for-himself technique of legislative decision-making in many committees is the presence of subject-matter experts. Committee members will acknowledge the expertise of one or two of their colleagues and will defer to them—not on matters of critical importance to themselves but on technical or factual matters. The expert may not be able ultimately to swing votes, but as the legislation works its way through subcommittee and committee, his views will carry substantial weight. It is important to realize, therefore, that there are no acknowledged experts on federal aid to education in the House of Representatives. If there were, they would be found on the Committee on Education and Labor. Yet every one of the factors thus far discussed militates against the unifying presence of expertise.

Inside the committee no deference is accorded even to the work of subcommittees. Though a subcommittee may have sat many days in hearings and worked long hours over its recommendations, these

---

[9] Powell set up a battery of three subcommittees to deal with educational matters but declined to assign them permanent areas of jurisdiction. He offered the chairmanship of the Special Subcommittee on Education to Landrum. Since, however, Powell had no intention of assigning any legislation to the subcommittee if Landrum became its chairman, Landrum declined to serve.

are almost always changed by the full committee. Long-time participants are hard put to remember occasions when substantial alterations have not been made; one senior member remarked:

> You can't take a bill before that group unless you know
> exactly what every section, every paragraph, every line, every
> word means. There are so many sharpies in there. . . . Some-
> one will try to put another interpretation on it, and if you
> can't refute it, it will stick. . . . Oh! it's a real circus.

The committee has, furthermore, never recruited a staff of experts
on education whose independent judgment has carried any weight
at all with the members.

Since the committee does not acknowledge within its own body
of supposed specialists any experts on federal aid, it is hardly likely
that the committee will be viewed as conveying expert opinion to
the floor. This committee's views as such ordinarily carry little persuasion with the House membership. The normal impression which
committee members manage to create in the floor is that of being
wholly unable to agree among themselves—both between and within
parties. Individual committee members often come to the floor prepared to introduce crippling amendments or, indeed, substitute bills.
Members are not usually daunted should a pet amendment, e.g., the
Powell Amendment, be defeated in committee. Said one Democrat
in reference to an education amendment:

> I tried it in the committee . . . and I'll try it again on the
> floor. I haven't told them [his committee colleagues] I'm going
> to, but they know that I tried it in committee, and I suppose
> they know I'll try again. . . . I just believe in it—that's all.

Other amendments come to the floor because the committee is
incapable of dealing with them: "Lots of times . . . if a person has
an amendment, he'll hold it back just so we can get the damn bill
on the floor. Then he'll propose it on the floor."

The House membership views the committee as "stacked" via the
appointment process; the additional picture of the committee in
wide disarray on the floor is not conducive to confidence. According
to one experienced committee member:

> Frankly, it's not one of the authoritative committees of the
> Congress—not one of those whose word you take automati-
> cally. . . . It lacks stature. In fact, most of the bills we report
> out get completely changed on the floor. . . . It's a power strug-

gle that counts on the floor and not respect for the committee or the influence of any one individual.

The committee's modest rank in the prestige hierarchy of House committees operates as both cause and effect of its internal conflicts. Because it is not regarded as having great prestige, House members are only moderately attracted to it. Of the twenty-one committee members interviewed, eight had designated it as their first choice for a committee assignment; six had listed it second or third; and seven members had been requested to go on or were simply put on the committee. Moderate attractiveness means a relatively high rate of turnover among committee personnel. Of the thirty members of the group in 1961, only three had been members since 1947; seven had been members since 1953; and less than half (fourteen) had been on the committee for as many as four years (since 1957). Instability of membership is, perhaps, a contributing factor to the committee's lack of tradition and lack of group-mindedness. These failures, in their turn, allow internal conflict to flourish, further decreasing the prestige of the group among House members.

Leadership

To write a politically viable federal aid to education bill and to maneuver it successfully through the House committee requires far more cohesion than the group normally displays. Only exceptional leadership within the committee or extraordinary pressure without—or both—can produce the requisite internal unity. The committee has had but one strong chairman since the war, Graham Barden (D.-N.C.). Among the members of his committee, Barden's legislative abilities are already legend. He is invariably described as "a shrewd, smart chairman," "a very effective chairman," "absolutely brilliant," "magnificent," and "one of the ablest congressmen in American history." For all of his eight years as chairman, Barden led the committee so as to create rather than resolve internal conflicts. Most of the time, he worked tirelessly to defeat federal aid legislation, and on the single occasion, in 1949, when he accepted a federal aid bill, he did so on such restrictive and uncomprising grounds that he triggered the most acrimonious of all committee conflicts.

His main tactics were to delay, divide, and conquer. And his successes were largely due to the fact that these tactics followed the natural grain of a conflict-ridden committee. "Barden was trying to keep things from being done," said a Democratic member. "He just wanted to filibuster and sow confusion. If it lagged, he would introduce some more." Another Democrat recalled, "He never shut any one up. He'd let you talk yourself around the clock and in circles if you would. One year, he brought in ninety-two witnesses from the Chamber of Commerce on the school bill and was going to let them all talk. That was his way of doing things." In support of these tactics, he relied heavily on the backstopping votes of the Republicans. A key Republican said, "He ran that committee 100 per cent. I must say that some of us on our side were in substantial sympathy with what he was doing. There was a good deal of support from the Republicans." From his perspective, a Democratic member concurred:

> You never had any leadership under Barden—not majority leadership. Under Barden, you had a club. He was a Republican; there's no doubt about that. He was a Democrat in name only. Under him, you had a coalition, and it was very skillful. The coalition ran things until 1959 when Ways and Means decided to enlarge the committee.

Barden used a skillful combination of formal prerogative, informal maneuver, and personal talent. During most of his tenure, for instance, he refused to institute formal committee rules. Among other things, the committee had no regular meeting day. "In my first year here," said one member, "we held our first committee meeting in April and the next one in June." There was, in addition, no time limit placed on the questioning of witnesses during hearings. "I remember once," said a Republican member, "when the very suggestion of a five minute limitation [for each member in questioning each witness] was made, and he hit the roof. He wouldn't hear of any such thing. And he carried the day by sheer bravado or strength of character, call it what you will."

Another prerogative which Barden employed dexterously was his authority to terminate committee meetings by declaring the absence of a quorum. "Even after 1959 Barden retained a lot of power," protested one Democrat, "we tried holding rump sessions without him but with a quorum. Barden would come in, look around and say, 'I see there's no quorum present,' bang his gavel, and it would be all over." A colleague recalled an occasion when the committee had recessed during a crucial executive session to enable the members to go to the floor to answer a roll call. Barden, however, stayed in the committee room and sent his clerk to the floor with instructions to call back as soon as the roll call was over and debate had resumed on the floor.

> I was one of the first ones back, and Barden was sitting there. He got a phone call, put down the phone, looked around and said, "No quorum" and banged the gavel. I jumped up and protested. He said, "No quorum," and left. . . . Technically, he was right. We were supposed to be sitting during debate and should have begun when the floor debate began again. . . . The timetable was such that if we didn't complete our work that day we couldn't meet for some time.

In 1956 Barden, who was opposed to the federal aid bill, refused to relinquish his right to control and manage the floor debate on the bill. His allocation of disproportionate time to the opponents plus his dramatic resignation as floor manager near the end of the proceedings added important increments to the unbelievable confusion which accompanied the floor defeat of that year. In the absence of particular committee rules and compensating informal tradition, the rules of the group had to be the same as the rules of the parent House. And in his knowledge of these, Barden far outdistanced the young and aggressive but legislatively naive liberals on his committee. "He was a master of parliamentary strategy," said one inexperienced opponent. "He'll lull you to sleep and then hit you with an uppercut. You wouldn't know what the hell had hit you." Another agreed, "We're a young committee . . . and it takes a lot of time to learn how the legislative process works. . . . We learned a lot from Barden."

As chairman, Barden could manipulate the subcommittees and staff. For considerable period of time, he refused to institute standing subcommittees with specific jurisdiction. The *ad hoc* nature of the committee structure enabled him to exert close control over the tasks of each subcommittee and over its Democratic membership. In 1957, for example, Barden used his power over subcommittees to head off an incipient liberal revolt in the committee. He won the support of one senior Democrat to his view on other procedural matters by agreeing to give him a permanent subcommittee of his own. As for the committee staff, Barden kept it small and inactive as befitted his tactical goals. Democratic committee members received so little research help they were ignorant of the names of the staff members. One staff assistant, a veteran Democrat, complained with great feeling:

> This committee has the most incompetent, inept staff of any of the Hill. Barden wanted it that way. He could manipulate a dumb staff easier than a smart one. . . . We haven't had a chief clerk or counsel on this committee for years that knew enough to come in out of the rain.

Whether accurate or not, this is the common perception of the staff shared by pro-federal aid members.

FEDERAL AID IN THE HOUSE COMMITTEE, 1945–1955

Between 1945 and 1955 the committee held federal aid hearings on seven separate occasions, but not until 1955 did a bill win the approval of a majority of the group. The peak years of controversy were 1949 and 1950—Barden was primarily responsible for the decisions adverse to federal aid in those years. In 1949 Chairman John Lesinski (D.-Mich.), whose interest was in labor matters, gave Barden the chairmanship of a thirteen-man Special Subcommittee on Federal Aid to Education. Barden selected an unrepresentative group of Democratic members—all four of the committee's southern Democrats, two of its four border-state members, and only two of its seven northern Democrats. The year 1949 was critical because for the first time, in both 1948 and 1949, the Senate had passed a federal aid bill. This bill contained both equalization (money distributed to states in accordance with criteria of need) and flat-grant (money distributed to states on some per capita basis) provisions. The money could be used for teachers' salaries and other current operating expenditures (no construction). The bill provided money for transportation and textbook aid to non-public schools in states where such "auxiliary services" were permitted by state law. The 1949 bill, S. 246, passed the Senate by a fifty-eight-to-fifteen margin on May 5. Twelve days later, when the House heard the first of its fifty-eight witnesses and took the first of its 953 pages of testimony, the prospects for federal aid legislation seemed brighter than ever.

Expressing his devotion to federal aid at every opportunity, Barden staged a counter-offensive by proposing a substitute bill and by refusing to entertain serious testimony on S. 246. At the outset, he set the ground rules. "There are some features in the Senate bill so objectionable to me that I could not find myself going over to it.

I am not going to accept it; that's all."[10] The distasteful provisions included those requiring reports to the Commissioner of Education (*i.e.*, federal control) and those providing for the possibility of aid to non-public schools. Barden dominated the hearings to a degree unequalled by any representative or senator in any federal aid hearing before or since. His colloquies with various witnesses consumed one-third of all the space devoted to questions and answers. Each witness was asked to testify and then subjected to questions on the Barden bill. Those groups, especially organized labor, who would not agree to support it were branded as uncooperative and given unsympathetic treatment. "I am frank to state to you that your idea will not pass" (to AF of L). "I wanted some help, my friend, and you have had a tendency to add chaos to confusion. . . . I don't believe you yourself have the slightest idea in the world there would be a Chinaman's chance of getting that bill through Congress, do you?" (to AF of L). "One ear is deaf and the other is partly closed when you talk to me" (to CIO).[11]

The issue which eventually rent the committee—that of aid to non-public schools—was systematically avoided. On one of the few occasions when the question faced him point blank, Barden stated, "My reason [for a public school aid bill] was that it is just so much easier and more comfortable to go around a mud hole than it is to go through it. . . . So in this bill and in this legislation, I pray that we will be spared any controversy over that point because it should not be in here."[12] To the countervailing arguments of National Catholic Welfare Conference representative he replied, "I am just as far in one direction as you can possibly be in the other. So we could not get together."[13] The fact that Barden's bill was a public school bill precipitated a national controversy as soon as it was reported (by a ten-to-three vote) from the subcommittee to the full committee. Chairman Lesinski attacked the bill as "anti-Catholic" and filled with "bigotry." "It will never be reported out of the Labor Committee . . . ," he said. "It is my opinion that he [Barden] drew it up that way purposely because he didn't want any aid to education and wanted to kill it."[14] The parallel dispute between

---

[10] House Committee on Education and Labor, *Public School Assistance Act of 1949*, 81st Cong., 1st sess. (1949), p. 102.

[11] *Ibid.*, pp. 628, 678, 768.

[12] *Ibid.*, p. 165.

[13] *Ibid.*, p. 744.

[14] *Congressional Quarterly Almanac*, V (1949), 266–69.

Cardinal Spellman and Eleanor Roosevelt flared and raged in the public press. The controversy over federal aid to non-public schools was not to dominate the educational policy struggle again until 1961. But in 1949 and 1950 it stirred a fatal division within the House committee.

Two key votes were taken by the committee in August of 1949. A motion to report out S. 246 was defeated eleven-to-fourteen, a vote for which there is no record. Following the heavy defeat of two substitute Republican measures, Representative John F. Kennedy (D.-Mass.) moved to postpone action until the next session. The motion, which would have killed federal aid legislation for that year, was lost thirteen-to-twelve. See Table II. Thus the

TABLE II

Federal Aid Votes—House Committee on Education and Labor, 1949 and 1950

	1949 Motion to Kill Federal Aid for 1949		1950 Motion to Report out S. 246	
	Yes	No	Yes	No
Democrats				
Lesinski (Mich.)	X			X
Barden (N.C.)		X		X
Kelley (Penna.)	X		X	
Powell (N.Y.)		X	X	
Wood (Ga.)		X	X	
Kennedy (Mass.)	X			X
Lucas (Texas)	X			X
Bailey (W.Va.)		X	X	
Irving (Mo.)		X	X	
Perkins (Ky.)		X	X	
Howell (N.J.)		X	X	
Sims (S.C.)		X	X	
Jacobs (Ind.)		X	X	
Burke (Ohio)	X			X
Steed (Okla.)		X		X
Wier (Minn.)		X	X	
Republicans				
McConnell (Penna.)	X			X
Gwinn (N.Y.)	X			X
Brehm (Ohio)	X		X	
Smith (Kans.)	X			X
Kearns (Penna.)		X		X
Nixon (Calif.)	X			X
Morton (Ky.)		X	X	
Werdel (Calif.)	X			X
Velde (Ill.)	X			X
TOTAL	12	13	12	13

Source: *Congressional Quarterly Almanac*, Vols. V, VI.

possibility of favorable action remained, but nothing more was, in fact, done. The vote on the Kennedy motion revealed the toll which the private school controversy had taken of the proponents of federal aid. Four Catholic members of the committee—Lesinski (Mich.), Kelley (Penna.), Kennedy (Mass.), and Burke (Ohio), all liberal Democrats, voted to kill federal aid legislation for that session. They were joined by the great bulk of the committee's conservative members. The majority group, on the other hand, could agree only to keep the issue alive. They could not, especially against the opposition of Chairman Lesinski that late in the session, agree on a bill to support. For Barden it was all or nothing, and not all of the thirteen were willing to pay his price.

Early in February of the next year, the committee met in executive session at the urging of President Truman to reconsider its negative action on S. 246. A motion to report out S. 246 again lost— this time by thirteen to twelve. The voting alignment (Table II) was similar to that of the previous August. Those who had voted to postpone the issue in 1949, voted against S. 246; those who had voted to keep the issue alive in 1949 voted in favor of S. 246. Among the five exceptions were Representative Augustine Kelley, who left his three colleagues to vote in favor of S. 246, and Representative Barden, who voted against S. 246 thus joining irrevocably with the committee group opposed to federal aid.

In view of the fact that S. 246 permitted state option on the question of auxiliary services for non-public schools, the continued opposition of Lesinski, Kennedy, and Thomas Burke requires further explanation. Since Kennedy proposed an amendment to S. 246 specifically allowing aid for transportation to non-public schools (rather than leaving it permissive), it seems likely that the three were still dissatisfied with the treatment of the question in S. 246. But it is also true that the three had spoken out against the equalization provisions of S. 246 and in favor of the flat-grant principle. All came from states which were scheduled to give far more than they would receive, and all came from districts which needed assistance. The reluctance of representatives from needy districts in wealthy states to support equalization provisions has always caused more acute problems in the House than in the Senate. Republican Carroll Kearns, a strong advocate of federal aid, reversed his decision and voted against S. 246 on precisely these grounds. From that vote until 1962, Kearns was adamant and rigid in his opposition to any equalization provision whatsoever. Since Kearns was the ranking minority member of the committee in the Eighty-sixth and Eighty-seventh Congresses, his inflexibility provided a significant example of the absence of maneuvering room within the group.

As chairman of the committee in 1951 and 1952, Barden did not allow the full committee to meet at all on federal aid questions. In 1953 and 1954, with the Republicans in control, a similar record was maintained by Chairman Samuel McConnell. In 1955, when the Republican administration sent its first program to Congress, Chairman Barden was again successful in bottling up federal aid legislation in his committee. In order to delay action, he designated the full committee as the unit to hold hearings and refused to limit questioning. He prolonged the hearings from March 2 to May 24 during which time the committee considered eleven separate bills, listened to fifty-two witnesses, and took 1,158 pages of oral and written testimony. Barden's foot-dragging ended only after he had been presented with an ultimatum by the fifteen non-southern Democrats.[15] On July 28, these Democrats plus seven Republicans formed the first federal aid majority on the committee, and they reported out a bill by a vote of twenty-two to eight. As Barden had planned, it was too late in the session for action by the Rules Committee and the House. Indeed, it was not until June of 1956, when faced with threats to bypass them and urgent proddings by the administration, that the Rules Committee consented to send the bill to the House floor. See Table III. The year-long delay furnished the first concrete evidence that majorities on the Education and Labor Committee could by no means guarantee majorities on the equally critical Rules Committee.

COMMITTEE AND CHAMBER ACTIVITY, 1956–1957

The conditions of partisanship gave basic shape to the federal aid struggles of 1956 and 1957. A Republican President faced a Democratic majority in Congress; and the Democratic majority was a slim one. In 1956, House membership stood at 232 Democrats and 203 Republicans; in 1957, it remained virtually the same, at 234 to 201. These conditions necessitated bipartisan majorities in and out of the committee if any federal aid bill were to be passed and signed into law. The bills which reached the floor in 1956 and 1957 did

---

[15] House Committee on Education and Labor, *Federal Aid to States for School Construction*, 84th Cong., 1st sess. (1955), pp. 1105–12.

command bipartisan majorities in the Committee on Education and Labor and in the Rules Committee, but supporting bipartisan majorities on the floor of the House never materialized.

An important factor in producing the committee majorities of those years was the successful effort to avoid the 1949–50 type of entanglement with parochial school issues. The technique was simply to write a different kind of bill—one embodying a type of aid for which parochial schools, by common agreement, were not eligible. The 1956 and 1957 bills, therefore, provided aid for school construction only. The 1956 "Kelley Bill" was sponsored by Representative Augustine Kelley (D.-Penna.), a devout and unmistakably Irish Catholic committee member. There was virtually no mention of private schools in the committee hearings of 1950, 1955, or 1957. Within the committee, informal taboos operated against raising "the religious issue." A former Republican member recalled:

> I guess I was the first to breach a rule on that. I made a speech on the floor about it. When I came back, Sam McConnell said to me, "That's one thing I wouldn't have said if I were you." I said, "Well, I believe it." And he said, "I know, but that's one subject we shy away from."

On the floor, majority leader John McCormack called attention to the forbearance of parochial school supporters. Said McCormack:

> No complaints, no opposition, no obstructionist proposals have come from private or parochial school sources. . . . [They have] refrained from any action that might impede passage of this bill even though it will bring no direct benefit to their schools. These people have an unselfish, statesmanlike attitude. . . . I do not know whether we shall again need to consider federal aid for current expenditures. If we do, I hope we will be spared a repetition of the ordeal of a few years ago. I hope public school authorities will have a tolerant cooperative attitude if an effort is made to try in a small way to help private and parochial school children. . . .[16]

Few, if any, committee decisions held up as well on the floor as the one which eliminated the issue of parochial school aid. In their other essentials, the 1956 and 1957 proposals represented the most fragile of compromises between the preferences of President Eisenhower and the preferences of a majority of committee Democrats.

---

[16] *Congressional Record*, 84th Cong., 2d sess. (1956), p. 11844.

The President was never more than a lukewarm advocate of federal aid. And committee Republicans, in the words of one of them, "went along holding their noses because it was the President's program." The majority of committee Democrats desired a far more ambitious program than could conceivably win presidential support. These differences were papered over by a mutual willingness to send a bill to the floor. But the coalition was not durable. Given an opportunity on the floor to act on its basic preferences, either faction might revert to a less flexible, more disruptive position.

President Eisenhower preferred a debt service approach to school construction. If he had to compromise on some sort of grant program, he preferred equalization grants, to be matched by the states. The 1956–57 bills combined a grant program with a debt service program to assist local districts in financing construction. The 1956 bill called for flat and equalization grants, also on a matching basis.

In 1956, the committee's Eisenhower Republicans accepted the compromise, but as soon as the bill reached the floor, they sought to exact a heavier price for their allegiance by changing the grant distribution formula to conform to the President's preference. Their proposal, sponsored by ranking minority member Representative Samuel McConnell (R.-Penna.), stirred confusion if not bitterness within the bipartisan coalition. Federal aid stalwart Cleveland Bailey (D.-W.Va.) protested:

> I feel compelled to question the good faith of the gentleman from Pennsylvania in offering this substitute plan. He was a member of the subcommittee that drafted the legislation and it was agreed that the Kelley Bill would be a nonpartisan-bipartisan approach to the solution of the problem. That is why the proponents of Title I, the federal grants-in-aid, agreed to accept Titles II and III of the President's program as a compromise measure to insure the approval of this legislation. The gentleman is not satisfied with two Titles of the President's plan, he wants to substitute Title III of the President's plan for Title I of the Kelley Bill.
>
> I can assure you the distinguished gentleman from Pennsylvania [Mr. Kearns] was a party to this agreement that this would be fought out on a nonpartisan-bipartisan basis and that the Kelley Bill was to be defended against all crippling amendments right down the line.[17]

Other Democrats complained that McConnell's formula was too complicated to be dealt with on the floor and added that they them-

---

[17] *Ibid.*, p. 11751.

selves could not understand it. Chairman Graham Barden further revealed the committee's disarray with his comment that "It is a little bit of an awkward position for the chairman to be caught in when the ranking minority member springs five pages of law on the committee of the whole without my ever having seen it."[18] The next day Barden formally withdrew as "floor manager" of the bill.

The public exhibition of committee disunity did no service to the bill's supporters and gave encouragement and a rationalization to its opponents. Representative Charles Halleck (R.-Ind.), a key Republican leader and a key opponent of federal aid, seized upon the division to argue that:

> The Kelley Bill never was the administration program; it is not the administration program now. . . . I hope a motion to recommit is offered, with instructions to incorporate the McConnell amendments thereby incorporating the President's recommendations.[19]

Representative McConnell did offer the recommittal motion. It was supported by eleven of the committee's thirteen Republicans (84.6 per cent) and by 76 per cent of the Republicans in the House as a whole. President Eisenhower was unwilling to state his own position positively enough to provide for Republican leadership one way or the other.

In 1957, on a bill that was said to contain "85 per cent of the specifications laid down by the President," Eisenhower's silence was even more disastrous for aid proponents. In this instance the bill was killed by a vote of 208 to 203. On the floor, committee Republicans vied with each other in attempts to fathom the presidential will. Representative Peter Frelinghuysen (R.-N.J.), the strongest Republican aid supporter on the committee, admitted, "Perhaps he has not given it his unequivocal wholehearted support, . . . [but] this bill in my opinion incorporates all the principles which the President declared are vital to sound legislation in the field."[20] Representative McConnell, senior committee Republican, attempted clarification:

> The President is in favor of a bill for school construction. This is not the most preferred bill he wishes. He has made that very clear. He also realizes that legislation is a matter of

---

[18] *Ibid.*, p. 11752.
[19] *Ibid.*, p. 11869.
[20] *Congressional Record*, 85th Cong., 1st sess. (1957), p. 12608.

compromise, and he understands an effort to compromise. He does say, however, that this is not his first preference; that he prefers a bill where financial need is more emphasized than in the compromise bill.[21]

Representative William Ayres (R.-Ohio), who had voted against reporting the bill out of committee, offered a substitute bill, saying, "This is the bill that the President is really for. This is the bill he supported in the last session. This is the bill, in my judgment, after having talked with him at a breakfast at the White House, his heart is really in."[22]

Members announced at several points that a presidential statement was imminent, but such a statement was not forthcoming. Its absence allowed each legislator to interpret the Eisenhower position to suit his own preconceptions. As Representative Halleck declared:

> I am going to follow the dictates of my own conscience. I am going to be mindful of the views of the people I represent. . . . Certainly I shall not be unmindful of the loyalties that are mine to my party and the stand of the administration insofar as I am able to determine how those various things will come up as a matter of application.[23]

Unemcumbered by presidential pressure, Halleck's conscience and that of 110 other Republicans dictated a vote to kill federal aid for 1957. A veteran federal aid supporter in the Senate summed up the sentiments of his cohorts when he stated later:

> It was what the administration did—or didn't do—that killed the legislation. The truth of the matter was that Eisenhower never wanted federal aid. I think some of his friends on the golf course must have told him that it was creeping socialism. I really do. In 1957, the bill lost in the House by five votes. He could have had a bill. A few phone calls to members of Congress, "This is the President of the United States calling congressman so and so"—and he'd have gotten the votes. If he had called up Charlie Halleck and Joe Martin and said "I want the votes," he could have gotten them. The struggle would never have been as close as it was. He just didn't want a bill. He did nothing. And in that situation, inaction meant, "No."

Amid great confusion on the floor, the Democratic supporters of

---

[21] *Ibid.*, p. 12723.
[22] *Ibid.*, p. 12750.
[23] *Ibid.*, p. 12721.

federal aid struggled to repair the damaged bipartisan coalition. When Ayres offered his substitute bill (the Eisenhower preference of 1956 and the one embodied in McConnell's amendment of that year), the committee's liberal Democrats agreed to support it. Representative Stewart Udall (D.-Ariz.) said, typically, "If in order to get the bipartisanship we need, we must have precisely the bill the President said he wanted last year, I . . . will support the amendment of the gentleman from Ohio, as I want a school bill."[24] Republicans and Democrats rose to pledge allegiance to this new coalition and, briefly, it looked as if a timely if not hardy majority might coalesce. But before any new alignment could take shape Chairman Howard Smith (D.-Va.) of the Rules Committee offered a preferential motion to strike the enacting clause of the bill, *i.e.* to kill it, and "be through with this rather futile debate." Representative Udall made a last impassioned plea:

> Finally, after two years of thrashing around in this thing, we have finally reached an agreement. We on this side have decided to go all the way with the President, cross every "t" and dot every "i" and go right down the line with precisely what the President wants. We can join hands with you. We have obviously worked out a working agreement. It is feasible in this body. We can pass a school bill today. Therefore the purpose of this motion is to derail this new coalition that we have.[25]

The motion was carried 208 to 203. The time was ripe, as Judge Smith doubtless sensed, for disrupting a coalition, not creating one. That which Republican and Democratic supporters could not accomplish over a period of years in committee or at the White House they could hardly hope to improvise in a period of minutes on the House floor.

Ineffective leadership contributed heavily to the federal aid failures of 1956–57. But even with the best of leadership, the bipartisan coalition might not have survived the effects of another deeply divisive social issue—segregation in the public schools. The crystallization of the issue by the Supreme Court's decision of 1954 had placed it before the committee with an intensity which had not existed in 1949 and 1950. Its potential for disrupting the bipartisan coalition was fully as great as the parochial school question. Where-

---

[24] *Ibid.*, p. 12751.
[25] *Ibid.*, p. 12753.

as a dearth of leadership had cost the coalition vital Republican support, the superimposition of racial issues upon federal aid issues deprived the coalitions of 1956–57 of equally vital Democratic support.

As might be expected, the segregated school issue nearly paralyzed the House committee. It was agitated by Adam Clayton Powell (D.-N.Y.) who, of all the members of that disharmonious group, was the least committee-oriented, the least legislatively oriented, and the least amenable to appeals based on the necessity for compromise and cohesion.[26] Powell was supported by some members of the bipartisan majority out of conviction; he was opposed by most of them; and, to confound the problem further, he was supported by some committee members who were strongly opposed to federal aid legislation under any circumstances. Debate of the issue inside the committee in 1955 was sufficiently heated to provoke at least one shoving incident between Powell and a Democratic opponent. The "Powell Amendment" prohibiting aid to segregated schools was ultimately rejected seventeen to ten in the committee. Six of the ten wrote additional views supporting Powell. Four of these were Democratic supporters of federal aid; two were Republicans opposed to it.[27] The lack of any committee tradition of unity in support of its votes served the cause of federal aid ill in this instance. The committee's inability to agree plus Powell's insistence on taking the issue to the floor forecast an even wider, more disastrous split within the bipartisan majority when the bill was debated and lost in 1956.

In 1956 the Powell Amendment was attached to the bill by a coalition of 77 northern Democrats and 148 Republicans. The amendment was opposed by 115 southern and border-state Democrats, 31 northern Democrats, and 46 Republicans. The voting

---

[26] Inside the committee, Powell was urged to adopt one of the following alternatives: attach his amendment to the appropriation bill for the Department of Health, Education, and Welfare; obtain a ruling from the executive branch that no funds would be distributed to segregated school districts; attach his amendment, as a first step, to the impacted areas program; or make a commitment in favor of federal aid regardless of the fate of his amendment. Powell declined to take any of these steps. Another Negro leader, Rep. William Dawson (D.- Ill.), took a more compromising stand, as did Powell himself when he became chairman of the committee. Rep. Powell's behavior can be explained in part by his great disaffection from the committee under Barden and by the political style he adopted in the light of his constituency. On the contrasting styles of Powell and Dawson, see James Wilson, "Two Negro Politicians: An Interpretation," *Midwest Journal of Political Science,* IV (November, 1960), 346–69.

[27] House Committee on Education and Labor, *House Report* 1504, 84th Cong., 1st sess., 1955.

alignment cut across and divided the ranks of proponents and opponents of federal aid. As such, it bore little resemblance to the final alignment on passage of the bill. Ninety-six of the 148 Republicans who had voted for the Powell Amendment voted against the bill. Twenty-nine of the thirty-one northern Democrats who had voted against the Powell Amendment voted for the bill, but they could not offset the large Republican swing in the other direction. The seventy-seven northern Democrats who voted for the Powell Amendment supported the bill, but they were unwilling to vote against their civil rights convictions in order to improve the chances of federal aid. The very passage of the amendment, however, irrevocably detached from the coalition some southern and border-state congressmen who might otherwise have voted in favor of the legislation. Whatever their motivation may have been, the consequences of 76.3 per cent Republican support for the Powell Amendment and 61.3 per cent Republican opposition to final passage were first to divide and then to defeat the federal aid coalition.

It is difficult to know precisely how many Democratic supporters were lost to the bill through the passage of the Powell Amendment. Some measure of that loss, however, can be gleaned from comparing the vote on passage in 1956 with the vote to strike the enacting clause in 1957. At the time the 1957 bill was killed, the pending business was a vote on the substitute bill supported by the coalition leaders. The effect of this amendment would have been to strike out the Powell Amendment which had been proposed by Representative Stuyvesant Wainwright (R.-N.Y.), an opponent of federal aid, and passed by a teller vote in the committee of the whole. A southerner who supported federal aid without the Powell Amendment could logically, therefore, have voted to keep the 1957 bill alive. Of the ninety-four southerners who voted against passage of the bill in 1956, only nine voted to keep the bill alive in 1957. Of the nine border-state members who voted against passage in 1956, four voted against killing the 1957 bill. Thirteen members, in other words, indicated by their 1957 votes that they might have been willing, in 1956, to support federal aid legislation free from desegregation provisions.[28]

The number of votes is not sufficient to have changed the result in 1956. How many other southern and border-state votes might

---

[28] The nine southerners were Representatives Andrews, Elliott, Grant, Huddleston, Jones, Rains, Roberts, and Selden, all of Alabama, plus Representatives Trimble and Hays of Arkansas. The four border-state representatives were Albert (Okla.), Steed (Okla.), Jones (Mo.), and Natcher (Ky.).

have been forthcoming in 1956 if the racial issue had not been raised at all is problematical. Enough, perhaps, to have produced the sixteen votes necessary to change the result. Certainly this was the contention of the northern liberals (including Negro Congressman William Dawson [D.-Ill.]) who voted against the Powell Amendment and pleaded with their fellow liberals to do likewise. By 1957, a greater number of northern liberals had been persuaded by this argument. They announced their change of mind and their intention to vote against all antisegregation amendments in the hope of passing a federal aid bill.

But the issue of school segregation had been crystallized by the Court, and no southerner needed a Powell Amendment to be reminded of it. The pre-1954 political climate simply could not be recreated. On the racial issue most southerners agreed with veteran Representative William Colmer (D.-Miss.) when he said of the Powell Amendment in 1957:

> This is a case of tweedledee and tweedledum. It is immaterial whether this amendment is adopted or not. . . . This will be offered as an amendment on an appropriations bill. If that is not done, it will be done administratively. If that is not done, is there anybody so naive as to believe that the Supreme Court . . . is going to permit you to receive money and have segregated schools. So you lose any way it goes.[29]

The absence of a Powell Amendment would doubtless have increased the chances of federal aid passage in the House. But its absence would not have guaranteed passage. The indisputable result of the 1956 and 1957 House battles was legislative stalemate. Comparing the final result of 1957 with that of 1956, the proponents of a new federal aid consensus increased their support by a very unimpressive nine votes. In 1958, the President withdrew his support for federal aid altogether, and, once again, Representatives Barden and Landrum plus thirteen Republicans kept the question bottled up in committee.

COMMITTEE AND CHAMBER ACTIVITY, 1959–1961

The congressional elections of 1958 decisively altered the balance of party power in the House. Democratic membership jumped from

---

[29] *Congressional Record*, 85th Cong., 1st sess. (1957), p. 12738.

234 to 283, increasing thereby potential chamber support for federal aid. The change in party ratios on the Committee on Education and Labor created a new all-Democratic majority which, beginning in 1959, "picked up the committee and ran away with it." As Democratic federal aid strength increased, however, President Eisenhower's enthusiasm for a massive program correspondingly waned—to the point where, from 1958 to 1960, any such bill faced the likelihood of a presidential veto. Bipartisanship in the committee gave way to a steadily growing partisanship as both the need and the disposition to compromise weakened. The new Democratic majority found the key to its own cohesiveness in a type of permanent, flat grant for construction and for teachers' salaries, a bill quite unacceptable to the President and to committee Republicans. In 1959 and 1961, therefore, the Democratic bill was opposed unanimously by the committee's Republicans. In 1960, two Republicans joined the Democrats, but this did not affect the outcome.

These conditions of increased partisanship did not prevent aid bills from clearing the committee, but they did cost the federal aid proponents critical increments of Republican and southern Democratic support at later legislative junctures. One such juncture was the Committee on Rules. To the degree that the new Democratic majority refused to compromise with the President and Republicans inside the Committee on Education and Labor, they increased Republican intransigence on the Rules Committee. In addition, a change of two Republican members of the Rules Committee increased the opposition of that side of that group. In 1959, an alliance between the four Republicans and two consistently anti-federal-aid southern Democrats forestalled even a committee vote on the subject. One of the architects of that bill recalled:

> We got that bill out of committee, and we knew it didn't stand a chance of getting through the Rules Committee. But we just let it sit there. It put a few feet to the fire. We got enough pressure built up so that the next year when we came back with a construction bill, we got one extra vote and got it through the Rules Committee.

In 1960, one Republican vote did come from Representative B. Carroll Reece (Tenn.), who reportedly was under heavy pressure from his needy constituency to support federal aid. The bill cleared the Rules Committee by a seven-to-five vote (see Table III) and subsequently passed the House. A fatal loss of Republican and southern Democratic support in the Rules Committee did occur, however, at an even later point in the process. Every problem of consensus-building in the House is compounded by the necessity of securing cohesive majorities in two separate and distinct committees.

TABLE III

Votes in the Rules Committee to Expedite Federal Aid Legislation, 1956–1961

CONGRESSMEN	1956		1960 1st		1960 2nd		1961 1st		1961 2nd	
	Yes	No	Yes	No	Yes	No	Yes	No	Yes	No
Democrats										
Smith (Va.)		X		X		X		X		X
Colmer (Miss.)		X		X		X		X		X
Madden (Ind.)	X		X		X		X		X	
Delaney (N.Y.)	X		X		X			X		X
Trimble (Ark.)	X		X			X	X		X	
Thornberry (Tex.)	*	*	X		X		X		X	
Bolling (Mo.)	X		X		X		X		X	
O'Neill (Mass.)	X		X		X			X	X	
Elliott (Ala.)							X		X	
Sisk (Calif.)							X		X	
Republicans										
Allen (Ill.)		X		X		X				
Brown (Ohio)	X			X		X		X		X
Ellsworth (Ore.)	X									
Latham (N.Y.)	X									
Reece (Tenn.)			X			X				
Budge (Ida.)				X		X				
St. George (N.Y.)								X		X
Smith (Calif.)								X		X
Hoffman (Ill.)								X		X
Avery (Kan.)								X		X
TOTAL	8 –	3	7 –	5	5 –	7	6 –	9	7 –	8

Source: *Congressional Quarterly Almanac*, Vols. XII, XIII, XVI, XVII. No record of 1957 and 1959 votes.
* Not present.

The 1960 House bill was, like its predecessors, a school construction measure. For lack of teachers' salaries provisions, it was far less than the legislative proponents of the 1959 bill and their allies from the National Education Association desired. It did, however, retain the flat-grant basis from the earlier bill, but in so doing, it eliminated the equalization provisions so basic to President Eisenhower's position. As a compromise with the Republicans, who were also devoted to the idea of matching grants, the bill provided direct grants for the first year and matching grants for the following two years

Representative Bailey, the chairman of the subcommittee which had drafted it, said, "It is particularly written and tailored to receive House approval. The job that faces me and other proponents of the legislation is to see that it is not muddied up from the introduction of a lot of side issues."[30]

The design of the bill did lead to the passage of the first twentieth-century federal aid-to-education legislation in the House. When the 206 to 189 vote for passage is compared with the 1956 vote—194 to 224 against passage—two facts emerge. First, the number of Democrats in favor of the bill increased by forty-three; whereas the number opposed dropped by only eight. That is to say, the pro-aid Democratic vote, the heaviest ever cast by that party in the House, was made possible by the augmented Democratic majority arising out of the 1958 elections. Of the forty-nine Democrats who took seats away from Republicans in that election, forty-three voted in favor of federal aid, two were paired in favor, three voted against it, and one had died. Second, one-third of the House's Republicans voted for the bill. This represented a sizeable drop in number (thirty-one), but only a slight drop in percentage (6.3 per cent). On the final vote, 162 Democrats (62.5 per cent) and 44 Republicans (32.4 per cent) combined to pass the bill. It was, however, the post-1958 Democrats who most directly altered the balance of power.

At the same time, floor action constituted failure for the federal aid advocates. Representative Bailey was unable to prevent the side issues of which he warned from "muddying up the bill." Bailey's difficulty was underlined by the fact that during the floor action, one of the key committee sponsors of the bill, Representative Frank Thompson (D.-N.J.), offered a compromise amendment (affecting the grant provisions and the duration of the program) which was subsequently passed over Bailey's own vigorous opposition. When finally other items were tacked on to the Thompson amendment, Thompson and Bailey voted against it.

The key item that was added to Thompson's amendment was the Powell Amendment denying aid to segregated schools—first approved by a teller vote in the committee of the whole and later confirmed by roll call. The northern Democratic floor generals and some others voted against the Powell Amendment. But one hundred northern and western Democrats, faced with a civil rights proposition and a fall election, voted for the amendment. Said Powell, "A

---

[30] *Congressional Record*, 86th Cong., 2nd sess. (May 25, 1960), p. 10270.

vote against this amendment is a vote against the Supreme Court. A vote against this amendment is a vote against civil rights."[31] The strategic situation, as recognized by the pro-aid floor leaders, was that a bill with a Powell Amendment might be endangered at several later points—even if it could be passed. Yet House Democrats joined the anti-aid Republicans, just as they had done in 1956, in voting it into the bill. The Republicans achieved their greatest cohesion on this roll call out of the six taken in 1960. In line with their classic whipsaw pattern, however, seventy-seven Republicans who voted for the Powell Amendment subsequently voted against the bill.

Since the Senate had already passed an aid bill, only the conference committee remained. House rules provide that unless there is unanimous consent to such a conference, the Rules Committee must grant a special rule sending the bill on its way. Following an objection by Representative August Johansen (R.-Mich.), the Rules Committee procedure was invoked. There, at the hands of the four Republicans and three southern Democrats, the bill perished. Representatives Reece of Tennessee and James Trimble, a moderate Democrat from Arkansas, changed their positions from the earlier vote. For Trimble, and probably for Reece, the primary reason was the addition of the Powell Amendment to the original bill. The Rules Committee took action on June 22; Congress did not adjourn until September 1. During that summer, some aid supporters worked for compromise, but positions became ever more inflexible. Republicans feared that if a bill were passed, it might draw a presidential veto, which would be a liability in the fall election campaign. Liberal Democrats were unenthusiastic because of the elimination of teachers' salaries from the bill; they preferred a campaign issue to a watered-down bill. This paralysis revealed, once again, the essential evanescence of federal aid majorities.

Flexibility and compromise would seem to be two of the prerequisites for federal aid passage in the House. Two reasons that these attributes may be difficult to achieve are the nature of House members' constituencies and the frequency of House elections. Large numbers of representatives find that they must respond to a single dominant constituency interest—be it that of private school aid, school integration, school construction, teachers' salaries, or federal control. To the degree that his district's interests are homo-

---

[31] *Ibid.*, May 6, 1960, p. 10486.

geneous, a congressman may be bound tightly to one position on certain aspects of the federal aid controversy. And his legislative maneuverability may be further restricted by the necessity of standing for election every two years. As one committee member said, "You're tied down a lot tighter to your constituency here than in the Senate. . . . Over there at least one-third of the senators can afford to be statesmen. Here, you've got to be a politician all the time because you have to run every two years." House members pride themselves on the fact that their short tenure keeps them "close to the people." But their constant accountability to their constituents may reduce their autonomy in committee and on the floor.

Among the decisive inflexibilities of the 1960–61 period one of the most interesting was that of the National Education Association. At a point of legislative impasse, where a skillful lobbying group could be especially effective, the NEA became deliberately inactive and uncompromising. It was enthusiastically behind a teachers' salary bill. Failing to get such a provision in the House bill, its zeal disappeared. Federal aid leaders were unable to state precisely what the NEA position was.[32] In the summer of 1960, the NEA preferred to "wait till next year" rather than work to promote a compromise construction bill in conference. The group did nothing, therefore, to move the House bill off dead center in the Rules Committee. *New York Times* education columnist Fred Hechinger placed a large share of the blame for the 1960 failure on "¿ . . the lack of enthusiasm for any realistically attainable compromise on the part of [the] . . . powerful association of public school educators representing more than 700,000 teachers."[33]

Since the NEA is the most important interest-group ally of the legislators favoring federal aid, its insistence on teachers' salary provisions as the price of its wholehearted support has severely restricted the legislative maneuverability of its congressional cohorts. At the beginning of the 1960 session, the NEA memorialized each member of Congress and stated its terms in flat, uncompromising language:

If no satisfactory school support bill embodying the principles of the Murray-Metcalf bill [of 1959] is enacted in the

---

[32] *Ibid.*, p. 10476.
[33] *New York Times*, September 4, 1960, p. 17.

next session of Congress, the association will endeavor to make this matter a major issue in the political campaigns of 1960 so that the American people may again express their mandate for the enactment of such legislation in 1961.[34]

The parliamentary inflexibility of the NEA is the cause of constant consternation and bitterness among its legislative friends. Two sympathetic members of the Education and Labor Committee commented in 1961:

> They are very disappointing. They want the moon. Their attitude is that they might as well try a big bite and go down fighting rather than to establish a new area of federal responsibility in a small-scale, reasonable way. I think they've done great damage to their own cause.

> They're the worst, most ineffective lobby around. . . . They don't get their people to do the one thing that gets bills passed around here—write letters. My desk should be piled that high with letters, but it isn't. They just don't do it.

A member of the committee staff summed up:

> Their pavement pounders, the boys who are up here all the time, came to me when the construction bill was up and said they wanted a teachers' salaries bill. They asked me what position they should take before their convention. I said they should certainly take a position in favor of school construction and teachers' salaries both, but I said that didn't mean they couldn't support the school construction bill if that was up. There was that wondering whether they should hold out for all of their program. The AFL-CIO is much more realistic. They never backed down one inch on their position for construction and teachers' salaries, but when the chips were down on the construction bill, they were in there pounding away in favor of the construction bill long before the NEA. . . . The AFL-CIO was willing to take half a loaf. But the NEA has a tendency to want the whole loaf. They don't realize that if you get half a loaf, you have taken the first step. That's the hardest step, and you may be able to get more. They're a little idealistic—and shortsighted. If you argue for a whole loaf and won't take half a loaf, you'll argue yourself right out of a job.

The task of majority-building was renewed in 1961 under conditions which seemed to eliminate a number of earlier obstacles. A

---

[34] Quoted in *Congressional Record,* 86th Cong., 2nd sess., (May 26, 1960), p. 10476.

sympathetic Democratic President occupied the White House. The retirement of Representative Barden and the accession of Representative Powell to the chairmanship placed the Education and Labor Committee completely in the hands of pro-aid liberals. And, in his new role, Powell agreed to exert all of his influence to oppose any amendment concerning aid to segregated schools. Finally, the prospects for success were increased when federal aid supporters secured, with the help of Speaker Rayburn and President Kennedy, an enlarged and more liberal Rules Committee. Progress would appear to have been made, but the pattern of majority-building in the House has been more characteristically cyclical. In 1961, the familiar problems of 1949–50 recurred, and the prospective federal aid majority foundered once again on the dilemmas of aid to parochial schools.

On the impetus of a strong statement in favor of parochial school aid by the Catholic bishops, a group of Education and Labor Committee members attempted to add a private school program to the public school bill. In the committee, one group of Democrats had to manipulate the committee machinery very sharply and skillfully to prevent another group of Democrats (with Republican assistance) from altering the basic nature of the administration's construction and/or salaries bill. They succeeded, and then drafted the bill carefully so that a point of order could be raised (under the rule of germaneness) against any private school amendments offered on the floor. Defeated on their first attempt, parochial school aid supporters on the committee then wrote a provision for long-term construction loans to private schools into the National Defense Education Act, which was being amended in the committee. The public school bill, the NDEA amendments, and a bill providing for aid to colleges were in the hands of separate subcommittees. The paternal interest of each subcommittee in its particular education bill certainly did not help matters when the bills became interlocked on the way to the House floor.

Relations between party contingents inside the committee had become badly frayed, leaving all problems to be resolved within the all-Democratic majority. A description by two leading spokesmen of the committee atmosphere of 1961 reflects the extent to which the bipartisanship of the earlier period had declined:

> [Republican:] The Democrats haven't made a single concession to us on anything. . . . We've dug our heels in. We

don't like their tactics, and they don't like ours. But what we're doing against the bill isn't any worse than what they are doing to pass the bill. If they aren't going to do some of the things we think are reasonable, we're going to have to oppose the whole thing right down the line.

[Democrat:] Boy were they mad. We were slick. But they were trying to be slick, too. They haven't got any interest in aiding parochial schools. They were trying to raise the issue, giggle, sit back and watch the bill die. They play the game right to the hilt.

Republican opposition to the committee's public school bill was unanimous.

The question which proved insoluble was whether the public school bill or the NDEA amendments with aid for parochial schools should be sent to the House floor first. The factional struggle inside the committee was resolved in favor of the public school bill, which was reported to the Rules Committee. But that committee voted nine to six (see Table III) to take no action on it until the other two bills had reached their committee. On this vote, the majority was comprised, as expected, of five Republicans and the two anti-federal-aid southerners. But they were joined, unexpectedly, by two liberal Democrats, both Catholics representing heavily Catholic constituencies—Thomas O'Neill from Cambridge, Mass. and James Delaney of New York City.

Once again, the separate problems of majority-building on the two House committees are apparent. The factional conflict which was eventually broken inside the Education and Labor Committee helped to precipitate a conflict which could not be resolved on the Rules Committee. Three weeks later when faced with all three education bills, the Rules Committee Democrats were still unable to agree on how to break the log jam. By an eight-to-seven majority, they voted to table all three education bills for the remainder of the year. On this vote, one of the two defecting Democrats, Representative O'Neill, changed his position; but the other, Representative Delaney, was still dissatisfied with the provisions for parochial school aid and again voted against sending the public school aid bill to the floor. A month later, an improvised federal aid bill was rushed to the floor on Calendar Wednesday—thus bypassing the Rules Committee—but it stood no chance of passage. The defeat in the Rules Committee and in the course of regular legislative processes was decisive.

The Rules Committee is, by the very nature of its jurisdiction over the House's program and procedure, subject to the directive influence of the majority party leadership. In 1961, the Democratic leadership group was itself badly split on the issue of priority and strategy. Speaker Rayburn, convinced that the only possibility for a public school program lay in its being considered first, insisted that the public school bill be taken up forthwith. Majority Leader John McCormack (D.-Mass.), fearful that the bill containing aid to parochial schools would fail unless it reached the floor first, argued against Rayburn. Each was allied with a faction in the Rules Committee. Because the Rayburn faction took the initiative inside the Rules Committee, it was the two members allied with McCormack, *i.e.*, O'Neill and Delaney, who delivered the *coup de grace* to federal aid. But, had McCormack's strategy been proposed in the committee, federal aid would just as surely have perished at the hands of the Rayburn faction—men such as James Trimble of Arkansas, Carl Elliott of Alabama, Homer Thornberry of Texas, and B. F. Sisk of California. The Rules Committee Democrats had been presented with the issue in a form which made it virtually insoluble.

The watered-down bill which administration and legislative leaders hastily drew up and sent to the floor via Calendar Wednesday requires comment only because it suffered the most lop-sided defeat in the history of federal aid. It died when an undebatable motion to consider it was lost by 170 to 242. The revealing feature of the vote was the complete disintegration on the floor as in committee of the moderate bipartisanship which had characterized the consensus-building attempts of the mid-fifties. See Table IV. Only six Republicans voted to consider the bill—a drop from a high of 41 per cent in 1957 to 3.6 per cent in 1961. During the same period, Democratic support for federal aid had steadily increased—from a low of 53.1 per cent in 1956 to 66.7 per cent in 1961.

TABLE IV

Increasing Partisanship on Federal Aid Final Votes 1956–1961

Congressmen	Per Cent Supporting Federal Aid			
	1956	1957	1960	1961
Democratic Representatives	53.1	56.5	62.5	66.7
Republican Representatives	38.7	41.0	32.4	3.6
House Index of Partisanship*	14.4	15.5	30.1	63.1

* The index of partisanship constitutes the difference between the percentages of Democrats and Republicans supporting federal aid. A value of 100 would indicate unanimous support by one party, unanimous opposition by the other; a zero value would demonstrate identical divisions within both parties.

Party tensions had been further exacerbated by the manner in which the new proposal had been concocted and rushed to the floor. A normally sympathetic Republican, Representative John Lindsay (N.Y.) explained his vote:

> It is insulting to those in the minority for the majority to slap a last-minute, strung-together, and totally inadequate compromise before us in this take-it-or-leave-it procedure. . . . My vote is a protest against the procedure used and the complete inability of the majority to put its legislative house in order.[35]

As in the case of the parochial school problem, a conflict which had been laboriously resolved at one point in time, *i.e.* partisanship, had returned to plague later efforts to build consensus.

Near the end of the 1961 session, Chairman Powell could only be guardedly pessimistic:

> It is my personal opinion, and I may be totally wrong, that the temper of this House is of such nature that Federal aid to school construction, per se, is dead at least for the next year. I think it is deplorable, but we must face the stark, brutal, and disheartening fact and not dissipate the energies of this Committee nor this House on that which will bring no results whatsoever.[36]

As prophecy, Powell's assessment remained accurate through the Eighty-seventh Congress and up to the congressional elections of 1962.

CONCLUSION

An epitaph for 1961 was pronounced by Secretary of Health, Education and Welfare Abraham Ribicoff when he said, "They expected a miracle and I couldn't produce a miracle. It was impossible to bring together a majority for a bill when most members didn't want one."[37] Ribicoff's lament summarizes many years of conflict over federal aid in the House. It also helps to restate the problem of majority-building in that chamber. The problem is not that a majority of representatives have not wanted a federal aid measure or could not be persuaded to want one. The problem is that an

---

[35] *Ibid.*, 87th Cong., 1st sess. (August 30, 1961), p. 16509.
[36] *Ibid.* (September 6, 1961), p. 17096.
[37] Quoted in *Wall Street Journal*, September 6, 1961, p. 14.

over-all majority—or a federal aid consensus—cannot be obtained at any one point in time for any one legislative proposal. To put it another way, any federal aid majority must be compounded of many submajorities. Different submajorities will be needed to resolve essentially different conflicts—that is to say, conflicts on different issues, in different decision-making units, at different points in time, and in different sets of society-wide circumstances. Furthermore, each submajority must be both flexible and cohesive—flexible enough to permit agreement with other submajorities and cohesive enough to make that agreement an asset in legislative maneuver.

At one time or another, submajorities have been obtained to resolve every identifiable conflict over federal aid. And, from time to time, each of these submajorities has combined considerable flexibility and cohesiveness. But, given the issues involved and given the institutional characteristics of the House of Representatives, an over-all House majority in support of general federal aid legislation is extraordinarily difficult to create. A new, stable House consensus remains as far from—yet as close to—realization as ever.

XIII

TWO STRATEGIES OF INFLUENCE: CHOOSING A MAJORITY LEADER, 1962*

Nelson W. Polsby

POLITICAL SCIENTISTS seem to be fond of debating whether traditional political theory in America is dead or only sleeping.[1] Either way, there is no argument that the speculations which occupied thinkers of other days have been little used to illuminate current political behavior. The argument, when there is one, concerns whether it is even possible to use traditional political theory in this way. Regrettably, optimists on this point have not always demonstrated that they were right in supposing that traditional political theory could contribute to the understanding of present-day politics. But this does not mean that they are wrong.

A major obstacle to the use of traditional political theory in modern political science has been theory's long-standing concern with prescriptive statements. Prescriptions are not necessarily the best instruments for organizing information about the empirical world, since the preferences which they assert may not correspond

---

* This paper was originally presented at the annual meetings of The American Political Science Association, Washington, D.C., 1962. Several members of Congress, who I am sure would prefer to remain anonymous, read an early draft of this chapter and made many useful comments. I should also like to thank Lewis A. Dexter, H. Douglas Price, and Robert L. Peabody. Others who have been helpful include Aaron B. Wildavsky, Lewis A. Froman, Jr., Norman O. Brown, Luigi Einaudi, Joseph Cooper, Alan L. Otten, and Neil MacNeil. Research assistance was provided by a Ford Foundation grant to Wesleyan University.
[1] The phrase "traditional political theory" refers in this context to the history of political thinking rather than to any specific political doctrines. See, for example, David Easton, *The Political System* (New York: Knopf, 1953); Harry V. Jaffa, "The Case Against Political Theory," *Journal of Politics*, XXII (May, 1960), 259–75; Robert A. Dahl, "The Science of Politics, New and Old," *World Politics*, VII (April, 1955), 479–89; Dahl, "Political Theory, Truth and Consequences," *World Politics*, XI (October, 1958), 89–102; Norman Jacobson, "The Unity of Political Theory," in R. Young (ed.), *Approaches to the Study of Politics* (Evanston: Northwestern University Press, 1958), pp. 115–24.

to any observed (or even observable) events. However, prescriptions may in fact point to quite interesting and genuine dilemmas in the real world. In these circumstances, we have the option of converting the language of prescription to that of description if we desire to put traditional political theory to more modern uses.

The possibilities of this device have lately been explored by a group of students of the legislative process, using as their text the celebrated speech to the Electors of Bristol by Edmund Burke.[2] In this speech, on the occasion of his election as Member of Parliament from Bristol, it will be recalled that Burke undertook to state and resolve a recurring dilemma of the representative:

> Certainly, gentlemen, it ought to be the happiness and glory of a representative to live in the strictest union, the closest correspondence, and the most unreserved communication with his constituents. Their wishes ought to have great weight with him; their opinion high respect; their business unremitted attention. . . . But his unbiased opinion, his native judgment, his enlightened conscience he ought not to sacrifice to you. . . . Your representative owes you, not his industry only, but his judgment. . . . Government and legislation are matters of reason and judgment, and not of inclination; and what sort of reason is that, in which the determination precedes the discussion; in which one set of men deliberate and another decide . . . Parliament is not a *congress* of ambassadors from different and hostile interests . . . but . . . a *deliberative* assembly of *one* nation. . . . We are now members for a rich commercial city; this city, however, is but part of a rich commercial nation, the interests of which are various, multiform, and intricate. . . . All these widespread interests must be considered; must be compared; must be reconciled if possible.[3]

Six years after Burke spoke these words, he stood for election once again, and on the same topic said:

> I could wish undoubtedly . . . to make every part of my conduct agreeable to every one of my constituents. . . . But . . . do you think, gentlemen, that every public act in six years since I stood in this place before you—that all the arduous things which have been done in this eventful period, which has

---

[2] Heinz Eulau, John C. Wahlke, Leroy C. Ferguson, and William Buchanan, "The Role of the Representative: Some Empirical Observations on the Theory of Edmund Burke," *American Political Science Review,* LIII (September, 1959), 742–56.

[3] "Speech to the Electors of Bristol," November 3, 1774, *Works* (London, etc.: Oxford University Press, 1906), II, 164–66.

crowded into a few years' space the revolutions of an age—can be opened to you on their fair grounds in half an hour's conversation? . . . Let me say with plainness . . . that if by a fair, by an indulgent, by a gentlemanly behavior to our representatives, we do not give confidence to their minds, and a liberal scope to their understandings; if we do not permit our members to act upon a *very* enlarged view of things, we shall at length infallibly degrade our national representation into a confused and scuffling bustle of local agency.[4]

A brief historical detour will suggest certain empirical problems related to Burke's position. Shortly after the second speech quoted here, Burke withdrew his candidacy, feeling he could not win. He and his constituents had disagreed over several matters, in particular his vote to free Irish trade from restrictions operating in favor of Bristol. Burke remained in Parliament, however, representing a pocket borough thereafter.[5] Although acting on his principle of independence from constituent pressures was costly to him, Burke was clearly in a position to take a more luxurious stand on such a question than another member could who did not have the protection of a pocket borough and the party list.

This raises still a more general empirical point: Under what conditions will the representative be more likely to respond to the demands of "local agency"? When is he more likely to respond to a political situation as it appears to him in the light of his experience at the seat of government? Under what conditions will attempts to influence the representative through his constituency bring better results than attempts to influence him through the network of loyalties and affiliations he has built up through service in his deliberative body—and vice versa?

The United States House of Representatives is one laboratory for the exploration of questions such as these. Indeed, where the stakes are as high as they often are in House decision-making, it is not surprising that full-scale campaigns are mounted in order to sway sometimes no more than a handful of marginal votes. But are these votes swayed from the inside or the outside? Do constituencies matter more or less than colleagues?[6]

---

[4] "Speech at Bristol," September 6, 1780 in *ibid.*, III, 2, 3, 4.

[5] *Ibid.*, and F. W. Raffety, "Preface" in *Works*, II, xiv–xv.

[6] One approach to some of these questions was made by Julius Turner, who used the analysis of roll calls as his major source of data in *Party and Constituency: Pressures on Congress* (Baltimore: Johns Hopkins, 1951). See also David B. Truman, *The Congressional Party* (New York: Wiley, 1959).

Sometimes the answer is reasonably clear and unequivocal. Here are examples of *inside* influences at work:

> Representative Cleveland Bailey is a genuinely dedicated opponent of reciprocal trade. . . . [He] is unusual among members—probably unique—in that protection is *the* most important issue to him and that he creates the sense of having a deep felt conviction on the subject. In 1953–54 he went around and pled individually with a number of members to vote against reciprocal trade and for the West Virginia miners. One member put it, "He was rough, real rough . . . I had to be rough with him." Another said, "In the 1954 vote, Cleve Bailey was worth 15 votes to his side easily."[7]

> The morning of one of the key votes on reciprocal trade [1955], Speaker Sam Rayburn attended a breakfast of the freshman Democrats in the House. I asked one of the Congressmen who was there about it. He chuckled: "Oh, you heard about that? . . . We'd just invited Mr. Sam to this breakfast. He turned it into a sort of speech and said he'd observed that *generally the new members got along better who went along*, but he didn't make any particular application—of course you could guess what he had in mind. . . ."[8]

On the other hand, it is sometimes possible to detect *outside* influences. The following example comes from the January, 1961, battle over the size of the House Rules Committee:

> It was learned that Representative Howard Smith, Southern leader and Rules Committee Chairman, has held several meetings in his office in recent weeks with representatives of the most powerful conservative lobbies in the country, trying to shape a campaign to beat Rayburn by applying pressure on members from home. The groups included the National Association of Manufacturers, the United States Chamber of Commerce, the American Medical Association and the American Farm Bureau. . . . Some members have reported heavy mail from business interests in their home districts. . . . On the other side, Northern Democrats have sent out an appeal to organized labor for help. Yesterday, Andrew J. Biemiller, chief AFL-CIO lobbyist, was at the Capitol trying to line up votes. . . .[9]

---

[7] Lewis Anthony Dexter, "Congressmen and the People They Listen To" (Cambridge: Center for International Studies, Massachusetts Institute of Technology, Ditto, 1955), chap. ii, p. 14, chap. viii, p. 7.

[8] *Ibid.*, chap. v, pp. 4–5.

[9] Richard L. Lyons, "Pressure Rises as House Moves to Vote on Rules," *Washington Post*, January 31, 1961.

During the aid to education debate [a Roman Catholic congressman] threatened to kill the public school measure by tagging on to it a parochial school amendment. [Presidential Assistant Lawrence] O'Brien appealed to [the congressman's home district party leader] who immediately telephoned [the congressman]. "Who sent you there, me or the Bishop?" he growled. "And who's going to keep you there, me or the Bishop?"[10]

At other times strong inside and outside influences are blurred together quite inextricably:

A newspaper correspondent told me: "Oh yes, you know those two boys [congressmen] . . . well you know why Jack voted against the leadership? Just to oblige Joe to whom he's very close; Joe was afraid he'd be the only fellow from the state to vote against the leadership and he'd get into trouble with the leadership and the party organization so Jack went along with him to prevent his sticking his neck out all alone. . . ."[11]

The whip from the area told me . . . "Tom rather wanted to go along with the leadership, but he found Dave and Don and four other guys from surrounding districts were against the leadership, and he decided he'd better go along with them, because after all he's hearing a lot from his district against it, and how could he explain his being for it and Dave and Don and the rest being against it?"[12]

The recent contest for the majority leadership of the House provides, as it happens, a rather good contrast between the two strategies of influence. In turn, the close examination of this case may begin to suggest answers to some of the questions posed above.

I

On January 10, 1962, the Democratic members of the House met in caucus in the House chamber and nominated John McCormack

---

[10] *Time* (September 1, 1961), p. 14. The congressman is not identified here, as he was in the *Time* article, first, because he denies the conversation took place (*Congressional Record*, 87th Cong., 1st sess. [August 29, 1961], p. 16318) and second, because the *Time* reporter's source for the quote told me that he had deliberately left ambiguous the identity of the congressman, and, while the event really happened, the *Time* reporter was misled about whom it happened to.

[11] Dexter, *op. cit.*, chap. viii, p. 4.

[12] *Ibid.*, pp. 4–5.

as their candidate for Speaker. Immediately following the conclusion of this business, Richard Bolling of Missouri asked that the
agenda of the caucus be expanded by unanimous consent to include
the selection of a Majority Leader, and Carl Albert of Oklahoma,
his party's whip and the only congressman put in nomination, was
elected to that post. Thus ended a period of skirmishing for the
majority leadership that had principally engaged Bolling and Albert
from the time of Speaker Rayburn's death on November 16 of the
previous year.

Most newspaper coverage of this event gave the impression that
the battle between these two men was drawn on liberal-conservative
lines. In Bolling's press conference on January 3 announcing his
withdrawal from the race, newsmen repeatedly suggested that the
contrast between them was predominantly ideological. A newspaper-
woman asked, rhetorically, "Don't the liberals *ever* win around here,
Mr. Bolling?" Another widely quoted colloquy went:

Reporter: "Mr. Bolling, do you regard your withdrawal . . . as a
defeat for liberalism?"

Bolling: "Well, I consider myself a liberal, and at the moment I
certainly feel defeated."[13]

Close observation suggests that the liberal-conservative distinction
has only a limited kind of utility for understanding the Bolling-
Albert fight for the majority leadership.[14] It is not necessary to base
this conclusion on a *Congressional Quarterly* tabulation showing
that Albert supported the Kennedy program 91 per cent of the time
in the first session of the Eighty-seventh Congress and Bolling 94
per cent—a fact continually cited by liberal supporters of Mr.
Albert.[15] Equally significant are the facts, first, that Albert indeed

---

[13] The best news coverage by far of this press conference that I saw occurred
in the *Baltimore Sun,* January 4, 1962. See Rodney Crowther, "House Race
Dropped by Bolling."

[14] Pursuit of this line of thinking at a McCormack-Albert press conference,
January 9, visibly irked Mr. McCormack. "A reporter . . . caught [Mr. Mc-
Cormack] at the door of the Speaker's lobby and asked him if he had asked
for complete support of President Kennedy's program. The new Speaker drew
back indignantly. 'I'm not trying to put words in your mouth,' said the reporter. 'Yes you are,' said Mr. McCormack, 'I've been voting for progressive
legislation for 30 years. I'm not a one-year man. Why don't you wake up?' "
Mary McGrory, "McCormack Speaks as His Own Master," *Washington Star,*
January 10, 1962.

[15] *Congressional Quarterly,* XIX (November 24, 1961), 1893–94. This tabulation also shows that throughout their careers in Congress, the voting records
of these men were quite close by several criteria.

had a great deal of support among members with impeccably liberal records of long standing and, second, that he was regarded at the White House as a genuine friend of the Kennedy program.[16]

If, then, the outcome of the Bolling-Albert contest cannot be explained by the usual ideological arithmetic one uses in analyzing the House, how can one explain what happened? In part, an explanation can be based on the strategies each of the main actors pursued. These strategies were in turn largely dictated by their respective positions and roles in the House during the final years of the Rayburn speakership.

Often great differences in resources between political actors are largely nullified by the fact that resources are generally employed at low levels of intensity and with indifferent skill. In this case, however, resources on both sides were employed with considerable skill and finesse, and hence the outcome comes closer to reflecting a common-sense notion of the logic of the situation than might otherwise have been the case. It makes sense to describe the "cards" that each man held because, in this instance, the man who held the better cards made no more mistakes than his opponent, and, in the end, he won.

It is worth stressing that only part of the explanation can be given by referring to the roles and strategies of the main participants and to the different ways in which their demands were communicated to other House members. Two other significant variables can be sketched in only very crudely. This battle took place in the very core of an institution about whose habits and practices precious little is known, and, second, it engaged the participation of a great many more facets of the human personality than political decisions in the House normally do. The mysteries of how men interact with one another, of what leads people into enmity, jealousy, friendship, all seem to me to have played a very significant part in this contest.

---

[16] These statements, and many others throughout this paper, are based on interviews and observations gathered during the summer of 1961 and from December to February, 1961–62, in Washington. During these months I spoke on matters connected with the subject of this paper to over 100 congressmen, congressional aides, newspapermen, and others, and during the latter period, I conducted interviews with twenty-six Democratic congressmen from all sections of the country on the leadership selection process then going on. Quotations are from notes taken during these interviews, and are occasionally slightly altered so as to preserve the anonymity of the respondent. My work in the summer of 1961 was supported by a grant-in-aid from the Social Science Research Council, whose assistance is gratefully acknowledged.

Obviously, the extent to which the outside observer can detect and extract meaning from these relationships is extremely limited, and this must inevitably weaken the plausibility and also the generality of the case I am about to construct, using, for the most part, more readily accessible materials.

II

The realization that Speaker Rayburn's health was failing seriously dawned on different members of the House at different times during the summer of 1961. That summer happened to have been an extremely hot and humid one in Washington. The House stayed in session continuously through the summer, one of the longest, bitterest, and most grueling sessions in the memory of veterans on Capitol Hill.[17] Over the course of this period, many members and observers, especially those who were close to the Speaker, could not help but notice the wasting of Mr. Rayburn's solid, imposing figure, the occasional, uncharacteristic wandering of his attention from the business of the House, his increased susceptibility to bouts of fatigue and irritability, the slowing of his gait.

The House is, in the words of one of its members, a "Council of Elders." It honors age and places much power and trust in the hands of its most senior and oldest men. One consequence of this fact is the necessary, calm preoccupation of members—especially those just below the top rungs of power—with the inevitable occurrence of death. To that large fraction of members for whom the House is a career and a vocation, the longevity of members above them in the many hierarchies of the House—not the entirely predictable congressional election returns in their home districts—is the key to the political future. This is not to say that members habitually rub their hands ghoulishly or enjoy the prospect of losing valued friends, but only that the norms and the rules of the House bring due rewards to men who accept the world as it is, who prudently make their plans and bide their time.

On the other hand, informal norms of the House also put constraints on members based on commonly accepted notions of decent

---

[17] The session lasted 277 days, the longest in ten years. Late one especially debilitating August afternoon, an elderly southern congressman shuffled over to where I was standing just outside the Speaker's lobby, and confided that he was going to sponsor a bill that would abolish the final month of each session of Congress.

behavior, decorum, and good taste. Hence it is impossible for an outsider to say when Mr. Albert and Mr. Bolling began thinking in any concrete way about the next step in their careers within the House. However, it seems safe to make two assumptions: First, that they each had entertained some general thoughts on the question of the majority leadership well in advance of the occurence of an actual vacancy (on January 9) or probable vacancy (on November 16) in the position. Second, both men knew Speaker Rayburn well, and both undoubtedly guessed earlier than most members that his health had permanently disintegrated.

III

On Saturday, November 18, Sam Rayburn was buried in Bonham, Texas. Mr. Albert reports that he had planned to wait until the following Wednesday to begin his campaign for Majority Leader. "I was in my office in McAlester on Sunday night," Mr. Albert said, "when Charlie Ward [his assistant] came in and said, 'Bolling has announced for Majority Leader.' I heard it on the radio that night and saw a copy of the press release from my hometown paper before I announced myself. It was an Associated Press report, and Bill Arbogast [who covers the House for AP] wrote the story."

As a result of this turn of events, Mr. Albert got into the race sooner than he had intended. Mr. Bolling had thrown down a challenge which he could ignore only at his peril. In addition, Mr. Bolling's action offered Mr. Albert an opportunity to run a campaign against him, rather than against any of the more popular or more senior members who had been mentioned for leadership positions.

To each side it appeared that the other had begun to make plans well before Mr. Rayburn's death. Observers partial to Mr. Albert noted that as long before as the previous spring, Mr. Bolling was being referred to in public as a prominent contender for a leadership post.[18] It was easy to infer that, at least in part, these references had been suggested or "inspired" by Mr. Bolling. On the other hand, observers partial to Mr. Bolling thought an alliance between Mr. Albert and the Speaker-to-be, John McCormack, was being announced

---

[18] For example, Mr. Bolling was introduced to a large public meeting at the Midwest Conference of Political Scientists on May 11, 1961, as "the next Speaker of the House of Representatives."

when Mr. Albert, as his chief deputy, led the tributes on September 26, 1961, in honor of Mr. McCormack's twenty-one years as Majority Leader.[19]

It seems plausible to suggest that the signs and portents friends of both men were reading did not reflect concious efforts by either man to organize a premature campaign for the majority leadership. Rather, each man appealed particularly to slightly different publics: Bolling to the press corps, Albert to various groups within the House itself. These groups may, without encouragement from either man, have initiated activity designed to facilitate their chances of advancement. "After Mr. Rayburn went home to Texas," Mr. Albert reported, "I had fifty or sixty members pull me aside and say to me, 'He's not coming back. Don't sit there and be done out of what you're entitled to.' But I refused to discuss the matter with them." Several members mentioned that they had volunteered their support to Mr. Albert, and some, apparently, had attempted to persuade him to run for Speaker. "I would never do that against John McCormack," Mr. Albert said. "Mr. Rayburn and Mr. McCormack picked me and made me whip, and to run against Mr. McCormack would have been the act of an ingrate."

Two groups were especially partial to Mr. Albert: his deputy whip organization and colleagues in the Oklahoma delegation. "We make a fetish of the fact that if you scratch one Okie you've scratched all of 'em," one member told me. As soon as Mr. Albert announced that he would run for Majority Leader, the members of the delegation did whatever they could to help his candidacy. The deputy whips gave Mr. Albert a party after Mr. Rayburn had gone to Texas, and attempted, without success, to induce Mr. Albert to begin work on his candidacy at that time.

Mr. Albert's announcement to the press followed the report of Mr. Bolling's by several hours. As soon as the announcement was made, Mr. Albert sent off a telegram to all members asking for their support and began telephoning each of them individually. "I bet you he was on the phone four days running," one member said.

Mr. Albert's intensive telephone campaign began with the west coast members. "James Roosevelt [congressman from Los Angeles] was the first man I called outside my own delegation," he said. By

---

[19] Mr. Albert's tribute on this occasion was much more elaborate than that tendered by any other member—save by Mr. McCormack's Massachusetts colleagues. See the *Congressional Record*, 87th Cong., 1st sess. (September 26, 1961), pp. 20084–96.

the end of the first day of telephoning, Mr. Albert thought he had all but five westerners committed to him. "If I wasn't sure of a senior man in a delegation," Mr. Albert said, "I started with the most junior men and asked them directly to support me. Then I'd work my way up the line so that when the senior man said, 'I'll have to check with my delegation,' I would have something to report to him. Of course on a thing like this, you call your friends first, but I had no set, written-out plan. I don't work that way."

The reasons members gave for supporting Mr. Albert are quite illuminating. They reflect two dominant themes, both of which illustrate the "inside" quality of his influence. On the one hand, Mr. Albert was his party's whip. Although there is no tradition which dictates that the whip shall be advanced to the majority leadership (as there is in promoting the Majority Leader to Speaker) many members felt that Mr. Albert nonetheless was "entitled" to the job by virtue of his six years service in the leadership hierarchy of the House. Some of them said:

> [From a liberal leader:] I made a commitment to Carl based on his years of service as whip and the fact that he was in line for this job from the standpoint of his long service as whip.

> [From a southwesterner:] Because I feel that he was entitled to it by reason of his effective part in the leadership of the House along with the Speaker and Mr. McCormack, I promised him my support.

> [From the elderly dean of a large delegation:] I am a firm believer in the rule that has governed the House for over 100 years, and that is that of seniority. If Congressman McCormack is to be promoted to the Speakership of the House on the premise of his seniority and being in line position, then obviously the majority leader and whip should pursue the same course.[20] I have had the honor of being a member of this great body for [many years] . . . and while I would be reluctant to

---

[20] Mr. Albert entered the House in 1947, Mr. Bolling in 1949, making them thirtieth (tied with nine others) and thirty-ninth (tied with nineteen others) in seniority respectively in the Democratic party in the House—not a very great difference. Mr. McCormack, on the other hand, was the benficiary of a long tradition of advancement from Majority Leader to Speaker, and, in addition, after the death of Speaker Rayburn, was third in seniority. He had never served as whip, incidentally, before his election as Majority Leader, nor had Speaker Rayburn. Both Mr. McCormack and Mr. Rayburn had held office for so many years it is highly probable that most members were unaware of the differences in the customs pertaining to the advancement of the Majority Leader and the whip.

say that the seniority process does not have some imperfections, nevertheless if any other procedure were to be applied, I am inclined to believe that rather a chaotic situation would immediately be evident.

A second theme illustrates Mr. Albert's personal popularity in the House. Many members could cite warm personal ties they had developed with Mr. Albert. The late John Riley of South Carolina said, "Carl Albert married a girl from Columbia, you know, and so he is practically a constituent of mine."

A northern liberal: "I'm in something of a special situation with Carl, since we're the only two members of the House who [belong to an exclusive, honorary organization]."

A congressman from a border state said, "In all good conscience, I had to agree to support Carl because of his great help and encouragement to me [on a pet bill]."

A southwesterner said, "As one of his deputy whips, I feel committed to Carl Albert."

A southerner: "I committed myself to Carl Albert, who is my neighbor in the House Office Building."

Another southerner: "My association with Carl Albert has been extremely intimate."

Three men who served with Mr. Albert on committees:

"Carl and I have sat side by side on [our] committee for fifteen years."

"Carl has been very kind to me in the committee work and has done several things for me which have been very important for my people. . . ."

"I sit right next to Carl Albert. . . . We have been close personal friends due to our connection on the committee. . . ."

Another member said, "Ordinarily I'm slow to make commitments, but due to a friendship with Carl which began when we were in the . . . Army together, I told him quite a while back that should he seek the position of Democratic leader, I would support him."

And some members, not unexpectedly, combined the themes. For example: "He is not only my neighbor but a member of my committee, and with it all a fine, able, conscientious man who has been doing the dirty work for the leadership for a long time. . . ."

It was characteristic of Mr. Albert's "inside" strategy of influence that he used the telephone energetically and extensively himself to make personal contacts with members as quickly as possible. As whip, he was the custodian of a complete set of home, office, and district telephone numbers for each member.[21] One member said:

> Albert got on the phone and tracked me down in the frozen wastes of northern Rockystate the first day after the Speaker was buried. You wouldn't think politicians would fall for that, but many of them did. They were impressed by the fact that he'd called them first. As a result he was able to line up a lot of the members, including many northern bleeding-heart liberals, in the first few days.

The principal argument which Mr. Albert used in asking the support of almost all the members I spoke with was the fact that he had already received a large number of commitments. This is instructive, because it evokes the almost obsessive preoccupation of congressmen with "getting along" and not sticking their necks out unnecessarily. "This House gives out no medals for individual bravery," said one congressman, "except posthumously."

Mr. Albert had an important further asset—the apparent backing of John McCormack. "I have heard McCormack say again and again that we have got to have a team player," one congressman said. "I guess he means by that a member of his team, and I suppose he favors Carl Albert." I asked a newspaperman who was following the situation closely to tell me who the most important congressman on Mr. Albert's side was, and he replied, "John McCormack." However, I could find no evidence that Mr. McCormack gave Mr. Albert any public endorsement.

Describing his campaign, Mr. Albert said:

> I didn't want to hurt Mr. Bolling's feelings. I never once threw knives or wrote mean things, although plenty of knives got thrown at me. I never once got on television. The sum total of my national publicity was a release when I got into the race and a release when I got up to Washington saying I thought I had enough votes to win. I refused to go on television although I was invited to go on most of the news and panel shows. I never mentioned Bolling's name at all. I never mentioned issues or anything. . . .

---

[21] Mr. Albert's administrative assistant said that this list happened to be in the Washington office while the telephoning was being done from McAlester, Oklahoma, where only the House telephone directory issued to all members was readily available.

IV

Mr. Bolling's campaign, in contrast, followed an "outside" strategy of influence. As in the Rules Committee fight at the opening of the Eighty-seventh Congress and on numerous other occasions where he had planned legislative strategy and tactics, he held aloof from direct contact with most members. "I seldom try to persuade people directly," he said. "Our districts persuade us—if we are going to be persuaded at all."

Bolling had an uphill battle on his hands. He was severely handicapped at the start by his unwillingness to do anything in his own behalf until well after the Speaker had died. "It's a funny thing that Dick was so dilatory," a friend said. Although he leaked an announcement of his candidacy for the majority leadership to the press on November 19, the day after the Speaker's funeral, it was not until November 28 that he sent a strikingly diffident letter to each of the Democrats in the House. This letter said:

> Just a note to confirm that I am running for Democratic floor leader and am seeking the support of my Democratic colleagues for that position. Reports during the past week have been encouraging and I am in this contest all the way.
> I am running on my legislative record and experience and hope that you will give my candidacy your consideration on that basis.

Several of his supporters expressed surprise at the mildness of this approach. The letter asked for "consideration," not support, and was not followed up by an energetic telephone campaign. Furthermore, Bolling had waited twelve precious days after the Speaker's death before making his move. Why?

Answers to a question of motive such as this one—even the answers given by Mr. Bolling himself—are bound to verge on speculation. My guess is that Mr. Bolling's hesitancy had something to do with the relationship he had had with Speaker Rayburn. According to the reports of numerous observers who had no axes to grind, Mr. Bolling and the Speaker had built a bond of affection between them that went well beyond the usual political alliance.[22] Mr. Sam, who

---

[22] Friends of Mr. Albert note that Mr. Albert was Speaker Rayburn's personal choice for whip in 1954 and further suggest that Mr. Albert was also a close personal friend of Mr. Rayburn's. One influential congressman said, "Mr. Sam thought the world of Carl Albert." But this same congressman indicated that he thought Mr. Bolling's relationship with the Speaker was unique. Without excluding the strong probability that Mr. Rayburn had a

had no immediate family, was well known for his habit of adopting political protégés with whom he could develop a relationship of warmth and trust similar to that found in the family situation. This was, apparently, Mr. Rayburn's way of overcoming the loneliness that otherwise might well have overtaken any elderly bachelor.

The need to overcome loneliness was strongly ingrained in Mr. Rayburn from childhood. Mr. Rayburn is quoted as saying:

> Many a time when I was a child and lived way out in the country, I'd sit on the fence and wish to God that somebody would ride by on a horse or drive by in a buggy—just anything to relieve my loneliness. Loneliness consumes people. It kills 'em eventually. God help the lonely. . . .[23]

Mr. Rayburn's advice to Presidents Truman, Eisenhower, and Kennedy reflect the same theme. As he reported afterward, on a conversation with Mr. Truman just after the latter had become President:

> "You've got many hazards," I said. "One of your great hazards is in this White House," I said. "I've been watching things around here a long time, and I've seen people in the White House try to build a fence around the White House and keep the various people away from the President that he should see. . . ."[24]

His biographer and research assistant, D. B. Hardeman says, "Mr. Sam was . . . annoyed by inactivity. When he could think of nothing else to do at home in Bonham he would get out all his shoes and polish them. He dreaded holidays and Sundays because visitors were few."[25]

Mr. Rayburn found it particularly congenial to work with younger men. D. B. Hardeman says, "Lyndon Johnson once con-

---

high personal regard for Mr. Albert (and, one supposes, several other members as well), the testimony of several knowledgeable and apparently unbiased observers was quite unanimous in indicating that for several years preceding his death Mr. Rayburn was particularly close to Mr. Bolling.

[23] David Cohn, "Mr. Speaker: An Atlantic Portrait," *Atlantic Monthly* (October, 1942), pp. 73–78. The quoted portion appears on p. 76. Mr. Cohn was a personal friend of the Speaker's. He comments on the quoted passage, "As he spoke, Rayburn relived the long, lean, lonely years of his childhood, and it was clear that he wished other children might be spared the bleakness of his youth."

[24] CBS News, "Mr. Sam: A Personal and Political Biography," telecast, November 16, 1961.

[25] D. B. Hardeman, "The Unseen Side of the Man They Called Mr. Speaker," *Life*, LI (December 1, 1961), 21.

fessed, 'The Speaker and I have always been very close but if we are not as close as we were once, it is because I'm almost 50. If you notice, he never has older men around him.' "[26]

"I always liked the House the best," Mr. Rayburn said. "There're more people there, usually they're younger people, and as I've advanced in years, I've stepped back in my associations, boys, young people ten, twenty years younger than I. Their bodies are not only resilient but their minds are too. They can learn faster than the fellow advanced in years."[27]

One of the things which no doubt drew Mr. Rayburn to Mr. Bolling was the exceptional resiliency and quickness of the latter's mind. On this quality, friends and political enemies of Mr. Bolling agreed. He is an extremely "quick study," and had several other things in common with the Speaker:

"Bolling loves the House," a judicious, slow spoken southern congressman who knows him rather well told me. "He loves it and has studied it. He has read everything that has been written about the House and has studied its power structure. He has a brilliant mind."

Although nearly thirty-five years separated them, both Mr. Rayburn and Mr. Bolling were strongly committed emotionally to many liberal programs. Bolling refers to himself quite frankly as a "gut liberal"; *Time* magazine has aptly characterized Rayburn as a "liberal of the heart."[28] In addition, both men shared a high sense of rectitude in their work, treating the majority of their colleagues with reserve and judging them rather severely. This social distance which both men maintained was no doubt related in some complex way to the intensity of their feelings about political issues. It is instructive in this connection to note the tendency of both men to become laconic in public when dealing with problems with which they had great personal involvement. Compare Bolling's prepared statement of withdrawal from the majority leadership race in 1962 with Rayburn's statement of withdrawal in 1934 from an unsuccessful race for the speakership.[29]

---

[26] *Ibid.*

[27] CBS News, "Mr. Sam . . .," *op. cit.*

[28] *Time,* LXXVII (February 10, 1961), p. 12. What is significant here, I think, is not the placement of either man on an ideological spectrum so much as the high degree of personal engagement which the references to parts of the body suggest.

[29] I was a witness to the events surrounding the composition of Bolling's statement of withdrawal, and am quite convinced that Bolling had no knowledge of Rayburn's statement. Rather, the striking resemblance between the two seems

In 1934 Rayburn said, "I am no longer a candidate for Speaker. There are no alibis. Under the circumstances, I cannot be elected."[30]

In 1962 Bolling said, "I am withdrawing from the race for leadership of the House. Developments of the last few days have convinced me that I don't have a chance to win."[31]

Bolling privately expressed an unwillingness amounting to an incapacity either to "do anything" until after a "decent" time had elapsed after the Speaker's death[32] or to canvass for votes in his own behalf. The major portion of this burden within the House was carried by Representative Frank Thompson of New Jersey and a group of four or five others. The brunt of Bolling's campaign was, however, carried on from outside the House.[33] Initially, he had to

---

to me to illustrate a remarkable similarity in the styles of the two men, not conscious imitation.

[30] Bascom N. Timmons, "Rayburn" (ditto, n.d.), part 4, p. 1. This series was supplied to certain newspapers at the time of Speaker Rayburn's death. Mr. Timmons is a newspaperman accredited to the House Press Galleries from a string of newspapers in the southwest. He is a Texan and was a friend and contemporary of Mr. Rayburn's.

[31] Rodney Crowther, *Baltimore Sun, loc. cit.* The psychologically-minded would also no doubt find it relevant that Mr. Bolling's father died when he was in his early teens. However, anyone concluding from data such as have been presented here that either Mr. Bolling or Mr. Rayburn gave indications in their behavior of being emotionally crippled or lacking in control could not possibly be further from the mark. The point here is simply that certain easily verified events and patterns in the lives of each man may well have predisposed him to like the other.

[32] Mr. Bolling's imputation of indecorousness (the news of which was communicated in such places as "Bitter Withdrawal," *Time,* LXXIX [January 12, 1962, 12]) was resented in the Albert camp. In their view, Mr. Bolling had himself precipitated the battle by first permitting word to leak to the newspapers that he was a candidate for Majority Leader.

[33] One index of this is the apparent fact that Mr. Thompson is generally not too popular in the House (a fact of which both he and Mr. Bolling are aware). Mr. Thompson is an able and gifted man with extremely good political connections outside the House, both "downtown" and in his home state. (See Richard L. Lyons, "Thompson Decision to Retain Seat Gives House Liberals Needed Lift," *Washington Post,* January 31, 1961.) But inside the House, he has a reputation for being sharp-tongued, supercilious, and too witty for his own good. He has a way of hanging nicknames that "stick" on friend and foe alike—to the delight of the former, the great chagrin of the latter. One political ally of Mr. Thompson's said, "He has got the reputation that whenever he is in favor of a bill, it is bound to lose. . . . Thompson is one of Bolling's major liabilities. I hear how the guys talk at the back of the room there [in the aisle behind the seats in the Hall of the House]. They say, 'Whose amendment is that? Thompson's? That guy? To hell with that!' And they vote it down." Another ally of Thompson's said, "Frank's always trying to talk silly with you when you're talking serious, and trying to talk serious when you're talking silly."

decide whether to run for Speaker or Majority Leader—which no doubt also contributed to the quality of hesitancy in his campaign.

Factors pointing to the speakership included the relative unpopularity of Mr. McCormack (1) with members, and (2) at the White House; but against this had to be weighed (1) Mr. McCormack's generally blameless voting record (from the standpoint of a pro-administration Democrat), (2) his long service in the second position, (3) the weight of a tradition which strongly favored the elevation of a Majority Leader, (4) Mr. Bolling's own relatively junior position, (5) the fact that Mr. McCormack, if he lost the speakership, would remain as a Majority Leader not especially favorably disposed toward the program of an administration that had just done him in politically, and, (6) the fact that opposing Mr. McCormack would unavoidably exacerbate the religious cleavage in the House and the country which the fight over school aid in the last session had revealed.[34]

And so, Mr. Bolling decided to run for Majority Leader against the extremely popular Mr. Albert. In a straight popularity contest, Mr. Bolling knew he was "born dead." His role in the House had been quite unlike Mr. Albert's; indeed, several congressmen contrasted them starkly.

A close friend described Mr. Albert's approach to the job of whip:

> The whip is more the eyes and ears of the leadership than anything. On controversial matters, they like to know what the chances of success are. . . . So the deputy whips count noses, and the whip's job is to evaluate the count—especially to assess the doubtfuls. . . . Albert developed quite a genius for knowing what people would do. . . .
>
> Another service he performed endears him to people. Carl's the kind of a guy everybody could find. He would talk to the leadership for [rank-and-file congressmen].
>
> A lot of these eastern guys have a Tuesday through Thursday club. The whip takes the duty on of telling them if the signals change so they can get back here if they're needed.
>
> He's done so many things for people. They trust him. They think of him, "Here's a man I can talk to when I need help." When the members go about picking a leader, they want personal services, not intellectuals.[35]

---

[34] See H. Douglas Price, "Race, Religion and the Rules Committee" in Alan Westin (ed.), *The Uses of Power* (New York: Harcourt, Brace & World, 1962), pp. 1–71.

[35] Mr. Albert's friend may, in reflecting unfavorably on Mr. Bolling, have done Mr. Albert a slight injustice. Mr. Albert was an honor graduate of the University of Oklahoma and a Rhodes Scholar—neither of which makes him an intellectual, but they clearly don't disqualify him either.

I dare you to find a member of Congress who said Bolling had lifted a finger for him.

A supporter of Mr. Bolling's (for whom Bolling had, according to this member's testimony, lifted many a finger) saw the roles of the two principals in much the same light, although his evaluation of their roles was quite different:

> Albert's approach to legislative matters is, well, everybody ought to vote his own district. . . . He brings his friends and his enemies in [to vote] both. . . . Why the hell get [a certain southern congressman] out [to vote]? He doesn't vote with us on anything. And he's a deputy whip! It's ridiculous. . . . The function of the whip [under Mr. Albert] is room service to members.
>
> Albert was the whip, but Bolling was doing the whipping. . . . When the heat was being put on in the Rules Committee and all the other fights, it was Bolling putting it on, and he wasn't making any friends doing it.[36]

Mr. Bolling was, as a friend of his described it, a "hatchet man" for Speaker Rayburn. This entailed a variety of activities on the Rules Committee, including monitoring the attendance of friends and foes, arranging for the disposition of bills, and keeping track of the intentions of the various (and numerous) factions in the House with respect to important legislation, in behalf of the Speaker. Occasionally, Mr. Bolling's job included putting the finger on members who were open to (or vulnerable to) persuasion, and he often had a crucial part in the process of persuading them—not always a pleasant task.[37]

Although Mr. Bolling is entirely in sympathy with policies espoused by liberals in the House, his position close to the Speaker precluded his joining in any formal way in the activities of the Democratic Study Group, the House liberal organization. As a friend of his put it, "Dick was aloof from the uprisings of the peasants."

[36] There are now several accounts of the 1961 battle over the Rules Committee in print, including a treatment of the episode in Price, *op. cit.;* the analysis of the vote by Cummings and Peabody in Chapter VII of this volume; a long chapter by Neil MacNeil in *Forge of Democracy* (New York: McKay, 1963), pp. 410–88; and a forthcoming case study in the Eagleton series by William MacKaye.

[37] See *Time,* LXXVII (February 10, 1961); William S. White, "The Invisible Gentleman from Kansas City," *Harper's* (May, 1961); Neil MacNeil, "The House Confronts Mr. Kennedy," *Fortune,* LXV (January 1962), 70–73.

"Bolling's got a sort of a chip on his shoulder," another member said.

"The thing you have to realize about Bolling," said an Albert backer, "is that he never bothers to speak to anyone else. I don't think Bolling understands politics."

Mr. Bolling's aloofness was, as I have suggested, probably something more than simply a reflection of his peculiar institutional position. A second friend of Bolling's said, "Despite a good deal of charm, Bolling just does not have a personality that inspires loyalty and friendship among men.[38] He's not a backslapping, how-the-hell-are-you type of guy. Bolling is personally quite pleasant, but reticent."

The late Clem Miller of California said, "Congress is a World War I rather than a World War II operation. You have to move huge bodies of men a few feet at a time. . . . Dick's spent the last few years divorcing himself from a base of fire. His job was right-hand man to the Speaker. He came to Democratic Study Group meetings but always identified himself as an observer, not as a participant. He came in a sense to lecture us like small children rather than lead us in our councils. There was a good deal of hostility toward him in the Study Group as a result of that. The Study Group was set up as a foil for the leadership. You can't have your foot in both camps, and so Dick alienated the base of support that he needed in the House."

Another member, often allied with Mr. Bolling, characterized him as "totally unfriendly."

Mr. Bolling's personal situation within the House was further complicated by a common enough phenomenon. As a relative newcomer, as an extremely able member performing difficult tasks well, and as an intimate of the Speaker, Mr. Bolling was, in the opinion of several observers, the victim of a certain amount of jealous resentment.

"Jealousy is a big factor," one congressman said. "Liberals have several characteristics that tend to make them ineffective, and vanity is one of them. They tend to be prima donnas."[39] Another said,

---

[38] Statements such as this one obviously are not intended to be taken with strict literalness. Most social scientists are agreed that the personal "qualities" of leaders vary according to the situation.

[39] Cf. a similar comment on Senate liberals by Tristam Coffin, "The Well Tempered Politician," *Holiday* (April, 1962), p. 107.

"Dick is not a popular man in the House, no doubt a surprise to newsmen. For one thing, he's resented because of his ability."

Liberals were clearly not the only group of congressmen susceptible to jealous feelings toward Mr. Bolling. His relative youth was offensive to some of his seniors. Mr. Bolling had risen very fast in the House and had been given many advantages by his friend, the Speaker. The record he had made thus far also suggested that, if elected, he would take many more initiatives than Mr. Albert and would more decisively challenge the powers of committee and subcommittee chairmen to control the flow and content of legislation— in behalf of programs for which many of these leaders had no particular liking.

Even to the superficial observer, Mr. Albert and Mr. Bolling are quite contrasting figures. Mr. Albert was fifty-three years old, exactly on the House median; Mr. Bolling was only forty-five. Albert is physically probably the shortest man in the House and looks nothing like the collegiate wrestler he once was. He has a softly lined, friendly, gentle face which, says a colleague, "always looks faintly worried." Bolling is a tall, husky, quite handsome and imposing-looking man who gives the appearance of great self-confidence and looks very much like the collegiate football player he was. Mr. Albert in conversation is homespun, soft-spoken, emotionally unengaged, and low-pressure. A colleague says, "You could vote impeachment of the President, and it wouldn't bother Carl." Mr. Bolling in conversation is articulate, expansive, sophisticated, intense; in short, one would surmise, a rather more threatening figure to someone of average inclinations than Mr. Albert.

Mr. Bolling has far greater acceptance in the higher echelons of the "downtown" bureaucracies and surely in the press corps than almost any other congressman, including Mr. Albert. Mr. Bolling is far more likely to spend his leisure hours among pundits, diplomats, and subcabinet officials than with congressmen, a pattern which Mr. Albert reverses. Mr. Albert prides himself, in fact, in spending a greater proportion of his time on the floor of the House than any other member, where he is continually accessible to his colleagues.[40]

---

[40] See John M. Virden, "Little Giant from Bug Tussle," *Saturday Evening Post*, CCXXXV (March 24, 1962), 94–97; Paul Duke, "Albert's Soft Sell," *Wall Street Journal*, March 6, 1962; "Carl Albert, Nose-Counter from Bug Tussle," *Time*, LXXIX (January 12, 1962), 13.

[Footnote continued on page 258.]

To a great extent, Mr. Bolling understood that a variety of institutional and personal "inside" factors were working against him, and so he launched an "outside" campaign.

V

Bolling's task, as he saw it, was divided into several phases of activity. First, he had to stall the Albert bandwagon. Then he had to receive enough commitments to win himself. His primary targets were the big state delegations of New York, California, Illinois, and Pennsylvania. Secondary targets included getting a firm grip on his home state delegation and going after younger, liberal congressmen and congressmen who had substantial labor and civil-rights-minded constituencies.

His strategy for accomplishing these ends had two major features. First, he intended to draw as sharp a contrast as he could between himself and Mr. Albert on issues and sell the contrast as hard as he could through the mass media. Second, he set about "pulling strings" on members, a process which he had practiced before in legislative battles.[41] This entailed identifying the men and interest groups favorable to his candidacy who for various reasons could reach and persuade members of Congress. Naturally, the foremost among these

---

Certain other characteristics place Mr. Albert closer to the rank and file of congressmen than Mr. Bolling. Mr. Albert was a small town boy, the son of a farmer and laborer, educated in public schools, and is a Methodist. Mr. Bolling was born in New York City, the son of a well-to-do physician. He grew up in comfortable circumstances and socially prominent circles in Huntsville, Alabama, after his father's death went to Exeter and the University of the South, has a Master's degree from Sewanee, and did further graduate work at Vanderbilt, and is an Episcopalian. If the script for this contest had been written by C. Wright Mills or one of his followers, Mr. Albert would have been the more "liberal" candidate and wouldn't have had a chance. (See Mills, *The Power Elite* [New York: Oxford University Press, 1956]). Mr. Mills carefully excludes Congress from his discussion of "the power elite" for reasons which seem to this reader designed to protect his thesis from evidence which would reject it.

[41] An example of this process was given in *Time*, Vol. LXXVII (February 10, 1961) at the time of the Rules Committee fight: *"Time* Correspondent Neil MacNeil listened as two Rayburn lieutenants were running down the list of doubtful members. On one: 'The General Services Administration ought to be able to get him.' On another: 'The Air Force can take care of him.' A third? 'If you can get the Post Office to issue that special stamp for him, you've got him.' And a fourth? 'The United Mine Workers can get him.' And a fifth? 'Hell, if we can't get him we might as well quit. Go talk to him.' A sixth? 'No, but I'll fix that bastard.' " *Time* gives the strong impression that the two lieutenants are Bolling and Thompson.

would have been the President, but at no time was presidential aid offered, and none was requested by Mr. Bolling.

The position of the White House in this battle was a complex one. While the mass media, on the whole, bought Mr. Bolling's contention that substantial differences in public policy separated him and Mr. Albert, the White House never did. It regarded both men as good friends of the Kennedy program, each having personal and political strengths and weaknesses. To intervene in behalf of one friend would have meant sacrificing another. For the White House to intervene and lose would have been disastrous for its prestige and legislative program. To intervene and win would have been more satisfactory but still would have involved (aside from the making of enemies) great exertion, the distribution of indulgences and the "cashing in" on favors owed, all of which could otherwise be employed to improve the chances for passage of controversial reciprocal trade, medical aid, tax reform, and education bills. Several members of the President's official family were close to Mr. Bolling and were almost certainly partial to him, but none participated in the fight.

Mr. Bolling and his backers in the House concurred in the White House policy of non-intervention and in the reasoning behind it. The major inside advantage of their side, as they saw it, was a professional ability to predict outcomes accurately and to recommend appropriate strategies. They understood fully that the risks to the White House were great, the probabilities of success dubious. If they could come close to winning on their own, within perhaps five or ten votes, then their recommendation might change, since the White House could then probably put them over the top. But it is not at all certain that even then the White House would have been ready to move.

If the administration was inactive, other keenly interested bystanders were not. The AFL-CIO backed Mr. Bolling strongly and performed several notable services in behalf of his candidacy. Labor lobbyists made a complete canvass of possible supporters in the House and, in several cases, made representations in Mr. Bolling's behalf with members. The NAACP was also active. Roy Wilkins, national chairman, telegraphed 153 selected branches of his organization, "Bolling right on 26 civil rights votes, Albert wrong. Wire, write or call your Congressman. This could affect civil rights legislation for years to come." The Democratic Reform Clubs of New York City were also interested in Bolling's candidacy, as were some local and national political leaders around the country and at least one farm organization.

An example of indirect influence in Mr. Bolling's behalf was described by an Albert supporter, "I heard that President Truman, a neighbor of Bolling's and a loyal Missourian, called Mayor Wagner of New York to try and get the New York delegation to support Bolling."

Mr. Bolling was especially successful in enlisting the aid of the mass media. Since the civil rights battle of 1957, when he anonymously kept newsmen briefed on the confusing tactical situation within the House, Mr. Bolling has been extremely popular with the Washington press corps.[42] He is asked to appear on broadcasts and telecasts much more often than the average member. He counts many Washington correspondents, including several famous ones, as close personal friends.

Hence, it is not altogether surprising that he was able to gain the endorsement of the *New York Times* as early as December 11. On Sunday, December 24, the *Times* reiterated its stand, saying, "The conservative coalition of Southern Democrats and Northern Republicans would find it much more difficult to exercise its suffocating veto over forward-looking legislation with the imaginative and hard-driving Mr. Bolling as majority floor chief."[43]

Five days previously, on December 19, James Wechsler, editor of the *New York Post,* gave a strong endorsement to Mr. Bolling, in which he printed a long verbatim extract of a letter endorsing Carl Albert which Bolling had received from Judge Howard W. Smith, leader of conservative southerners in the House.[44] Wechsler commented, "This is not to say Albert has faithfully followed Smith's gospel. He is a moderate, pleasant man whose voting record might be far more impressive if he came from a state more congenial to the advance of civil rights and less dominated by the natural gas interests. Despite their differences on a variety of matters, Smith is

---

[42] A Washington correspondent commented: "[Bolling] was a good news source and popular among newsmen from the time he first got on the House Banking Committee and became even more popular when he was moved to Rules as Rayburn's obvious protégé."

[43] *New York Times,* December 24, 1961.

[44] This letter was sent in response to Mr. Bolling's November 28 request for "consideration" from each Democrat. Supporters of Mr. Albert were dismayed by the fact that while they had not solicited Judge Smith's support and Mr. Bolling had, the Smith endorsement was being used by Mr. Bolling against Mr. Albert with the press.

plainly confident that he can handle Albert; he is equally convinced that Bolling spells trouble. . . ."[45]

On December 29, Marquis Childs[46] and Edward P. Morgan both urged the selection of Mr. Bolling, referring once again to the Smith letter and to issues separating the two candidates. Mr. Morgan was especially vigorous in his commentary:

> . . . where Bolling has been consistently for them, Albert has been basically against civil rights legislation, federal aid to education, full foreign aid and regulation of the oil and gas industry. It is reliably reported that one Texas congressman told a southern colleague that "with Albert in there, oil will be safe for twenty years. . . ."[47]

What of the outcomes of these activities? The relations between outside "pressures" and congressmen have been variously described in popular and academic literature. There is an old tradition which regards these relations as essentially nefarious.[48] Descriptively, the congressman is sometimes thought to be a relatively passive creature who is pulled and hauled about according to the play of pressures

---

[45] James Wechsler, "Hill Battle," *New York Post,* December 19, 1961. Mr. Bolling's constituency is the Fifth District of Missouri, which includes most of Kansas City. Mr. Albert represents the thirteen counties of Oklahoma's Third District, an area known as "Little Dixie." This district is predominantly rural and is somewhat depressed economically. Its major products are timber, peanuts, cotton, and livestock. Several Albert supporters suggested that a generally liberal record such as Mr. Albert had made in the House was in some ways a more creditable performance for a man from a district of this kind than for a man from a big city. Although this argument has some plausibility, it should also be noted that several of the most respected southern liberals and moderates in the House have come from districts very similar to Mr. Albert's. Sam Rayburn himself was one such example. Others would be Carl Elliott of Alabama, Frank Smith of Mississippi, and James Trimble of Arkansas. This argument may, in other words, be an attempt to appeal to a popular stereotype which automatically classifies big-city districts as "liberal" and rural southern districts as "conservative." But it may be that on the vast majority of issues coming to a vote in Congress, representatives from southern, rural, economically depressed areas have constituencies as liberal as any in the country.

[46] Marquis Childs, "The High Stakes in House Battle," *Washington Post* December 29, 1961—and elsewhere.

[47] "Edward P. Morgan and the News," American Broadcasting Company, December 29, 1961. The documentation of this case has never, to my knowledge, been made. I suggest that at the least the reference to Mr. Albert's position on federal aid to education would be difficult to defend.

[48] See, for examples of this tradition, H. H. Wilson, *Congress: Corruption and Compromise* (New York: Rinehart, 1951), Karl Schriftgiesser, *The Lobbyists* (Boston: Little, Brown, 1951).

upon him and whose final decision is determined by the relative strength of outside forces.[49] More recently, political scientists have become preoccupied with the qualities of reciprocity in the relations of interest groups and politicians. This literature calls attention to mutually beneficial aspects of the relationship and lays stress on the ways in which politicians may act to govern the outside pressures placed on them.[50]

My information on the impact of Bolling's outside campaign is necessarily incomplete. It is apparent at a minimum that a sufficient number of congressmen were never reached by this campaign. One congressman said:

> Bolling's best hope was forces outside the House—labor and civil rights groups. But I received not one communication in his behalf from anybody. There was nobody campaigning for him. Nobody knew if he was serious or not. Where was the heat?

Another congressman, from a heavily populated area, said:

> Our delegation was never put on the spot. Bolling never tried to wage a campaign in our delegation. Apparently he tried to get labor leaders to pressure Cautious [the state party leader] to put pressure on our congressmen. This is OK, but you really have to put the pressure on because if you know Cautious, he won't ever move unless he's really in a box.

In other cases, congressmen were able quite easily to *resist* pressure. "The word got around," one liberal congressman said, "that this wasn't like the Rules Committee fight, where there was a legitimate issue. Rather, it was all in the family, and any outside interference, even from the White House, would be resented."

---

[49] An excellent example of this mode of thinking is contained in Max Lerner, *America as a Civilization* (New York: Simon & Schuster, 1957), pp. 415 ff. and especially p. 424. More generally, see Arthur F. Bentley, *The Process of Government* (Evanston: Principia, 1949), Earl Latham, *The Group Basis of Politics* (Ithaca: Cornell University Press, 1952), Oliver Garceau, "Interest Group Theory in Political Research," *The Annals*, CCCXIX (September, 1958), and David B. Truman, *The Governmental Process* (New York: Knopf, 1955). Truman explicitly rejects the notion that congressmen are wholly passive.

[50] Lewis A. Dexter, *op. cit.*, and Dexter, "The Representative and His District," *Human Organization*, XVI (Summer, 1947), 2–13, reprinted as Chapter I of the present volume; Dexter, "What Do Congressmen Hear: The Mail," *Public Opinion Quarterly*, XX (Spring, 1956), 16–26. See also Donald R. Matthews, *U.S. Senators and Their World* (Chapel Hill: University of North Carolina Press, 1960), esp. chaps. viii, ix.

Harlem's Representative Adam Clayton Powell, announcing his support of Albert, charged that some organized labor representatives were putting pressure on some Democratic members of his committee. He added, "I can't understand why labor union leaders would do this. Frankly, this is Democratic party business, not labor business."[51]

On the other hand, Bolling's campaign from the outside made several converts. Representative Leonard Farbstein of New York City, for example, announced that he would vote for Mr. Bolling on the basis of Mr. Wechsler's column.[52]

Another congressman, a conservative veteran, wrote Bolling and detailed the substantial political disagreements between them, concluding, "But Famous Farmer tells me he is supporting you, and if he is supporting you, I am supporting you."

A leader of another interest group, in another part of the country, wrote, "I have just been informed by Congressman Dean Delegation's home secretary that Dean will be supporting you for majority leader. If there are any particular targets in [this state], I'm still available to apply whatever other pressures I can."

In aggregate, however, the impact of this campaign was not sufficient to accomplish Mr. Bolling's major goal. Edward Morgan commented with some asperity on the failure of Mr. Bolling to consolidate his support on an ideological basis, and at the same time he renewed the plea that the battle be defined in ideological terms:

> If they voted . . . in support of their constituencies' needs
> for protection on gas prices, housing, civil rights and the like,
> the big city and industrial area representatives would have to
> come down almost unanimously for Bolling over Albert on
> their voting records alone and the man from Missouri would
> have it cinched. But he doesn't have it cinched. . . . At least one
> Massachusetts congressman has already committed himself to
> Albert in writing . . . Adam Clayton Powell is looking south
> . . . So are a couple of New Jersey Representatives. . . . Most
> surprisingly, perhaps, two leading California Congressmen,
> Holifield and Roosevelt, have not dashed to Bolling's aid. . . .[53]

---

[51] Robert C. Albright, "Powell Backs Albert for House Post," *Washington Post*, December 1, 1961. Powell, unlike the congressman just quoted, checked with the White House before he made his announcement, obviously taking the position that the President had a legitimate interest in the outcome.

[52] *New York Post*, December 21, 1961.

[53] "Edward P. Morgan and the News," American Broadcasting Company, December 29, 1961. This account may be contrasted with a column put out by

Over the long New Year's weekend, Bolling, Thompson, and Andrew Biemiller of the AFL-CIO met and assessed Bolling's "hard" strength at between sixty-five and seventy votes. Perhaps fifty more would have joined them if Bolling were going to win, but otherwise, they faded. A Bolling lieutenant said, "Everybody wanted to know, 'What's his chances?' The typical response was, 'I'll lie low. I'm with you if you've got a chance; otherwise, nix.' "

By the most realistic calculations, however, Mr. Bolling fell short of the 130 or more votes that he needed. He decided to withdraw his candidacy rather than embarrass his supporters in their state delegations and possibly jeopardize their future effectiveness in Congress.

VI

It is possible to identify at least four reasons why Mr. Bolling's attempt to win from the outside failed. The first two have already been mentioned: Mr. Albert's extreme popularity and Bolling's relative isolation provided little incentive for individual members to seek outside excuses of their own accord to do what they could more conveniently do for inside reasons. Second, the hands-off policy of the White House deprived Mr. Bolling's campaign of what would have been a major outside weapon had the President chosen to come in on Mr. Bolling's side.

The third major obstacle to the success of the outside campaign was the fact that, through no fault of Mr. Bolling's, a few of his supporters unwittingly blunted one of his principal weapons, the ideological contrast between himself and Mr. Albert. Just before the opening of the second session of the Eighty-seventh Congress, and at the same time the struggle over the majority leadership was going on, a group of liberal congressmen proposed that a policy committee be created in the Democratic party to be elected by the members

---

William S. White, a former Capitol Hill reporter. White's explanation of what happened is: "Whatever chance [Bolling] might have had, however, was sunk without a trace by the ultra-liberals themselves. They rushed forward to gather him into their arms, through zealous indorsements by such too-gooder groups as Americans for Democratic Action. No man in a House which—like the country itself—is essentially moderate could possibly have survived such embarrassing public embraces. So Mr. Bolling had to withdraw his candidacy. ∴ . ." *Washington Star*, January 5, 1962—and elsewhere. I could discover little evidence which would lend credibility to this analysis. Regrettably, Mr. White offers none.

from each of the eighteen whip zones. This committee was to advise and counsel with the leadership, and it was contemplated that it would be "more representative" (and presumably more liberal) than the leadership, unaided, would be.

Congressmen favoring this proposal circulated it among their Democratic colleagues in an attempt to get the fifty signatures necessary to place it on the agenda of the caucus which was to elect a new Speaker. Several liberals favoring Mr. Albert promptly signed, thus furnishing themselves with an excellent alibi, if they were challenged on ideological grounds by constituents and interest groups. They could claim that the fight over the majority leadership was not really significant since Bolling and Albert were, in their voting records, so close. But on the basic issue, on the institutional structure of leadership in the House, they were, as always, for liberalization.

This proposal went through several stages. At one point, it was seriously proposed that Mr. Bolling accept the chairmanship of this committee as the price for withdrawing his candidacy for the majority leadership. This proposal implied that the new Speaker had accepted the policy committee in principle.[54] Mr. Bolling was him-

---

[54] The rate at which tentative proposals and counterproposals of this sort fly around Washington is perfectly phenomenal. Theodore H. White rhapsodizes about the kinds of people who often act in the capacity of carrier pigeon: "Washington holds perhaps fifty or a hundred . . . men, lawyers all, successful all, who in their dark-paneled law chambers nurse an amateur's love for politics and dabble in it whenever their practices permit. Where, in the regions, cities and states of the country, provincial lawyers love to counsel local politicians, promote names for the local judiciary, arrange the candidacies of lesser men, in Washington lawyers dabble in national politics, in appointments to places of high political destiny. Their influence, collectively, can never be ignored, because, collectively, they possess a larger fund of wisdom, experience, contacts, memories, running back over thirty years of national politics, than most candidates on the national scene can ever hope to acquire on their own . . . ." *The Making of the President, 1960* (New York: Atheneum, 1961), p. 33. Newspaper people also quite often undertake this sort of activity, and occasionally lobbyists do, too.

Fortuitously, much of the activity described in this paper took place during the Christmas-Debutante-New Year's social season in Washington. As a result, many of the participants in these events kept running into each other at parties. Political science may some day catch up with the slick magazines and novels in comprehending the true significance of Washington parties. In this case, it appears that much of the negotiating on whether or not Mr. Bolling would join the leadership group as head of the policy committee took place on an informal basis, through intermediaries and without any soul-stirring confrontations of rivals such as are found in Allen Drury's *Advise and Consent.*

self dubious about the chances that such a committee could perform the tasks its supporters envisaged for it. Counterproposals and negotiations buzzed back and forth about the possibility of putting "teeth" into the committee and about prior agreements as to its membership. At another level, Mr. Bolling and Mr. Thompson had to avoid being mousetrapped by the petition to put the policy committee on the agenda. To have signed the petition might have looked to Albert-McCormack forces like a proposal of terms and an acknowledgment of defeat. The fact that supporters of the Bolling candidacy were leading the fight for the policy committee was compromising enough as it was.

In the end, the whole idea came to nothing.[55] The proposal never received enough signatures to gain a place on the agenda, and at John McCormack's first press conference upon his nomination for the speakership, he said, "A policy committee is out."[56] But the policy committee plan served one significant purpose. It softened and blurred Bolling's attempt to define the issue between himself and Mr. Albert in such a way as to embarrass liberals who were not supporting him.

The fourth reason for the failure of the outside campaign is probably the most important. It has to do with the conditions under which the actual choice was going to be made. Normally, a congressman has considerable leeway in the casting of his vote because the issues are complex and technical, because the ways in which they are framed sometimes inspires no sharp cleavages of opinion, because interest groups are often disinterested and inattentive. But when an issue heats up and reaches the final stages of the legislative process,

---

[55] That is, it came to almost nothing. In mid-March, 1962, three months after the events described here took place, the Democrats reactivated a "steering" committee along the lines of the "policy" committee proposed at the opening of the session. Mr. Bolling did not become a member. A leading Democrat in the House observed to me that the members of this committee, including James Davis of Georgia, William Colmer of Mississippi, Paul Kitchin of North Carolina, Clarence Cannon of Missouri, were likely, if anything, to be *less* liberal than the leadership they were supposed to advise. This was an outcome exactly opposite to the one envisaged by proponents of the policy committee idea.

[56] For the story at various stages, see: Robert C. Albright, "Drive is Begun for Democratic Steering Group," *Washington Post,* December 30, 1961; Mary McGrory, "McCormack Silent on Liberals Plan," *Washington Star,* December 31, 1961; Robert K. Walsh, "Party Harmony Setup Seen by House Liberals," *Washington Star,* January 5, 1962; Richard L. Lyons, "Liberal Democrats Defer Demands," *Washington Post,* January 9, 1962; Rowland Evans, Jr., "Democrats Unanimous," *New York Herald Tribune,* January 10, 1962.

leeway dissipates. Interest groups become active. The mail begins to pour in.[57] Newsmen appear on the scene. Congressmen stick close to the Floor, listen to debate, mill around, stand ready to answer quorum calls or to vote on amendments.

There are four procedures for voting in the House: voices, standing, tellers, and roll call, in the order in which they expose members to public view. In the Committee on the Whole House, only the first three types of votes are taken. A diligent reporter or lobbyist can, however, even without benefit of a roll call, usually find out how a given member votes. The procedure is not foolproof, but, from the gallery, an outsider can always keep his eye fixed on one or a few congressmen whose votes are of interest to him. Corroboration, if any is needed, can be obtained by asking around among other congressmen.

The caucus at which voting for Majority Leader was to have taken place provided no such opportunities for outside surveillance. No spectators were admitted. Congressmen were even protected from the scrutiny of their colleagues; Representative Francis Walter, chairman of the caucus, sent word that the balloting for Majority Leader, when the time came, would be secret. The rules of the caucus say nothing about a secret ballot; rather, general parliamentary law governs the caucus meetings, and there is a special provision that "the yeas and nays on any question shall, at the desire of one fifth of those present, be entered on the journal"—all of which did not alter the fact that the balloting would be secret.

In spite of the interest which Mr. Bolling had stirred up among outside groups, these groups were operating under an insuperable handicap. The voting procedure maximized the chances that a congressman cross-pressured between the demands of "local agency" and his own personal feelings could vote his private preferences with impunity.

VII

What does this case suggest about the general relations between inside and outside influences in the decision-making processes of

---

[57] Lewis Dexter makes the point that the mail usually comes too late to affect the substance of legislation. However mail is used here only as an index of attentiveness to issues on the part of publics. See Dexter, "What Do Congressmen Hear . . . ," *op. cit.*

the House?[58] Several things. First, it shows the extent to which inside and outside strategies tend to encourage different modes of communication among members and to evoke different definitions of the decision-making situation. The inside strategy is likely to define situations as "family matters," and to feature face-to-face interaction among members. The outside strategy is likely to evoke a more ideological, issue-oriented definition of the situation. Interaction among members is more likely to take place through third persons, lobbyists, and the press. Second, this case suggests conditions tending to promote the success of each strategy of influence. Inside strategies are favored when: (1) the matter to be decided can be rationalized as in some sense procedural rather than substantive; (2) there are great differences in the inside strengths of the two sides, but their outside strengths approach equality; (3) members are protected from surveillance by outsiders. Outside strategies are favored, presumably, when these conditions are reversed.

Additional conditions bearing on the effectiveness of inside and outside strategies may be imagined. Presumably, the autonomy of a representative from constituent pressures diminishes as his constituency approaches unanimity in its preferences *or* as the intensity of preference for a given alternative by any substantial portion of his constituency increases. We know that few decisions before Congress are likely to unite constituencies in this way or to inflame their passions to such a great extent. In addition, Congress takes routine steps to insulate its decision-making from certain kinds of outside influences.

One such device is the consideration of business in the Committee of the Whole, where substantial revisions of legislation can be made on the Floor without binding congressmen to a record vote. The committees—whose composition and behavior sometimes reflect outside interests[59] and sometimes inside distributions of influence[60]—

---

[58] Obviously, no real-world case will fit a typology perfectly. It may be well to remind the reader that the predominant strategies of the major actors were as I have indicated, but that Mr. Albert had some support from outside the House (such as from Senators Kerr and Monroney and Goveror Edmondson of Oklahoma), and many of Bolling's supporters within the House backed him for reasons other than outside "pressures" which he might have been able to bring to bear on them. These included some members from the South whose position on civil rights was more accurately reflected by Mr. Albert.

[59] As for example, the Agriculture Committee. See Charles O. Jones, "Representation in Congress: The Case of the House Agriculture Committee," *American Political Science Review*, LV (June, 1961), 358–67. Reprinted as Chapter V of the present volume.

[60] There are numerous examples of this—e.g., the operation of the seniority

mark up bills and vote on them in executive sessions only. A third device favoring inside distributions of influence in the House is the Rules Committee. One of the prerequisites for appointment to service on this committee is ability to "take the heat" and resist constituency pressures to report out bills which the House leadership wants killed.[61]

The enumeration of these devices hints at some of the problems facing two significant groups of outsiders: Presidents of the United States and political scientists. The President has a never-ending battle of converting decisions in the House choices from inside ones to outside ones. Most of his attempts to influence decisions are direct, but his efforts to dramatize issues before relevant publics may also be interpreted as attempts to activate interest groups and unify constituencies so as to make the employment of inside strategies of influence in the House difficult.

For political scientists, the lesson is clear. In order to understand the context within which decisions in the House are being made sufficiently well so that we can identify the goals in terms of which outcomes may be seen as "rational," it will be necessary to study the House at close range. On the whole, political scientists have taken a somewhat Olympian view of congressional behavior. We have tended to organize our conceptions of rationality and legitimacy around presidential goals and presidential party platforms.[62] This has operated to obscure the constraints on the behavior of those in the House who share the policy preferences these political theories imply. It has also, I think, bred a kind of impatience with the study of strategies

---

system. See George Goodwin, "The Seniority System in Congress," *American Political Science Review*, LIII (June 1959), 412–36. On the influence of state delegations on committee assignments and the force of tradition in determining the allocation of seats, see in general, Nicholas Masters, "Committee Assignments in the House of Representatives," *American Political Science Review*, LV (June, 1961), 345–57. Reprinted as Chapter II of the present volume.

[61] On the Rules Committee, see Robert L. Peabody, "The Enlarged Rules Committee," Chapter VII of the present volume, and the following articles by James A. Robinson, "Organizational and Constituency Backgrounds of the House Rules Committee" in Joseph R. Fiszman (ed.), *The American Political Arena* (Boston: Little, Brown, 1962); "The Role of the Rules Committee in Regulating Debate in the U.S. House of Representatives," *Midwest Journal of Political Science*, V (February, 1961), 59–69; "Decision Making in the House Rules Committee," *Administrative Science Quarterly*, III (June, 1958), 73–86; "The Role of the Rules Committee in Arranging the Program of the U.S. House of Representatives," *Western Political Quarterly*, XII (September, 1959), 653–69.

[62] This comment may be anachronistic, judging from much of the recent work on the House. It agrees with Ralph K. Huitt's similar judgment in "Democratic Party Leadership in the Senate," *American Political Science Review*, LV (June, 1961), 333 f.

and tactics of House decision-making, which study, I believe, is a necessary step in understanding why the House operates as it does.

XIV

PARTY LEADERSHIP CHANGE IN THE UNITED STATES HOUSE OF REPRESENTATIVES*

Robert L. Peabody

LONG PERIODS of one-party domination, increased average tenure in office for Representatives, and the institutionalization of patterns of succession to the Speakership, have all contributed to a tendency toward leadership stability in the 20th-century House of Representatives. The elections of Sam Rayburn (D., Texas) and John McCormack (D., Mass.) to the offices of Speaker and Majority Leader in 1940, of Joseph Martin (R., Mass.) to the office of Minority Leader in 1939, and of Leslie Arends (R., Ill.) to the position of Republican Whip in 1943, mark the beginnings of the longest tenures in these four positions for any incumbents in the history of Congress.[1] When changes in top leadership occur— as with the overthrow of Minority Leader Charles A. Halleck by Republican Representative Gerald R. Ford, Jr., in 1965, or the succession of Majority Leader McCormack to the office of the Speaker in 1962 following the death of Rayburn—the consequences

* Reprinted from *The American Political Science Review*, Vol. LXI, No. 3, September 1967.

This article was stimulated by an opportunity to study the 1965 Ford-Halleck minority leadership contest at first hand. The resulting case study led to speculation on the general problem of leadership change in the House of Representatives. I would like to acknowledge my indebtedness to numerous readers of earlier drafts, especially James D. Barber, Milton C. Cummings, Jr., Richard F. Fenno, Jr., Ralph K. Huitt, Charles O. Jones, Nelson W. Polsby, Randall B. Ripley, and Francis E. Rourke. Financial assistance was provided by grants from the Social Science Research Council Committee on Political Behavior and the Johns Hopkins University Committee on Public Affairs.
[1] George B. Galloway, *History of the House of Representatives* (New York, 1962), pp. 287–292; Randall B. Ripley, "The Party Whip Organizations in the United States House of Representatives," *APSA Review*, 58 (September, 1964), p. 563.

are considerable. In the case of revolt, individual careers are made and broken. The organization and policy orientations of a congressional party may be extensively altered. While orderly succession has less dramatic impact, it too has a significant effect on "who gets what, when and how." Some members move closer to the seats of power and others fall out of favor. Key committee assignments, and hence the development of entire legislative careers, are likely to ride or fall on the outcomes. A congressional party's philosophical approach, the kinds of legislation it promotes, its strategies of implementation—all hinge to a considerable degree on the individual personalities, political backgrounds, and state and regional outlooks of its principal leaders. Only the contest for the control of the White House and the occasional elections which convert one party from a minority into a majority within Congress are likely to have a more significant consequence for party fortunes.

Despite its acknowledged importance, our overall understanding of the workings of congressional party leadership is rudimentary.[2] The day-to-day observations of newspaper reporters provide some insights, but journalists seldom generalize about their impressions.[3] With increasing frequency political scientists can profit from the writings of more analytically-oriented congressmen.[4] Unfortunately, good biographies on House members are relatively rare compared with presidential, judicial or even senatorial biography.[5] Most full-

---

[2] As David B. Truman observed in 1959: "Everyone knows something of leaders and leadership of various sorts, but no one knows very much. Leadership, especially in the political realm, unavoidably or by design often is suffused by an atmosphere of the mystic and the magical, and these mysteries have been little penetrated by systematic observation": *The Congressional Party* (New York, 1959), p. 94.

[3] The most notable exceptions in recent years are William S. White, *Citadel: The Story of the U. S. Senate* (New York, 1956) and Neil MacNeil, *Forge of Democracy: The House of Representatives* (New York, 1963). A masterpiece from the past is Ben Perley Poore, *Perley's Reminiscences of Sixty Years in the National Metropolis*, 2 vols. (Philadelphia: 1886).

[4] Two of the best examples are Clem Miller, *Member of the House* (New York, 1962) and Richard Bolling, *House Out of Order* (New York, 1965).

[5] Treatment of Speakers seems to be an exception. See, for example, James A. Barnes, *John G. Carlisle* (New York, 1931); James G. Blaine, *Twenty Years of Congress, from Lincoln to Garfield*, 2 vols. (Norwich, Conn., 1884); Samuel W. McCall, *The Life of Thomas B. Reed* (Cambridge, 1919); William A. Robinson, *Thomas B. Reed, Parliamentarian* (New York, 1930); L. White Busbey, *Uncle Joe Cannon* (New York, 1927); Champ Clark, *My Quarter Century of American Politics* (New York, 1920); and Bascom N. Timmons, *Garner of Texas* (New York, 1948). A forthcoming political biography of the

length studies of party leadership have long been outdated.[6] Only within the past decade have political scientists begun to set forth propositions about congressional leadership developed from intensive field research.[7]

Much less is known about change in leadership. Newspaper accounts of all but the most recent contests are likely to be fragmentary and superficial. Biographies rarely describe leadership contests in any detail and usually these accounts are anecdotal and one-sided. Only two studies exist of contests analyzed in depth by political scientists on the scene.[8] Lack of knowledge about types, the conditions which promote one type rather than another, and the consequences of leadership change are further complicated by the hazards of generalizing from what must inevitably be a limited number of cases. Yet, research on congressional leadership must move in the direction of generaliza-

---

late Speaker Rayburn by his staff assistant, D. B. Hardeman, should correct the shortcomings of the only full-length existing biography, C. Dwight Dorough, *Mr. Sam* (New York, 1962), which tells us almost nothing about Rayburn, the legislative leader.

[6] Chang-wei Chiu, *The Speaker of the House of Representatives Since 1896* (New York, 1927). This Columbia doctoral dissertation builds on a much better Radcliffe thesis first published in 1896: Mary Parker Follett, *The Speaker of the House of Representatives* (New York, 1909). Among the more useful older studies on party leadership, see DeAlva S. Alexander, *History and Procedure of the House of Representatives* (Boston, 1916); George R. Brown, *The Leadership of Congress* (Indianapolis, 1922); and Paul D. Hasbrouck, *Party Government in the House of Representatives* (New York, 1927).

[7] See, for example, Truman, *op. cit.,* Donald R. Matthews, *U. S. Senators and Their World* (Chapel Hill, 1960); Ralph K. Huitt, "Democratic Party Leadership in the Senate," *APSA Review* 55 (June, 1961), 333–344; Nelson W. Polsby, "Two Strategies of Influence: Choosing a Majority Leader, 1962," in Robert L. Peabody and Nelson W. Polsby (eds.), *New Perspectives on the House of Representatives* (Chicago, 1963); James A. Robinson, *The House Rules Committee* (Indianapolis, 1963); Randall B. Ripley, "The Party Whip Organizations in the United States House of Representatives," *op. cit.,* 561–576; Lewis A. Froman and Randall B. Ripley, "Conditions for Party Leadership: The Case of the House Democrats," *APSA Review* 59 (March, 1965), 52–63; and Charles O. Jones, *Party and Policy-Making: The House Republican Policy Committee* (New Brunswick, 1964).

[8] The analysis which follows is dependent upon Nelson W. Polsby's study of the Albert-Bolling contest, "Two Strategies of Influence: Choosing a Majority Leader, 1962," *op. cit.;* and Robert L. Peabody, "The Ford-Halleck Minority Leadership Contest, 1965," Eagleton Institute Cases in Practical Politics (New York, 1966), No. 40. The latter study is based on eighty-five interviews with over forty Republican Representatives and staff members during and immediately following the several contests which preoccupied House Republicans from early December, 1964 through February, 1965.

tion over a series of Congresses if a theory of party leadership and its consequences for the legislative process is to be developed.

This article begins by outlining a scheme for classifying types of intra-party leadership change in legislatures. This scheme is illustrated with nineteen cases of change or attempted change taking place in the United States House of Representatives in the 84th–89th Congresses (1955–1966). After noting the rather striking differences in the degree to which the Republican minority resorts to contested change as compared with relatively peaceful patterns of leadership succession in the Democratic majority, some of the conditions which seem to facilitate one type of change rather than another are discussed. Finally, some of the consequences of leadership change for individual careers, legislation, party fortunes and the representative process are suggested.

I. TYPES OF INTRA-PARTY LEADERSHIP CHANGE

Change in party leadership in legislatures comes about in three principal ways. *Inter-party turnover*, the replacement of one party's set of leaders by those of another party, occurs when the results of national elections convert a minority into a majority. Such change is relatively rare. For example, in the United States House of Representatives, party control has switched but twenty-four times in the 90 Congresses elected every two years since 1788.[9] This article focuses upon a more common type, *intra-party change*, or the replacement of one or more incumbents within a party hierarchy by other members of the same party. A third type, *institutional reform*, is characterized not by the replacement of leaders, but by alterations in party organization or the rules of a legislature which modify the powers of an existing office or create a new position. In the absence of inter-party turnover and as an alternative to institutional reform, legislators frequently turn to intra-party change, both as a means of fulfilling vacancies and as a device to promote leadership more favorable to their own interests.

Three variables have been selected as a means of classifying types of intra-party leadership change: (1) whether or not a vacancy exists in a leadership position, (2) the presence or absence of an established pattern of succession, and (3) the extent to which

---

[9] U. S. Bureau of the Census, *Historical Statistics of the United States, Colonial Times to 1957* (Washington, D. C., 1960), pp. 691–692.

the change is contested. When dichotomized these variables lead to a six-fold classification scheme as outlined in Table 1. The first

TABLE I

Types of Intra-Party Leadership Change

	No Contest	Contest
NO VACANCY	Status quo	(5) Revolt or its after-math
VACANCY Established pattern of succession	(1) Routine advancement	(4) Challenge to the heir apparent
No established pattern of succession	(2) Appointment or emergence of a consensus choice	(3) Open competition

variable is discrete: either a vacancy exists in a given position such as the Speakership, or it does not. The vacancy may come about for a variety of reasons, including death, resignation, retirement, or election defeat. The remaining two variables are not as easily dichotomized. Patterns of succession may be quite firmly established as with elevation from the Minority or Majority Leader to the office of Speaker in the House of Representatives. Other patterns, such as succession to the Majority Leader from the position of party Whip, are only tentative and emerging. The final variable, the extent to which a given change is contested, is even more difficult to define in operational terms. For purposes of this analysis, a "contest" takes place when two or more legislators announce their candidacies and work actively to align support. For simplicity of classification the "contest—no contest" variable has been dichotomized, although as with most variables in the social sciences, it is continuous rather than discrete.[10] That is to say, there are a number of finer gradations along a continuum which a more fully developed scheme would have to take into account. For example, the "no contest" classification may include situations where a contest is considered but abandoned short of announcement because the dissident party faction decides it does not have the necessary votes to make a successful challenge.[11] Contests may

---

[10] For discussion of this problem in the determination of causality, see Hubert M. Blalock, Jr., *Causal Inferences in Nonexperimental Research* (Chapel Hill, 1964), pp. 32–33.

[11] The attention of journalists and political scientists is naturally drawn to instances of organized revolt. For newspapermen, it is conflict, of course, which

range from (a) situations in which two or more candidates announce but all but one withdraw before the final vote, to (b) controversies which force concessions, although the leaders survive, or (c) instances of successful revolt.[12]

These distinctions will become more meaningful after discussion and illustration of the types of intra-party leadership change suggested by this classification scheme: (1) routine advancement, (2) appointment or emergence of a consensus choice, (3) open competition, (4) challenge to the heir apparent, and (5) revolt or its aftermath.

These types are ordered in terms of the amount of credit expenditure (time, energy, number of members involved, and so on) which each is likely to engender.[13] Routine advancement involves little or no expenditure of resources. Dissident members may invest some time conducting an informal poll of the membership to see if a contest has any chance of succeeding. Typically, no commitments are sought, and the campaign is never launched for lack of a single candidate which all opposing factions can rally behind. The second and third types usually involve lower party positions where the stakes are not as high. Leadership appointments may be challenged in a party conference or caucus, but at some cost. If no consensus choice emerges, several candidates may run. Friends, committee associates, and state or regional delegations may be brought in on either side. When the party posi-

---

makes news. But political scientists need to explore situations where the threatened change does not get beyond the discussion stage, as for example, threats to replace Thomas Kuchel, the incumbent Minority Whip in the United States Senate, at the opening of the 89th Congress, and disgruntlement with Speaker McCormack's leadership at the beginning of the 90th Congress.

[12] In the Republican Party (a) is illustrated by the Miller-McCulloch contest of 1960; (b) by the unsuccessful challenge against Minority Whip Arends in 1965 as well as the famed "revolt" against Speaker Cannon in 1910; and (c) by the minority leadership contests of 1959 and 1965.

[13] For general discussion of a theory of social exchange, see Talcott Parsons, "On the Concept of Influence," James S. Coleman, "Comment on 'On the Concept of Influence,'" *Public Opinion Quarterly*, 27 (Spring, 1963), 37–62; 63–82; George C. Homans, "Social Behavior as Exchange," *American Journal of Sociology*, 65 (May, 1960), 545–556; and Peter M. Blau, *Exchange and Power in Social Life* (New York, 1964). For more specific applications of exchange theory to legislatures, see Robert L. Peabody, "Organization Theory and Legislative Behavior: Bargaining, Hierarchy and Change in the U. S. House of Representatives" (paper delivered before the American Political Science Association, New York City, September 7, 1963); James S. Coleman, "Collective Decisions," *Sociological Inquiry* (Spring, 1964), 166–181; and James D. Barber, "Leadership Strategies for Legislative Party Cohesion," *Journal of Politics*, 28 (May, 1966), 347–367.

tion is important for the resources it controls, such as the campaign committee chairmanship, or because it is seen as a stepping stone to higher office, then more members are recruited to work actively in behalf of the candidates. If the contest goes to a formal vote, the pressures to align uncommitted members become intense. The greatest credit expenditures are likely to occur in challenges to an heir apparent, or contests which attempt to remove incumbent party leaders. Revolts may end up involving the full time and energy of as many as a third of the party membership over periods of several weeks or longer.

The upper left-hand cell of Table I or the *status quo* is, of course, the routine situation. No vacancy in a leadership position exists and no contest takes place. Continuity in office is the general practice in the House of Representatives, as in most organizations. For example, Representative Joseph Martin, Jr., of Massachusetts was first elected to Congress in 1924. He became Republican Minority Leader in 1939. He was re-elected Minority Leader seven times and Speaker twice before the one instance of his defeat in 1959 by his former Majority Leader in the 80th and 83rd Congresses, Charles Halleck of Indiana. Halleck was twice re-elected Minority Leader before his overthrow by Ford in 1965. Republican Whip Leslie Arends, first elected Whip in 1943, has maintained his position under three different Minority Leaders, Martin, Halleck and Ford.

The late Speaker Sam Rayburn of Texas was first elected to Congress in 1912. He became Chairman of the Interstate and Foreign Commerce Committee in 1931. In 1934 he briefly challenged Joseph W. Byrns of Tennessee, the incumbent Majority Leader, for the nomination for Speaker. However, Rayburn withdrew from the race before a vote in the Democratic Caucus. Rayburn went on to defeat Rules Committee Chairman John J. O'Connor of New York in a contest for Majority Leader in 1937. He was elevated to the Speakership in 1940. His occupancy of the top Democratic House position during the next 21 years was never challenged.

The ability of incumbents to retain office is not difficult to explain. Party leaders, particularly Speakers, have multiple opportunities to grant favors, create obligations, and build credit, all of which they can use to maintain a network of continuing support. A Speaker or floor leader has available, in addition, a number of sanctions, including the withholding of patronage and the vetoing of committee assignments, the threat of which can act as strong deterrents on contested change. In addition, there are a number of benefits to be gained from continuity of party leadership, not the least of which is experienced floor management. Contests, and particularly revolts against incumbent leadership, are likely to generate high costs in terms of subsequent party harmony. For all these reasons, the predominant pattern in congressional parties is the retention of incumbents rather than frequent leadership turnover.

II. FREQUENCY OF CHANGE

Evidence of the frequency of change in five major party-wide positions in both the Democratic and Republican parties for a twelve-year period, 1955–1966, is presented in Tables II and III.

TABLE II

Democratic (Majority) Party Leaders, House of Representatives, 1955–1966

Congress	Speaker	Majority Leader	Majority Whip	Caucus Chairman	Congressional (Campaign) Comm. Chairman
84th: 1955 1956	Sam Rayburn,[a] Texas	John McCormack,[b] Mass.	Carl Albert, Okla.	John Rooney, N.Y.	Michael Kirwan,[c] Ohio
85th: 1957 1958	Rayburn	McCormack	Albert	Melvin Price, Ill.	Kirwan
86th: 1959 1960	Rayburn	McCormack	Albert	Price	Kirwan
87th: 1961 1962	Rayburn McCormack	McCormack Albert	Albert Hale Boggs, La.	Francis Walter, Pa.	Kirwan
88th: 1963 1964	McCormack	Albert	Boggs	Walter Albert Thomas, Texas	Kirwan
89th: 1965 1966	McCormack	Albert	Boggs	Eugene Keogh, N.Y.	Kirwan

[a] Rayburn was first elected Speaker in the 76th Congress on September 16, 1940.
[b] McCormack was first elected Majority Leader in the 76th Congress on September 25, 1940.
[c] Kirwan was first elected Chairman of the Democratic National Congressional (Campaign) Committee midway in the 80th Congress (1948).
Sources: George Galloway, *History of the House of Representatives* (New York: Crowell, 1961); Randall B. Ripley, "The Party Whip Organizations in the United States House of Representatives," *APSA Review* LVIII (September, 1964), 561–576; *Biographical Directory of the American Congress, 1774–1961; Congressional Record; Congressional Quarterly Almanacs;* Michael J. Kirwan, *How to Succeed in Politics* (New York, 1964), p. 9.

TABLE III

Republican (Minority) Party Leaders, House of Representatives, 1955–1966

Congress	Minority Leader	Whip	Policy Comm. Chairman	Conference Chairman	Congressional (Campaign) Comm. Chairman
84th: 1955 1956	Joseph Martin,[a] Mass.	Leslie Arends,[b] Ill.	Joseph Martin,[c] Mass.	Clifford Hope,[d] Kan.	Richard Simpson,[e] Pa.
85th: 1957 1958	Martin	Arends	Martin	Charles Hoeven, Iowa	Simpson
86th: 1959 1960	Charles Halleck, Indiana	Arends	John Byrnes, Wisc.	Hoeven	Simpson William Miller, N.Y.
87th: 1961 1962	Halleck	Arends	Byrnes	Hoeven	Bob Wilson,[f] Calif.
88th: 1963 1964	Halleck	Arends	Byrnes	Gerald Ford, Mich.	Wilson
89th: 1965 1966	Gerald Ford, Mich.	Arends	John Rhodes, Ariz.	Melvin Laird, Wisc.	Wilson

[a] Martin was first elected Minority Leader at the opening of the 76th Congress, January 3, 1939.
[b] Arends was first elected Minority Whip midway in the 78th Congress (1943).
[c] Martin served as both Minority Leader and Policy Committee Chairman from 1949 until 1959.
[d] Hope served as Conference Chairman from the 82nd Congress until his retirement at the end of the 84th Congress (1951–1956).
[e] Simpson served as Chairman of the Republican Congressional (Campaign) Committee from 1953 until his death on January 7, 1960. He was succeeded by Miller in late January, 1960.
[f] Wilson was elected Chairman of the Republican Congressional (Campaign) Committee on June 29, 1961 following Miller's selection as National Chairman of the Republican Party.
Sources: George Galloway, *History of the House of Representatives* (New York: Crowell, 1961); Randall B. Ripley, "The Party Whip Organizations in the United States House of Representatives," *APSA Review* LVIII (September, 1964), 561–576; *Biographical Directory of the American Congress, 1774–1961; Congressional Record; Congressional Quarterly Almanacs;* Charles O. Jones, *The Republican Party in American Politics* (New York, 1965).

This period was selected because it encompasses the six complete Congresses since the last election bringing about inter-party change in the organization of the House, the midterm election of 1954.[14]

---

[14] Only one instance of leadership change took place at the opening of the 90th Congress in January, 1967. Representative Dan Rostenkowski of Chicago was elected Chairman of the Democratic Caucus, replacing Eugene Keogh of New York, who had retired at the end of the 89th Congress. All other incumbent leaders, Democrats and Republicans, were re-elected to the positions

For the Democratic Party, the majority party in the House of Representatives throughout this period, the five major party-wide leadership positions are the Speaker, the Majority Leader, the Majority Whip, the Chairman of the Democratic Caucus, and the Chairman of the Democratic National Congressional (Campaign) Committee.[15] With the exception of the Whip, all of these positions are elective. The Democratic Whip is appointed by the Majority Leader in consultation with the Speaker. Nominations to lesser party positions are largely controlled by the Speaker and Majority Leader, but their choice must be ratified by the Democratic Caucus, composed of all Democratic House members. Table II lists the incumbents for these five positions since 1955.

For the Republican Party, the minority party throughout this period, the five major party positions are Minority Leader, Minority Whip, Chairman of the Republican Conference, Chairman of the Republican Policy Committee and Chairman of the Republican Congressional (Campaign) Committee. All of these positions are elective in the sense that the nominees must ultimately be approved by the Republican Conference, counterpart to the Democratic Caucus. For two offices during most of this period the selection process has been made by separate committees. From 1919 until 1963 the choice of the Republican Whip was formally made by the Republican Committee on Committees, acting on the recommendation of the Speaker or Minority Leader. In 1965 the Republican Whip was directly elected by the Republican Conference. The Chairman of the Republican Congressional Committee, the counterpart to the Democratic National Congressional Committee, is elected by that committee. As with the Republican Committee on Committees, each state with Republican members is entitled to one Representative with as many votes as there are Republican House members in his state delegation. Table III lists the incumbents for these five Republican leadership positions for the 84th–89th Congresses.

---

they held in the previous Congress. In addition, House Republicans converted the Chairmanship of their Committee on Planning and Research from an appointive to an elective position.

[15] A sixth leadership position, Chairman of the Democratic Steering Committee, has been omitted from consideration. This committee, the counterpart to the Republican Policy Committee, was largely dormant throughout this period. Reactivated briefly in 1962 and again in 1965, its chairman is thirteen-term Representative Ray Madden of Indiana, senior administration supporter on the Committee on Rules.

As Tables II and III suggest, the prevailing practice is continuity in office rather than leadership change. At first glance, Republicans are no more susceptible to change than Democrats. Of the thirty changes in each party which could be hypothetically expected (a change in each position with each Congress) each party has made but nine.[16] It should be noted, however, that five of the nine Democratic cases are accounted for by the practice of rotating the largely honorary position of Caucus Chairman among senior Democrats who have not yet become chairman of standing committees. As will become more apparent, the way in which change comes about has far more important consequences than the number of changes *per se*.

III. LEADERSHIP CHANGE, 84TH–89TH CONGRESSES

The utility of a classification scheme is demonstrated both by its ability to order phenomena as well as the fruitfulness of the hypotheses it generates. Before suggesting why one party resorts to conflict as a means of change more frequently than the other party, each of the five types of intra-party leadership change needs further elaboration. Four of the five types are illustrated by nineteen cases of change or attempted change which took place during the 84th–89th Congresses (Table IV). Two earlier contests for the nomination for Speaker within the Republican Party in 1919 and 1931 provide more clear-cut cases of the remaining type, challenge to an heir apparent.

(1) Routine Advancement

This first type of intra-party leadership change takes place when a vacancy occurs in a top leadership position, a clear pattern of succession exists, and the next-ranking member in the party

---

[16] For the Democrats these nine changes consist of the choice of McCormack for Speaker in 1962; Albert for Majority Leader in 1962; Albert and Boggs for Whip in 1955 and 1962; and the five choices for Chairman of the Democratic Caucus (see Table 2). The nine Republican changes in leadership would include the selections of Halleck and Ford for Minority Leader in 1959 and 1965; Byrnes and Rhodes for Policy Committee Chairman in 1959 and 1965; Hoeven, Ford and Laird for Chairman of the Republican Conference in 1957, 1963, and 1965; and Miller and Wilson for Chairman of the Campaign Committee in 1960 and 1961 (see Table 3). In the following section one further case is added, the unsuccessful attempt to remove Arends as Minority Whip in 1965.

TABLE IV

Types of Intra-Party Leadership Change, House of Representatives, 84th–89th Congresses (1955–1966)

	No Contest		Contest[a]	
	Democratic Majority	*Republican Minority*	*Democratic Majority*	*Republican Minority*
NO VACANCY	*Status quo*		**(5)** *Revolt or its aftermath*	Minority Leader Halleck vs. Martin, 1959; Ford vs. Halleck, 1965; Conference Chairman Ford vs. Hoeven, 1963; Minority Whip Arends vs. Frelinghuysen, 1965[b]
			(4) *Challenge to heir apparent*	
			(3) *Open competition*	
			Majority Leader Albert vs. Bolling, 1962	Conference Chairman Laird vs. Frelinghuysen, 1965; Congressional (Campaign) Comm. Chairman Miller vs. McCulloch, 1960; Wilson vs. McCulloch, 1961
VACANCY				
Established pattern of succession	**(1)** *Routine advancement* Floor leader to Speaker McCormack, 1962			
No established pattern of succession	**(2)** *Appointment or emergence of a consensus choice* Majority Whip Albert, 1955; Boggs, 1962; Caucus Chairman Rooney, 1955; Price, 1957; Walter, 1961; Thomas, 1964; Keogh, 1965	Conference Chairman Hoeven, 1957; Policy Comm. Chairman Byrnes, 1959; Rhodes, 1965		
Total number of changes	8	3	1	7

[a] In cases of contest, the winning candidate is listed first.

[b] Strictly speaking, the Arends-Frelinghuysen contest is not an illustration of a change in leadership since the incumbent Whip Arends withstood the challenge.

hierarchy is elevated without challenge. One index of the increasing institutionalization of the House has been the development of patterns of succession to top leadership. Eleven of the twelve Speakers in the twentieth century have been elevated from either the majority leadership or from the minority leadership following congressional election victories. The one exception to this established pattern was Gillett's defeat of Minority Leader Mann for the Republican nomination for Speaker after Republicans regained control of the House in 1919.

McCormack's succession to the Speakership in January, 1962, following the death of Rayburn, illustrates the prevailing practice of routine advancement. Rayburn and McCormack had served together in the principal Democratic leadership positions in the House since September, 1940. When Speaker Bankhead of Alabama died in 1940, Majority Leader Rayburn was elevated without contest. McCormack, with White House backing, defeated Clifton Woodrum of Virginia for the office of Majority Leader by a vote of 141 to 67. Prior to his selection, McCormack was Chairman of the Democratic Caucus and fourth-ranking member on the Ways and Means Committee. His northern background, which complemented Rayburn's, was a strong factor in his election. The two men served in tandem throughout the 1940's and 1950's, dropping down to Minority Leader and Minority Whip, respectively, during the two Republican-controlled Congresses, the 80th and 83rd.

Rayburn's health began to fail in the summer of 1961. Before he left for his home in Bonham, Texas in late August he designated Majority Leader McCormack as Speaker pro tempore. McCormack served out the remaining month of the session in that capacity. Rayburn died on November 16, 1961.

None of McCormack's possible liabilities—his age, religion, or lack of popularity with some elements of the House, particularly Democratic Study Group members—proved serious enough to bring on a challenge. Some members feared that McCormack, at 71, was slowing down and would not provide the strong leadership necessary to get the Kennedy legislative program enacted. Others were hostile to the elevation of another Roman Catholic to a position of national leadership along with President Kennedy and Senate Majority Leader Mansfield. Although not particularly popular with Northern liberals and some Southern members, McCormack had the support and respect of a number of the senior oligarchs of the House, especially Carl Vinson of Georgia and

Howard W. Smith of Virginia. The inability of his opponents to rally around one of the several possible candidates and the hands-off policy adopted by President Kennedy and his White House assistants made McCormack's election inevitable. On January 10, 1962, he became the 45th Speaker of the House.

(2) Appointment or Emergence of a Consensus Choice

This second type of change is illustrated by a number of appointments or unchallenged elections at the lower levels of the party hierarchy where patterns of succession are not yet established. The appointments of Majority Whips Carl Albert in 1955 and Hale Boggs in 1962 are illustrative. When the Democrats regained control of the House in the 84th Congress (1955–56), a vacancy had been created in the Whip position by Tennessee Representative Percy Priest's elevation to the Chairmanship of the Committee on Interstate and Foreign Commerce. Albert, who was beginning his fifth term, had come to Rayburn's attention as the Representative of the Oklahoma district adjacent to Rayburn's own Texas district and through parliamentary skills displayed in floor debate. At the same time that Rayburn and McCormack were appointing Albert as Majority Whip, they created a new position of Deputy Whip for another talented young Representative, Hale Boggs of Louisiana. In January, 1962, after Albert was elected Majority Leader, he appointed Boggs as Majority Whip. John Moss of California advanced from a regional whip position to Deputy Whip at the same time.

The selection of the Chairmen of the Democratic Caucus for these six Congresses also illustrates this second type. Since the principal responsibility of this party official is to preside over the party caucus at the opening of each session of Congress, a caucus which seldom meets again, the position is primarily honorary. By tradition, incumbents serve for one, or at the most, two terms. They are nominated by the leadership and selected from a pool of loyal, senior members who are not yet chairmen of standing committees.

Until 1963, the Chairman of the Republican Conference was also an honorary title with few duties beyond presiding over infrequent meetings of House Republicans. Unlike the Democrats, the Republicans have not rotated the position. Thus, Clifford Hope of Kansas served in this capacity from 1951 until his retirement in 1956. Charles Hoeven of Iowa, first selected in 1957, served until his defeat by Gerald Ford at the opening of the 88th Congress. Since Ford's election in 1963, and particularly since Melvin Laird's election in 1965, the responsibility of the Republican Conference Chairman has undergone considerable reorganization and upgrading.

Two uncontested choices for Chairman of the Republican Policy Committee also illustrate emergence of a consensus choice. In response to the disastrous 1948 election, Republicans seeking to improve their organizational structure converted a defunct steering committee into a policy committee. Little was made of it, however. Republican Minority Leader Martin served as Chairman of a largely inoperative committee for the next ten years. In 1959, following Charles Halleck's overthrow of Martin, the Chairmanship was given independent status. John W. Byrnes of Wisconsin, the most senior available member save for Halleck among several members considered as possible challengers to Martin, was elected without opposition.

The selection of John Rhodes of Arizona as Byrnes' successor in 1965 is a less clear-cut case of a consensus choice. Byrnes resigned from the Chairmanship of the Republican Policy Committee in late January, 1965 in order to devote his full time to serving as ranking minority member of the Ways and Means Committee. With Byrnes' endorsement, the Republican Conference adopted a resolution on January 14, 1965 which prohibits its five principal party leaders from serving as chairman or ranking minority member on standing committees. Byrnes' intention to resign had cleared the way for another Wisconsin Republican, Melvin Laird, to be elected Chairman of the Republican Conference. The selection of Rhodes was not challenged, even though he was not the new Minority Leader Ford's first choice. Rhodes, first elected to Congress in 1952, had served as Chairman of the Policy Committee's subcommittee on special projects since 1961. A friend of Ford's, he had nevertheless backed Halleck in the 1965 contest against Ford. After Rhodes announced his candidacy, Ford considered putting up a candidate of his own choice, but because of the potential costs to his own prestige and to party harmony, he decided to avoid a direct confrontation. With the support of Laird and Arends, he created a separate Committee on Planning and Research to coordinate the task forces. Ford's first choice to head the Republican Policy Committee had been four-term Representative Charles Goodell of New York. Goodell, co-manager of Ford's successful challenge to Halleck, was appointed Chairman of the newly created Committee on Planning and Research. His appointment was confirmed on February 23, 1965, the same day that Rhodes was unanimously elected Chairman of a restructured Republican Policy Committee.

(3) Open Competition

When a vacancy occurs in a party leadership position which is not appointive and where no pattern of succession has been established, open competition between two or more candidates may take place. The two contests for Chairmanship of the Republican Congressional (Campaign) Committee in 1960 and 1961 illustrate this type. Richard Simpson of Pennsylvania, Chairman from 1953 to 1960, died on January 7, 1960. Many of the Republican members who had backed Martin against Halleck in 1959, aligned themselves behind William McCulloch of Ohio. On January 20, 1960 the Halleck forces won a further victory when their candidate, William E. Miller of New York, was elected Chairman. Miller had behind-the-scenes support from Vice President Richard M. Nixon, and was also acceptable to another prospective presidential candidate, Governor Nelson Rockefeller of New York. When Miller was elevated to Chairman of the Republican National Committee in June, 1961, another non-mid-westerner, Bob Wilson of California, emerged from a field of potential candidates which included Laird of Wisconsin, Rhodes of Arizona, and Ford of Michigan, in addition to McCulloch. While the selection of Miller and Wilson cannot be divorced from prior House contests and political maneuvering on the national scene, they also reflected successful efforts to widen geographical and expand suburban representation within the House Republican leadership.

Both regional and ideological differences were at issue in another example of open competition, the contest between Laird of Wisconsin and Peter Frelinghuysen of New Jersey for Chairman of the Republican Conference in 1965. Ford, the Chairman in the previous Congress, had announced his intention to resign regardless of the outcome of his open challenge to Minority Leader Halleck. Laird, sympathetic to Ford's candidacy, announced his own independent bid for the Conference Chairmanship on December 29, 1964, the week before the 89th Congress convened. First elected to Congress in 1952, Laird had risen to fourth-ranking Republican on Appropriations and served as Chairman of the Republican Platform Committee at San Francisco in 1964. His firm management of the drafting of the platform, which Goldwater and Miller later campaigned on, led to intensified criticism of Laird from eastern seaboard liberals such as John Lindsay of New York and Bradford Morse and Silvio Conte of Massachusetts. Together with some twenty House colleagues organized as the Wednesday Club, they decided to field a last-minute candidate of their own. Meeting on Sunday night before the January 4, 1965 vote, the Wednesday Club selected Frelinghuysen as their choice. He had only recently joined their group but he was one of the few members with a seniority equivalent to Laird's. Despite Frelinghuysen's late announcement he received 62 votes to 77 cast for Laird.

Richard Bolling's abortive effort to prevent Carl Albert's advancement from Democratic Whip to Majority Leader at the opening of the second session of the 87th Congress in 1962 represents still another example of open competition. Following Rayburn's death in 1961, Bolling at first considered a challenge to McCormack. He finally concluded he would have a better chance to defeat Albert, although he realized that in both cases the odds were severely stacked against him. Strong support for Bolling's candidacy failed to materialize. Just before Congress reconvened his hard count was estimated at sixty-five to seventy votes, far short of the 130 votes needed to win in the Democratic Caucus. Bolling announced his withdrawal on January 3rd, 1962. One week later at the opening caucus Carl Albert was unanimously elected Majority Leader.[17]

(4) Challenge to an Heir Apparent

This fourth type of contest takes place when a vacancy occurs through death, defeat or retirement, but the apparent successor's claim is contested. No clear-cut case took place in the House during

---

[17] This contest comes close to qualifying as the fourth type, *challenge to the heir apparent*. Excerpts from the interviews reported in Polsby's detailed study of this contest clearly reveal the extent to which members perceived Albert as " 'entitled' to the job by virtue of his six years' service in the leadership hierarchy of the House." *op. cit.*, p. 247. But while the pattern of succession from Floor Leader to Speaker has been firmly established, there is only limited precedent for elevating the party Whip to Floor Leader. Oscar Underwood of Alabama served briefly as Minority Whip in 1900–1901, but ten years intervened before he became Majority Floor Leader in 1911. With the possible exception of John Garner of Texas, no other Floor Leader save for Albert had previously served as Whip *prior* to his first selection as Floor Leader: Ripley, *op. cit.*, p. 563, p. 564, n. 19. Albert, however, was able to capitalize on McCormack's two related experiences of serving as Minority Whip and then moving back up to Majority Leader following the 80th and 83rd Congresses. Boggs' elevation from Deputy Whip to Whip in 1962 was further evidence of a developing pattern.

the 84th–89th Congresses. Several earlier contests in this century, the Gillett-Mann struggle over the nomination for Speakership in 1919, and the upset of former Majority Leader Tilson by Republican Rules Committee Chairman Snell in 1931 just prior to the organization of the 72nd Congress, are illustrative examples. The Republican Party had endured minority status and the rather arbitrary rule of Minority Leader James R. Mann of Illinois, successor to Speaker Cannon, for eight years before they regained control of the House in the election of 1918. Favorable election results did not inhibit national party leaders and House opponents of Mann from putting together enough support within the Republican Conference to win the nomination, and ultimately, the Speakership, for Frederick H. Gillett of Massachusetts. Gillett, first elected in 1892, was one of two Republicans in the House who had served longer than any other member, save for ex-Speaker Cannon. Gillett, the ranking Republican member on the Committee on Appropriations, had few personal enemies. Mann, in contrast, had antagonized many members in both parties with his relentless and caustic criticisms of legislation. In addition to his strong identification with the Cannon regime, his opponents accused him of conflict of interest in his relations with the Chicago meat packing industry. On February 27, 1919, Gillett defeated Mann by 138 votes to 69 with three other candidates receiving 18 votes.[18] Gillett served as a rather ineffective Speaker from 1919 to 1924, when he resigned to run for the Senate.

In 1931, Halleck's predecessor, Joseph Martin of Massachusetts, backed Bertrand H. Snell of New York in a bitter Conference struggle resulting in the overthrow of Republican Speaker Nicholas Longworth's apparent successor, 73-year old John Q. Tilson of Connecticut.[19] Longworth had died on April 9, 1931, before the 72nd Congress convened. Tilson had served as Republican Majority Leader under Longworth since 1925, the year in which Martin was first elected to the House. This contest followed a 49-seat election setback for the Republicans in 1930. The deaths of several Republican incumbents before December, 1931 allowed the Democrats to gain control of the House and frustrated Snell's ambitions to

---

[18] *New York Times,* February 28, 1919, p. 1; Chiu, *op. cit.,* pp. 25–27.

[19] Snell moved from 55 votes on the first ballot to a 96 to 64 lead over Tilson on the seventh ballot but still one short of a majority. Before the eighth ballot began, Tilson moved to make the nomination unanimous. *New York Times,* December 1, 1931, pp. 1, 4; December 8, 1931, pp. 1, 16.

be Speaker. Snell voluntarily retired from the House in 1938. Martin, the eastern Assistant Whip and the Republican Campaign Chairman in a year in which the Republicans won back 80 seats, was elected Minority Leader in 1939, without any serious challenge.[20]

(5) Revolt or its Aftermath

This last type, usually the most costly in terms of the investment of resources required, takes place when: (1) no vacancy in a leadership position exists, (2) the incumbent cannot be persuaded to step aside, and (3) an intra-party contest ensues. The Halleck-Martin struggle for the Minority Leadership in 1959, the Ford-Hoeven fight over the Chairmanship of the Republican Conference in 1963, and the Ford-Halleck contest for the Minority Leadership in 1965, all illustrate this type of intra-party change. Ford's unsuccessful attempt to remove incumbent Minority Whip Arends represents a quite different form of revolt.

In the late 1950's, when Martin's health began to fail, a number of younger Republicans sought more vigorous party leadership. The election disaster of 1958 provided a further impetus for change. In mid-December, more than a dozen Republicans met in the office of Representative Bob Wilson of California to discuss what could be done to improve party fortunes. While they were agreed that new leadership was needed, they were divided in their choice among Halleck of Indiana, Byrnes of Wisconsin, Ford of Michigan, and Simpson of Pennsylvania. In an informal poll of members, they found widespread sentiment for change, but only one active candidate, former Majority Leader Halleck. After determining that the White House would remain neutral, Halleck announced his candidacy. On the eve of the vote, his backers estimated they had more than eighty votes of the 154 Republican Representatives-elect. Martin, like Halleck six years later, did not take the challenge seriously until it was too late.

At the afternoon conference on Tuesday, January 6, 1959, the Martin forces led by Richard Simpson of Pennsylvania, Leo Allen and Leslie Arends of Illinois, and Clarence Brown of Ohio, lost a move to avoid a secret ballot by a vote of 96 to 50. Halleck edged Martin on the first ballot by a vote of 73 to 72 with one ballot re-

---

[20] Joe Martin, *My First Fifty Years in Politics* (as told to Robert J. Donovan) (New York, 1960), pp. 81–82.

jected as illegible. Since neither candidate received a majority another ballot was necessary. Halleck won on the second ballot by a vote of 74 to 70.[21]

The Ford-Hoeven contest of 1963 was an important precursor of the 1965 minority leadership struggle. It was initiated at the opening of the 88th Congress by two junior members on the House Education and Labor Committee, Robert P. Griffin of Michigan (first elected in 1956) and Charles E. Goodell of New York (first elected in a special election on May 26, 1959). After considering and rejecting challenges to either Halleck or Arends, Griffin and Goodell decided to go after the Republican Conference Chairmanship as a further step toward revitalizing party machinery. With the active support of most of the House members elected in 1958, 1960 and 1962, and the tacit approval of many of the same activists who had promoted the Halleck upset of Martin, they launched an over-the-weekend campaign against Hoeven, the incumbent Conference Chairman since 1957. On January 8, 1963, their candidate, the 49-year-old Ford, defeated the 67-year-old Hoeven, by a secret ballot vote of 86 to 78.[22]

A necessary, but not sufficient, cause of the 1965 revolt was the Republican election disaster of November, 1964. The Goldwater defeat and the net loss of thirty-eight Republican House seats created a psychological climate within which revolt flourished. But the seeds of dissatisfaction with Halleck's leadership extended back to bitterness engendered by Halleck's defeat of Martin in

---

[21] The best single review of this contest is Jones, *op. cit.*, pp. 29–38. His summary contains one questionable statement: "A poll of members showed that John W. Byrnes of Wisconsin had the most support, Gerald R. Ford, Jr., of Michigan was second, and Halleck was third." (p. 35). A more plausible interpretation is that the informal polls taken in late December and early January were too indefinite to do much more than suggest that there were several possible candidates with Halleck and Byrnes the front-runners. The insurgents discussed going with Byrnes, but found him reluctant to step out in front of Halleck, an experienced floor leader. When one of their group, former Representative Jack Westland of Washington, discussed the possibilities of a revolt with Halleck in Florida, Halleck insisted on his right as the former Majority Leader to make the challenge. Other contemporary accounts seem to support this interpretation. See, for example, Richard Fryklund, "Story of G.O.P. Revolt Has Varied Chapters," *Washington Star*, January 11, 1959, p. A-1; John L. Steele, "G.O.P. Tactics That Toppled A Veteran Leader," *Life*, January 19, 1959; and Martin's own version, *op. cit.*, pp. 3–19. I am indebted to Representative Bob Wilson for making available a 69-page scrapbook of clippings and other materials which he kept on this contest.

[22] "Ford's Election Sparks Shifts in GOP House Strategy," *Congressional Quarterly Weekly Report*, 21 (February 8, 1963), 149–156.

1959. This irritation and unrest was compounded by the continuing frustrations of minority status. Agitation for change, only temporarily dampened by Ford's defeat of Hoeven in 1963, intensified throughout the long and trying sessions of the 88th Congress.

A post-election House Republican Conference held on December 16, 1964 put Halleck to test. Although called to evaluate Republican party organization and policy positions, its principal consequence was to bring back to Washington a diversified group of younger activists who were convinced that the first step toward achieving majority status was new leadership. Two likely challengers emerged, Gerald R. Ford, Jr. of Michigan and Melvin R. Laird of Wisconsin. Ford, with four more years of seniority, was selected as the candidate with the best chance of defeating Halleck.

Ford announced his candidacy on December 19, 1964. By dint of superior organization and hard campaigning the young activists, led by Griffin of Michigan, Goodell of New York, Quie of Minnesota, Ellsworth of Kansas, and Rumsfeld of Illinois, got off to an early lead which they never relinquished. Halleck's counterattack was a classic illustration of "too little and too late." Only a few members worked actively in his behalf. Most of his contacts were made in the final week of the campaign. Only in the closing days did he begin to cash in on his credits outstanding. On January 4, 1965, at the opening of the 89th Congress, Ford defeated Halleck by a secret ballot vote of 73 to 67. In the final analysis, it was the two-thirds of the House Republican Party in the five most junior classes which made victory possible for Ford. The bulk of his support, and certainly the organizational nucleus of his campaign, came from members elected in 1956 and subsequent elections.[23]

A fourth contest, New Jersey Representative Frelinghuysen's unsuccessful challenge to the incumbent Minority Whip, Leslie Arends of Illinois, ten days after Ford's defeat of Halleck in 1965, came about as an aftermath of revolt. In this instance, the challenger ran with the new Minority Leader's endorsement in a losing effort to consolidate the revolt and provide wider geographical and ideological representation within the minority leadership. Arends's early start in the defense of his incumbency, his more than twenty years of service as party Whip, and his wide-spread personal

---

[23] Peabody, "The Ford-Halleck Minority Leadership Contest, 1965," *op. cit.*, pp. 32–35.

popularity proved to be too strong. He won by 70 votes to 59. Frelinghuysen's personal reserve and rather aristocratic background cost him some support. So did his identification with the Wednesday Club. Conservatives, already smarting under National Chairman Burch's resignation, found Frelinghuysen's stand on the nuclear policy plank at San Francisco and his general liberal voting record on foreign affairs further reasons for opposing Ford's choice. In any event, Ford, like Martin and Halleck before him, came to understand more fully that members are more hesitant to reveal their true preferences to an incumbent Minority Leader.

IV. CONDITIONS WHICH FACILITATE OR INHIBIT CHANGE

The differences between the dominant types of intra-party change adopted by the two parties are quite striking. As Table IV illustrates, all but one of the nine instances of leadership selection in the Democratic majority were uncontested. Even in this one instance —the Albert-Bolling fight for Majority Leader in 1961–62—the challenger withdrew before the contest reached the voting stage in the Democratic Caucus. In contrast, seven of the ten Republican leadership changes were decided by intra-party combat. Four of the seven contests involved challenges to incumbents.

Why has the Democratic majority developed patterns of succession and utilized relatively peaceful means of leadership change? What causes the Republican minority to seldom resort to change short of contests? Among the most important factors which combine to facilitate or inhibit one type of change rather than another are (1) the skill of the incumbent, (2) majority-minority status, (3) election results, and (4) differences in hierarchy and structure in the two congressional parties.

(1) Skill of the Incumbent

The age, personality and skill of the incumbent in contrast to his potential or actual challengers, are clearly among the most crucial factors affecting patterns of leadership change. In contrast to their Democratic counterparts, first Martin and later Halleck seemed to have lost touch with their colleagues, particularly junior Republicans. Halleck and his supporters used this criticism to telling advantage in the 1959 minority leadership contest. The same charge was leveled against Halleck in 1965. As one of his supporters admitted: "I don't know anyone who was really close to him. That was one of Charlie's problems—communication I presume he ate by himself. He didn't show up at the Republican luncheon in the Capitol. He shielded himself from other members. He was out of touch with the team to an unnecessary degree." Truman's analysis of voting patterns in an earlier Congress, the 81st, provides some corroborating evidence. Neither Martin nor Halleck appeared to be very influential with the more junior members of the Republican minority; Democratic junior members were much more likely to vote in accordance with their party floor leader, McCormack.[24]

One characteristic of successful leadership is an ability to recruit and develop younger talent for positions of future leadership. Rayburn had this reputation. One of Ford's principal campaign themes was his promise to be accessible to all and to make 60-minute ball players out of all 140 House Republicans. Assessments of personality played a prominent role in the outcomes of other contests, for example, Albert's popularity and Bolling's relative estrangement in 1962.

Leadership contests are won by the side which can mobilize the greatest number of members who are willing to work long and intensively in an effort to convert their fellow congressmen. Here, more than in typical battles over legislative issues, personal loyalties and animosities developed over a series of Congresses are crucial. Respect, trust and affection are usually more crucial than explicit bargaining based on such tangible objects of exchange as committee assignments or the promise of additional patronage. Over the long run, however, the majority leadership enjoys greater stability, in part, because of its superior resources, both tangible and intangible.

(2) Majority-minority Status

Congressional leaders have many opportunities to help their colleagues achieve their personal and legislative objectives. A leader's endorsement frequently decides which one of several candidates will receive a preferred committee assignment. A floor leader may interrupt a freshman member's speech to argue in favor of his public works project and in the process, convert enough wavering members to make the difference. Party leaders appear at fund-raising dinners. They provide the kind of personal endorse-

---

[24] Truman, *op. cit.*, pp. 212–227.

ment which will enhance a member's chances for re-election. Both majority and minority party leaders are constantly involved in such credit-building endeavors. But majority party leaders enjoy superior resources. They work within a climate of expanding rather than contracting credit.

Credit expands because of the multiple benefits which accrue with majority status. There are more committee assignments and appointments to prestige boards and commissions to be distributed. It is the majority which receives most of the credit when legislation is passed. Their projects receive higher priority. Majority members chair the committees and subcommittees. With position comes staff, superior access to executive officialdom, and greater influence on legislative outcomes. Since there are more benefits to go around, majority members are more satisfied and less critical of their leadership. Majority status promotes a search for compromise, accommodation and the acceptance of the established patterns of succession.

In contrast, the minority party operates in an environment of continuing frustration and increasing discord. There are fewer choice committee assignments to go around. The majority controls most of the prestige appointments. Political patronage and staff assistance are not as abundant. Opportunities for constructive participation in the drafting and implementing of major legislation are more limited. Limited resources, contracting credit, an inability to adequately reward the party faithful, the prospects of continuing defeat in floor struggles—all foster internal dissension and further undermine the leadership. If election results continue to run against the minority party, as they have with House Republicans during this period with the single exception of 1960, then party juniors are motivated to take their frustrations out through change in leadership.

(3) Election Results

Party structure and leadership change in the House of Representatives are intimately related to congressional election results. In the first place, the party which wins a majority of the 435 seats earns the right to organize the House, choose the Speaker and select the committee chairmen. What has not been so clearly understood is the relationship between the aggregate size of the net gain or loss and its implications for intra-party leadership change. Strong victories promote good will and generally reflect to the benefit of party leaders. Conversely, defeat results in pessimism, hostility and a search for scapegoats. If the net losses are particularly severe, as many as thirty to fifty seats, then the possibilities of minority leadership change through revolt are greatly enhanced.

TABLE V

Party Line-up, House of Representatives, and President, 1954–1964

| Election Year | Congress | House of Representatives | | | | President |
| | | Members Elected | | Gains/Losses* | | |
		Dem.	Rep.	Dem.	Rep.	
1954	84th	232	203	+19	−18	Eisenhower (R)
1956	85th	234	201	+ 2	− 2	
1958	86th	283	154	+49	−47	
1960	87th	263	174	−20	+20	Kennedy (D)
1962	88th	259	176	− 4	+ 2	
1964	89th	295	140	+38	−38	Johnson (D)

* Gains and losses do not always balance because of independent candidates or increases and decreases in the size of the House as a result of the admission of Hawaii and Alaska and reapportionment.
Source: *Congress and the Nation* (Washington: Congressional Quarterly Service, 1965), p. 63.

Table 5 summarizes the congressional election results and party line-ups from 1954 to 1964. This period was a particularly trying one for House Republicans. Eisenhower was in the White House from 1952 to 1960, but Republicans lost control of Congress after 1954. They continued as a minority party through the mid-sixties. Halleck apparently considered the possibility of a contest against Martin after the elections of 1954 and 1956, but did not make a bid because White House neutrality was not forthcoming. At least three, and perhaps all four cases of revolt were preceded by election disappointments. In the 1958 election, House Republicans suffered a further net loss of 47 seats. Halleck's defeat of Martin followed. Under Halleck's leadership and with Nixon at the head of the ticket, House Republicans made moderate gains in 1960.

When traditional midterm gains were not forthcoming in 1962, junior Republicans led by Goodell and Griffin took out their frustrations on Republican Conference Chairman Hoeven. In 1964, with Goldwater at the head of the Republican ticket, House

Republicans lost 48 House seats and picked up only 10 seats previously held by Democrats. Ford's defeat of Halleck and the attempt to remove Arends followed. A senior Republican, who played a prominent role in both the 1959 and 1965 minority leadership contests, summed up the climate created by election defeats:

> Such elections normally make minorities anxious. A climate is created. Members are seeking some way to make a change. It is in the nature of things. If the results are downhill, you make the change. If you hold your own or win, you don't. The election defeat creates an environment which makes members look for some change. It's a sense of unrest, a subconscious searching for something to ease individual consciences. The result is often "let's change our leadership."

The Democratic majority fared far better throughout this period, a factor which contributed to stable leadership. After regaining control of the House in 1954, Speaker Rayburn and Majority Leader McCormack picked Albert as Whip and created the new position of Deputy Whip for Boggs. In the face of Eisenhower's overwhelming victory in 1956, the Democratic leadership was content to hold its own. Inability to capitalize on large Democratic majorities achieved in 1958 led to the formation of the Democratic Study Group.[25] Composed of mostly Northern moderates and liberals, the DSG played a crucial role in the 1961 fight to enlarge the principal scheduling body of the House, the Committee on Rules. But Rayburn also needed 22 Republican votes to offset 1960 election losses in his narrow 217–212 win.[26] After Rayburn's death, McCormack, Albert and Boggs each advanced one step in the party hierarchy. Following decisive election gains in 1964, the DSG promoted caucus action which stripped two Southern Democrats of their committee seniority and brought about further liberalization of the House rules.

Election defeat tends to produce party leadership conflict within the Republican minority. Conversely, election successes have enhanced leadership stability in the House Democratic majority.[27]

---

[25] Kenneth Kofmehl, "The Institutionalization of a Voting Bloc," *Western Political Quarterly,* 17 (June, 1964), 256–272.

[26] Milton C. Cummings, Jr. and Robert L. Peabody, "The Decision to Enlarge the Committee on Rules: An Analysis of the 1961 Vote," in Peabody and Polsby, *op. cit.,* pp. 167–194.

[27] The impact of the midterm election of 1966 on prospective leadership change at the beginning of the 90th Congress adds further support to these

But it is not just the climate created by the election, but its impact on hierarchy and party structure within the two House parties which promotes or deters change.

(4) Hierarchy and Party Structure

The Republican minority has been more prone to leadership change through contested means for two further reasons. First, unlike the Democratic majority, Republicans in recent Congresses have suffered from a disproportionate number of junior members to senior members. This problem becomes particularly acute after major election defeats, such as 1958 and 1964. For example, following the Goldwater disaster, 93 of the 140 House Republicans (66.4 percent) were members of the five most junior classes (1956, 1958, 1960, 1962 and 1964). Even with the large class of entering freshmen, the comparable figure for Democrats was 169 members out of 295 (57.3 percent). What was more striking, however, was not relatively greater average seniority among Democrats, but much more depth among its senior members. Of 72 members in the 89th Congress who had served 10 terms or more, only 11 (15.6 percent) were Republicans. Just as Martin before him, it was Halleck who suffered most from the loss of loyal senior supporters in 1964.

Conversely, it was the very existence of this pool of senior Democrats, many of them committee chairmen and heads of state delegations, which helps to explain the development of hierarchical patterns of leadership succession and the reluctance to challenge incumbents characteristic of the Democratic majority. A Representative must have substantial service, a minimum of five terms, before he can be considered a candidate for leadership. Seniority is not the only factor. The dissident factions must settle on a candidate capable of winning. When a vacancy occurs there are likely to be two or three equally plausible prospects, no one of whom is preferable to all of the factions within the party: Hierarchical balance is bolstered by traditions of the majority party which foster moderation and acceptance of the existing leadership. "Above all, in the House, one must *last*. If one does last, influence

---

generalizations. Republicans made a net gain of 47 House seats, but fell 31 seats short of winning control. The party breakdown for the 90th Congress was 248 Democrats and 187 Republicans. A principal effect of the election was to consolidate Ford's position as Minority Leader. Although the House Democratic majority leadership came in for some criticism and floor setbacks in the opening months, their leadership positions were not directly contested.

will accrue, but this power is diluted with any defeat. So a congressman, however strong or senior, does not commit himself carelessly. He waits."[28]

Differences in party structure also contribute to the pronounced variations in types of leadership change characteristic of the two House parties. At the risk of oversimplification and ignoring variations from Congress to Congress, the Democratic majority is composed of more than two Northern moderates and liberals for every Southern conservative. Urban machine Democrats and border state congressmen, epitomized by Speaker McCormack and Majority Leader Albert, have traditionally formed a moderating nucleus between the ideological extremes of the party. Neither wing can organize the House nor reap the benefits of majority status without the other. Although this dominant cleavage makes House Democrats less cohesive than Republicans in their voting patterns, majority status and the need to promote a presidential program lead to greater accommodation among elective leaders and seniority leaders than is the case among minority Republicans.[29]

In contrast, the Republican minority, although characterized by greater voting cohesiveness, is less susceptible to compromise and accommodation. Its rather monolithic voting structure is skewed heavily in the conservative direction. There appears to be little attempt by conservatives, who outnumber liberals by six or seven to one, to tolerate dissent or accord liberals positions in the party leadership. If the activities of the Wednesday Club in a series of contests taking place at the opening of the 89th Congress are at all characteristic, liberals have seldom been cohesive enough to form a balance of power between personal or sectional interests within the predominantly conservative Republican ranks.

Lacking a better historical perspective the full import of party structure for leadership change must remain speculative. But it would appear that the basic bimodal distribution within the Democratic majority is a strength as well as a weakness, since it promotes compromise and a trading off of major leadership positions between North and South. The relatively monolithic structure of the House Republican party may lend itself to party harmony and centralization of leadership when the G.O.P. controls Con-

---

[28] Excerpt from an unpublished newsletter of the late Representative Clem Miller, January-February, 1962, p. 3.

[29] For evidence of such effects in an earlier Congress, the 81st, see Truman, *op. cit.*, pp. 231–246.

gress, but this same structure seems to discourage accommodation and the selection of its leaders short of contests in times of minority status.

V. CONSEQUENCES

What difference does it make when a Halleck upsets a Martin or a McCormack succeeds a Rayburn? More broadly, what are the consequences when one party, the Democratic majority, develops patterns of succession to top leadership, while the other, the Republican minority, seldom stops short of contests in the selection of its party leaders? As Truman, Huitt and others have pointed out, the discretionary aspects of congressional leadership are considerable.[30] Their personalities and backgrounds not only shape the positions they occupy, but also have important implications for the careers of their supporters and the success or failure of legislation. The predominant mode of change adopted by the two House parties has additional consequences for national elections, the two-party system, and representative government.

Within the confines of this article it is impossible to assess fully the impact of even the most important leadership choices made by the two House parties during this twelve year period. It is possible, however, to use two examples—Halleck's defeat of Martin in 1959 and McCormack's elevation to the Speakership in 1962— to briefly illustrate some of the most important kinds of consequences of replacing one incumbent leader by another.[31]

Revolt, by its very nature, results in more wholesale change than orderly succession. Following his defeat of Martin, Halleck brought new vigor to the Republican party leadership. A canny, aggressive "gut-fighter," he was at his best in the give-and-take of floor debate and behind-the-scenes maneuvering. In contrast to Martin, he seldom cooperated with Rayburn, McCormack and the more liberal wing of the Democratic majority, but instead actively cultivated ties with conservative Southern Democrats. Moderate Republicans on the Committee on Rules who had retired or advanced to the Senate were replaced with solid conservatives. The dormant Re-

---

[30] Truman, *op. cit.*, p. 245; Huitt, *op. cit.*, pp. 336–337.

[31] For an attempt to more fully analyze the consequences of Ford's defeat of Halleck in 1965, see Robert L. Peabody, "House Republican Leadership: Change and Consolidation in a Minority Party" (paper delivered before the American Political Science Association, New York City, September 9, 1966).

publican Policy Committee was reinstituted, John Byrnes of Wisconsin was elected Chairman, and arrangements were made to provide professional staff. Under Byrnes and John Rhodes of Arizona, task forces were created to investigate problems which cut across committee lines or which might serve as the basis of campaign issues. Freshman members were given representation on the executive subcommittee of the Republican Committee on Committees.

When Halleck took over as Minority Leader in 1959 Republicans had 154 House members. At one time during the 88th Congress, the number increased to 178. For a majority of 140 Republicans-elect at the beginning of the 89th Congress, however, Halleck's ability to promote party solidarity and to administer defeat to Democratic proposals was not enough. Ford's promise to "promote and communicate the image of a fighting, forward-looking party seeking responsible and constructive solutions to national problems" struck a receptive chord. The intensive efforts of some 30 members working in Ford's behalf led to Halleck's defeat only six years after his own coup.

Peaceful succession brings on more incremental change, but the impact of such different personalities as Rayburn and McCormack on the office of the Speaker is considerable. McCormack's style is both more institutional and partisan than Rayburn's. He calls more meetings to discuss legislative strategy and involves the Majority Leader and Whip to a much greater extent than Rayburn did. Under his leadership, the Democratic Steering Committee has been revived and the Caucus has come into greater use. The telephone is one of McCormack's most effective weapons—"I'd call the devil if I thought it would do any good." In contrast, Rayburn operated on a more independent and personal basis. He preferred the intimacy and informality of after-the-session gatherings of the "Board of Education."[32] The Whip organization was used less frequently and Rayburn almost never called a party caucus beyond the opening meeting.

McCormack's shift from partisan Majority Leader to impartial presiding officer was not an easy transition. His strong partisan identifications reflect his South Boston organizational ties. Rayburn's rural Texas background and more conservative political out-

---

[32] For a discussion of Rayburn's use of this informal institution, see MacNeil, *op. cit.*, pp. 82–84.

look made him more acceptable to most Southern Democrats. He was more inclined to cooperate with Republicans, a relationship facilitated by his close friendship with former Minority Leader Martin.

With the selection of a new Speaker or Minority Leader, some congressmen exercise more influence and others fall out of favor. The relationship of members of the Committee on Rules to the new Speaker provides an illustration. The influence of Bolling of Missouri and Thornberry of Texas declined; O'Neill of Massachusetts and, to a lesser extent, Madden of Indiana, gained influence. Committee assignments in 1963 also reflected the composition of the new leadership. For example, McCormack was instrumental in packing the Committee on Appropriations with five Northern liberals over the objections of its conservative Chairman, Cannon of Missouri.

Leadership change also has a direct impact on legislation. Certainly, a bill to enlarge the House of Representatives to 438 members by adding one additional member from Massachusetts, Missouri, and Pennsylvania would not have advanced as far as it did without the new Speaker's support.[33] McCormack's Catholicism made it even more mandatory that any federal-aid-to-education bill be accompanied by some resolution of the church-state issue. The possibilities of strong civil rights, medicare, and mass transit legislation improved as a more sympathetic leader advanced to the Speakership. Since ideological differences between Martin, Halleck and Ford were less pronounced and the minority has far less control over scheduling, the impact of leadership change on Republican legislative goals is more difficult to trace.

The relatively peaceful modes of leadership change practiced by House Democrats in recent years have promoted party harmony, facilitated the passage of legislation, and thus aided the re-election of Democrats. But the development of patterns of succession is by no means universally endorsed by House Democrats. A junior member, a potential candidate for leadership, summed up some of the disenchantment:

A man shouldn't become a leader just because sometime fifteen or twenty years ago somebody made an obscure decision

---

[33] McCormack disavowed his support of H.R. 10264 after an uneasy bipartisan coalition came apart on the floor of the House during the amendment stage: *Congressional Quarterly Weekly Report*, 20 (March 16, 1962), p. 429.

to put someone in as whip or deputy whip, and then, he advances up the hierarchy. There's a real problem in the House. It's a kind of hardening of the arteries, too much bureaucracy. We're beginning to be more like the people we criticize downtown. Leadership should come from a man's proven ability, not just because he got started on the ladder. . . .

I think what the Republicans have done is a healthy development. If Joe Martin were a Democrat, we'd still have him as our leader.

Change through contested means has a number of opposite consequences. Few House Republicans are complaining about bureaucratized patterns of succession since none exist. In any future change, the incumbent Whip would be bypassed as he has been in the past. Should Ford falter, the closest approximation to an heir apparent is Conference Chairman Laird. But other potential candidates—among them Wilson, Rhodes, and Goodell—wait in the wings. House Republicans can take some consolation from one by-product of overwhelming election defeats—it moves able younger members into positions of high rank far quicker than any other means. The overall costs to internal party harmony from frequent contests are difficult to estimate. More latent than manifest, they seldom reveal themselves in legislative voting patterns. But the animosities and bitterness flowing from leadership contests remain an underlying source of tension and distrust. One contest tends to promote another. Continuing frustrations at the polls will quite likely lead to further contests.

To an extent not adequately stressed, congressional leadership change has important consequences for national politics and the strength of the two-party system. The House provides a pool of talent for nominations to the Senate or state-wide offices. The Senate has produced more presidential candidates in recent years, but the House is frequently a mid-career stage for aspiring national leaders. House members continue to participate intensively in the selection of candidates, the writing of party platforms and the management of national conventions. The party which does not control the White House turns to its congressional leaders for the nucleus of opposition party leadership. As leaders of the congressional majority, Rayburn and Johnson had more resources at their command, including better press coverage, than Republican minority leaders like Dirksen, Halleck and Ford. Currently the Joint Senate-House Republican Leadership and the Republican Coordinating Committee play dominant roles in the selection of domestic campaign issues and the structuring of debate on foreign policy. Thus, a change in House leadership has implications far beyond the internal activities of Congress.

VI. CONCLUSIONS

Collective decisions made by the electorates of 435 House districts have a number of important consequences for representative government in the United States. First, the election results advance or limit the careers of some 800 promising politicians, not a few of whom are destined for national leadership as party spokesmen, committee chairmen, and presidential aspirants. Second, the aggregate outcome of seats won and lost determines which congressional party shall be the majority with the right to organize the House of Representatives. Third, the size of the majority sets the limits for success or failure of the President's legislative program. If Congress is controlled by the opposition party, or if his own party does not have a working majority, then a President's expectations as to what is politically feasible must be lowered. He may even have to shift from a policy largely oriented toward passing legislation to one primarily designed to promote campaign issues, two or four years hence. Finally, as the findings of this article suggest, the size of the net gain or loss sets the climate for continuity or change in House party leadership. These aggregate election results provide the clearest instruction offered by the electorate in what is at best a generalized and largely uninformed evaluation of administration and congressional performance.[34] Congressmen

---

[34] "In Detroit in January, 1957 only 18 percent of the people could correctly name the Congressman from their own district, and only 13 percent knew the names of both United States Senators from Michigan. . . . The world of the political activists and the newspapers which report political events is much more remote from the world of the average citizen than is generally realized": Daniel Katz and Samuel J. Eldersveld, "The Impact of Local Party Activity Upon the Electorate," *Public Opinion Quarterly*, 25 (Spring, 1961), 1–24, 20. "The electorate sees very little altogether of what goes on in the national legislature. Few judgments of legislative performance are associated with the parties, and much of the public is unaware even of which party has control of Congress. As a result, the absence of party discipline or legislative results is unlikely to bring down electoral sanctions on the ineffective party or the errant Congressman": Donald E. Stokes and Warren E. Miller, "Party Government and the Saliency of Congress," *Public Opinion Quarterly*, 26 (Winter, 1962), 531–546, 545. It seems clear that the electorate does not bring down electoral sanctions upon the ineffective party in the sense of the responsible party doctrine. However, members of Congress, particularly Representatives in the minority party, seem to interpret large-scale shifts in seats won or lost as a judgment on their party image and the calibre of its leadership.

translate these instructions into mandates for continuing support or opportunities for change in congressional party leadership.

This analysis began by distinguishing three basic kinds of leadership change in legislatures, inter-party turnover, intra-party change, and institutional reform. After noting that continuity rather than change is the predominant pattern of congressional leadership, five types of intra-party leadership change were set forth: (1) routine succession, (2) appointment, or the emergence of a consensus choice, (3) open competition, (4) challenge to an heir apparent, and (5) revolt, or its aftermath. All but one of these types were illustrated by nineteen instances of leadership change or attempted change which took place in the five top party-wide leadership positions in both House parties during the 84th to 89th Congresses (1955–1966). The remaining type, challenge to an heir apparent, was illustrated by two earlier contests in 1919 and 1931.

Some rather striking differences were revealed in the predominant mode of change practiced by the two House parties during this twelve-year period. The Democratic majority was able to resolve its problems of leadership change through relatively peaceful means in eight out of nine cases. In contrast, the Republican minority resorted to contested means in seven out of ten cases. In four instances, most notably the minority leadership contests of 1959 and 1965, change in Republican party leadership was sought through organized revolt. Two sets of findings emerge from analysis of these cases:

1. Democratic majority:

   a. The Democratic majority is much more likely than the Republican minority to resolve questions of leadership change through non-contested elections or appointments.

   b. The longer the period of majority status, the more likely the majority party is to develop established patterns of succession.

   c. When contests take place in the Democratic majority, they will most likely occur at the middle or lower levels of the party hierarchy.

2. Republican minority:

   a. The Republican minority is more prone to intra-party leadership change through contested means.

   b. The longer the period of minority status, the more prone the minority party is to leadership change through revolt.

c. Revolts are most likely to occur following congressional election disasters (the net loss of thirty or more seats).

Further historical research is needed to determine the extent to which these findings are limited to this twelve-year period or have broader applicability. In order to prove or disprove hypotheses relating party differences and majority-minority status to types of leadership change, it will be necessary to examine in detail the periods 1894 to 1930 and 1931 to 1954. During the earlier period the Republican party was in the majority save for a Democratic interlude from 1910 until 1918. To what extent were the Cannon revolt and the Gillett-Mann and Snell-Tilson contests the exceptions rather than the rule? How was the Democratic party, as the minority party, able to avoid leadership contests during the 1920's? Were the series of leadership contests which preoccupied the Democratic majority in the 1930's a spilling over of the frustrations of minority status in the 1920's and a reflection of its new and unwieldy party structure? What other factors were at work in the selection of party leaders throughout these periods?

The outcome of future leadership change in both parties will provide a further test and opportunity for modification of these findings. Given the high component of chance, prediction in politics is always hazardous. Yet, in the long run, a science of politics is as dependent upon its ability to predict as on its capacity for explanation.[35] When change comes about in the Democratic party, it is most likely to occur through the death or retirement of the 75-year-old Speaker, John W. McCormack of Massachusetts. The incumbent Majority Leader, Carl Albert of Oklahoma, should routinely advance to the Speakership, contingent upon his full recovery from a September, 1966 heart attack. If a contest develops in the majority party, it is most likely to occur when and if the incumbent Whip, Hale Boggs of Louisiana, attempts to move up to Majority Leader. The problem for his opponents, just as it was in the 1959 and 1965 minority leadership contests, will be to agree upon a candidate with sufficient seniority, demonstrated leadership skills, and popularity around whom a majority might coalesce. Should Boggs succeed, and should the incumbent Deputy Whip, John Moss of California, be appointed Whip, then leadership succession in the House of Representatives, at least as it reflects majority practices,

---

[35] Abraham Kaplan, *The Conduct of Inquiry* (San Francisco, 1964), pp. 346–351.

will have undergone further institutionalization. The return in 1968 of a sizeable number of the Democratic freshman members who lost in 1966 could sufficiently strengthen the Democratic Study Group so as to give it a decisive voice in subsequent leadership contests.

Leadership change in the Republican minority party will depend heavily upon the results of the presidential election of 1968 and the congressional election of 1970. Minority Leader Ford needed a substantial victory in 1966 to consolidate his leadership. He got it—a net gain of 47 House seats. But should his party stumble in the next two campaigns, then he, like Martin and Halleck before him, is likely to be asked to step down or face the consequences of further revolt.

Studies in depth of past and future leadership change in the House of Representatives, as well as the modification of these hypotheses as they apply to other legislatures such as the United States Senate or the British House of Commons, should improve our understanding of the workings of legislative parties. They would also provide an opportunity for further examination of such important explanatory variables as the personality and skill of party leaders, majority and minority status, and the impact of election results on party structure and hierarchy.

BIBLIOGRAPHY

From among the vast number of books on the Congress of the United States, we have limited our selection, in the main, to books which focus primarily on the House of Representatives—particularly, empirical studies conducted since World War II. In addition, we have included a number of the most important official and semi-official reference works which all students of Congress find invaluable in their research. For more extended comment on the use of these reference works, the reader is directed to Roland Young's "Research Guide," *The American Congress* (New York: Harper, 1958), pp. 281–324. We have found the mimeographed bibliographies of Edward N. MacConomy and Walter Kravitz of considerable assistance in the preparation of this bibliography (Washington, D.C.: Legislative Reference Service, Library of Congress, 1959, 1962). John F. Manley has contributed an excellent up-to-date bibliography to Tacheron and Udall, cited below. See also Robert L. Peabody, "Research on Congress: A Coming of Age," in Ralph K. Huitt and R. L. Peabody, *Congress: Two Decades of Analysis* (New York: Harper and Row, 1968).

Bailey, Stephen K. *Congress Makes a Law*. New York: Columbia University Press, 1950.
_____. *The New Congress*. New York: St. Martin's Press, 1966.

_____, and Samuel, Howard D. *Congress at Work*. New York: Holt, 1952.

Baker, Gorden E. *The Reapportionment Revolution*. New York: Random House, 1966.

Bauer, Raymond A.; Pool, Ithiel de Sola; and Dexter, Lewis A. *American Business and Public Policy: The Politics of Foreign Trade*. New York: Atherton, 1963.

Bendiner, Robert. *Obstacle Course on Capitol Hill*. Toronto: McGraw-Hill, 1964.

Bibby, John, and Davidson, Roger. *On Capitol Hill*. New York: Holt, Rinehart, and Winston, 1967.

Bolling, Richard. *House Out of Order*. New York: Dutton, 1966.

_____. *Power in the House*. New York: Dutton, 1968.

Carroll, Holbert N. *The House of Representatives and Foreign Affairs*. Pittsburgh: University of Pittsburgh Press, 1958.

Clapp, Charles L. *The Congressman: His Work as He Sees It*. Washington, D.C.: The Brookings Institution, 1963.

Clark, Joseph S. (ed.). *Congressional Reform*. New York: Crowell, 1965.

Congressional Quarterly Almanac. Washington, D.C.: Congressional Quarterly, Inc., 1945–, Vols. I–.

Congressional Quarterly Weekly Report. Washington, D.C., Congressional Quarterly, Inc., 1945–, Vols. I–.

Cooper, Joseph. *Reorganization and Reform in the U.S. House of Representatives*. Washington, D.C.: Brookings Institution, 1969.

Cummings, Milton C., Jr. *Congressmen and the Electorate*. New York: Free Press, 1966.

Davidson, Roger; Kovenock, David; and O'Leary, Michael. *Congress in Crisis: Politics and Congressional Reform*. Belmont, California: Wadsworth, 1966.

De Grazia, Alfred (Coord.). *Congress: the First Branch of Government*. Washington, D.C.: American Enterprise Institute for Public Policy Research, 1964.

Ewing, C.A.M. *Congressional Elections, 1896–1944*. Norman: University of Oklahoma Press, 1947.

Fenno, Richard F., Jr. *The Power of the Purse*. Boston: Little, Brown, 1966.

Froman, Lewis A., Jr. *The Congressional Process*. Boston: Little, Brown, 1967.

_____. *Congressmen and Their Constituencies*. Chicago: Rand McNally, 1963.

Galloway, George B. *History of the House of Representatives.* New York: Crowell, 1962.

_____. *The Legislative Process in Congress.* New York: Crowell, 1953.

Green, Harold P., and Rosenthal, Alan. *Government of the Atom: The Integration of Powers.* New York: Atherton, 1963.

Griffith, Ernest. *Congress, Its Contemporary Role.* 4th rev. ed.; New York: New York University Press, 1967.

Gross, Bertram. *The Legislative Struggle.* New York: McGraw-Hill, 1953.

Hacker, Andrew. *Congressional Districting.* Washington, D.C.: The Brookings Institution, 1963.

Harris, Richard. *The Real Voice.* New York: Macmillan, 1964.

Jewell, Malcolm E., and Patterson, Samuel C. *The Legislative Process in the United States.* New York: Random House, 1966.

Jones, Charles O. *Minority Party Leadership in Congress.* Boston: Little, Brown, forthcoming.

_____. *Party and Policy-Making.* New Brunswick: Rutgers University Press, 1964.

Keefe, William J., and Ogul, Morris S. *The American Legislative Process: Congress and the States.* Englewood Cliffs: Prentice-Hall, 1965. Rev. ed., 1968.

Kofmehl, Kenneth. *Professional Staffs of Congress.* West Lafayette, Ind.: Purdue University Press, 1961.

McAdams, Alan K. *Power and Politics in Labor Legislation.* New York: Columbia University Press, 1964.

McInnis, Mary (ed.). *We Propose: A Modern Congress.* New York: McGraw-Hill, 1966.

MacKaye, William R. "A New Coalition Takes Control: The House Rules Committee Fight of 1961." *Eagleton Cases in Practical Politics.* New York: McGraw-Hill, 1963.

MacNeil, Neil. *Forge of Democracy: The House of Representatives.* New York: McKay, 1963.

Martin, Joe. *My First Fifty Years in Politics.* New York: McGraw-Hill, 1960.

Mayhew, David R. *Party Loyalty among Congressmen.* Cambridge: Harvard University Press, 1966.

Miller, Clem. *Member of the House: Letters of a Congressman.* (ed., John W. Baker.) New York: Scribner, 1962.

Mooney, Booth. *Mr. Speaker.* Chicago: Follett Publishing, 1964.

Peabody, Robert L. "The Ford-Halleck Minority Leadership Contest, 1965," *Eagleton Cases in Practical Politics.* New York: McGraw-Hill, 1966.

_____. "Political Parties: House Republican Leadership" in Allan P. Sindler (ed.). *American Political Institutions and Public Policy.* Boston: Little, Brown, 1969.

Polsby, Nelson W. *Congress and the Presidency.* Englewood Cliffs: Prentice-Hall, 1964.

Pressman, Jeffrey L. *House vs. Senate: Conflict in the Appropriations Process.* New Haven: Yale University Press, 1966.

Price, H. Douglas. "Race, Religion, and the Rules Committee: The Kennedy Aid-to-Education Bills," in Alan F. Westin (ed.). *The Uses of Power.* New York: Harcourt, 1962.

Riddick, Floyd Millard. *The United States Congress: Organization and Procedure.* Manassas, Va.: National Capitol Publishers, 1949.

Rieselbach, Leroy N. *The Roots of Isolationism.* Indianapolis: Bobbs-Merrill, 1966.

Ripley, Randall B. *Majority Party Leadership in Congress*. Boston: Little, Brown, 1969.

_____. *Party Leaders in the House of Representatives*. Washington, D.C.: Brookings Institution, 1967.

Robinson, James A. *Congress and Foreign Policy Making*. Illinois: Dorsey Press, Rev. ed., 1967.

_____. *The House Rules Committee*. Indianapolis: Bobbs-Merrill, 1963.

Saloma, John S. *The Responsible Use of Power, A Critical Analysis of the Congressional Budget Process*. Washington, D.C.: American Enterprise Institute for Public Policy Research, 1964.

_____. *Congress and the New Politics*. Boston: Little, Brown, 1969.

Scammon, Richard (ed.). *American Votes*. Vols. I-VII. New York: Macmillan, 1956, 1957. Pittsburgh: University of Pittsburgh Press, 1958–.

Schubert, Glendon (ed.). *Reapportionment*. New York: Scribner's, 1965.

Smith, Frank E., *Congressman from Mississippi*. New York: Pantheon, 1964.

Tacheron, Donald G., and Udall, Morris K. *The Job of the Congressman*. Indianapolis: Bobbs-Merrill, 1966.

Thomas, Norman C., and Lamb, Karl A. *Congress: Politics and Practice*. New York: Random House, 1964.

Truman, David B. (ed.). *Congress and America's Future*. Englewood Cliffs: Prentice Hall, 1965.

_____. *The Congressional Party*. New York: Wiley, 1959.

Turner, Julius. *Party and Constituency: Pressures on Congress*. Baltimore: The Johns Hopkins Press, 1951.

U.S. Bureau of the Census. *Congressional District Data Book*. Washington, D.C.: Government Printing Office, 1961.

U.S. Congress. *Biographical Directory of the American Congress, 1774–1961*. Washington, D.C.: Government Printing Office, 1961.

_____. *Congressional Record*. Washington, D.C.: Government Printing Office, 1873–, Vols. I–. (Begins with 43rd Cong.)

_____. *Congressional Directory*. Washington, D.C., Government Printing Office, 1807–. (Begins with 10th Cong.)

Voorhis, Jerry. *Confessions of a Congressman*. Garden City, N.Y.: Doubleday, 1947.

Wilson, Woodrow. *Congressional Government*. New York: Meridian, 1956. (Originally published 1885.)

Young, James Sterling. *The Washington Community, 1800–1828*. New York: Columbia University Press, 1966.

Young, Roland. *The American Congress*. New York: Harper, 1958.